UNDERSTANDING EARLY CLASSIC COPAN

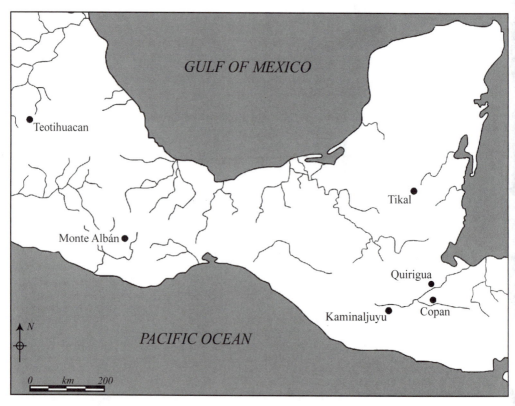

GULF OF MEXICO

Teotihuacan

Tikal

Monte Albán

Quirigua

Copan

Kaminaljuyu

N

PACIFIC OCEAN

0   km   200

Mesoamerica with locations of major Precolumbian sites featured in this volume.

UNDERSTANDING
EARLY
CLASSIC
COPAN

Edited by

Ellen E. Bell, Marcello A. Canuto, & Robert J. Sharer

 UNIVERSITY OF PENNSYLVANIA MUSEUM OF ARCHAEOLOGY AND ANTHROPOLOGY

University of Pennsylvania Museum of Archaeology and Anthropology
3260 South Street • Philadelphia, PA 19104–6324

Unless otherwise credited, illustrations are by chapter authors.

Library of Congress Cataloging-in-Publication Data

Understanding early classic Copan / edited by Ellen E. Bell, Marcello A.
Canuto, Robert J. Sharer.
　　　p.　cm.
"An outgrowth of a symposium of the same name organized for the 65th
Annual Meeting of the Society for American Archaeology in Philadelphia
in April 2000"—Pref.
Includes bibliographical references and index.
　　ISBN 1-931707-51-0 (alk. paper)
　　1.　Copâan Site (Honduras)—Congresses. 2.
Mayas—Antiquities—Congresses. 3.　Mayas—Funeral customs and rites.
4.　Archaeological surveying—Honduras—Copâan Site. 5.　Excavations
(Archaeology)—Honduras—Copâan Site. 6.　Maya
architecture—Honduras—Copâan Site. 7.　Tombs—Honduras—Copâan Site.
8.　Honduras—Antiquities.　I. Bell, Ellen E.　II. Canuto, Marcello A.,
1969–　III. Sharer, Robert J.　IV. Society for American Archaeology.
Meeting (65th : 2000 : Philadelphia, Pa.)
　　F1435.1.C7U63 2004
　　972.83'84—dc22

　　　　　　　　　　　　　　　　　　　　　　　　　2003020812

To the memory of

Gordon R. Willey

whose vision, prescience, and expertise
allowed for modern archaeology to flourish at Copan.

CONTENTS

ILLUSTRATIONS

PLATES following p. 318

TABLES

PREFACE

T his volume is an outgrowth of a symposium of the same name organized for the 65th Annual Meeting of the Society for American Archaeology in Philadelphia, PA, in April 2000. This session emerged from the foundation laid by Loa P. Traxler and E. Wyllys Andrews V, who organized symposia on the Early Classic Acropolis and Classic period Copan for the 61st Annual Meeting of the Society for American Archaeology in 1996.

We believe that independent, yet interrelated, work at the Classic Maya center of Copan, located on the southeastern edge of the Maya area in what is now northwestern Honduras, has reached a critical mass, a point at which an increasingly cohesive picture of the center in the Early Classic period (A.D. 400–600) is emerging. We sought to provide a forum in which researchers approaching Early Classic Copan in a variety of ways—including archaeological, epigraphic, iconographic, palynological, osteological and geophysical investigations—could come together to share their results with one another and anyone else who might be interested.

Much to our delight, the symposium spurred debate, generated new interpretations, and opened dialogues among those who participated and attended. This volume represents a continuation of the dialogues begun in that symposium; it is a first step, not the last word, which we hope will continue to foster discussion and urge people on to a deeper and more nuanced understanding of the Early Classic at Copan and elsewhere.

To thank the innumerable people who have preceded, helped, encouraged, and guided us throughout this process would be nearly impossible. In this brief space, we can only hope to mention a few of those who deserve our thanks and deepest gratitude: residents of the town of Copán Ruinas, our colleagues in the U.S. and abroad (many of whom generously contributed to the present volume), the Instituto Hondureño de Antropología e Historia, the government of Honduras, the University of Pennsylvania Museum of Archaeology and Anthropology (Boyer and Shoemaker Chair Research Funds and the Kolb Society), the University of Pennsylvania Research Foundation, the National Science Foundation, the National Geographic Society, the Fulbright Program, the Foundation for the Advancement of Mesoamerican Studies, the Maya Workshop Foundation, the Kislak Foundation, the Seltz Foundation, the Holt Family Foundation, and numerous private donors. We would also like to thank the dedicated University of Pennsylvania Museum Publications staff, Matthew Manieri and James Mathieu, our editor, Walda Metcalf, and our families and friends for their help and support.

CHRONOLOGY

Period	AD/BC	Copan		Kaminaljuyu	Chalchuapa	Tikal	Oaxaca
		Phase	Facet	(Wetherington 1978)	(Sharer 1978)	(Harrison 1999)	(Marcus and Flannery 1996)
POST-CLASSIC	1400	EJAR			Ahal		Late Monte Albán V
	1300						
	1200						Early Monte Albán V
	1100			Ayumpuc	Matzin	Caban	
	950						
CLASSIC — Terminal	850	CONER	Terminal II	Pamplona		Eznab	Monte Albán IV
CLASSIC — Late	750		Terminal I	Amatle 2	Payu	Imix	
	650		Transition			Ik	Monte Albán IIIb
CLASSIC — (Middle)		ACBI	Late	Amatle 1 Esperanza	Xocco		
CLASSIC — Early	500		Early			Manik	Monte Albán IIIa
	400						
PROTO-CLASSIC — Late	250	BIJAC	Late	Aurora	Vec		
	150					Cimi	
PROTO-CLASSIC — Early	50			Arenal	Late Caynac	Cauac	Monte Albán II
	50	CHABIJ	Early	Miraflores Verbena	Early Caynac		
	150					Chuen	Monte Albán Ic
PRECLASSIC — Late	250	SEBITO		Providencia	Chul		
	350						Monte Albán Ia
	450	BOSQUE			Kal	Tzec	
PRECLASSIC — Middle	550			Las Charcas			Rosario
	650				Cholos	Eb	
	750	UIR					Guadalupe
	850			Arevalo	Tok		
	1000	GORDON		???	???		San José
	1100	PLATA					
PRECLASSIC — Early	1200						Tierras Larges
	1300	RAYO					
	1400						Espiridión
	1500	???					

ABBREVIATIONS

cal	Calibrated radiocarbon date
ECAP	Early Copan Acropolis Program
IHAH	Instituto Hondureño de Antropología e Historia
masl	Meters above sea level
PAC	Proyecto Arqueológico Copan
PAAC	Proyecto Arqueológico Acrópolis Copan

NOTE

In accordance with Acuerdos 1046-87 and 129-88 of the Congress of Guatemala, we have not used accent marks in the names of archaeological sites or ceramic phases derived from indigenous words (e.g., Copan, Kaminaljuyu, Teotihuacan, Quirigua). Accent marks have been retained in place names of Spanish origin and in indigenous words used in modern political designations (e.g., Copán Ruinas, Departamento de Petén, Guatemala). We extend our thanks to Juan Antonio Valdés for bringing this issue to our attention.

I

UNDERSTANDING EARLY CLASSIC COPAN:
A CLASSIC MAYA CENTER AND ITS INVESTIGATION

Marcello A. Canuto, Ellen E. Bell, and Robert J. Sharer

I n the quarter century since Gordon R. Willey initiated the modern era of archaeological research in the Copan Valley of northwestern Honduras (Willey et al. 1976),
an almost continuous series of research projects has investigated numerous facets
of ancient Copan, ranging from the monumental architecture of the polity capital to
the humble households of the surrounding hinterland settlement. However, as is the
case at most Classic Maya sites, the material remains of Copan's final phase of occupation—that is, the Late Classic period (ca. A.D. 600-850)—dominate both the data and,
consequently, much of our thinking about the polity and its people (Webster et al.
2000). It has been far more difficult to develop a comprehensive model of earlier periods both in the polity capital and throughout the Copan drainage. This difficulty is
especially salient in regards to the critical earlier portion of Copan's Classic period, the
Protoclassic (ca. A.D. 100-400) and the Early Classic (ca. A.D. 400-600), during which
Copan, along with many other Classic Maya polities, was transformed into an
autonomous state system (see Chronology).[*] Therefore, although much evidence for
the final centuries and eventual collapse of the Copan polity has long been available
to scholars, its origins and development have remained obscure.

The archaeological research presented in this volume reflects one of the first
concerted attempts to correct this all-too-common emphasis on the Late Classic period in Maya research. This volume unites the results of multiple research programs and
perspectives from both the site of Copan itself and its surrounding valley. This purposeful coordination of recent research makes possible a balanced view of Copan's
development during the entire span of the Classic period (ca. A.D. 100–900).

---

[*] For the purpose of the present study we refer to the Early Classic period at Copan as
defined by the Acbi ceramic phase (ca. A.D. 400-600) and equated with the early kings of the
Copan dynasty (Rulers 1-10). The Late Classic period at Copan (sometimes also known as the
"Full Classic") is defined by the Coner ceramic phase (ca. A.D. 600-850) and is equated with the
later kings of the Copan dynasty (Rulers 11-16). The Classic period was preceded by the
Protoclassic period (defined by the Bijac ceramic phase, ca. A.D. 100-400) and generally equated with the "Predynastic period."

Figure I.1 Southeast Maya area.

Geographical Setting and Site Layout

The site of Copan (Figure I.1) is located in a mountainous region along the southeastern edge of the Maya area, within what is now northwestern Honduras, five kilometers east of the border with Guatemala. The Copan Principal Group defines the remains of the Classic Maya polity capital. It dominates the largest in a series of intermontaine pockets carved out by the Copan River (Figure I.2), which eventually joins the Motagua River system some 60 km southwest of the Classic Maya site of Quirigua in eastern Guatemala. The remains of ancient settlement are found throughout 24 km^2 of alluvial bottomlands as well as in adjacent terrace and upland zones located along the Copan River and its various tributaries. The Principal Group sits on the western bank of the Copan River on the bottomlands near the eastern edge of the Copan pocket.

The Principal Group (Figure I. 3) consists of a series of relatively open plazas to the north and a massive complex of superimposed construction to the south, with the ballcourt and associated structures, including Structure 10L-26 (Temple of the Hieroglyphic Stairway), acting as the boundary between the two. The publicly accessible Great Plaza and the freestanding monuments (stelae and altars) it contains form the focal point of the northern portion of the Principal Group. The Great Plaza is

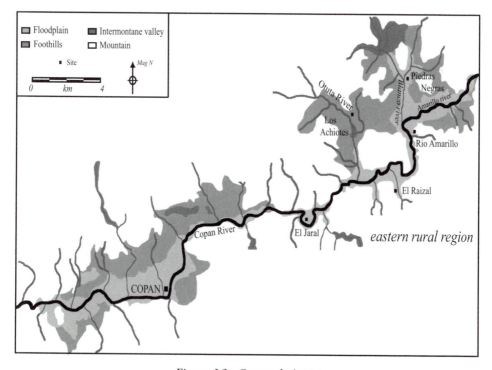

Figure I.2 Copan drainage.

flanked on the east by a raised platform and on the west by a small acropolis known as the Northwest Platform that dates to the Early Classic—and possibly even the Late Preclassic—period (Viel and Hall 2000b). To the south, the Hieroglyphic Stairway Plaza is bounded by the massive stairs of Structure 10L-11 on the south, the Hieroglyphic Stairway on Structure 10L-26 to the east, and the ballcourt on the north.

The stairways of Structures 10L-11 and 10L-26 lead upward to the massive, elevated Acropolis. Because of their elevation, the surface structures of this Late Classic royal complex are far less accessible than the more public areas to the north. Moreover, the Acropolis is divided into two enclosed courtyards (the East and West Courts) surrounded by raised constructions and separated by Structure 10L-25 (also known as the Dance Platform) and Structure 10L-16. This latter structure supports the highest of Copan's surviving buildings and therefore represents the pivotal point of the Acropolis. As the West Court is dominated on its north side by the already-mentioned Structure 10L-11, the East Court is dominated by the series of platforms and associated buildings also on its northern margin, Structure 10L-22a (also known as Popol Na), Structure 10L-22, Structure 10L-21a, and the remnants of Structure 10L-21. On its western margin is the Jaguar Stairway that leads to the lower platform of Structure 10L-25. Many of the buildings located on the eastern side of the East Court were swept away by the Copan River as it undercut this portion of the Acropolis (including Structures 10L-19 and 10L-20). Eventually the river was successfully diverted by the Carnegie Institution of Washington in the 1930s (Stromsvik 1935; Trik 1939), contributing to the survival of Structure 10L-18 on the southeast corner of this court.

The Principal Group is surrounded by heavy concentrations of settlement, consisting of large elite residential compounds to the south (El Cementerio) and west (El Bosque) and slightly more distantly to the northeast (Las Sepulturas). The areas to the east and west of the Principal Group were connected to the Great Plaza by causeways. Although the majority of surface-visible architecture within the surrounding residential compounds dates to the Late Classic period (A.D. 600–850), all these compounds are multicomponent constructions. The Cementerio Group, for instance, includes an Early Classic component; moreover, both Late Preclassic and Early Postclassic remains have been found in the Bosque area (Manahan 2003), and a sizable Middle Preclassic cemetery (with an Early Classic level above it) was uncovered in Group 9N-8 within the Las Sepulturas settlement area (Fash 2001).

Overall, settlement in the Copan Valley has been divided into three zones— urban, pocket, and rural (Figure I.2)—each exhibiting different densities and distributions of established settlement types (Baudez 1983; Fash 1983c; Sanders 1986; Sanders and Webster 1988; Willey et al. 1979). Since the outlying rural areas consisted mostly of smaller sites (Sanders and Webster 1988; Webster 1985), with only a few elite centers, such as Río Amarillo, these rural populations were seen as smaller and simpler social groups loosely affiliated with the Copan polity (Freter 1988, 1994, 1996; Webster et al. 1992; Webster and Freter 1990a; Wingard 1996). Recent research (Canuto 2002;

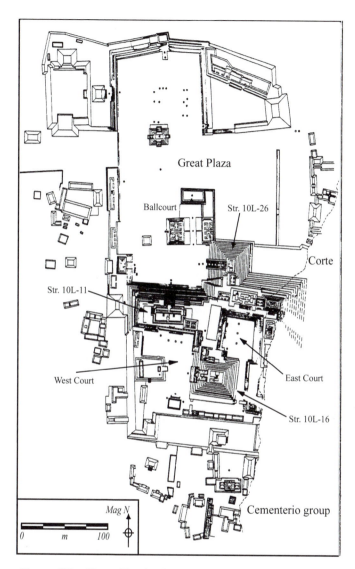

Figure I.3 "Late Classic Copan Principal Group" (ca. A.D. 600–850) with the Acropolis, showing locations of three interconnected PAAC tunneling programs excavated beneath Structure 10L-16 (from the West Court), Structure 10L-26 (from the Plaza of the Hieroglyphic Stairway), and the East Court (from the Corte; after Fash 2001 with additions by Marcello A. Canuto).

Saturno 2000) has shown, however, that these rural areas also consisted of important and notable Late Preclassic and Early Classic populations. Furthermore, these results accord well with previous settlement research within the Copan pocket that interpreted the Early Classic period as a time of great settlement growth that expanded from the polity center (Fash 1983c). The most recent settlement research shows that during the Early Classic, the rural populations were integrated with developments at the polity center.

Research at Copan

As one of the most intensively and extensively investigated centers in the Classic Maya area, Copan has a history of research that extends back to the mid-1800s. The first recorded visit to the site was made by the Spanish conquistador and explorer Diego García de Palacio in 1576 (García de Palacio 1983[1576]). The site was next visited by Colonel Juan Galindo in 1834. In contrast to García de Palacio's brief stay, Galindo spent several months at Copan taking notes and making plans, sketches, and renderings of the buildings, sculpture, and inscriptions. He also undertook the first documented excavations in the Acropolis, investigating a vaulted tomb located below Structure 10L-19 (Galindo 1836, 1935; Graham 1963; Morley 1920:596). A few years later Stephens and Catherwood documented many of Copan's monuments and buildings during their famous tour through Central America (Stephens 1963[1841]).

At the end of the 19th century, Alfred Maudslay mapped the Acropolis and cleared a number of buildings on its summit, including Structures 10L-16, 10L-22, and 10L-20; the latter collapsed into the Copan River shortly thereafter (Maudslay 1886, 1889-1902). The Peabody Museum of Harvard University continued Maudslay's clearing work atop the Acropolis, exposing Structures 10L-21a and 10L-21. Most of the latter was eventually lost to erosion along the river cut (Gordon 1896, 1902). Concurrently, Sylvanus G. Morley made visits to Copan at the turn of the last century to document its sculpture, which was eventually published in his mammoth work *The Inscriptions at Copan* (1920). In the 1930s and 1940s, the Carnegie Institution of Washington conducted an extensive program of excavation and restoration within the site. It was during this phase of research that the Copan River was finally diverted from the eastern side of the Acropolis, avoiding further destruction of the architectural complex (Longyear 1952; Stromsvik 1941, 1952; Trik 1939).

In 1974, the Instituto Hondureño de Antropología e Historia (IHAH) invited Gordon R. Willey of the Peabody Museum of Archaeology and Ethnology to design a program of research and conservation at Copan. The resulting comprehensive research proposal (Willey et al. 1976) emphasized the integration of investigations in the site core with the study of settlement in and beyond the Copan Valley that has provided the uniquely rich data set we enjoy today. In many ways, all of the work reported in this volume is an outgrowth of that original research design. The Copan Valley

Project (1976-1977), directed by Gordon R. Willey, opened the modern era of research at Copan with the mapping and excavation of settlement surrounding the Principal Group (Fash 1983; Willey and Leventhal 1979; Willey et al. 1994).

Settlement research was later continued and expanded by the Copan Archaeological Project in 1977, which also began renewed investigations in the Principal Group. The Copan Archaeological Project had two phases (PAC I and II), the first directed by Claude Baudez (1977-1980; Baudez 1983) and the second by William T. Sanders (1980-1985; Sanders 1986). This latter effort was followed by the Rural Sites Project (1985-1988) directed by David Webster (Abrams 1994; Diamanti 1991; Freter 1988; Gerstle 1988; Gonlin 1993; Hendon 1987; Webster 1989) and the Copan Mosaic Project (1985-2002) under the direction of Barbara and William L. Fash (Fash 1991, 2000; Fash and Sharer 1991; B. Fash et al. 1992; Fash 1993; W. Fash et al. 1992). The Rural Sites Project surveyed and tested settlement remains outside the main pocket of the Copan Valley, while the Copan Mosaic Project documented and reconstructed elements of architectural sculpture throughout the region.

Although some investigations undertaken in Las Sepulturas and areas adjacent to the Principal Group by William L. Fash and René Viel focused on Preclassic remains, most of the successive research programs over the last quarter of the 20th century focused on surface-visible, Late Classic remains. While reasonable and appropriate, this focus did little to reveal the origins and development of the Copan polity during the Early Classic period. It is only since the early 1990s that these issues have been addressed by a concentrated and concerted research effort focused on this little known period of Copan's history.

Recent Research at Copan (1988-2002)

Improvements in the method and structure of archaeological research in the last decade of the 20th century have revolutionized our understanding of the Classic Maya. On the one hand, advances in research techniques, methodology, and material analysis have refined and enhanced archaeological interpretations. On the other hand, the development and flourishing of such related disciplines as conservation sciences, art history, epigraphy, osteology, palynology, geomorphology, and zoology have provided access to data previously thought irretrievable or, at best, indecipherable.

Much of this progress, however, has remained confined to the investigation of the most readily accessible archaeological materials. That is, the increased precision and detail allowed by enhanced methods and new technology has been applied most often to cultural levels relating to the Late Classic period. Early Classic contexts, ordinarily deeply buried or encased within Late Classic buildings, were rarely accessible by traditional excavation techniques. In fact, archaeological research at Copan, despite almost a century of continuous investigations, had offered only vague assertions about the nature of the polity's founding and subsequent development. Ironically, the basis for these assertions was derived principally from Late Classic monuments that retrospectively mention earlier events in the polity's history. However, with the establishment of the Copan Acropolis Archaeological Project (PAAC) in the late–1980s, William L. Fash initiated the first project designed to investigate the full history of the Classic Copan polity, including the crucial Early Classic era in which the Classic period ruling dynasty was founded.

The Conjunctive Approach at Copan

One of the most salient characteristics of recent research at Copan is its explicit adoption of a conjunctive approach to its investigations (Fash and Sharer 1991), coupled with implementing a series of new techniques for the gathering and analysis of data. Originally defined by Walter Taylor (1948), the conjunctive approach has been adapted to conditions at Copan. In its Copan setting, the conjunctive approach refers to archaeological research designed to solve specific questions about the past. A broad range of specialists has address these questions by studying everything from the construction, styles, and decoration of buildings, to the remains of Copan's ancient people and their activities. These data are combined with a historical perspective based on the decipherment of texts. The resulting multiple data sets are then applied to the original research questions; consistent and complementary findings provide answers, while inconsistent and contrary findings create the need for further research. Many of the results reported in this volume derive directly from this conjunctive research.

The application of the conjunctive approach to questions about Early Classic Copan was facilitated by several new and innovative data-gathering techniques that made the comprehensive investigation of the deeply buried Early Classic levels of the Acropolis possible. The PAAC and later research programs directed by William L. Fash, Ricardo Agurcia Fasquelle, Robert J. Sharer, and Rudy V. Larios initiated this focus on Early Classic Copan through the adoption of an extensive tunnel methodology rarely used at other sites. Where previous efforts in the Classic Maya area had produced only scant and adumbrated views of the Early Classic antecedents to Late Classic structures, research within Copan's monumental Acropolis achieved unprecedented exposures of multiple Early Classic contexts without the collateral damage to overlying later structures that other more traditional excavation methodologies would have occasioned. Remains of long buried Early Classic architecture were often well preserved, and could be accurately recorded using the latest electronic survey equipment (Topcon Total Station) and computer-aided design software.

Given the large scale of these tunnel excavations, the PAAC project objectives were divided among the principal researchers. William L. Fash of Harvard University directed the work under the Temple of the Hieroglyphic Stairway, uncovering an elaborate tomb thought to be that of the 12th Ruler of the Copan dynasty, Smoke Imix God K. Beneath this tomb, Fash and his collaborators encountered Early Classic buildings and associated remains dating back to the founding era (Fash 1991; W. Fash et al. 1992; Williamson 1997). Ricardo Agurcia Fasquelle of the Asociación Copan tunneled into the series of constructions within the elevated mass of Structure 10L-16, the central and dominant point of the Acropolis. His work resulted in the discovery of the structure nicknamed Rosalila, an elaborately decorated Early Classic building buried almost completely intact below the Late Classic Structure 10L-16 (Agurcia F. 1996; Agurcia F. and Fash 1991; Agurcia F. and Valdés 1994). Rudy Larios V. undertook the consolidation of the exposed river cut, or *corte*, to prevent further erosion and collapse, thus preserving the greatest stratigraphic section in Mesoamerica which spans the Early and Late Classic phases of Acropolis construction (Larios et al. 1993). Excavations directed by E. Wyllys Andrews V of Tulane University investigated El Cementerio, the elite residential group to the south of the Acropolis, which might have been the residence of members of the ruler's family in the Late Classic and included an important Early Classic component as well (Andrews and Fash 1992; Bill 1996; Doonan 1996).

Finally, the tunnel excavations directed by Robert J. Sharer of the University of Pennsylvania examined the area beneath the eastern portion of the Acropolis. He and his collaborators uncovered a complex sequence of temples, palaces, and courts that date to the founding of the Copan dynasty in the Early Classic period (Sharer et al. 1992; Sharer, Traxler, et al. 1999). This sequence of architecture preserves the entire architectural history of the eastern half of the Acropolis, from its modest beginnings, through a succession of expansions, to its presently visible form. Within the successive stages of the Early Classic Acropolis these excavations revealed what may be the tomb of the 8th Ruler of the Copan dynasty as well as a funerary complex in the basal levels below Structure 10L-16 that contained the two earliest royal tombs found at Copan. The earliest chamber might hold the remains of the dynastic founder, K'inich Yax K'uk' Mo', while the slightly later tomb contained the remains of a royal woman who could have been his wife.

Other research programs outside of the Acropolis were undertaken in conjunction with PAAC's tunneling efforts. These programs deployed new techniques and approaches to infuse traditional settlement research with new perspectives and questions relating to concurrent research within the Acropolis. Investigations in the Copan pocket conducted by Fash and his students, and by Jay Hall and René Viel, have revealed important Late Preclassic and Early Classic materials. In the Río Amarillo pocket of the Copan drainage, some 20 km to the east of the Copan pocket, research by Marcello A. Canuto (2002) has yielded new data crucial to our understanding of the Early Classic as well. The combined efforts of these programs to achieve singular access to traditionally elusive archaeological contexts have led to an unparalleled focus on the founding and development of the Classic Maya polity of Copan.

As already mentioned, the broad scope of this Early Classic research at Copan exemplifies the interdisciplinary, i.e. conjunctive, nature of the PAAC project. In fact, from its inception, PAAC has deployed a wide range of research. In this time, different research disciplines at Copan have come together to provide new information and to contribute to the development of new interpretative models. The proximity of, and cooperation among, these research programs has fomented the cross-pollination of ideas and theories that has helped build a series of new interpretations informed by multiple lines of independent evidence.

As a result of this conjunctive research, it has become clear that, in the Early Classic period, the polity of Copan underwent massive and irreversible organizational and scalar changes that established the patterns of later sociopolitical organization (as reflected in settlement, monumental constructions, iconography, and hieroglyphic inscriptions within the polity). Furthermore, it appears that these changes involved a fusion of well established and diverse local traditions with those derived from the southern Maya lowlands, the Maya highlands, central Mexico, and from non-Maya areas of central Honduras.

The Present Volume

The principal goal of this volume is to present a synthesis of what has been learned about Early Classic Copan from the conjunctive research applied over the last decade of the 20th century. Its contributions represent innovative and multifaceted research that contradict, enhance and supplement previous work. We offer the results of this research in a series of contributions presented here in thirteen chapters divided into four topics: landscape and settlement, monumental architecture, burials, and epigraphy and iconography. The final four chapters synthesize information and interpretations that place Early Classic Copan within the wider context of the Maya area and Mesoamerica.

Landscape and Settlement

The first section discusses research on the Early Classic landscape and settlement of the Copan region. It includes two chapters that examine the wider ecological and demographic context within which the Copan dynasty was established in the 5th century A. D. In the first chapter, Hall and Viel examine the development of an anthropogenic landscape in the Copan Valley, noting that processes of hydraulic control and land management in the Copan pocket were initially passive but became increasingly more active through time. They track this transformation from an uncontrolled and dynamic landscape into a more controlled and stable hydraulic regime during the Early Classic period.

In the second chapter, Canuto discusses how the existence of a rural occupation around the Copan pocket reflects the changes wrought by the establishment of a ruling dynasty at Copan in the Early Classic period. He discusses the Late Preclassic heterarchical political system of loosely connected centers that belonged to the

Southeastern cultural sphere. He then tracks the replacement of this system in the Early Classic period by a more centralized hierarchy of centers that reflected Petén based forms of social organization, spatial aesthetics, construction techniques, and resource procurement.

Monumental Architecture

At the core of the polity capital, the Acropolis represents four centuries of accumulated architecture and is the defining architectural expression of the Copan dynasty. The five chapters in this section focus on the construction of monumental architecture in the Principal Group as a marker of Early Classic polity origins and development.

Traxler, drawing on Acropolis excavations during the 1990s and on new interpretations of the Great Plaza excavations conducted during the PAC I two decades earlier, marshals evidence for the existence of numerous Early Classic earthen structures buried under later masonry constructions. She traces these construction sequences in order to propose how the dynastic founder and his son, Copan's second ruler, drastically redesigned a small predynastic center into their new royal capital, thereby setting a spatial template followed for the rest of Copan's dynastic history.

Fash, Fash, and Davis-Salazar also discuss the establishment of the new royal center at Copan. The earliest dynastic rulers produced the first versions of several key public monumental constructions, including the initial ballcourt and the first in a sequence of dynastic temples buried beneath Structure 10L-26 and its Hieroglyphic Stairway. They note that these original public buildings reveal the cosmopolitan context and connections used by the dynastic founder and his successors.

Sedat and López investigate the southern portion of the Acropolis. They discuss the earliest royal complex, located deep beneath Structure 10L-16, associated with the beginnings of the Copan dynasty. In its initial stage during the Early Classic period, this architectural complex belonged stylistically to the Southeastern earthen architectural tradition. As the complex expanded, it was used by early dynasts to showcase several sophisticated foreign construction styles and methods.

Agurcia Fasquelle continues the architectural history of this core sequence of buildings beneath Structure 10L-16 by discussing the culmination of Early Classic architecture at Copan, a building informally named Rosalila that dates to the 6th century A.D. This structure represents one of the few completely preserved examples of Early Classic art and architecture uncovered anywhere in the Maya area. Based on his excavations of this unique building and its archaeological context and iconography, he demonstrates how Rosalila interrelates cosmology with Early Classic kingship, providing a unique view of the development of the Early Classic Copan dynasty.

Concluding this section, Carrelli outlines her new energetics research at Copan. Focusing on diachronic changes in construction methods and materials as well as the varying size and complexity of Early Classic royal architecture, she undertakes a scientific analysis of the varying amounts of labor utilized by Copan's first dynasts to illustrate the high degree of control they exercised over human and material resources. Her findings suggest that during the Early Classic period the initial dynasts wielded a degree of power comparable to rulers of other early preindustrial states.

Burials

The third section presents the latest interpretations derived from human interments found within the Early Classic Acropolis. These three chapters represent conjunctive research based on thorough archaeological documentation combined with the newest scientific analyses.

To begin this section, Bell, Sharer, Traxler, Sedat, Carrelli, and Grant present a synopsis of the Early Classic tombs and burials excavated since the early 1990s. This chapter provides the essential context for the analyses and interpretations presented in the remainder of this section.

Reents-Budet, Bell, Bishop, and Traxler then examine the stylistic and instrumental neutron activation analyses of pottery vessels from three Early Classic royal tombs. Based on the conjunction of all available evidence, it is proposed that these tombs contained the remains of the dynastic founder, a royal woman who was probably his wife, and Ruler 8. Stylistic markers, ceramic composition, and spatial patterning both complement and amplify the historical and archaeological data.

Buikstra, Price, Wright, and Burton investigate the same three royal tombs, as well as four additional Early Classic interments from the Acropolis. The authors utilize strontium isotope ratio analysis and other methods as the basis for inferences about diet, traumas, and life histories for each of these buried individuals, suggesting that several of these individuals were born and raised in areas outside the Copan Valley.

Epigraphy and Iconography

The three chapters in this section focus on the epigraphic and iconographic record from Early Classic Copan. They provide key historical information that, combined with other data sets, furnishes a richer understanding of Copan's dynastic origins and its development as a polity capital.

Stuart presents his analyses of Copan inscriptions that refer to the predynastic and early dynastic periods, including the text of Altar Q, a carved stone monument which provides the best account of Copan's dynastic founding by K'inich Yax K'uk' Mo'. Stuart notes that this text implies that the founder was an outsider who brought profound political and religious change to the polity. He also discusses new readings for previously undeciphered predynastic inscriptions and traces the importance of Teotihuacan in legitimizing the dynastic founder's power.

B. Fash focuses on *in situ* sculptures which, once integrated into the archaeological chronology, help map the development of the Early Classic sculptural tradition at Copan. Noting that iconographic language informs our understanding of the religious and cultural beliefs displayed on public monuments, she demonstrates that this language absorbed traditions from Copan's neighbors during this critical period in its history and influenced sculptural conventions at other Maya sites.

Taube concludes this section with a discussion of the iconography of the superimposed sequence of buildings beneath Structure 10L-16, located at the core of the Acropolis. The central motif of the final building in this series, Structure 10L-16, concerns the fiery resurrection of the dynastic founder as the sun-god, a theme associated with several of the preceding Early Classic structures buried below and consistent with central Mexican mortuary ritual and symbolism.

Regional Context

The four concluding chapters place Copan within a wider Mesoamerican context, seeking to correlate Early Classic events at Copan with those in the southeast Maya area, the Maya highlands, the southern Maya lowlands, and the Valley of Oaxaca.

Sharer shows how the archaeological and historical evidence reveals interactions with some of the leading polities in Mesoamerica during Copan's Early Classic dynastic founding era. He proposes that the southern Maya lowlands played a critical role in the formation of the Early Classic Copan state, reconstructed as a Tikal-orchestrated takeover of Copan led by K'inich Yax K'uk' Mo'. Broken monuments and destroyed architecture suggest that a violent event occurred at Copan in the mid-6th century, most likely also originating in the Maya lowlands.

Urban and Schortman examine the neighboring central Honduran region where the proliferation of local material styles suggests the definition of localized zones where hierarchy-building advanced in some cases and faltered in others. The rapid transformations experienced by Copan's rulers and subjects must be understood within this context. They examine the varied trajectories of Early Classic central Honduran societies, relations among these paths, events at Copan, and some of the reasons underlying the variety observed in the archaeological record.

Valdés and Wright address the close ties between Copan and Kaminaljuyu, one of the premier highland centers in adjacent Guatemala. They amplify our understanding of the history and autonomy of this important polity from its Middle Preclassic origins to its Early Classic political transformation, when populations at Kaminaljuyu may have moved into the Copan region. Drawing on isotopic data, Valdés and Wright investigate shifts in diet and identify foreigners from the Maya lowlands in Early Classic Esperanza phase tombs at Kaminaljuyu.

Marcus provides a comparative context for the rise of the Early Classic Copan state. In the Valley of Oaxaca, primary states evolved from the rise and fall of rival local chiefdoms as each attempted to incorporate its neighbors into a larger polity. Copan, however, is seen as the product of secondary state formation, created by the arrival of K'inich Yax K'uk' Mo' from an already established state. Accompanied by ambitious public construction, new royal texts, marriages to prominent local women, and the acquisition of new territory, his arrival follows a pattern seen elsewhere in Mesoamerica.

Final Words

Individually, the contributions to this volume represent the coordinated efforts of multiple research programs undertaken at Copan since 1988 by a wide variety of researchers. However, taken as unit, these contributions constitute a research approach unparalleled in the Classic Maya area in its duration, complexity, and interdisciplinary effort. We offer this volume, therefore, not only as a collection of the findings of many research programs, but also as a testament to the efficacy of the conjunctive approach—a comprehensive, inclusive, and multiscalar research design that extends far beyond the parameters of any single research program. We hope that both the research questions asked and the answers supplied by this research provide a model for not only future and larger research initiatives at Copan, but also elsewhere in the Maya area.

I SETTLEMENT AND LANDSCAPE

1

THE EARLY CLASSIC COPAN LANDSCAPE: A VIEW FROM THE PRECLASSIC

Jay Hall and René Viel

C opan has been investigated for longer and has been subjected to a greater variety of archaeological investigations than any other major Maya site. Monumental and multifaceted research efforts have produced a level of understanding about fully Classic Copan (A.D. 600-900) perhaps unrivaled for the lowland Maya (Webster et al. 2000:vii–ix), but we need a clear picture of the developments that preceded A.D. 426 when K'inich Yax K'uk' Mo' took power and began monumental construction on a grander scale. It is somewhat ironic and certainly tantalizing that Copan is also the only lowland Maya site to have yielded unequivocal evidence for an Early Preclassic occupation (Marcus 1995:9): the Rayo phase living surface, dated around 1400 B.C., found in the Las Sepulturas group below a Gordon phase cemetery (Fash 1991:65–66) dated around 1000 B.C.

We find it curious that so little of Preclassic Copan was revealed despite the over 1,000 test pits that have been dug by earlier projects in a pattern designed to gain a representative sample of sites in the Copan pocket (Webster et al. 2000). Was it simply that this earlier occupation was too ephemeral or limited in area to have left many traces? Was the historically changeable Copan River responsible for destroying the evidence? Were the earlier excavations not dug deeply enough through sterile lower sediments? Or, was this lack of information simply the result of a research design that focused too narrowly on the Classic period (see Marcus 1995:30)? On evidence, none of the answers to the above questions provides a particularly compelling argument for this lack of evidence, although there seems to be a partial case for all of them.

Driven by this curiosity and holding to the premise that it is not possible to understand fully Classic Copan without understanding its Late Preclassic roots, we designed an archaeological research program aimed at revealing more of the nature and extent of those early roots. In presenting the preliminary results of this project, this chapter tangentially relates to Copan's Early Classic period by using evidence for the Preclassic landscape to propose an updated environmental backdrop to the important cultural events in and after A.D. 426. It also seeks to provide a fuller appreciation of how dramatically the local landscape was modified and managed by the Maya when they took power in the Copan Valley. A key element underlying that modification process was the Copan River system and its capacity to disrupt an orderly farming life centered on its fertile floodplain.

Copan: The Valley and the River

The urban core of Copan is constructed within the confines of the largest of five small alluvial pockets nestled along a sinuous 38 km stretch of the relatively narrow and steeply sloped Copan River Valley system (Turner et al. 1983). The waters of this steeply graded river flow in a southwesterly direction from headwaters at the Sierra Gallinero divide (1,100 m above sea level) down to the Honduras-Guatemala border (550 m above sea level) some 12 km downstream from Copan, where its name changes to the Camotan River, before eventually joining the great Motagua River.

In their pioneering work for the PAC I, Turner et al. (1983), identified a number of environmental zones and associated geomorphic features across the Copan segment of this river system. Situated at an elevation of some 600 m above sea level, the fertile alluvial bottomlands (ca. 12.5 km long and up to 4 km wide) include the present inundation zone and older alluvial terraces of two different elevations ("high" and "low"). The higher terrace meets a relatively wide and gently sloping piedmont and foothill zone (at ca. 650–700 m) before slopes rise steeply and develop into rugged mountainous terrain that peaks at about 1,400 m.

Almost 85% of the Copan Valley's soils are quite low in fertility; the highly fertile *entisols* and *mollisols* that compose the remaining 15% are found in the bottomland and foothill zones. In fact, the latter were and still are the most agriculturally productive (Webster et al. 2000:17; Wingard 1996). In addition, due to the valley's high slope gradients (75% of the land lies on a slope gradient of over 8%, and 40% lies on a gradient of over 16%), erosion is a potential problem that is exacerbated by agriculturally motivated forest clearing (Webster et al. 2000:17). In such scenarios, increased slope runoff of water and sediment would significantly affect the geomorphic characteristics of the Copan River system, especially in the bottomlands.

Particularly relevant to this chapter is the geomorphic history of the Copan River, which was developed by Turner et al. (1983:80) under the auspices of PAC I. Their investigation of the river channel, terrace, and archaeological sediments demonstrated dramatic change over the past several millennia. This documented history begins in late Pleistocene times that saw alluviation of the valley from a level near bedrock up to 35 m or more. During the terminal Pleistocene, after a short period of stabilization, a down-cutting phase created the high terrace, and the system again stabilized for sufficient time to permit alluvial soil development. During a period estimated at between 1000 B.C. and A.D. 500, the bottomlands are inferred to have witnessed frequent periods of aggradation and lateral movements of the river channel, a process which widened the inundation plain. However, such changes were considered of insufficient magnitude to cause significant cultural disturbance (Turner et al. 1983:86).

The last major change appears to have been cultural: at some point during the middle of the Classic period (ca. A.D. 700), the Maya themselves diverted the river channel and no doubt undertook other civil engineering projects to mitigate the undesirable effects of an active river system. This natural process, while held partially in check by the labors of a great many inhabitants of Copan, resumed when this polity fell into decline after A.D. 800. Between 1,000 and 500 years ago the river began downcutting, resulting in the current low terrace (Turner et al. 1983:86). Subsequently, the river stabilized vertically, and its new meandering course over a widened floodplain became responsible for the undercutting and destruction of a large portion of the Acropolis and other valuable segments of the archaeological record in the bottomlands of the Copan pocket (Fash 1991:43-44). With this scenario of an active and restless riverine landscape outlined, we turn now to our search for the Preclassic record of Copan.

The Copan Formative Project

When fieldwork commenced in 1992, the Preclassic was represented by four rather small ceramic assemblages: Rayo, Gordon, Uir, and Chabij (Viel 1993a, 1993b). During 1993, the University of Queensland team excavated 26 2 x 2 m test excavation units within a transect that extends from the Copan Sculpture Museum, along the former airstrip, to the base of the Chinchilla Mound, just north of the Great Plaza (Figure 1.1). Excavation units were usually excavated to the underlying riverbed (up to 7 m below the modern surface) as there was a concern that the PAC I units might not have been deep enough to reveal deeply buried Preclassic material. This testing yielded several facts pertinent to our understanding of the early Copan landscape (Hall and Viel 1994; Viel and Hall 1994). First, we recovered a full sequence of ceramic assemblages, ranging from Early Preclassic Rayo (Locona horizon: 1200-1400 B.C.) to Protoclassic Bijac (A.D. 50-400), which lay below Classic occupation debris (mostly Coner, very little Acbi). Second, no Preclassic cultural features were encountered. Third, the stratigraphy exhibited alternating horizontal layers of clays, silts, and sands and gravels, and thick (>30 cm) sterile deposits often separated artifact-bearing strata. Fourth, ceramic sherds from below Classic period deposits were generally small and/or abraded and rounded.

From the above facts we inferred that, with respect to deposits below the surface remnants of Classic period structures, we had been excavating alluvial and colluvial deposits related to flooding and other products of torrential weather conditions. In short, the Preclassic materials recovered were the product of at least secondary deposition with their exact origin unknown. In 1994, the testing focus was shifted to a level area between the Chinchilla Mound and the northern limit of the Great Plaza. Here the results were mixed: excavation units nearer the plaza exhibited cultural stratigraphy and features relating to plaza construction while those farther to the north were stratigraphically similar to those dug on the old airstrip northwest of the Principal Group in 1993.

Although the results of two seasons' testing were disappointing because no Preclassic cultural features were discovered, it led to a fruitful reconsideration of the influence of the Copan River on the early landscape, especially on the floodplain. What seemed puzzling to us at the time was the depth and distance of these laminated alluvial deposits in relation to the current river channel. Returning to the evidence marshaled by Turner et al. (1983) to postulate shifts in the main river channel during the Middle Preclassic, we began to investigate the possibility that the river had changed course during pre-Rayo times and had actually cut a new channel well to the north. However, consultation with a geo-morphologist, Jean-Pierre Tihay, led to a closer field investigation of sediments exposed in our test pits as well as in the current Copan River channel. The outcome of this study produced a somewhat different hypothesis, one that better accounts for our current evidence.

We now postulate that torrential events during Copan's early settlement produced an overflow channel that ran through the northern end of the Principal Group, debouching into the Copan River west of the El Bosque ward (Figure 1.1). This channel was probably spawned not so much by over-bank spillage of a rain-swollen Copan River but rather by significant volumes of sediment-loaded water coming down the steep valley slopes in tributary channels and as surface runoff during periods of torrential rain. This hypothesis also predicted the coexistence of smaller transverse defluviation channels running from the main overflow channel through the El Bosque ward to the main river channel.

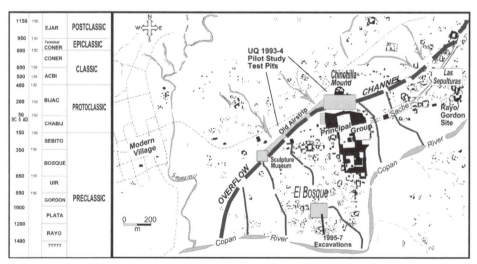

Figure 1.1 Copan study area showing localities and features noted in text plus a simplified version of the revised chronology (re-drawn after Viel and Hall 1998).

This textbook scenario provided a useful working model with testable implications, and it subsequently served to shift the focus of our testing program southwest
of the Principal Group to the El Bosque ward where remnants of Preclassic life-ways
were predicted to have survived the effects of flooding and gully erosion. Promising
test excavation units sunk at a Bosque locality near Ballcourt B in 1995 were expanded in 1996 and 1997 to expose larger areas relating to predicted paleo-channels and
main stratigraphic disconformities. We now summarize the results from two of these
enlarged pits.

Pit 9

This pit is a T-shaped aggregation of 16 2 x 2 m excavation units dug on the eastern
edge of Structures 14 and 15. Figure 1.2 shows aspects of the western segment while
Figure 1.3 is a composite stratigraphic profile of this segment. Both figures display a
number of salient points pertaining to the postulated model. First, some 40–50 cm
below Late Classic (Coner) fill and construction (Stratigraphic Unit I [SU I]) lies a dis-
conforming, culturally sterile, and homogenous silty clay deposit (SU III) which in turn
overlies culturally sterile gravelly sand (SU IV). Second, the surface of this deposit is
relatively level until it slopes sharply to the south and becomes associated with a feature interpreted as a collapsed house lying at the top of the current water table and
radiocarbon dated to 800–500 B.C. [cal] (Hall and Viel 1998). This elevated and fairly
level surface is pitted with several other cultural features that have been interpreted as
ovens, kilns, and trash pits. Dating of these surface features from *in situ* ceramics and
a single radiocarbon determination from one excavation unit (100 B.C.–A.D. 30 [cal])
puts the SU III surface between Late Preclassic (Sebito) and Early Protoclassic (Chabij)
times.

We interpret SU III as an exposure of the extensive alluvium identified by
Turner et al. (1983) that originated in the terminal Pleistocene and on which soil developed during a relatively stable period in the river's history. In this particular locality
we observe an exposed patch of arable land where local farmers worked, built their
houses, and carried out daily subsistence activities near the main river channel. At this
locality, the land's southern edge overlooked a body of water, perhaps a tranquil pond
within a defluviation channel or an oxbow relating to a former river channel. This
edge was slowly eroded by lateral water seepage into the fine alluvium base, causing
subsequent slumping of the bank.

A simple stone-and-adobe house, with a human burial beneath and numerous
domestic artifacts in and around it, was located near this bank. As the erosion process
incorporated it, the house slowly dissolved and disarticulated as it settled into the
pond mud, coming to rest some 50 cm below its original position on the bank (Hall
and Viel 1998). Structural remains of this house (river-worn cobbles) are associated
with exceptionally well-preserved and barely disturbed, although broken, ceramic ves-

Figure 1.2 Two aspects of Pit 9 (Op. 57/9) highlighting features noted in text.

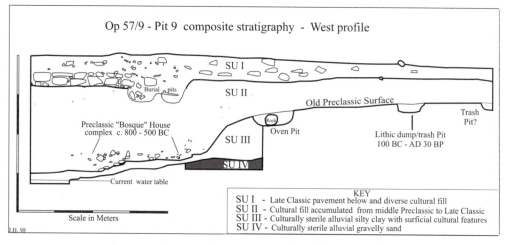

Figure 1.3 Composite western profile of Pit 9 (Op. 57/9)
showing key strata and cultural features.

sels belonging to the newly defined Bosque complex which, according to the recently revised Copan chronology, dates to 650–350 B.C. (Viel and Hall 1998; Viel 1999a). The fauna associated with this complex, while predominately deer and peccary, included the tapir, an animal that is normally found in a wetter habitat than that seen in Copan today.

Pit 3

Located roughly 50 m east and 20 m north of Pit 9, this pit is a roughly square aggregation of 2 x 2 m pits (ca. 100 m^2 in area) that were excavated below a Late Classic house-group plaza (between Structures 20, 22, 23; Figure 1.1). Removal of Classic period deposits below the plaza's stone pavement revealed a sharp discontinuity between a dark upper unit (SU II) with abundant *cascajo* inclusions (rubble from stone masonry) and a lower silty clay unit (SU III; see Figure 1.4). While the upper part of SU III contains cultural material, this thick alluvium becomes culturally sterile before giving way to sorted sands, gravels, pebbles, and cobbles relating to a former riverbed. Since the stratigraphy in SU III is almost identical in character to its counterpart in neighboring Pit 9, we consider the two as probably contemporary, with both exposures representing windows into the older Preclassic landscape.

The lowest cultural remains found in SU III comprise a small and isolated patch of Middle Preclassic (Uir) sherds. Most other artifacts and several features associated with SU III date to the Protoclassic period (A.D. 150–400). Notable features

SU I

SU II

Rubble
fill

Old Channel

SU III

Figure 1.4 Northern exposure of Pit 3 (Op. 57/9) showing strata,
old alluvial surface, and channel scar.

include a large circular earthen oven (with a central stone surrounded by several kilo-grams of well-preserved charcoal) and a small earthen mound associated with an extended burial containing Bijac ceramics (Hall and Viel 1998). A calibrated radiocar-bon date of A.D. 240 was obtained on charcoal from the oven. This date places this SU II/SU III interface prior to the Early Classic.

An interesting feature of this interface is that, unlike the level surfaces between Classic Maya building mounds, it is quite uneven. Figure 1.4 highlights the northern profile of a notable topographic feature of this earlier surface. Essentially, it is a shallow (up to 80 cm deep) U-shaped channel that fits the morphology of those predicted in the defluviation zone. The large river cobbles shown on pedestals in Figure 1.4 lie in a linear fashion across the bottom of this channel. Since they are too large and too regularly sorted and aligned to have arrived there by natural means, we currently interpret them as "stepping stones" through shallow muddy water.

This channel differs from that noted in Pit 9 in that its sides appear too regular to have been shaped and maintained by nature. Furthermore, while its base contained a thin accumulation of ceramics and stones of varying shapes and sizes, the channel did not exhibit an expected deposit of gravels and sands which should have been quite well sorted in the base of a defluviation channel. These observations led us to hypothesize that the channel was regularly maintained by the local inhabitants during Protoclassic and Early Classic times; that is, sands, silts, and debris were regularly scooped up onto the banks to keep the channel clear and perhaps to provide added nutrients for local soils.

Discussion

While these summarized preliminary results simplify what is undoubtedly a more com-plicated picture, they at least permit useful inferences concerning a Preclassic land-scape about which little was previously known. First, the topography of the low allu-vial terrace and associated inundation zone upon which the Principal Group and urban core were constructed was quite different from the relatively level one of Classic Copan (or that seen today). That earlier terrain, represented by the SU III alluvium in the Bosque locality as well as in numerous test excavations on the airstrip, was more undulating, dissected by sinuous channels of varying depth and width, and probably also wetter and muddier than today.

This scenario is supported by subsequent investigation of other lines of evi-dence. A review of the stratigraphic profiles of PAC I test excavations (e.g., Cheek

1983a, 1983b; Fash 1983c; Valdés and Cheek 1983) reveals not only old alluvial sediments from which Johnson identified paleosol remnants (Turner et al. 1983), but these sediments also indicate an uneven and dissected terrain. Also, Tihay interprets the fine lamellar clay sediments exposed by the Early Copan Acropolis Program (ECAP) at the very base of the Acropolis as indicative of a marshy, perhaps even lacustrine environment (Sharer, Traxler, et al. 1999:5).

Second, we infer on chrono-stratigraphic grounds that the Maya filled these gullies or channels in order to level the ground for urban expansion. Much of that fill included the rubble created by Copan's masons as they shaped cut stone blocks for the buildings. As the dating of features directly associated with the SU III surface shows it to have been occupied from perhaps as early as 800 B.C. and certainly up to and including the Late Protoclassic period of ca. A.D. 200–400, such terrain leveling could not have been undertaken until quite late. Since Coner ceramics dominate the record and Acbi sherds are rare in the rubble fill, this terraforming expansion, at least into this part of the Bosque ward, appears to have occurred during the Late Classic, and certainly after A.D. 550–600. In this connection, preliminary results from another of our excavations in the Bosque (Pit 6) that reveal an unusually high proportion of Acbi ceramics and construction features, indicate that this Early Classic occupation also rested on undulating rather than leveled terrain. Since these people appear to have used river cobbles rather than cut stone for construction, they cannot be responsible for the fairly large-scale expansion into the Bosque inferred from Pit 3.

Thus, it would appear that the landscape of the Copan pocket at the time of K'inich Yax K'uk' Mo' was probably little changed from the one that had been around for at least 1,000 years and perhaps much longer. It was certainly nothing like the landscape at the end of the recorded dynasty in A.D. 822. This later landscape had undergone massive alteration through sophisticated engineering and architectural development during the Late Classic. Moreover, these alterations would have required a large, specialized, and well-organized labor force (see Abrams 1994). Nevertheless, the Early Classic was also a period of building and population expansion and, in order to counter the periodic and potentially disastrous effects of torrential conditions in the valley, significant engineering adjustments were also necessary.

In fact, one of our test excavation units at the northern edge of the Northwest Platform revealed a stone wall associated with Acbi ceramics. We currently interpret this construction as a protective measure against floodwaters, perhaps a rock lining for the postulated overflow channel which directed the course of the waters around important buildings within the defluviation zone. In addition, the bulk of the Acropolis was constructed in the Early Classic, overlying initial episodes of filling and platform construction dated to the introduction of Acbi ceramics (Sharer, Traxler, et al. 1999:8–9). Outside the Acropolis, cultural mitigation of nature's deleterious effects during the Early Classic should not be considered at anything like the scale witnessed during the Late Classic. It was no doubt much more planned and proactive than that of the preceding periods.

For some time now, we have considered this apparent difference in scale of cultural modification of the local environment in terms of changing land management practices in the valley. Since we can now view parts of the old Preclassic landscape through "windows" created by our excavations, we are in a position to advance and test notions of cultural agency in its manipulation. Unsurprisingly, our investigations lead us to argue strongly for the Copan River system as the most influential element in shaping the Preclassic cultural landscape. On this evidence we argue for relatively passive land management by the inhabitants of Copan throughout Preclassic times (1400 B.C.–A.D. 400). Although they depended on the alluvial soils in the inundation zone of the Copan pocket for their subsistence crops, there is nothing to suggest that residents were anything but passive recipients of nature's wrath.

During the Late Classic, the pendulum swung heavily in the opposite direction, with a huge investment by local inhabitants in engineering projects designed to tame the effects of torrential conditions. In fact, their works terra-formed the pocket and protected the Principal Group so well against the effects of torrential weather that modern events such as Hurricane Mitch in 1998 did not damage the site, while it destroyed modern bridges and sealed roads throughout the country (Viel and Hall 2000a).

Although we can see the two ends of this pendulum's arc with relative ease, it is more difficult to assess its middle section, or the rate at which the change occurred. However, test excavation units provide tantalizing hints that during late Bijac and early Acbi times some more active or at least "less" passive activities were undertaken to mitigate flooding. As noted above, the presence of regular-sided channels in the Bosque with "scoured" bottoms suggest that people might have kept the watercourses clear of clogging debris and vegetation (as well as perhaps incorporating them into a raised field cultivation system) and the "Acbi wall" north of the Great Plaza was possibly built to control overflow channel waters (Hall and Viel 1998).

Rather than viewing this inferred change from passive to active human agency as a gradual one, we see it consisting of several quantum steps. While it is too soon to argue for such steps in the Preclassic, we think that one occurred after about 150 B.C., another at ca. A.D. 400, and another after A.D. 600. These changes perhaps coincided respectively with postulated influences from the Guatemalan Highlands, the accession of K'inich Yax K'uk' Mo', and the accession of Ruler 12.

Conclusion

We have emphasized that the model is based on coarse-grained evidence and that only detailed investigation, which is planned for future years, will serve to test its explanatory utility. One critical piece of research planned for the near future is a comprehensive non-invasive subsurface testing program (magnetometer and ground-penetrating radar) aimed at identifying and determining the extent and character of the old alluvial surface. Once the face of that long-lived alluvial surface has been identified and mapped, we shall be better able to assess the model and to more accurately target areas for future investigation of the Preclassic without the trial-and-error aspect of normal test excavation that destroys the integrity of cultural deposits of later periods.

Acknowledgments

The Copan Formative Project was variously funded by The Australian Research Council, The French Ministry of Foreign Affairs through the CEMCA, and the University of Queensland. We owe a debt of gratitude to the Instituto Hondureño de Antropología e Historia (IHAH) and its staff both in Tegucigalpa and Copan for generous support and cooperation. A special debt is owed to Dr. Jean-Pierre Tihay for giving so freely of his geo-morphological expertise. Our sincerest thanks to Ricardo Agurcia Fasquelle for continuous support of our project, both personally and in his capacity as Director of the Asociación Copan. Finally, we warmly thank all those excellent excavators from Copan who dug with such diligence and precision and the numerous University of Queensland archaeology students who have assisted us so well in the field and the laboratory.

2

THE RURAL SETTLEMENT OF COPAN:
CHANGES THROUGH THE EARLY CLASSIC

Marcello A. Canuto

T his chapter is concerned with the interaction between Copan and its surrounding rural settlement before and after the Early Classic. During this period, settlement in the hinterland area to the east of the Copan Valley (known as the
Río Amarillo Valley) exhibits marked changes in settlement pattern, spatial organization, architectural style, resource exploitation, and ritual activity. These changes reflect
a much broader development within the Copan drainage, namely the formation of a
dynastic state in the 5th and 6th centuries A.D. at Copan. The following discussion
attempts to provide a fresh perspective on the nature of this development by examining the transformation of the rural community as a consequence of the unique changes
triggered in A.D. 426 when K'inich Yax K'uk' Mo' took power and established his
dynastic rule in Copan.

A Question of Scale

At Copan, top-down analyses of dynastic history (Fash 1983b, 1988; B. Fash et al. 1992;
W. Fash et al. 1992; Sanders and Webster 1988; Sharer, Traxler, et al. 1999; Viel 1999b),
monumental architecture (Agurcia F. 1996, 1997c; Andrews and Fash 1992; Sharer et al.
1992; Sharer, Traxler, et al. 1999; Williamson 1996), and elite compounds (Hendon 1987,
1989; Sanders 1986; Traxler 2001) show that the 5th century A.D. was a pivotal period
in Copan's history. These studies also demonstrate that Copan's early dynasty was
capable of commandeering labor and resources (Carrelli, this volume) at unexpected
levels to alter both its natural (see Hall and Viel, this volume) and architectural land-
scapes (see Agurcia F.; Fash et al.; Sedat and López; and Traxler, this volume).
Furthermore, related work (see Grube et al. 1995; Martin and Grube 1995, 2000;
Reents-Budet et al., this volume; and Sharer, this volume) has shown the many connec-

tions this early dynasty had with the larger and more powerful polities of its time. Recognizing the development of this dynasty and a powerful elite class, the increased conflicts between polities, and an eventually over-taxed ecological system, this research concludes that the Copan dynasty controlled a large territorial state which over-extended itself and eventually retracted and collapsed in the beginning of the 9th century A.D. (see Marcus 1992a, 1993).

Curiously, bottom-up research at Copan—settlement analysis (Freter 1988, 1994, 1996; Leventhal 1979; Webster 1985; Webster and Freter 1990b; Willey et al. 1979), ecological and palynological analyses (Rue 1987; Wingard 1996), and household archaeology (Gonlin 1993, 1994; Webster and Gonlin 1988)—has developed quite a contrasting model for Classic Copan's political development. This settlement research addresses broad issues of socioeconomic organization and social evolution (see Blanton 1994; Netting et al. 1984; Rathje 1983; Wilk and Rathje 1982) in the rural regions. Focused on changes in demographic patterns, social organization, and agricultural strategy, these studies generally concluded that the Copan dynasty was only loosely influential in the developments of its rural population. Noting that Copan's dynastic collapse was not accompanied by a decline in rural population (Freter 1988, 1994), this research claims that the Copan dynasty had nominal control over a loose confederation of autonomous lineages inclined to sociopolitical fragmentation rather than unity—a segmentary state (Sanders 1989; Sanders and Webster 1988).

These two top-down and bottom-up models of center-periphery interaction are contradictory because they are the result of incompatible research approaches. However, a mid-level approach focusing on the sociopolitical unit known as the *rural community* can resolve this epistemological and empirical impasse. Because of its integrative role both on a regional and local scale, the rural community proves pivotal to our understanding of how a large polity and its surrounding population interacted. Despite recent interest in the community from other quarters in archaeology (see Canuto and Yaeger 2000; Kolb and Snead 1997; Rogers and Smith 1995; Schwartz and Falconer 1994; Wills and Leonard 1994, for examples), at Copan this important social unit has been largely overlooked (see Fash 1983a for an exception). However, recent research (Canuto 1997, 1998, 1999a, 1999b, 2002) has adopted this social category as its basic unit of analysis in order to address the nature of polity-settlement interaction.

Settlement Research and the Segmentary Model

Settlement research at Copan began with systematic survey and test excavations within the Copan Valley (Willey et al. 1978). This work categorized settlement within a four-tiered hierarchy based on the architectural and physical criteria of each site. Furthermore, the Copan region was divided into three zones—urban, pocket, and rural (Figure 2.1)—each exhibiting different densities and distributions of the established

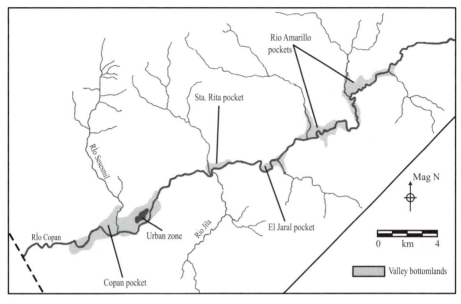

Figure 2.1 Copan drainage settlement zones
(re-drawn after Webster and Gonlin 1988: 171, fig. 1).

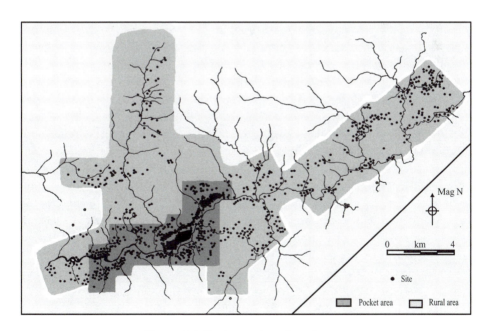

Figure 2.2 Pocket and rural settlement
(re-drawn after Webster and Freter 1992: 118, fig. 1).

settlement types (see Baudez 1983; Fash 1983c; Sanders 1986; Sanders and Webster 1988). These categorical and regional divisions allowed subsequent research to focus on the dynamics—movement, growth, migration, and colonization—of the various settlement types within the distinct zones (Figure 2.2). This research identified the Early Classic period (A.D. 400-600) as a time of great demographic expansion from the polity center (Fash 1983c). As settlement filled the urban zone, covering and rendering unusable the agricultural lands of the Copan Valley (see Hall and Viel, this volume), populations were forced into more marginal regions of the valley (Fash 1983a) and into the rural area (Freter 1988, 1994, 1996; Webster et al. 1992; Webster and Freter 1990a; Wingard 1996).

When settlement survey expanded by 135 km^2 to encompass surrounding rural regions like the Río Amarillo Valley to the east (see Sanders and Webster 1988; Webster 1985), investigations demonstrated that rural settlement could not be categorized with the same types used for the Copan Valley survey. Because the rural settlement consisted much more heavily of smaller residences, new settlement categories were devised to capture the full range of this variation (Webster 1985). These smaller rural residences were interpreted as reflective of the low socioeconomic status of the rural population.

A program of household archaeology followed this survey in order to assess the nature of rural socioeconomic status and to determine if there existed distinctions among the various rural populations (see Johnston and Gonlin 1998). This investigation recognized that the rural population was characterized by (1) a simpler settlement hierarchy, (2) the predominance of utilitarian Late Classic ceramics, and (3) obsidian-hydration dates ranging centuries beyond the collapse of the Copan dynasty. Research concluded that the hinterland population consisted of dispersed, self-sufficient, and "humble" homesteaders (Gonlin 1993, 1994; Webster and Gonlin 1988) with little or no supra-household organization. Furthermore, the interaction of this population with Copan was inferred to be economic: as there would have been less cultivable land available within the Copan Valley (Webster et al. 1992; Wingard 1996), the rural population would have provided the polity the foodstuffs it could no longer produce itself.

These regional survey and household approaches recognized the economically self-sufficient and kinship-affiliated *household* as the rural population's most complex form of social organization. The larger settlement clusters in the rural areas (Figure 2.3) represented successful multi-generational households organized along lineage affiliations. These localized lineages, moreover, were only loosely tethered to maximal lineage heads at Copan (Freter 1988; Sanders 1981, 1989) and largely impervious to dynastic collapse. The autonomy of rural lineage groups resulted in a model for polity-hinterland interaction that emphasized the dispersed, centrifugal, and segmentary nature of Classic Maya society.

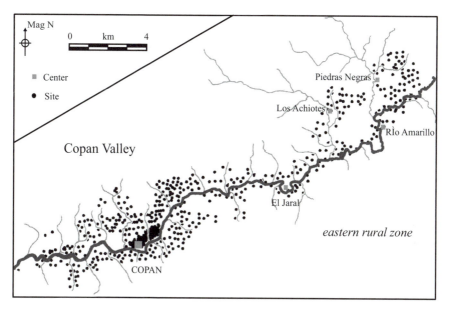

Figure 2.3 Copan Drainage Settlement.
(redrawn after Freter 1992: 129, Fig. 6)

Importance of Community Research

At Copan, between the rural household and the rural population, however, there exists another unit of sociopolitical organization—the rural community. This midrange unit of social organization integrates local and regional forms of interaction. In fact, the community, rather than either the *population* or the *household*, represents both the physical location and social context for all salient forms of supra-household interaction (see Yaeger and Canuto 2000; Yaeger 2000). Consequently, the study of center-periphery interaction cannot reside in the study of the elite center, population, or household; rather, it can only be recognized in the development, organization, and dynamics of the community in which all these various spheres of interaction intersected.

Research on the organization and dynamics of the rural community proves indispensable to understanding the impact the elite center had on rural settlement, especially during the development of the Early Classic Copan dynasty. Focusing on various micro-regions (Figure 2.4; see Gaffney and Gaffney 1988; Gaffney and Tingle 1988) within the Río Amarillo Valley region rather than on single households, particular elite

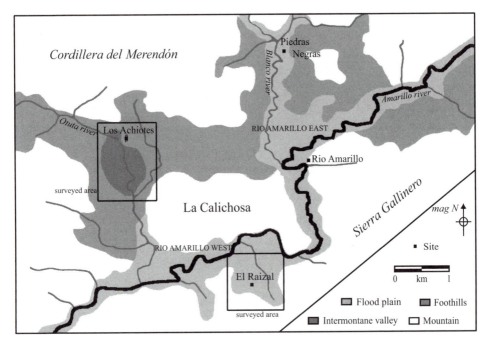

Figure 2.4 Río Amarillo rural zone.

polities, or even whole regions, I investigated two rural communities—Los Achiotes and El Raizal—on their own terms. The preliminary results of these investigations, presented below (see Canuto 2002 for greater detail), helped characterize center-hinterland interaction more precisely and, consequently, assess the development of state organization at Copan.

Los Achiotes and El Raizal: An Initial Comparison

The site of Los Achiotes (Figure 2.5) is located roughly 20 km east of Copan in a small pocket of the Río Otuta—a Río Amarillo tributary—with a deep and fertile stratum of topsoil (Olson 1979). The occupation of this site precedes the Early Classic dynastic expansion of Copan. Los Achiotes ceramics belong to the Chabij and Bijac ceramic phases, suggesting a Late Preclassic and Protoclassic occupation; furthermore, three radiocarbon dates from wood posts defined an occupational span from ca. 250 B.C. to A.D. 150. The central site and its coeval settlement are located, without exception, on the hilltops surrounding the floodplain. While the largest site sits atop an ancient alluvial spur, the surrounding mound groups are located on separate knolls overlooking

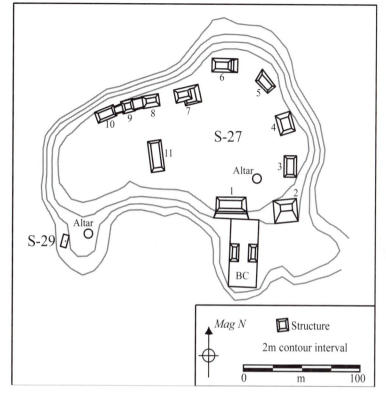

Figure 2.5 Los Achiotes.

the floodplain. The inhabitants of this community refrained from living on the floodplain, preferring the security of higher ground. This pattern of site location near, rather
than on, the agriculturally fertile land is also seen in the Copan Valley in this time period (see Fash 1983b, 1991; Hall and Viel, this volume).

The site of El Raizal (Figure 2.6) is also located some 20 km east of Copan (3
km south of Los Achiotes) in a small valley drained by the Quebrada Raizal which also
feeds into the Río Amarillo. The site was established and occupied during the apogee
of the Copan dynasty, roughly A.D. 500 to A.D. 800. The ceramics indicate that occupation began during the Acbi phase and extended into Coner times. Consistent with the
ceramic data, radiocarbon samples date the occupation from A.D. 600 to A.D. 800.
Moreover, the earliest radiocarbon date was located above an Acbi midden, suggesting
that occupation had begun even earlier—ca.A.D. 500. In fact, a dedicatory cache with
a Chilanga ceramic vessel indicates the Acbi beginnings of this site's occupation.
Found on the actual floodplain of the valley, the site and its contiguous settlement are

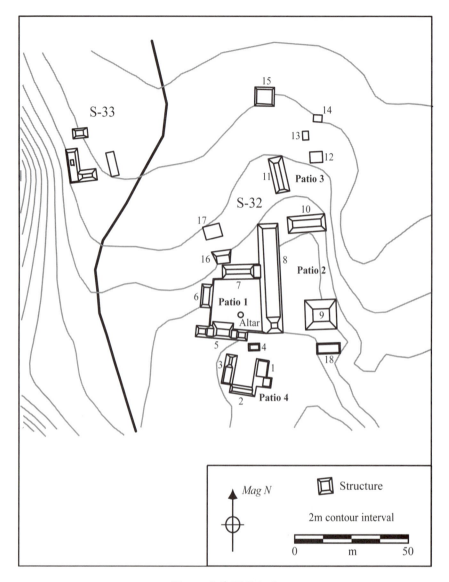

Figure 2.6 El Raizal.

surrounded by foothills on all sides save north. The settlers of this community did not choose to locate their homesteads on strategically advantageous hilltops like those of Los Achiotes. El Raizal's location on the floodplain has no obvious strategic or defensive advantage other than to allow its inhabitants to lay direct claim to the land itself.

The preceding evidence suggests that the rural settlement cannot be seen as a single generic homesteading population: one community represents a Late Preclassic/Protoclassic, pre-dynastic occupation, while the other community indicates occupation beginning in the Early Classic period and coeval with the early dynastic developments in Copan.[*] This chronological information alone poses some problems for an indiscriminate population-based settlement analysis. The temporal discontinuity of this occupation data suggests that Copan's hinterlands were not settled by a homogeneous population in a single wave of centrifugal emigration from Copan. Furthermore, the location of these two communities, relative to the agricultural land that their members exploited, might indicate different forms of intra-community organization. The combination of chronological discontinuity and potential differences in terms of socioeconomic organization makes a community-centered analysis necessary for the development of a more precise model of center-hinterland interaction.

What follows is a preliminary inter- and intra-community comparison of Los Achiotes and El Raizal according to four broad categories: (1) spatial organization, (2) architectural style, (3) material goods, and (4) special deposits and features. Although it might prove impossible to account for these differences precisely, it is clear that ecological or environmental factors cannot be relied upon as explanations. Both sites are located in almost identical topographical and ecological niches, and neither site has differential access to any particular resource. Whatever differences these two communities do exhibit can only be a result of the actions and predispositions of their respective members. Furthermore, it is hoped that these differences can be interpreted as evidence of structural and organizational variation and contribute to the development of a new model for Classic Maya rural sociopolitical organization and its relationship to the polity center.

Spatial Organization

In terms of spatial organization, Los Achiotes and El Raizal differ greatly. Overall, as a community, Los Achiotes has been described as "out of the range of variation of site layout and planning of anything found in the Copan Valley, and appear[ing] to reflect distinct conceptualizations of space" (Vlcek and Fash 1986:109–10). The main group at Los Achiotes (Figure 2.6) consists of household platforms arranged around a large open plaza roughly 75 m^2. Except to the west, each structure is located on the edge of the hilltop. Furthermore, two large terraced platform structures and an altar are located in

---

[*] The occupational span of El Raizal remains very important. The early dates indicate that population incursions into the rural areas happened long before the Copan Valley shows evidence of over-population (see Webster et al. 1992; Wingard 1996). Furthermore, few Coner II (see Bill 1997) and absolutely no Postclassic Ejar ceramics were recovered from this entire area. This ceramic evidence suggests little to no activity at the site much beyond the 9th century A.D.

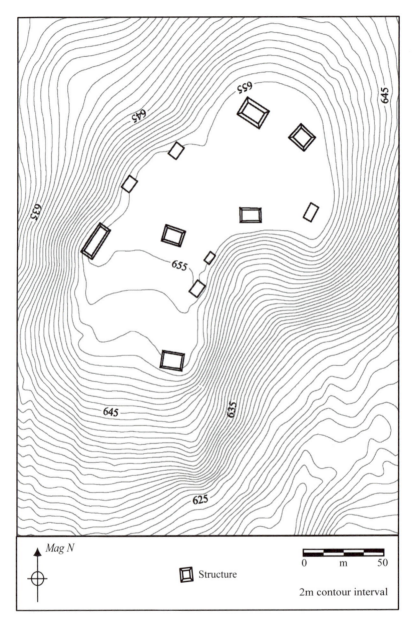

Mag N

Structure

0   m   50

2m contour interval

Figure 2.7 Cerro Chino.

the southern sector of the community.* Although some residences are closer to them than others, none is particularly associated with this sector spatially. The settlement surrounding the main site replicates this pattern at a smaller scale: each group is composed of structures located at the edge of a knoll, creating open and accessible internal patios.

Despite its distinctiveness, the Los Achiotes site plan is not unique within this area. Cerro Chino (see Canuto and McFarlane 2000; Fash and Fash 2000:447) in the Copan Valley is located on a flat hilltop with platforms arranged around a plaza roughly 50 m in diameter (Figure 2.7). Moreover, it is contemporary with Los Achiotes. The correspondence of these two sites could indicate the presence of a spatial and architectural template distinct from that which would follow the imposition of a Petén-based dynasty at Copan. These two sites might represent examples of a pre-dynastic indigenous conception of space and formal planning.

At El Raizal, in contrast to Los Achiotes, the nonresidential structures of the site are contiguous with the main residential patio, suggesting preferential access to non-private sectors of the community for some of its members. The largest cluster of structures is located along an ancient river bank (Figure 2.7). The main structures form a tight, spatially nucleated cluster organized around two restricted-access patios. Divided by a single range structure, the western patio is sunken and surrounded by three residential structures. The eastern patio is limited to the east by the riverbank terrace and by large nonresidential structures to the north and south. Outside of this dual-patio cluster lie smaller ancillary structures organized around enclosed patios.

Overall, the spatial patterning of El Raizal resembles the much larger elite compounds in the Copan Valley, which developed from Acbi times into extensive residential complexes (Fash 1983c). El Raizal's spatial plan also resembles that of another rural site known as Río Amarillo. In fact, this latter site was closely associated with dynastic Copan (Saturno 1996, 2000). El Raizal appears to have been a typical rural community of Copan-based people whose predilection for restricted/enclosed areas as well as for the intermingling of domestic and ritual spaces was replicated at a smaller scale.

Household spatial organization further distinguishes these two communities from each other. Killion (1990, 1992) has related the spatial organization of residential patio groups to agricultural strategies in Mesoamerica, developing a house-lot area model in which a residential patio group household comprises both the structures and the open space surrounding them. In this model, the surrounding space is divided con-

---

* These structures—Structures 1 and 2—differ from others at the site in size and construction. While their precise function remains uncertain, they can be considered as distinct from the rest.

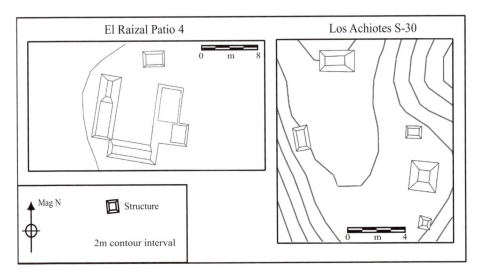

Figure 2.8 Spatial comparison of El Raizal and Los Achiotes households.

centrically into clear, intermediate, and garden-refuse areas. Following Killion's model, equivalently sized patio groups from these two communities (such as S-30 from Los Achiotes and Patio 4 from El Raizal; see Figure 2.8) were compared according to three spatial attributes: (1) spatial openness, (2) size of cleared area around the patio, and (3) size of refuse-garden area.

In terms of openness, the Los Achiotes patio group is easily accessible from three different directions, while the El Raizal patio group is enclosed on all four sides with only one entrance to the northwest. The internal patios, therefore, are very distinct. In terms of cleared area in the patio group, extensive excavations and post hole tests revealed very different patterns. At Los Achiotes, the cleared area of the patio group was very hard to define precisely since the group did not have clear boundaries. However, an area of 1,800 m^2 with an artifact density of ca. 15/m^3 corresponded to the area circumscribed by the residential structures. Outside of this area, artifact density rose threefold. At El Raizal, the cleared area was much more easily recognized since it corresponded perfectly with the internal patio space defined by the four surrounding residential structures. Within an area of 450 m^2, the average artifact density was ca. 20/m^3. Outside the internal patio, the density rose sharply to seventeen times that of the internal patio. Therefore, while both residential patio groups had cleared areas, that of the Los Achiotes group was four times larger.

Finally, the refuse-garden area of each patio group—here defined as the unbroken flat open space surrounding the group—also differed greatly in size. At Los

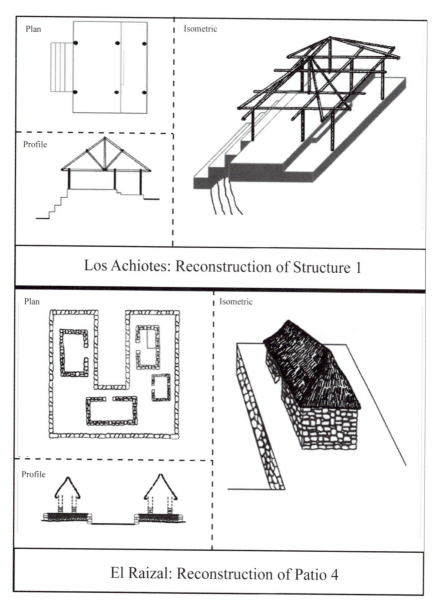

Plan

Isometric

Profile

Los Achiotes: Reconstruction of Structure 1

Plan

Isometric

Profile

El Raizal: Reconstruction of Patio 4

Figure 2.9 Architectural comparison of El Raizal and Los Achiotes households (drawing by Fernando López).

Achiotes, given the patio group's placement on top of a knoll, the refuse-garden—ca. 4,500 m^2—was limited by topography. By contrast, the El Raizal patio group was surrounded on three sides by land amenable to intensive horticulture measuring as large as ca. 5,500 m^2.

Killion (1992) notes that if the cleared area surrounding the residential structures is large and the refuse-garden is small, there exists an emphasis on close-to-house, in-field agriculture. However, where residential structures are surrounded by a small cleared area and a large garden-refuse area, then the residents often engage in far-from-household, out-field agriculture. In broad terms, if this contrast holds for Los Achiotes and El Raizal, these household spatial patterns suggest the existence of very different forms of social organization and subsistence adaptation, despite the ecologically similar locations of both communities.

The Los Achiotes pattern suggests an intensive in-field agricultural system with little emphasis on household horticulture. The nearest fields that Los Achiotes community members would have exploited lie only meters away at the base of the hills they settled. Moreover, because the community was not built on the fertile floodplain, no resident could claim exclusive use of the land (Urban and Schortman, this volume). These fields would have been communally used and owned. If true, the Los Achiotes residents participated in a socially-integrating agricultural system that involved communal farming of nearby lands. The consequent emphasis on the redistribution of agricultural goods through social interaction and ritual would have reduced the need for autonomous household horticulture to supplement family income.

The opposite spatial pattern—a small cleared area and a large garden-refuse area—at El Raizal suggests that most of the families traveled a distance to reach their particular fields. In fact, an exclusive land-tenure pattern might also be indicated by the fact that members of the largest El Raizal residence settled on the best locally available agricultural land. This exclusion would have required other families to farm more distant fields. In fact, it is possible that surrounding families were required to provide tribute labor to the central family as payment for the use of such lands. Furthermore, the larger garden-refuse area around the El Raizal patio group might indicate that its inhabitants, as a household, invested more heavily in horticulture in order to supplement their yields from such fields. This subsistence system would reflect a greater level of household autonomy and responsibility in the absence of the communal strategies inferred for Los Achiotes.

Architecture

The structures from Los Achiotes and El Raizal reflect not only distinct stylistic affiliations but also different forms of social organization. A comparison of the architectural construction and nonresidential structures of both communities demonstrates that El Raizal was characterized by greater intra-community variation than Los Achiotes.

At Los Achiotes, the architecture consists of earthen substructures supporting pole-and-thatch superstructures covered by a large roof (Figure 2.9). Some of the larger substructures are terraced and surrounded by an *argamasa* apron-flooring extending up to 3 m from the base of the substructure. No stone masonry structures, save one (Structure 2), were encountered in the extensive excavations of this site (65% was tested). In this time period, this earthen architectural style is common throughout the southeastern Maya area (e.g., at Chalchuapa; Sharer 1978e) as well as in the Guatemalan highlands (e.g., at Kaminaljuyu; Kidder et al. 1946). Interestingly, predynastic structures from the Copan Acropolis are also constructed using this technique (Sedat and Lopez, this volume) as are the structures of the coeval site of Cerro Chino.

Intra-community architectural variability within Los Achiotes was negligible. Some structures, like Structure 1, were larger than others; however, the overall variation among residential structures was due more to intra-household variability resulting from distinct function than to any symbolic or economic difference. Even the larger structures (except Structure 2) were built in the same manner as the residences. Structure 2 was the sole stone masonry building at the site. As the tallest building, measuring ca. 2 m, it looks more like a shrine temple than a residence. Located in the far south-eastern corner of the hilltop, it overlooks a flat and wide area to the south where residents could have congregated. To the west of this space lies the most prominent nonresidential complex of the community—one of only two known ballcourts in this region ouside Copan.[*] An I-shaped court, measuring 54 m in length, with an 8.2 m wide alley oriented north-south, this ballcourt is also earthen in construction. This open space to the east could also have easily accommodated residents to observe the activities in and around the ballcourt.

The presence of this structure and its surrounding space imply not only a community's political autonomy, enabling it to host such activities, but also the importance of communal activity in general. Given the coordination of labor required for both its construction and multiple ensuing ritual gatherings, the ballcourt area represents the physical space where periodic events would have enforced a communal identity. Moreover, the extra-community interactions, implied by the ballcourt's function as an arena for competition, enhanced the group identity (see Schortman and Nakamura 1991) of the Los Achiotes residents in relation to external visitors.

Turning to El Raizal, the majority of its architecture is cobble masonry used to construct simple platforms supporting superstructures made of cobbles, wattle-and-daub, and perishable roofs (Figure 2.9). Early Classic evidence from monumental centers like Copan, Quirigua (Sharer 1978a), and even Río Amarillo (Saturno 2000) suggest that they also consisted primarily of cobble architecture in their initial phases.

---

[*] The other is located at the site of Los Orquídeas in the Paraíso Valley Department of Copan, Honduras (Canuto and Bell 2003).

Intra-community architectural variation is evident at El Raizal. Markers of prestige such as cut-stone masonry façades, internal stone benches, and non-domestic buildings were not distributed evenly throughout the community. Cut-stone masonry, for instance, was associated exclusively with structures of the central patio group. The conspicuousness of this rare architectural feature attests to the important role this expensive commodity played as a marker of uniqueness. Furthermore, all three benches encountered in excavations belonged to structures of the central patio group.

All non-domestic structures at El Raizal were annexed to this central patio group. This architecture is located to the east of the central patio group and consists of a 40-m-long range structure (Structure 8) to the west, another 18-m-long structure to the north (Structure 10), and a 3.5-m-tall shrine (Structure 9) to the south. Excavation of the shrine structure to the south revealed a three-terraced substructure and outset staircase leading to a perishable superstructure. It was clear that this structure faced north onto another enclosed patio to the east of the central patio group. Activities associated with these nonresidential structures would have been closely associated with the residents of this contiguous patio group. Attendance at these activities might have even have been restricted.

Los Achiotes shared cultural attributes typical of the region in its time. However, internally, Los Achiotes was a community of relatively equivalent families whose group identity provided the basic framework for interaction—both agricultural and ritual. El Raizal exhibits many more complex architectural features than Los Achiotes. The uneven presence of markers of wealth and prestige suggests that El Raizal's intra-community integration was less overtly egalitarian than that of Los Achiotes. Rather, it appears that the central family of El Raizal attempted to align itself with the Copan Valley elite rather than associating itself with its co-communitarians.

The presence of a ballcourt (see Santley et al. 1991) at Los Achiotes suggests its political autonomy. However, the absence of a ballcourt at El Raizal and anywhere else outside of the Copan Principal Group after the rise of Copan's dynasty suggests that the central polity was capable of denying certain rights and privileges to its rural subordinates. Overall, therefore, during Copan's early dynastic period, the integration of rural communities, like El Raizal, within the Copan drainage was more hierarchical than the horizontal integration of Los Achiotes in its contemporaneous political system.

Material Goods

Los Achiotes belongs to the southeastern cultural region (Demarest and Sharer 1986; Sharer 1974; Sharer and Gifford 1970) in terms of ceramics. Its Late Preclassic ceramic assemblage lacks fine-line painted vessels but does include Usulutan fine wares (see Schortman and Urban, this volume). The majority of the utilitarian wares consists of either unslipped burnished vessels (some with incisions in zones) or simple red/orange-slipped vessels. Interestingly, although the fine wares at Los Achiotes appear identical to those of Copan at this time, their utilitarian assemblages differ—possibly a result of different local production traditions (more precise INAA chemical composition tests are in progress. Furthermore, griddles (*comales*) are rare at Los Achiotes. At Copan, the general absence of griddles in the pre-dynastic period has been attributed to the lack of certain griddle-prepared staple foods—like the Maya tortilla—in the Copan diet. It has been noted (Viel 1983) that the griddle becomes ubiquitous in Copan in the Bijac period when Guatemalan highland groups migrated into the Copan area from the west (see Valdés and Wright, this volume). The Los Achiotes community predated this arrival, leaving the ethnic identity of its members as potentially non-Maya.

The lithics from Los Achiotes demonstrate the community's almost equal reliance on local chert and obsidian for stone tools. Obsidian blades are relatively rare, and there is little evidence for any local production of them. These patterns suggest that obsidian blades were imported already manufactured (McFarlane and Canuto 2000) from both Ixtepeque (to the southwest of Copan) and the more distant El Chayal (near Kaminaljuyu). At Los Achiotes, the percentage of El Chayal obsidian is almost twenty times higher than at Copan in the same time period (Canuto and McFarlane 2000; see Aoyama 1996). Normally, El Chayal obsidian is present at Copan in minute quantities, while obsidian from the closer Ixtepeque source predominates. However, the elevated quantity of El Chayal obsidian at Los Achiotes indicates a down-the-line trade southward from the Motagua River Valley, via El Paraíso, to Los Achiotes, perhaps ending in Copan. This trade route allowed members of the Los Achiotes community direct access to an alternate exchange system, and thereby avoiding a dependence on the redistribution of goods at Copan.

In terms of intra-community patterns of material goods, refuse middens show the greatest difference between residences in the central site and its peripheries (since analysis of these materials is ongoing, this description should be understood as preliminary). For instance, the high concentration of obsidian blades in the central site suggests that only certain central households were managing the acquisition of foreign goods within the community (McFarlane and Canuto 2000). These same residences have the highest incidence of Usulutan wares in their refuse. Curiously, however, almost no other types of "exotic" goods (shell, jade, stingray spines, eccentric flints) were recovered—only a few shell and slate beads were found. In fact, the most common markers of prestige were in the form of ceramic vessels and obsidian blades—portable objects that could easily be used for community-based feasting and ritual ceremonies rather than only being the permanent property of individuals.

At El Raizal, the ceramics place this community within the Classic period Copan sphere of ceramic production. Both its utilitarian and fine-paste assemblages correspond almost identically to those found in the Copan Valley at the same time. Visual assessment finds remarkably little difference in these ceramics from the general range of variation seen within the Copan Valley (see Bill 1997; Viel 1983). Unlike previous analyses claiming reduced variation among rural ceramics (Freter 1996), evidence from the entire El Raizal community exhibits the full gamut of Copan utilitarian wares (such as both the red-pasted Sepulturas and the gray-pasted Zico groups). In terms of fine-paste wares, the cream-pasted Chilanga and Copador are prevalent. Although present, the more finely decorated Surlo types are much less frequent than in the Copan Valley. One example of this type from El Raizal was even incised with the Copan emblem glyph.

In terms of lithics, members of El Raizal imported and relied heavily on obsidian, which represents more than 95% of all the lithic material used within the community. Unlike Los Achiotes, little or no chert was used. The instance of El Chayal obsidian within the community is ca. 1%, while prismatic blades make up roughly 60% of the assemblage. Both these percentages are not only different from those of Los Achiotes, but also equivalent to the contemporaneous levels within the Copan Valley. There was limited evidence of on-site blade production, suggesting that the inhabitants had to purchase some finished products rather than only importing raw material.

In regard to intra-community comparisons, the complement of utilitarian goods found in El Raizal patio groups demonstrates the self-sufficiency and economic autonomy typical of the rural hinterlands (Gonlin 1993, 1994). However, the uneven distribution of the imported goods encountered within the El Raizal community belies the equivalence of these patio groups and attests to intra-community socioeconomic stratification. Prestige goods like jade pendants, ritual flints, and a few examples of elite Surlo pottery were associated only with the central patio group. Other fine wares—Chilanga and Copador—were ubiquitous, although to varying degrees. By its intra-community distribution, it appears that the Surlo types were exchanged exclusively among the more powerful within the larger polity—along horizontal lines of class affiliation. Conversely, the more commonly found cream-pasted wares appear to have been distributed along vertical lines based on local patronage and kin affiliation (see LeCount 1999).

In conclusion, members of Los Achiotes interacted as a community of equivalent families that used strategies of communal action to procure and redistribute foreign goods. Perhaps some incipient stratification is evident in the spatial distribution of some of the prestige goods recovered. As Cohen (1985) exhorts, no rural community, however "simple," is entirely egalitarian; and Los Achiotes was surely no exception. It is, however, the nature of this inequality that suggests the overarching ideological importance of a community identity among its members. This identity, moreover, appears much attenuated among the members of El Raizal, whose household autonomy was more explicitly expressed. Furthermore, the obvious symbols of personal and household distinction within the community made internal socioeconomic distinction commonly and perhaps even constantly visible.

Special Deposits and Features

The evidence for ritual activity—such as caches, special features, public monuments—further distinguishes these two communities from each other. At Los Achiotes, no evidence for ritual practice—such as dedicatory caches or special deposits—was associated with individual structures; rather, it was centered on public spaces. For instance, two caches were related to the ballcourt—in its southern and eastern axis points. Moreover, in the refuse surrounding the ballcourt, a high percentage of Usulutan mammiform tetrapods—perhaps functioning as ritual serving vessels for feasting activities associated with the ballgame (Fox 1996)—was recovered. As another indicator of ritual behavior, a large cut-stone altar was located in southeastern sector of the community—in the nonresidential sector of the site. Located in an open area and resting on a prepared floor that extended outward to cover ca 8 m^2, it would have been visible and accessible to all residents.

At El Raizal, evidence for ritual practice was found in direct association with particular patio groups, each of which exhibited a greater or lesser degree of such ritual investment, perhaps as a function of family group prestige. Dedication rituals were recognized in the form of caches located on the center axes of patio structures and consisting of fine-ware vessels. In most cases, these caches were dug into the adjacent ground; however, in one case, a small cist was constructed within architectural fill for the placement of objects (all three of the vessels recovered from these caches will be analyzed for organic remains).

In terms of the aboveground markers, a round altar with a dedicatory cache of seventeen obsidian blades—perhaps used for bloodletting—was encountered in the private patio space enclosed by central patio structures. Furthermore, the large shrine-like structure was directly associated with this same patio group. Excavation of this shrine structure revealed evidence of ritual burning ceremonies within its superstructure in the form of a ritual hearth (lined with small flat cobblestones and filled with ash) and the remains of multiple censer pieces. This excavation also demonstrated that this shrine had originally been a domestic structure.

When considered within a community context, the variation in these expressions of symbolic and ritual behavior represents a contrast in which the El Raizal inhabitants seemed more inclined to undertake noninclusive family rites, while those of Los Achiotes focused on rituals they undertook communally. Moreover, the distinctions in household ritual behavior would have been more evident at El Raizal given the variation in the practices—from simple earthen caches to masonry offering cists to shrine structures—the inhabitants of El Raizal would have recognized as many differences as similarities amongst themselves. By contrast, the little evidence of inter-family variation in ritual practice encountered at Los Achiotes might be considered indirect evidence for a more overtly communal identity.

Discussion

The hinterland community of Los Achiotes precedes Copan's dynastic expansion. This community exhibits greater household inter-dependence and community autonomy. The material record suggests that the inhabitants of this community undertook quotidian practices like cooperative farming, shared household activities, and minimization of inter-household difference that fomented a sense of practical solidarity. These daily practices would have involved a constant reinforcement and reproduction of a community-based *habitus* (see Bourdieu 1973, 1977, 1990; Pauketat 1994, 2000). More periodic activities involving common access to ritual areas, construction of public architecture, and participation in public rituals further enhanced this sense of community unity. These activities could have provided an alternative form of identification for community members beyond that of their individual households.

Members of Los Achiotes also interacted with extra-community groups as evinced by the presence of a ballcourt and their importation of obsidian goods. These interactions reinforced local community identity since neither marker of extra-community interaction was found in greater association with any particular household. The ballcourt, therefore, may have represented an icon of local community identity, rather than asymmetrical access to external interaction.

Soon after the rise of Copan's dynasty, the hinterland community of El Raizal reflects drastic realignments in rural social organization. Research has shown that members of this community undertook daily activities such as household horticulture and overt expressions of social differences that would have fostered a very different sense of community than that of Los Achiotes. The greater fragmentation of daily practice along household lines would have engendered a greater sense of household and family identity. Furthermore, periodic activities would have taken place in enclosed patios, where only certain members would participate in noninclusive activities. These periodic practices would have enhanced the compartmentalization of the community by actively demonstrating socioeconomic differences among its members.

The El Raizal community also lacks an overt expression of its own identity. Rather than symbols of autonomy, it was permeated with markers reflecting the attempts of its central members to affiliate with the Copan elite. Resulting in the use of symbols like elite pottery, exotic goods, and even architectural style, the extra-community interactions of some members of the El Raizal community transcended their own intra-community interaction. Furthermore, the larger ritual buildings of El Raizal functioned differently from the Los Achiotes ballcourt because they were exclusively associated with the central patio group. In other words, the physical and interactive world of El Raizal reinforced an atomized sense of identity closely tied to the household rather than the community. The absence of community-forming icons like a ballcourt combined with the proliferation of Copan-derived symbols reinforced the rural-wide dependence on integrative mechanisms based on interaction and access to symbols emanating from the polity center.

As a result of the uneven distribution of such symbols, select households were promoted (*sensu* Flannery 1972) to become nodal centers through which a regional identity of "eliteness" was fostered based on periodic extra-community interaction of the selected household. These nodal households became the local proxies for the polity elite among the rural population. As a result, rural group identity was based less on unifying daily and periodic practices than on the distribution and access to symbolic goods. In this manner, the rural community identity, while still kin based, became less salient and more limited to the household.

Conclusion

The evidence discussed here contradicts the interpretation that the Copan polity was inconsequent to the developments of rural settlement. A model for Classic Maya rural society must now interpret the chronological coincidence of the rise of dynastic rule at Copan, the decline of community independence, and the rise in household autonomy. In fact, the Preclassic heterarchical political system loosely connecting centers within the southeastern cultural sphere (Demarest and Sharer 1986, Sharer 1974; Sharer and Gifford 1970) was replaced in the Early Classic period by a more centralized hierarchy reflecting Petén-based forms of social organization, spatial aesthetics, architectural techniques, and resource procurement. In other words, the dynasty of K'inich Yax K'uk' Mo' brought massive changes to how the Copan polity integrated its hinterlands. So much so that pre-dynastic Copan's lack of influence on Los Achiotes compares sharply with dynastic Copan's influence on rural communities like El Raizal.

The variegated landscape of the Preclassic was transformed into a more unitary and consistent territory of a large, expanding and young Early Classic state at Copan. The early Copan dynasty quickly attempted to co-opt, subsume, and integrate as much territory and population as possible. The leading El Raizal household would thus be one of many examples in the Copan polity of rural households located in areas on important communication and exchange routes seeking both control and representation within the polity to the detriment of local identity and autonomy. Since the segmentary lineage model for Classic Maya society has been placed in some doubt (Sharer 1993; Gillespie 2001b), it might be possible to understand the difference between Preclassic Los Achiotes and Classic El Raizal as the Copan-aided undermining of rural community autonomy through the bolstering of a "house" form of rural sociopolitical organization (see Gillespie 2001b) that rendered center-hinterland interaction more compatible with early dynastic designs.

Acknowledgments

I would like to acknowledge both the generous support received during this research as well as the numerous people who have provided me with help, counsel, and insights regarding these interpretations. My dissertation research was made possible by a fellowship from the Fullbright-IIE program (1997), a grant from the Foundation for the Advancement of Mesoamerican Studies (1998), a grant from the National Science Foundation Dissertation Improvement Program (1999), as well as numerous donations from the Segy Foundation (1996–2000).

The interpretations presented here are the outgrowth of several years of research critically supplemented and enhanced by countless discussions with my mentors and colleagues in the field, for which I am extremely grateful. Thanks especially go to Robert Sharer and Ellen Bell for their honest and fruitful comments. I would also like to thank Thomas Tartaron and the numerous Yale graduate students who read earlier versions of this chapter. Their comments proved invaluable. Though I am indebted to all those who have helped me, all errors, mistakes, and misrepresentations remain my own responsibility.

II ARCHITECTURE AT EARLY CLASSIC COPAN

3

REDESIGNING COPAN:
EARLY ARCHITECTURE OF THE POLITY CENTER

Loa P. Traxler

T he Maya site of Copan preserves generations of royal architecture and shows dramatic changes in the design of the polity center during the Early Classic period. Recent excavations suggest that the dynastic founder, K'inich Yax K'uk' Mo', and his son and successor, Ruler 2, redesigned their political center, shifting the location of monumental construction and changing the layout of the central complex, known today as the Principal Group (Sharer, Fash, et al. 1999; Sharer, Traxler, et al. 1999; Traxler 2001). Architectural groups, newly established in the early 5th century A.D., set the architectural pattern of the center for centuries. This chapter reconstructs the early development of the polity center and proposes revisions to the interpretation of the Great Plaza sequence.

Through the efforts of several major excavation projects we are now better able to link architectural sequences within the Principal Group. The initial sequences of Structures 10L-11 and 10L-26 were established through tunnel excavation by the Carnegie Institution of Washington project, directed by Gustav Strömsvik, in the years preceding and after World War II (see Baudez 1983). In the late 1970s, the Great Plaza sequence was established through remote sensing and excavations supervised by Charles Cheek in the first phase of the Copan Archaeological Project (PAC I), directed by Claude Baudez (1983). Surrounding the Principal Group, valley settlement test excavations supervised by William L. Fash encountered occupation remains and architecture related to the early history of the center (Fash 1983a, 1983b). PAC I also contributed the ceramic analyses by René Viel which provided a temporal frame to the architecture and artifacts recovered (see Viel 1983).

Most recently, the Copan Acropolis Archaeological Project (PAAC), directed by Fash, has revised and expanded the Acropolis architectural sequences through major tunneling programs, including the Structure 10L-16 excavations directed by Ricardo

Figure 3.1 Southwestern corner of Cominos Structure
as exposed in Tunnel Sub-op. I/32
(photograph by Loa P. Traxler).

Agurcia Fasquelle, the Structure 10L-26 excavations directed by Fash, and the extensive tunnel excavations beneath the eastern Acropolis directed by Robert Sharer (see Agurcia F., this volume; Fash et al., this volume; Fash and Sharer 1991; Sharer et al. 1992; Sharer, Fash, et al. 1999).

Results from additional research projects around the Principal Group help refine our understanding of the origins and development of Early Classic Copan. The recent excavations near the Principal Group by Hall and Viel (this volume) have aided the definition of the Preclassic landscape and its settlement. The excavations conducted by Harvard field school teams led by Fash and coordinated in areas with Hall and Viel's project have contributed important data on this period as well. One locus requiring further investigation is Platform 10L-1, located in the northwest quadrant of the Principal Group. Preliminary testing on the platform surface by Fash and additional excavations by Hall and Viel suggest that this structure may have been an important area of predynastic Early Classic activity.

In light of continuing research, this chapter attempts to integrate the architectural data from the Principal Group excavations conducted since 1975. The goal is to provide an overview of the earliest architecture within the polity center. This synthesis remains preliminary, and the suggested revisions to previous interpretations should be examined critically by the original excavators. It is my hope that this synthesis will promote a dialogue on these ideas and that, as a result, we can forge a more complete reconstruction of the development of the Principal Group as the center of the Copan kingdom.

Strong evidence suggests that the polity center located at Copan in Late Protoclassic to Early Classic times (ca. A.D. 150–600) was redesigned at the beginning of the 5th century A.D. This architectural enterprise seems to correlate with the beginning of the dynastic era inaugurated by the accession of K'inich Yax K'uk' Mo' to the Copan throne in A.D. 426 (Sharer 1996; Sharer, Fash, et al. 1999). At this time different architectural traditions existed within the polity center. In the redesign process we note an emphasis on distinct traditions and an increase in the construction investment within these traditions. These patterns may speak to the different regional affiliations and perhaps different regional origins of the elite, the nobility, and the royalty of the Early Classic era Copan kingdom (Sharer 2003a; Traxler 2001).

The architecture within the redesigned polity center includes cut-stone masonry structures of Lowland Maya and central Mexican styles as well as cobble structures typical of the Southeastern Region (Sharer, Traxler, et al. 1999). Prominent among the varied architectural types are earthen structures documented by the recent Early Copan Acropolis Program (ECAP) excavations (Sharer, Traxler, et al. 1999; Traxler 2003). Well-preserved earthen structures exist at the lowest levels beneath the Acropolis (Figure 3.1). Additional structures located elsewhere in the Principal Group likely are part of this early earthen architectural tradition. Based on numerous pub-

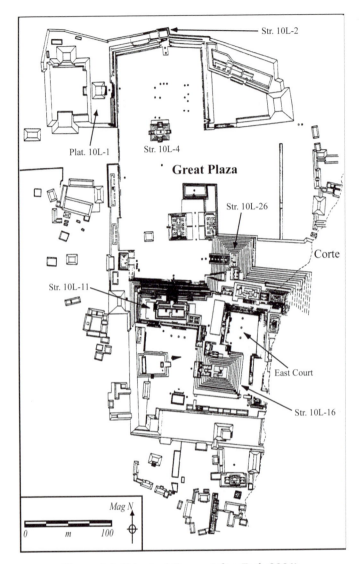

Figure 3.2 Principal Group (after Fash 2001).

lished reports and unpublished records of previous research, it seems clear that other excavations have uncovered the remains of this type of architecture.

Reconstructing the Early Development of the Polity Center

Excavations by Hall and Viel (this volume) indicate that areas surrounding the Principal Group were subject to periodic flooding in the Late Preclassic period. Sparse occupa-

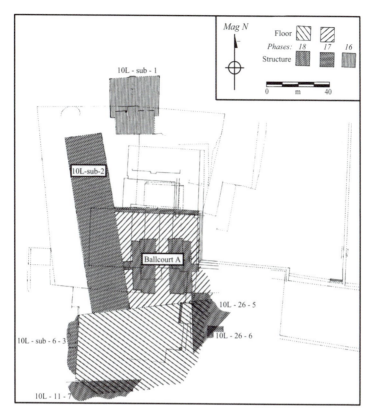

Figure 3.3 Early architecture of the Great Plaza
(after Cheek 1983:fig. C-6).

tion debris and the limited number of Preclassic structures documented by the Harvard and PAC I settlement excavations (Fash 1983a, 1991; Willey et al. 1979) suggest that settlement in the Copan Valley relocated periodically in response to the shifting course of the river and seasonal floods.

A more stable settlement formed during Protoclassic and initial Early Classic times at Copan represented by architecture and occupation debris containing Bijac phase ceramics (ranging from ca. A.D. 150–400; Cheek 1983a; Fash 1983b). This settlement remains poorly defined in architectural terms. It is represented by one or two structures containing Bijac fills located ca. 200 m west of the Great Plaza (Fash 1983b:181–183) and possibly the core architecture of Platform 10L-1 (Figure 3.2). Two Bijac phase caches beneath Structure 10L-sub-1 in the Great Plaza (Figure 3.3) provide clear evidence of the ritual marking of space during this time (Cheek 1983a:270–271 and fig. C-24). When these deposits are considered along with the few and brief hieroglyphic texts that refer to events during this time (Schele 1987b; Stuart this volume, 1986, 1989), the evidence suggests that a polity center emerged at some time preceding A.D. 400.

A dramatic change in the Principal Group occurs during the time of transition from Bijac to Acbi phase ceramics (ca. A.D. 400–425). Test excavations along the base of the Acropolis Corte by Murillo (1989) revealed deeply buried small-scale cobble structures that likely predate this interval. These earliest structures were covered by extensive terraces, at least one low platform, known as Yune (see Sedat and López, this volume), and patio groups, some of which are bounded by cobble and earthen walls (Sharer, Fash, et al. 1999; Traxler 2003). Compared to their underlying predecessors, the sheer size of these later structures suggests they were associated with elite activity and a change in the organization and function of architecture. In fact, the Yune group is the core from which the southern portion of the Acropolis evolved over time (Sharer, Fash, et al. 1999; Sharer, Traxler, et al. 1999). Some of this construction, dated to the earliest phases of Yune Platform, is discussed by Sedat and López (this volume).

At about this time, large structures began to appear elsewhere. Although only a few of these can be dated with any precision, it seems that this architectural expansion roughly coincided with the founding of the royal Copan dynasty of K'inich Yax K'uk' Mo' in A.D. 426. Construction of the earliest group of large-scale earthen structures began to the northeast of Yune Platform. Initially composed of earthen substructures supporting multiroomed buildings arranged around open patios, this group was eventually replaced by masonry architecture following the same group plan (Traxler 1996, 2001, 2003). Structures on the early phase of Yune Platform were also earthen, but by its middle stage at least two buildings were constructed of masonry (Sedat and López, this volume). One of these early masonry structures, Hunal, stands out because its substructure exhibits the central Mexican *talud-tablero* architectural style (Sharer, Traxler, et al. 1999).

The ECAP excavations suggest that much of the elite architecture from this time relates to the earthen architecture of the Maya Highlands and adjacent sites within the general Southeastern Region. This tradition is represented in the Late Preclassic architecture at highland sites including Kaminaljuyu (Cheek 1977; Kidder et al. 1946), at the southeastern site of Chalchuapa (Sharer 1978e), and closer at hand at Los Achiotes in the Río Amarillo Valley (Canuto, this volume). Earthen structures at Kaminaljuyu and Chalchuapa resemble those in the Copan Principal Group in their form and general use of earthen-core substructures. They differ, however, in the techniques used to finish the substructure façades. Typically Late Preclassic structures at both Kaminaljuyu and Chalchuapa have a surface finish consisting of a thick layer of crushed *talpetate* (consolidated volcanic ash) mixed with clay. At Copan, the earthen substructures typically display a thin surface finish of red pigment mixed with clay.

While earthen architecture underlies most Acropolis loci, the earliest-known entity in the Structure 10L-26 sequence, called Yax Structure, was built of masonry on an extensive layer of fill (Fash 1998; Williamson 1996). Although Yax is too poorly preserved to examine for architectural style, its immediate successor, Motmot Structure, and adjacent Ballcourt I were built in a Lowland Maya architectural style (Fash 1998; Fash et al., this volume). According to Fash et al. (this volume), the Motmot Structure and Ballcourt I were probably erected for the 9.0.0.0.0 period ending in A.D. 435. This period ending date is inscribed on the Motmot Marker along with the portrait and name of both the dynastic founder, K'inich Yax K'uk' Mo', and his son, Ruler 2 (Stuart, this volume). This monument was set in the plaster courtyard floor shared by Ballcourt I, along with an early version of Structure 10L-11, and an early version of Structure 10L-sub-6. The Motmot Marker and its date provide a secure *end* to the time range for the design shift of the polity center.

In the Great Plaza, Cheek (1983) documented the extensive leveling and construction episodes which created the plaza area still seen today. From its southern to northern limits the early plaza fill deposits contain a mix of Bijac and Acbi phase materials, along with a small amount of Preclassic Uir phase sherds in some areas. These plaza fills underlie and, in many excavated trench sections, merge with the construction fills of Structure 10L-2 at the north end of the Great Plaza and Structures 10L-sub-1, 10L-sub-2, and probably 10L-sub-5, all located in the central area of the plaza.

Combined with the recent Acropolis data, the available evidence suggests a coordinated and large-scale expansion of architecture over much of the area of the Principal Group, from the Yune Platform in the south to the limits of the Great Plaza in the north. This architectural enterprise seems to correlate with the first years of the dynastic era ushered in by K'inich Yax K'uk' Mo' in A.D. 426, based on the available dating evidence, including ceramics, stratigraphy, and the reference to the dynastic founder on the Motmot Marker (with its 9.0.0.0.0 date).

According to the inscription on Altar Q, K'inich Yax K'uk' Mo' came from somewhere outside of Copan (Stuart, this volume). This external origin may explain the introduction of at least two foreign architectural styles associated with the newly expanded polity center. The masonry apron-molding design seen in Motmot Structure derived from the Petén region of the Maya lowlands (Fash 1998). The *talud-tablero* design of Hunal Structure derived from the architectural traditions of central Mexico, but this style was also used at both highland and lowland Maya sites during the Early Classic (Sharer 2003a). At Tikal, masonry *talud-tablero* architecture was built for a century or more before K'inich Yax K'uk' Mo' arrived at Copan (Laporte and Fialko 1990). Moreover, at Kaminaljuyu, earthen architecture built in *talud-tablero* style frequently incorporated stone to stabilize the complex façades. The fact that the construction methods used at Copan to build Hunal were masonry techniques with plaster finish like those at Tikal, rather than earth and stone techniques with a clay-*talpetate* finish like those used at Kaminaljuyu may indicate that K'inich Yax K'uk' Mo' had closer ties with the Maya Lowlands than with the Maya Highlands. These architectural patterns indicating closer ties to the Maya Lowlands than to the Maya Highlands are consistent with the manufacture and stylistic patterns of the elite ceramics found in the Early Classic royal tombs of the Copan Acropolis (see Reents-Budet et al., this volume)

Earthen Architecture and the Great Plaza

Following the documentation of earthen architecture in Acropolis excavations (Sharer, Traxler, et al. 1999), other evidence for this architectural tradition was sought in the data from previous research programs at Copan. A review of the published reports and section drawings from the PAC I excavations in the Great Plaza (Baudez 1983; Cheek 1983a) revealed important evidence for earthen architecture beneath later masonry structures. The excavations carried out by Cheek documented early stages of masonry construction at the site center (Cheek 1983a, 1986; Cheek and Spink 1986), and they also exposed the remains of what now are recognized as earthen structures beneath several Great Plaza locations.

During two field seasons for the PAC I, Cheek opened excavation units covering the entire expanse of the Great Plaza. This important program sought to establish the architectural development of the Great Plaza and to link its stratigraphy with the Acropolis sequences known at that time from the Carnegie tunnels in Structures 10L-11 and 10L-26. In addition to the plaza excavations, Cheek supervised the excavation and restoration of Structure 10L-4 in the central area of the Great Plaza (Cheek and Milla Villeda 1983) and Structure 10L-2 (Figure 3.2) at its northern limit (Cheek and Kennedy Embree 1983).

In his report Cheek characterized the initial level of the Great Plaza's northern sector as fill deposits resulting from an extensive leveling operation. This effort was contemporary with the construction of the initial masonry architecture of the Plaza's southern sector. Beneath Structure 10L-2 at the northern limit of the Great Plaza, Cheek and Kennedy Embree (1983:fig. F-6) identified the vestiges of a structure based on a pavement of flat stones and a series of post holes within a mass of construction fill (Figure 3.4). They interpreted the remains as the core of a masonry structure (designated as Structure 10L-2-3rd) built in the 6th century A.D. which had been largely destroyed (Cheek and Kennedy Embree 1983:105, 130). In light of similar features documented in ECAP tunnels beneath the Acropolis—especially an association between post holes and earthen substructures (e.g., Cab Structure on Early Yune Platform; Sedat and López, this volume)—it is likely that the fill (Layer 10e) and the post hole features (Features 35 and 37) associated with Structure 10L-2-3rd are the remains of an earthen substructure with supports for perishable roofing timbers. The roofing may have been similar to that proposed for the earthen Maravilla Structure beneath the Acropolis which included the preserved remains of sizable wooden corner posts (Sedat 1996). The remains also resemble structures at the site of Los Achiotes in the adjacent Río Amarillo Valley (Canuto, this volume).

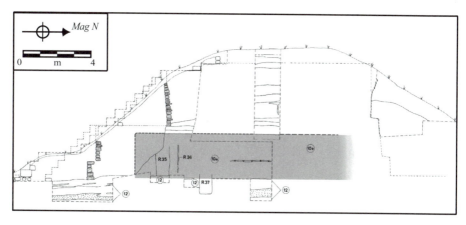

Figure 3.4 Section drawing of Structure 10L-2-3rd. The grey area represents the possible extent of the initial earthen substructure located beneath later masonry versions of the building (after Cheek and Kennedy Embree 1983:fig. F-6, with additions by Loa P. Traxler).

It is quite possible that there were two earthen versions of Structure 10L-2-3rd, based on the stratigraphy represented in the published section drawing (Cheek and Kennedy Embree 1983:fig. F-6). A carbon lens indicated within fill Layer 10e may represent burned material on the summit of an initial earthen structure. Carbon deposits are found in association with several earthen structures in the early Acropolis levels (Traxler 2003). If this is the case, Feature 36 may represent the burned south façade of the initial version of Structure 10L-2-3rd. Feature 37 may well have been the remains of a post set within this version of the structure, given the lower elevation of the post base in comparison to Feature 35.

In any case, the earthen construction fill of the base of Structure 10L-2-3rd was the same as that used to level the Plaza in this northern area. This relates its construction to the initial masonry architecture of the southern sector. There is no clearly preserved façade for 10L-2-3rd, but the fill mass (Layer 10e) viewed in section suggests that it measured at least 2 m in height. It is likely that Feature 35 is the remains of a post hole within the base of this structure (Cheek and Kennedy Embree 1983:fig. F-6). This burned-clay feature produced one unequivocal archeo-magnetic date of A.D. 575 +/-17 (Cheek and Kennedy Embree 1983:108). This date, however, probably relates to the burning and demolition of the earthen structure prior to the construction of its masonry successor, Structure 10L-2-2nd.

In the central area of the plaza beneath Structure 10L-4, Cheek and Milla Villeda (1983) documented fill layers which may represent earthen architecture in this location. The stratigraphy of the initial layers in the sequence was difficult for the archaeologists to interpret due to excavations conducted in the 19th century. In his early site explorations, Maudslay dug a deep pit into the center of Structure 10L-4 (Figure 3.2; Maudslay 1889-1902:20). His pit reached a depth of 12 feet below the plaza surface, cutting through fill he described as "hard-rammed earth, free from stones," before ending at the level of undisturbed soil. At a depth of 8 to 9 feet below the plaza level, Maudslay encountered a jaguar burial under a layer of charcoal. The PAC I excavations in this structure explored fill levels that likely covered the animal burial and charcoal layer, since the lowest levels described by Cheek were all slightly higher in elevation than the bottom of Maudslay's pit (Cheek and Milla Villeda. 1983:49-53 and Fig. G-5).

Cheek and Milla Villeda proposed that the first structure at this location was a low masonry platform that they called Structure 10L-4-4th. This structure may have encased or been attached to an earlier structure represented by a fill layer of sandy clay and river cobbles (Layer 7b on the published section drawing, Cheek and Milla Villeda 1983:Fig. G-5). This fill was interpreted as the core of Structure 10L-4-3rd although its base was lower in elevation than the masonry of 10L-4-4th. It is likely that Layer 7b represents an early structure of earth and cobbles. Below it lies fill of dark brown sandy clay (Layer 3g) that may have covered the jaguar burial and charcoal deposit. This fill may represent an earthen structure through which Maudslay excavated, but further investigation is needed to resolve these details.

Continuing south in the central area of the Great Plaza, Structure 10L-sub-1 stood facing north (Figure 3.3), oriented toward Structure 10L-2-3rd. The remnants of the northern facade of 10L-sub-1 are shown as a vertical profile of fill (Layer 4) in Cheek's excavation section (1983:fig. C-14d). Cheek interpreted this layer as the remains of a destroyed masonry structure, but it is likely that this fill represents another earthen structure. Fill Layer 4 contained ceramics assigned to the Bijac-Acbi Phase transition. Based on the fill descriptions and ceramic associations, it is likely that Structure 10L-sub-1 was contemporary with or even predated the masonry Structure 10L-sub-2, located just to the southwest (Figure 3.3). Cheek reported Structure 10L-sub-2 as the earliest Great Plaza structure (Cheek 1983a:fig. C-6).

Farther to the southeast of Structure 10L-sub-1, Cheek defined Structure 10L-sub-5 and dated its construction to the fifth century A.D. (Cheek 1983:245, see also Fig. C-3). As with others in the plaza, he interpreted its remains as the core of a destroyed masonry structure (Cheek 1983:Fig. C-4c, Layer 31). Based on similarities with architecture beneath the Acropolis, 10L-sub-5 was probably an earthen structure that had its summit building cut away. This destruction is similar to the demolition pattern of earthen patio buildings located northeast of Yune Platform. Although unclear at present, Structure 10L-sub-5 likely integrates in some fashion with the eastern structure of Ballcourt I, the east end of Structure 10L-sub-7, and the initial buildings of the Structure 10L-26 sequence.

Finally, Cheek defined Structure 10L-sub-2 by means of several excavation units (Figure 3.3). Its remains comprise the earliest masonry structure of the Great Plaza (Cheek 1983:218-223). Cheek noted that its fills, which contained ceramics dated to the Bijac-Acbi transition, were quite variable from one area to another. Future research may be able to test if this structure incorporated low earthen substructures within its masonry confines.

Based on the information available from the published accounts, it appears that the Great Plaza entities summarized here are directly comparable to the earthen structures documented by ECAP excavations beneath the Acropolis. The similarity is apparent in their fills of rather homogenous earth with few artifact inclusions, the minimal of use of construction stone, and the use of wooden posts, presumably to support roofing for superstructures. The Great Plaza and Acropolis also share a tendency for early earthen structures to be succeeded by later masonry architecture. This indicates a general continuity of construction at certain locations that, once established, continued to be used for long spans of time.

Conclusion

The Great Plaza was part of a major construction program that redesigned the polity center at Copan and probably coincided with the dynastic founding. As such, the Great Plaza was an extensive area with formal boundaries marked by earthen architecture from the beginning of its construction sequence. The northern, southern, and southwestern limits of the Great Plaza preserve evidence of construction contemporary with the leveling of these plaza sectors. The stratigraphy of the southern sector ties directly into the stratigraphy of the Acropolis and its architecture associated with inscribed hieroglyphic dates. These connections suggest the entire polity center from Yune Platform to the Great Plaza was reconfigured in the early 5th century A.D. The extent of this monumental construction effort measures some 400 m from north to south.

One important element of the Principal Group remains to be thoroughly documented. This is Platform 10L-1, which fronts the Great Plaza on its east side and dominates the northwest quadrant of the polity center (Figure 3.2). Future excavations will hopefully establish the chronology of Platform 10L-1 and determine whether it began as an earthen or masonry complex. If further synthesis of the recent excavation data continues to support the proposition that K'inich Yax K'uk' Mo' was the instigator of this redesign and expansion of the polity center after his accession in A.D. 426, then discussion can begin to explore the possible motivations for this enterprise (Sharer 1996; Traxler 2001).

Acknowledgments

The author would like to acknowledge the generous support of the Selz Foundation for a three-year grant (1996–1998) that made possible the completion of the architectual mapping effort of the Early Copan Acropolis Program. Previous support came through grants from the National Science Foundation (#9123390), the Committee for Research and Exploration of the National Geographic Society, and Apple Computer. Thanks also go to our colleagues in the Museum Applied Science for Archaeology at the University of Pennsylvania Museum and its Scientific Director, Stuart Fleming, for the development of mapping and surveying software and support for its field application. Thanks go to our field crews and ECAP staff for their efforts that enabled the architectural mapping program to achieve its goals. Any error in the representation of their hard work is the responsibility of the author.

4

SETTING THE STAGE:
ORIGINS OF THE HIEROGLYPHIC STAIRWAY PLAZA
ON THE GREAT PERIOD ENDING

William L. Fash, Barbara W. Fash, and Karla Davis-Salazar

W ith the advent of the "Epigraphic Revolution" in Maya studies during the last half of the 20th century, scholars have had access to historical data that enables them to ask many new kinds of questions of the archaeological record. Copan has long been recognized as the ancient Maya site with the greatest number and variety of hieroglyphic inscriptions (Morley 1920). The study of the Early Classic archaeological remains in the Copan Valley has led to considerable debate regarding the dating, content, and cultural context of the earliest Classic Maya monuments in this southeastern-most great center (Baudez 1994; Fash and Sharer 1991; Longyear 1952; Morley 1920; Viel 1983, 1993b).

One locus of long-standing interest for historical analysis has been the area north of the Acropolis, including the Plaza of the Hieroglyphic Stairway. The publication of the Early Classic dates on the Hieroglyphic Stairway by George B. Gordon (1902) led Gustav Strömsvik of the Carnegie Institution of Washington to seek the remains of earlier buildings buried inside the pyramidal substructure of the Hieroglyphic Stairway and the final version of the Copan Ballcourt (Strömsvik 1952). Charles Cheek (1983b) incorporated this work in his own reconstruction of the building sequence of the northern part of the Principal Group at the same time that Barbara Fash was re-drawing the inscription of the Hieroglyphic Stairway for epigraphic analysis by Berthold Riese (1986). In 1985, William Fash, Barbara Fash, and Rudy Larios renewed the investigations of the final-phase structures of the ballcourt and Hieroglyphic Stairway of Structure 10L-26 in a modest effort named the Copan Mosaics Project. The following year we initiated the Hieroglyphic Stairway Project and, in 1988, the Copan Acropolis Archaeological Project (PAAC), in part to continue with the Late Classic mosaic sculpture conservation, documentation, and analysis (Fash 1988).

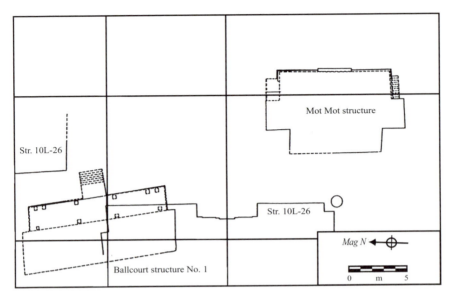

Figure 4.1 Plan view of Motmot Structure, Motmot floor marker,
and eastern building of Ballcourt I, showing outlines
of final phase Hieroglyphic Stairway and ballcourt.

But these new endeavors were also designed to systematically delve into the architecture buried beneath the final-phase buildings in the Acropolis and adjacent courtyards. This was to be achieved through tunneling into the massive temple-pyramids to document the architectural history of the Acropolis and test the historical accuracy of the inscription that graces the final-phase stairway and its surmounting temple. In contexts where inscriptions were found *in situ*, it would also be possible to tie the earlier, buried buildings and associated activities to the reigns of particular rulers. Subsequently, the work on the Stairway and its ancestors was followed up by further research on the Acropolis river cut, and a new series of tunnels was cut into its face by Robert Sharer and his colleagues from the University of Pennsylvania as an integral component of PAAC.

When we began this work, many archaeologists questioned the veracity of the Late Classic historical accounts of Early Classic rulers. Some even went so far as to refer to the first ten dynasts as "putative kings," fabricated from whole cloth to lend legitimacy to what these scholars believed was essentially a 7th and 8th century kingdom (Webster and Freter 1990a). Others took issue with the method of tunneling, admonishing that it had yielded only spotty results at other Maya sites (Black 1990). The Hieroglyphic Stairway Project and PAAC have demonstrated that the rulers carved on the sides of Altar Q were real historical individuals, whose lives and works are amply attested in the archaeological record. Collectively, we have also shown that carefully designed and executed tunnel excavations can be extraordinarily informative in exploring buried architecture at Copan (Fash 1999; Sharer, Fash, et al. 1999; Sharer, Traxler, et al. 1999).

As Robert Sharer is fond of stating, investigations of the Lowland Classic Maya can now be considered historical archaeology. We remain ever alert to the possibility of contradictions—as well as the numerous remarkable cases of overlap and agreement—between the different data sets that the PAAC (and other research programs in Copan) have produced. Nonetheless, to date, all evidence that has come to light supports our earlier observations (W. Fash et al. 1992) that nothing buried beneath the Hieroglyphic Stairway contradicts, in any way, the official history commissioned by the final rulers of Copan.

In this chapter, we chart the origins of the central part of the Principal Group, which bridges the Acropolis on the south with the Central and Great Plaza areas to the north. To do so we will briefly summarize the sequence of buildings, texts, and offerings which we and previous investigators have documented in our research there, with thanks and appreciation to the tireless efforts of Rudy Larios, David Stuart, Richard Williamson, Linda Schele, Fernando López, and Joel Palka.

K'inich Yax K'uk' Mo' and the Earliest Constructions

Our investigations revealed that K'inich Yax K'uk' Mo' and his son and successor Ruler 2 (see Stuart, this volume) chose the Bak'tun Ending 9.0.0.0.0 (A.D. 435) to lay out the building plan for this part of the Principal Group that all of his successors were to follow. The earliest two buildings, given the field designations "Yax" and "Motmot," are both ascribed to the reign of the founder, based on their associated ceramics, radiocarbon dates, and in Motmot's case, an associated, dated hieroglyphic text. Motmot Structure, built directly on top of Yax, was located on the east side of a complex of four buildings and shared a common plaster plaza floor with the earliest ballcourt on the north, the first version of Structure 10L-11 to the south, and the initial construction of Structure 10L-7, to the west. Set into that shared plaza floor was an inscribed circular floor marker (Figure 4.1) dedicated by the founder and his son on the Period Ending 9.0.0.0.0, declaring that they conceived and commissioned the entire building complex to be consecrated on that hallowed date in the Long Count.

The very earliest construction beneath Structure 19L-26, Yax Structure, was built atop sterile alluvium in the early 5th century A.D. Cheek (1983b) documented this same layer beneath the other structures built to the west and north, as well (Traxler, this volume). The fill laid down to level the ground contained Bijac pottery and a high proportion of green obsidian artifacts (Aoyama 1999:93), leading its discoverer, Richard Williamson (1996), to nickname this building "Yax" (blue-green). This structure and all its successors at this locus faced west. Its substructure consisted of a

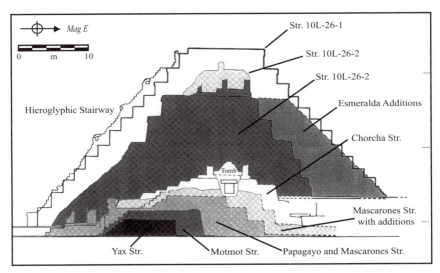

Figure 4.2 Schematic E–W cross-section of construction sequence
of Structure 10L-26 and antecedents.

single terrace, built on a slight batter, adorned with a small, U-shaped stucco panel on
its back wall. This axially-placed motif was the only part of the building's decorative
program that survived. The upper part of Yax Structure was removed when its successor Motmot was constructed, a pattern that would characterize renovation projects
throughout the Acropolis.

It should be emphasized at the outset that this pattern of willful destruction
of buildings and sculptures is found throughout the construction sequence here and
in the rest of the Acropolis, from start to finish (Figure 4.2). Individual buildings and
sculptures had a finite life cycle in the same way that maize and people did, in an end-
lessly repeating cycle of life and death. In each instance offerings were made, first to
pay respects (and, ritually "terminate") the building about to be buried, and next to give
life and a "soul" to the new one that succeeded it.

In the case of the death of Yax Structure and the birth of its successor
Motmot, a remarkable feature takes center stage. On the central axis of Yax Structure,
a cylindrical stone-lined cist 1 m wide and 1 m deep was built. It became the final resting place for a young adult woman who was buried cross-legged on a reed mat found
on the floor of the cist (Burial XXXVII-9; Figure 4.3). Shortly after her burial, the tomb
was re-visited. The re-visitation involved the scenario familiar now to epigraphers
James Fitzsimmons (1998) and David Stuart (1998). "Fire enters his house," is a phrase
often cited in Classic Maya texts, and in this case fire entered her funerary chamber (as

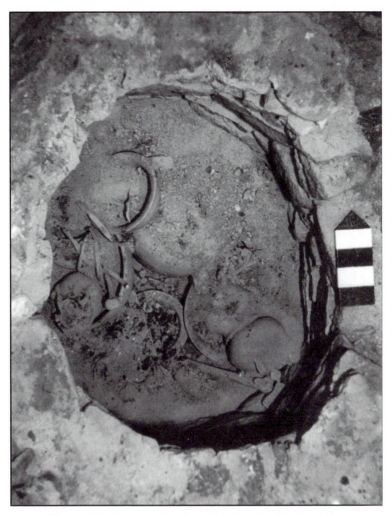

Figure 4.3 Interior of Motmot Tomb and cylindrical cist.

meticulously documented in Karla Davis-Salazar's excavations; Williamson 1996). The lower legs were left *in situ*, on the floor of the tomb along with offerings of a deer skull and a decapitated human skull with the cervical vertebrae still attached. The upper skeleton of this young woman was highly disturbed and blackened by fire, as were the ceramic offerings and puma skeleton found intermixed with her bones.

Many of the offerings in the Motmot burial are analogous to paraphernalia used in divination and curing ceremonies among the living Maya. We believe that this

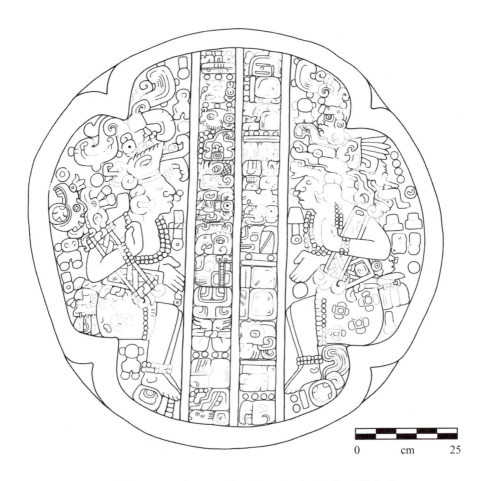

Figure 4.4 Motmot floor marker (drawing by Barbara W. Fash,
incorporating 1999 suggestions of David Stuart
and James Fitzsimmons).

woman was an accomplished day-keeper, buried with her spiritual co-essence or *way*,
a puma. It is intriguing to note that while the Altar Q dedicatory cache indicates that
jaguars were the preferred *wayob* of rulers (Fash 2001), this young woman instead had
a puma as a spirit-companion. The whole complex was sealed by capstones of tuff, and
another offering was placed and burned atop the covered burial chamber. The offering was that of a decapitated deer, positioned atop a crocodilian skin represented by
numerous scutes (identified *in situ* by Randolph Widmer).

Figure 4.5 Central floor marker of Ballcourt IIa
(drawing by Barbara W. Fash).

The date of the Motmot deer offering is given in the hieroglyphic text of the stone that was set directly above this remarkable burial, which we refer to as the Motmot floor marker (Figure 4.4). This text records the tied deer hooves expression seen in the Madrid codex in association with deer sacrifices. Here the glyph is linked with the name of K'inich Yax K'uk' Mo', and the Calendar Round date 8 Ajaw 14 K'ej, corresponding to the Bak'tun Ending 9.0.0.0.0. David Stuart (this volume) believes that Ruler 2 is the main protagonist of the period ending celebration, since the second dynast's name is the one that follows the period ending date. Stuart is unable to deter-

Figure 4.6 Modeled stucco on the southwest corner of
Motmot Structure (drawing by Nathan C. Fash).

mine from present evidence whether the founder was still alive at this date, but leans toward the view that he was and that he was acting as a co-regent with his son during this event (Stuart, this volume). The whole indicates that the re-visitation of the tomb and its closure, the deer sacrifice, and the dedication of the Motmot floor marker took place as part of the Bak'tun-ending ritual performed by Ruler 2, and likely also K'inich Yax K'uk' Mo', on the date 9.0.0.0.0.

We have consistently referred to this stone as a floor marker because of its design, carvings, and use. It is quite clear that the design was pedestaled on the top of this immense, irregularly shaped piece of limestone, precisely so that a plaster floor could be lipped up to the surface of the relief. Its contours are remarkably similar to those of other well-known floor markers in Mesoamerica, including the much later Mexica Sun Stone and Coyolxauhqui Stone of the Templo Mayor in Tenochtitlan; Altar 4 of Polol (Hammond 1991) constitutes a contemporary exemplar from the Maya Lowlands. It is also noteworthy that the diameter of the carving precisely matches that of the cylindrical cist, above which it was directly placed. We believe the marker was commissioned and designed as an integral part of the Motmot cist to match the diameter and physically seal the cist itself, at the appointed hour.

The Motmot floor marker bears the seated portraits of the founder K'inich Yax K'uk' Mo' on the left, and his son and successor Ruler 2, on the right. Each is named in both the text and the central element of his headdress. The inscription takes

Figure 4.7 Reconstruction of modeled stucco macaw that adorned Ballcourt I (drawing by Barbara W. Fash).

the form of two parallel columns on a central shaft that looks like a stela. This format has its earliest known antecedents in Protoclassic Stelae 2 and 5 of Abaj Takalik and a later example from Polol (B. Fash, this volume). At Copan, this same format was later to be taken up on the central floor marker of Ballcourt IIa (Figure 4.5), and the famed Peccary Skull of Tomb 1 (Fash 2001:fig. 24; see also Stuart, this volume). The dividing line in the center of the text indicates that one reads the left-hand column in sequence from top to bottom and then proceeds to the right-hand column. This symmetry nicely matches the iconography since the (viewer's) left-hand figure and text column refer to the founder, and the right-hand text column and figure refer to his successor.

The Motmot inscription also refers to several features that have been identified in the archaeological record. The first is the aforementioned sacrifice of a deer
(represented by tied deer hooves in the text). The second is a reference to the dedication of a "4-sky structure," which describes Motmot Structure's four sky-bands, modeled
in stucco on the east and west sides of its substructure (Figure 4.6). The third is a reference to "smoke entering," which is what happened when the subfloor burial chamber was re-entered and the bones of its young female occupant were purified by fire.
The fourth reference we can tie to this complex is the final glyph in the text, "4
macaw," a literal description of the founder's ballcourt with its four huge modeled stucco macaws, again on the east and west sides of the architectural monument.

The archaeological, iconographic, and textual records conjoin to relate that
on that momentous occasion, Ruler 2 and his father K'inich Yax K'uk' Mo' dedicated
the ballcourt, Motmot Structure, and the earliest versions of Structures 10L-7 and 11 by
making a food offering of a deer above the capstones of the re-entered burial chamber,
which was purified by fire.

The floor that lipped up to the carving on the floor marker was shared by
Motmot Structure, the first ballcourt at Copan, and ancestral versions of Structures 10L-
7 and 10L-11, tying them all to the Bak'tun ending 9.0.0.0.0 and the vision of Ruler 2
and his father. On this momentous period ending, they established the layout of the
most public part of the Principal Group which would survive until the end of the
dynasty. The four large macaws modeled in stucco on the ballcourt each sported the
head of a feathered serpent in the mid-section, in whose mouth was a severed right
arm (Figure 4.7). The arm bears a single large circle or "dot" (for the numeral one). The
most parsimonious explanation for this imagery is that it represents the severed arm
of Hunahpu (1 Lord), as recounted much later in the Quiche version of this myth.

However, we have taken pains to note that the feathered serpent head on the
Ballcourt I stucco bird bears an uncanny resemblance to those of contemporary
Teotihuacan (Fash and Fash 2000), which we believe can hardly be attributed to
chance. Burned and disturbed burials in a cylindrical elite burial pit (Motmot
Structure), and the importation of Pachuca obsidian (in the fill of Yax Structure) are evidence for the exchange of both goods and ideas with Teotihuacan on or before the
date 9.0.0.0.0. The feathered serpent on the ballcourt that was built at the same time
likely represents the transliteration of Teotihuacan ideology and attendant architectural sculpture into local media and ideological constructs. The great highland metropolis, however, was certainly not the only place whose traditions inspired the founder's,
and his successor's, public works.

Motmot Structure was clearly built in emulation of Early Classic Maya buildings in the Petén, with large, impressive apron moldings on all four sides and a frontal
stairway facing west. On the back side of the substructure was a large raised central

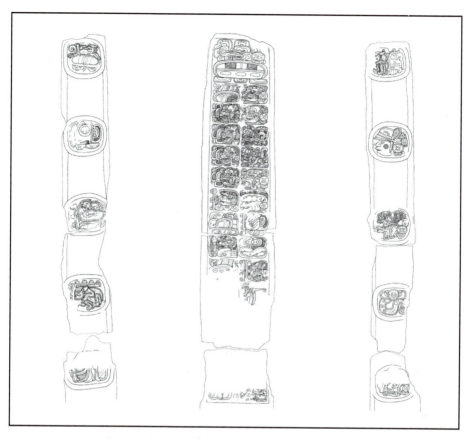

Figure 4.8 Stela 63 (drawing by Barbara W. Fash).

panel with a "G-1" mask, facing the rising sun. Crowning the head of the G-1 mask is a
bird emerging from a large Yax sign. Although the beak and facial features of the bird
were not preserved, it does not seem too unreasonable to suggest that this iconographic assemblage represents a large, pictorial version of the name of the founder, K'inich
Yax K'uk' Mo'. Framing the battered remains of the mask are sky-bands, also modeled
in clay, and also only partially preserved. This is precisely the arrangement shown on
the stucco panel on the contemporary Margarita Structure, to name the founder. Just
to the east and south of the Motmot central panel, three patolli boards were scratched
into the plaster floor behind the structure.

Ruler 2 and Papagayo

A short time later, the son and successor of K'inich Yax K'uk' Mo' decided to build over
Motmot and construct its successor, which we call Papagayo Structure. Before so
doing, he honored both his father and the locus of the Bak'tun Ending ritual by placing an elaborate offering on the Motmot floor marker. Barbara Fash's meticulous excavations of this offering recovered jade earflares at the four cardinal points, a series of
fine layers of pigments, and a three-stoned hearth used to burn offerings, including
Spondylus shell, jade, and feathers. The whole offering was then sealed by another
large limestone slab and finally covered with fill. A pattern was clearly emerging: fire,
jade, pigments, and/or mercury were all to be offered as part of the termination rituals
of buildings and their associated monuments.

Two burials were also placed in association with the back (east) side of Motmot
before it was buried. Burial XXXVII-1 was an adult male placed in a masonry cist directly at the foot of the G-1 mask, with the base of the apron molding serving as the west
side of the cist. Due east and slightly higher was another cist containing the remains of
a highly robust young adult male skeleton, Burial XXXVII-2, in whose mouth had been
placed a highly burnished jade bead carved in the form of a *ti* ("ajaw") vulture. Virtually
the entire superstructure of Motmot was razed, and most of the stucco adornments on
both the front and back were obliterated, as part of the ritual "killing" of the building.

Stela 63 was erected in the succeeding temple, Papagayo. This monument
bears the Long Count date 9.0.0.0.0 8 Ajaw 14 Kej, followed by a Lunar Series and, finally, the name of the founder, K'inich Yax K'uk' Mo' (Figure 4.8). The text records that
the stela was placed by Ruler 2 to honor the founder. Ruler 2 also proclaims that he
was the son of (*hu-ne*) K'inich Yax K'uk' Mo'. Stela 63's format is remarkably similar
to that of Stela 9 at Lamanai, which was also placed inside of a temple and carved on
three sides (Pendergast 1988). On the back side of Papagayo Structure is a depiction
in modeled stucco of a huge crocodilian, situated above signs for stone and water. This
is in keeping with the broader Mesoamerican world view that the surface of the earth
is the back of a giant saurian that swims in an immense body of water.

In summary, we have reviewed the evidence for a burial, feathered serpent
sculpture, and green obsidian signaling ties to Teotihuacan; a floor marker whose closest parallel is with stelae at the Guatemalan Pacific piedmont site of Abaj Takalik; an initial stela most like that of Lamanai, Belize; and architectural features like those found at
many Maya Southern Lowlands sites. Overall these artifacts, art, architecture, and
inscriptions from this central part of the Principal Group indeed show that Early
Classic Copan was a cosmopolitan center.

Two generations later, Ruler 4 refurbished the interior of Papagayo by placing
a hieroglyphic step at the base of Stela 63 and a new stucco floor inside the temple.
When the second floor was laid down inside Papagayo atop the original floor, it was
designed and built to lip-up to the base of the newly created hieroglyphic step. The
step actually obscured the carving on the base of the stela on the front side, and the

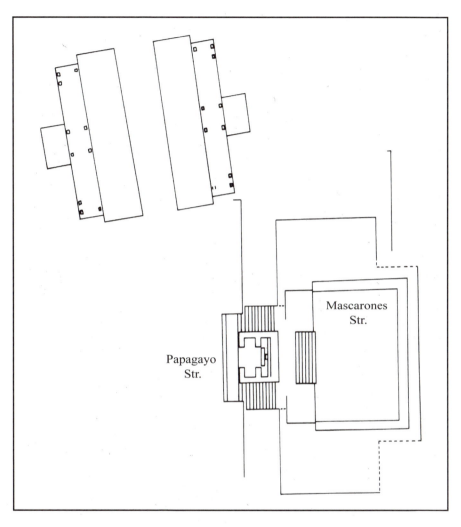

Figure 4.9 Plan of Papagayo and Mascarones Structures
(drawing by Fernando López).

fill behind the step created a low bench or platform in the back of the temple. This bench obscured the glyphs on the side of Stela 63, just as the step obscured the glyphs on the front side. Indeed, the fact that the name of the founder survived the later fire and breakage of the base of the stela owes entirely to the fact that the step and bench covered, and protected, that part of the stela. Clearly, the two were not erected at the same time, and Ruler 4's name appears on the riser of the step, confirming textually what the archaeological record demonstrates architecturally.

The hieroglyphs carved on the riser of the step, curiously enough, were carved perpendicular to the floor and designed to be read from right to left (see Stuart, and B. Fash, this volume). The text also cites the glyph *pu* or bulrush, leading David Stuart (2000) to believe that this relates Copan to a place of the reeds or bulrushes. This reference, he notes, is later found in the final-phase temple inscription, with its Teotihuacan "font" text, leading Stuart to believe that both references have to do with the central Mexican metropolis. Again, we find clear evidence from the earlier records (both archaeological and textual) in support of the historical claims made by the Late Classic kings.

Built directly behind Papagayo was an imposing pyramid-temple we call Mascarones (Figure 4.9) because of the modeled plaster mask first discovered on its substructure by Strömsvik (1952:fig. 5). The building faced west, with a central stair-case directly behind the back wall of Papagayo, on its central axis. The modeled stuc-co mask that Strömsvik uncovered was the only one to survive, with only the stone armatures being preserved on the symmetrical outset panel south of the staircase. We believe that another pair of masks would have adorned the second terrace of the pyra-mid on its west side, but that terrace was obliterated when the building was partially dismantled to make way for the next construction. Likewise, the superstructure was also destroyed by the Maya, and we are uncertain whether it was of masonry or per-ishable materials. The back side of the substructure was added onto, so this building must have been in use for at least two generations before it was buried. Of particular interest in the present context is that the stucco decoration that Strömsvik uncovered included the basal part of a sky-band, just north or the central stairway of Mascarones. Symmetry would dictate that there would have been another on the terrace wall south of the stairs. This pattern, of course, recalls the four sky-bands that decorated Mascarones's predecessor Motmot and were codified in the text of the floor marker.

This continuity in decoration and function was to last for all four of the struc-tures in this courtyard of public ceremonials, now known as the Plaza of the Hieroglyphic Stairway. The vision and the architectural template established by K'inich Yax K'uk' Mo' (and his son) was apparently considered a sacred proposition, respect-ed and emulated by his successors even as they expanded the scale and enhanced the meanings of these public buildings and the open court they shared. Papagayo Structure and Stela 63 were to be left open to allow visitation to that sacred space for more than two centuries, even as larger buildings engulfed all but its front side. When it was finally buried at the time of the death and burial of Ruler 12 in A.D. 695, the new version of the building continued to function as a dynastic temple. Furthermore, the great 9.0.0.0.0 date and the name of the founder were cited on Ruler 13's first stela (J), at the eastern entrance to the Principal Group. Structure 10L-11 continued to serve as a lineage or rulership house, according to the inscriptions (Stuart 1992). The ballcourt consecrated by K'inich Yax K'uk' Mo' continued to be decorated by large full-figure macaws.

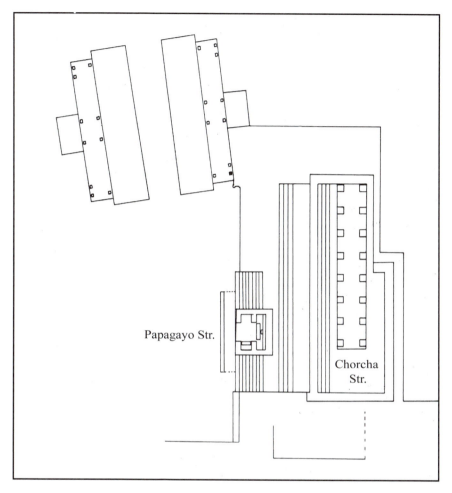

Figure 4.10 Plan of Papagayo and Chorcha Structures
(drawing by Fernando López).

End of the Early Classic Period

The 6th century construction of the building we call Chorcha buried its predecessor,
Mascarones and also engulfed the back and short sides of Papagayo Structure (Figure
4.10). As noted above, the superstructure, second terrace, and parts of the decoration
of the first terrace were all destroyed when this took place. Vast quantities of broken
polychrome pottery and carbon were laid in front of the destroyed mask south of the

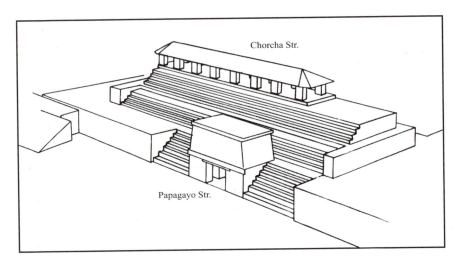

Figure 4.11 Isometric reconstruction of Papagayo and
Chorcha Structures (drawing by Fernando López).

central stairs as part of the fill that covered it. A formal termination ritual consisting of a number of jades in varying stages of manufacture, cinnabar, and a *Spondylus* shell were burned in a circular offering placed on the floor between the stairs of Mascarones and the back wall of Papagayo just prior to the filling in of the area and the construction of Chorcha (Fash 1988). This circular offering and its content recall those of the termination ritual offering placed on top of the Motmot floor marker on the very same axis during the reign of Ruler 2.

The superstructure of Chorcha was an unusual one compared to those that preceded and succeeded it on this locus (Figures 4.10, 4.11). Measuring 30.5 m north-south by 6 m east-west, it was a large, gallery-like building with eight rectangular columns framing seven doorways on both its front and back sides. This arrangement mimicked the superstructure of the adjacent Ballcourt II, which likewise had a series of paired columns supporting a thatch roof. It would seem that the "temple" function was fully met by Papagayo, while other functions that were more open and may have involved more participants were carried out in Mascarones. This was the final Early Classic structure built at this locus, and at the end of its long life was used to house one of the largest and most richly stocked royal tombs yet discovered in Copan, that of Ruler 12 (Fash 2001).

Papagayo and Stela 63 were apparently very important to the budding kingdom of Copan, because they were left accessible for quite some time. One of us (W. Fash 2001:105), originally sustained that Papagayo was open and in use for some 200 years, which our most recent work now obliges us to extend another fifty years. The fill placed inside Papagayo building when it was finally buried contained Copador ceramics. Architectural stratigraphy (documented by Fernando López) demonstrates that the ritual destruction and burial of Papagayo Structure coincided with that of Chorcha, the colonnaded building in back of Papagayo selected as the final resting place of Ruler 12 (Smoke Imix God K), in A.D. 695. Once again, both the building and its sculptures were ritually de-activated, the superstructure roofs demolished, and most of the stucco embellishments on the exterior surfaces effaced when Ruler 12 was buried. As part of this process, the human effigy censers that were placed around the perimeter of the royal tomb were fired up and then smashed.

In Papagayo Structure fire was used to deface the text of the inscribed stone step and the lower part of Stela 63, which was deliberately broken. Five of the six macaw head markers of Ballcourt IIa were also placed inside the building, indicating that Ruler 13 was dismantling Papagayo and Ballcourt IIa to make way for newer versions of each. Offerings were once again made as part of the de-activation of these buildings and their sculptures, including ceramic braziers placed at the foot of Stela 63 with the ballcourt markers. Once the burning, breaking, and offerings were completed, Papagayo, Ruler 12's tomb, and Chorcha were filled in. A sixth and final macaw head ballcourt marker was placed amidst the rubble, about halfway up the fill inside Papagayo. Those who placed the offerings and burned the sculptures inside Papagayo also filled it in and deposited one last offering of a macaw head marker toward the top of the fill. The same pattern was followed above the burial chamber of Ruler 12, where we found the final, 12th effigy censer perched atop the protective vault above the tomb. Thereafter, Ruler 13 erected Stela J perhaps as a substitute for Stela 63 and its predecessor the Motmot marker. All three cite the Bak'tun Ending 9.0.0.0.0 and its protagonist, K'inich Yax K'uk' Mo', as a cornerstone in the city's history.

The death and burial of Papagayo and its ancient monuments, as well as those of Ruler 12, heralded a new era in the life history of this ancestral temple-pyramid. With the construction of Esmeralda Structure, the central axis of the building with the dynastic inscription shifted to the north of its original locus, due to the encroachment of the construction mass of the adjacent Acropolis. Likewise, the manner of presentation of the dynastic texts shifted dramatically, from a lone stela and hieroglyphic step tucked up against the back wall of a temple, to a grandiose stairway with the largest glyphs ever carved in the history of the city. Elsewhere, the senior author has documented the life history of the stairway from its original locus on the east side of Structure 10L-26-2nd's substructure to its re-location and considerable augmentation on the final version on the west side (Fash 2002). However much the decoration and the medium of expression of dynastic lore may have shifted during the Late Classic period, these did not alter the function of the building as first set out by the founder in the early 5th century A.D. In textual terms, as Stuart (this volume) provocatively asserts, the monument went from a long-term focus on a single, foundational event in time to a focus on the passage of time itself. Structure 10L-26 continued to serve as a dynastic temple, a place where accounts of the deeds of all successive rulers were to be understood in the context of the royal charter of sacred places, buildings, and behaviors established by K'inich Yax K'uk' Mo'.

Conclusions

In looking at the broad historical sweep of construction in this central part of the Principal Group, we see considerable continuity and conservatism in the use of sacred space through time, at specific loci, for specific rituals and other activities. Yet we must also acknowledge the tremendous innovations that characterized the architecture and associated art and inscriptions here. The first floor marker was laid in place here, as a cornerstone of dynastic history in Copan. Its successor markers, placed in the playing alleys of the ballcourts, initially carried through on the themes of the Motmot marker but eventually diverged from them in new directions, both thematically and stylistically. The first known hieroglyphic stela (63) of Copan was also erected here. So, too, were the first ballcourt and its successors. The macaw imagery on the ballcourt was a first in the Maya area, incorporating as it did central Mexican imagery and an ancestral version of the Popol Vuh myth. The macaw imagery was a font of inspiration for numerous other, later ballcourts in the Copan region, but interestingly enough, nowhere else in the Maya area. The "four macaw" reference to Ballcourt I on the Motmot floor marker constitutes the first "named monument" we know of in Copan, along with the "four sky" nominal, a reference to Motmot Structure itself.

Returning briefly to the origins of the Principal Group, two final issues merit discussion. The first is that we still have not determined just how far back in time the constructions beneath Structure 10L-11 go. We know the Motmot floor lips up to an early, very large version of Structure 10L-11. We did not penetrate that stairway and at this point have no idea how large the platform that it provides access to might be. It remains for future investigations to determine whether earlier buildings, built during or even before the reign of K'inich Yax K'uk' Mo', may be found there. Given the importance accorded this largest Copan structure by Yax Pahsaj, and also by Ruler 7, who refers to it as the "lineage house of Yax K'uk' Mo'(Stuart 1992), one would think that it must have been equally important during the reign of the founder, if not before. Stuart's considerations (this volume) of the Yehnal Structure stucco mask as a potential emblematic name of a pre-K'inich Yax K'uk' Mo' ruler bear noting in this context.

Second, we do know of another important building complex, north of the Acropolis, whose origins pre-date the arrival of K'inich Yax K'uk' Mo'. We refer to the Northwest Platform and its underlying features, where René Viel and Jay Hall have test-pitted at the base and found Preclassic period deposits (personal communications, 1998; Traxler, this volume). In consultation with them, the Harvard Field School did some preliminary test-pitting on the summit of the platform and to the east of it in

1999. In each case, these recovered some Bijac and Acbi pottery beneath a superficial Late Classic stucco floor. Ongoing and future research by Viel and Hall may give us more concrete indications of precisely how much, if any, of this monumental platform pre-dates the arrival of K'inich Yax K'uk' Mo'.

Significantly, a boulder sculpture reminiscent of the pot-bellies found in stelae caches in Copan was found on the top of the Northwest Platform in our 1999 excavations. Broken in several pieces, it was clearly the object of veneration by Terminal Classic peoples, who left rectangular cache vessels beneath each of the two largest fragments. Thus, the references on Great Plaza stelae to important events in A.D. 159 and 160 (see Stuart, this volume) may refer to actions that took place on or near the Northwest Platform. The potbelly tradition has its origins and greatest expressions in the highlands and Pacific piedmont of Guatemala, indicating that the earliest Copan elites drew inspiration, if not biological ancestry, from that part of the Maya world. If the core of the Northwest Platform—or even just a significant part of the remains underlying it—proves to be of Late Preclassic and Protoclassic date, that would be significant. It may prove to be the center of a vigorous chiefdom in the Copan Valley prior to the much-heralded entrance of a now well-known "Lord of the West" onto the stage of Early Classic Maya history. With his arrival, the large public areas, buildings, and associated activities to the north of the Acropolis were re-configured in a template that was to be revamped and renewed—but never reformulated—for the duration of Copan's life as a Classic Maya kingdom.

5

INITIAL STAGES IN THE FORMATION OF THE COPAN ACROPOLIS

David W. Sedat and Fernando López

Since 1989, the Early Copan Acropolis Program (ECAP) has conducted archaeological investigations within the Copan Acropolis (Sharer, Traxler, et al. 1999). This research has focused on tracing the construction of early levels buried beneath the southern half of the Acropolis, where Rosalila (Agurcia F., this volume) and Structure 10L-16 were later built. The earliest complex of structures located in this area was arranged over the surface of a low but extensive earthen platform, named Yune (Sedat 1996; Sedat and López 1999). Located approximately 60 m south of the area known as the Great Plaza, this platform measures ca. 70 m square and resulted from the leveling of the clayey soils on the west bank of the Copan River.

Differences in the composition and architectural style of the sequent structures on this platform have led to the definition of at least three stages of development: early, middle, and late. This chapter will examine the sequence of these stages. However, it is important to note that because of Yune's deeply buried location and limited exposure, the reconstruction presented here is to be considered preliminary.

Early Yune Platform Stage

Evaluation of the features both underlying and associated with the stucco surfaces that define the summit and edges of Yune Platform (Figure 5.1) suggests that: (1) over the northern half of Yune the construction of the platform and associated substructures was apparently a single coordinated event that almost completely transformed what seems to have been an earlier complex of river-cobble structures or pavements; (2) for an unknown period of time, structures both on and to the north of Yune Platform were in existence without the benefit of stucco surfacing; and (3) the structure(s) on the southern half of Yune or surfaces to the north of Yune might be older than those on the northern half of the Yune Platform itself.

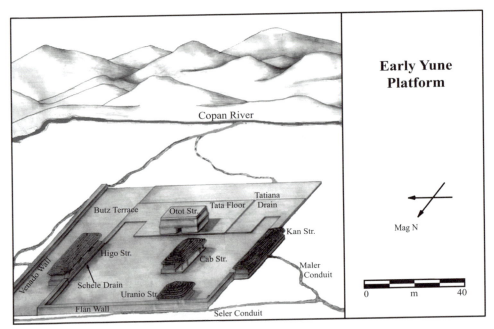

Figure 5.1 Hypothetical reconstruction of Early Yune Platform
(drawing by Fernando López).

During the Early Yune stage (Figure 5.1), the eastern edge of the platform was marked by an earthen and cobble substructure (Higo) whose foundation was a cobble-cored embankment which stepped down to a lower, narrower terrace bounded by a 2-m-wide cobble wall of unknown height. Although this wall might have served a defensive function or protected the site from flooding (see Hall and Viel, this volume), the cobble-cored terrace it sits on might be a vestige of a monumental pre-Yune construction largely transformed and obliterated during later construction episodes. Underneath this entire cobble construction ran a cobble-lined drain that siphoned water from the eastern part of the platform's surface toward the Copan River. The presence of a round stopper-like stone found near the mouth of the eastern drainage passageway, and the construction of other specialized channels designed to drain water, suggest that water on the surface of Yune Platform was controlled and managed.

The northern limits of Early Yune were marked by an earthen wall of unknown height. In its northwestern quadrant there existed an earthen substructure designated Uranio, the first in a series of three such structures at this location. The latest and largest version (Maravilla) remained in use until the 6th century A.D. Uranio's extent and orientation are unknown, but it contained a buried individual with jade-inlaid teeth (Burial 93-1; see Bell et al., this volume).

An earthen substructure of unknown extent bounded Yune's west side. Under this structure ran a stone-lined conduit (Maler). The conduit could have brought gravity-fed water onto the platform, possibly in order to create a ritually significant shallow reflecting pool over the central area of the platform. Moreover, this conduit could have also provided drinking water to residents living on and near Yune.

The southern limits of Early Yune are unknown. However, new evidence suggests that an accumulation of superimposed cobble floors associated with one or more cobble-and-earthen entities (collectively named Mamá) was initially situated in this area. If the sizable later Yune constructions (like Wilin Structure) built over the southern portion of Early Yune are a good indication of the extent of prior construction, Mamá might have been a low substructure for a perishable building possibly 18 m or more in length, probably oriented to the north. After an unknown interval, Mamá was succeeded by Otot, a small masonry building.

At the center of Early Yune, there was an earthen substructure designated Cab that appears to have been about 0.8 m high and measured 11.0 m (N-S) x 8.5 m (E-W). Cab appears to have had a complex and still poorly understood construction sequence and use span. The core of the substructure appears to have been surrounded by flat river cobbles that formed a pavement; a construction feature that appears elsewhere under the first stucco surface that forms the summit of Yune, as well as in areas to the north of Yune. Evidence of post holes around the substructure's perimeter indicates that the vulnerable earthen construction material was protected by a perishable roof that sheltered both the core of the substructure and what may have been a somewhat later addition, a lower porch-like area on the west, the direction that this structure probably faced. There is evidence that the support posts for a building on top of Cab (presumed to have been perishable) were renewed at least once, implying that the structure may have continued to have been used for two decades or more, based on modern estimates in the Copan area of the longevity of wooden posts.

The renewal of Cab involved placing a cobble-and-earth fill component (named Bac) immediately east of the main body of the substructure. It is unknown, however, whether Bac was intended as an expansion of the Cab summit to support a new and larger building or whether Bac related to subsequent construction at this locus—the building of the Hunal Structure. This unknown relationship remains critical because the northwestern corner of a sub-floor masonry chamber (at least 1.2 m high and of unknown extent) was found to be integral to the southeastern quadrant of Bac. We assume this corner represents the remnants of a chamber because its lower extent was intruded roughly 1 m below the initial stucco surfacing of Cab and into sub-platform levels.

Details of the chamber's original form and function are unknown, however, because of the extensive modifications made by successive constructions in this locus. The chamber was largely demolished, and only a vestige was incorporated into later chambers at the same location. However, what is particularly intriguing about Bac is that, after four later transformations and modifications, this spot ultimately became the tomb for a woman richly arrayed with great quantities of jade, shell, and other offerings. The latter, known as the Margarita Tomb, is discussed further below (see also Bell et al. and Buikstra et al., this volume). Since several modest jade offerings on Cab's west side appear to confirm the westward orientation of this structure, they might indicate that this structure was associated with ritual activities. This reconstruction becomes even more plausible if the Bac feature were indeed built and used during Cab's use period.

Overall, Early Yune was a large-scale low platform that supported a coherently planned arrangement of structures made from readily available local materials that did not require significant additional preparation or modification. Delimiting structures (walls and substructures) would have defined the internal open spaces and provided possible advantages for defense or flood mitigation. Drainage of rainfall and introduction of gravity-fed water was anticipated with special stone-lined conduits, and the stucco surfacing over the platform undoubtedly enhanced both drainage and human traffic. Intriguingly, three structures (Uranio, Cab, and Mamá/Otot) seem to define a court group, with eastern Cab showing possible ritual function. This arrangement of structures recalls a common Maya court layout which is cataloged as Plaza Plan 2 for the central Lowlands (Becker 1971). However, the limited excavations on this level of the Early Acropolis cannot confirm this or any other pattern.

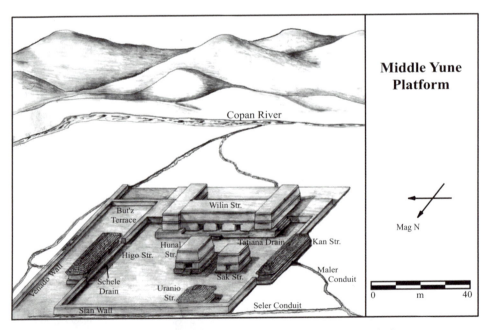

Figure 5.2 Hypothetical reconstruction of Middle Yune Platform
(drawing by Fernando López).

Middle Yune Platform Stage

The middle stage in the development of Yune Platform (Figure 5.2) is marked by the replacement of Cab by a 1 m-high masonry substructure designated Hunal, which exhibits a *talud-tablero* style (of 4:1 ratio). Because Hunal was so extensively demolished by later construction (only its northeastern quarter survives), many crucial details relating to its form are not available. Initially, Hunal was thought to be a north-facing structure based on an unbalustraded staircase found on its north side (Sedat 1997b; Sharer, Fash, et al. 1999). However, new evidence has revealed that there was a balustraded staircase on its east side as well. This eastern staircase suggests that the primary access into the building was on the east, while the unbalustraded northern staircase led to a secondary access. Because the ancient demolition on the west and south sides is so extensive, we might never know whether there were staircases on these sides, or the full dimension of the north-south and east-west axes. Without this crucial information, we cannot say whether Hunal was exclusively oriented to the east (with secondary accesses on the north and possibly south sides), or whether there had been accesses on both east and west sides as well as entrances on the north and south. Even so, we assume Hunal was bilaterally symmetrical with respect to its east-west axis, and that there were at least three rooms (a northern, central, and southern) for the building, even though the presence of the postulated south room has not been confirmed.

The masonry building on Hunal had at least two phases, Hunal K'ak and Hunal Mo'. The earlier version—Hunal K'ak—had walls ca. 1 m thick, but the size of the central room suggests that the building was not vaulted. This building's original thick stucco floor was refurbished at least once with a red-painted surface in the north room and the eastern part of the central room. Given our reconstruction of Hunal K'ak, the Bac Chamber was situated centrally underneath the eastern end of the central room, that is, at the top of the balustraded staircase. It remains unknown, however, whether Bac was an integral part of Hunal's construction, or if Hunal was a stucco renovation of a preexisting Cab-Bac substructure. Regardless, Bac's dense cobble-and-clayey fill seems to have been intentionally placed by ancient builders to solidify the construction of this chamber.

Assuming the Hunal K'ak stage followed the same general room layout as the later building stage on Hunal, there would have been a doorway between the north and central room. There are indications that the red-painted floor of the north room continued through this doorway to the central room's eastern doorway area, while the floor of the western portion of the central room remained unpainted. This pattern suggests that Bac's sub-floor location might have been marked by special embellishment, possibly including a shallow depression over the area. Enigmatically, there are traces of a 0.25-m-wide boundary between the painted and unpainted areas of the floor in the central room, and a single post hole was preserved within this area.

Based on our observations of similar features associated with later structures within the Copan Acropolis, we believe that there was once a north-south wattle-and-

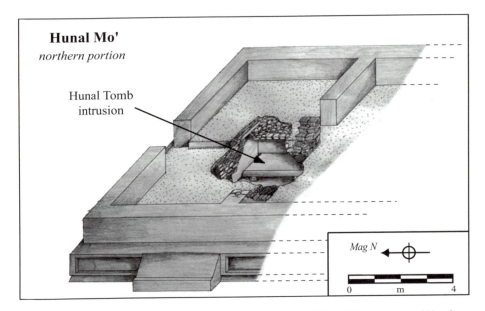

Figure 5.3 Reconstruction of the northern portion of Hunal Structure and Tomb (drawing by Fernando López).

daub wall (supported by upright wooden poles set in the floor around this red-painted area) enclosing either a special, shrine-like area over Bac or forming a screen to cut off the view from the doorway toward the western part of the central room, making this interior space more private. West of this feature, the floor has numerous small round burnmarks, which may have been caused by small *incensarios* or *candeleros*. While these features might be interpreted as evidence of activity related to a sub-floor deposit, there is no way to determine the original form or function of Bac during either stage of Hunal.

The later version of Hunal's building, designated Hunal Mo' (Figure 5.3), had much thinner walls (0.6 m) than its predecessor, indicating that it too was probably roofed with timbers. The substructure appears unchanged, although Hunal Mo's building walls were moved closer to the edge, apparently to maximize interior building space. Hunal Mo' had an interior red-painted doorway through the wall (offset to the east) dividing the central and north rooms. This doorway had cord holders on the central room side, indicating that it could be closed off.

The new building plan for Hunal Mo' significantly increased the size of the north room and seemingly reduced the size of the central room. The largely hypothetical shrine proposed to have marked the area of the Bac Chamber seems to have been covered over by the new stucco floor for this building. We presume that one motivation for this change was to prepare a suitably-sized covered space for the vaulted chamber that was eventually intruded beneath the eastern end of the northern room. Curiously, the positioning of this intruded chamber made it analogous in location to the proposed location of the Bac Chamber under the central room. In any case, the evidence is clear that an intrusive cut somewhat over 2 m in depth was made within the eastern portion of the north room of the Hunal Mo' building (Figure 5.3).

This intrusion was used to construct a north-south oriented vaulted masonry chamber (named the Hunal Tomb), whose interior dimensions were 2.7 m by 1.5 m, and 1.8 m in height. Before the vault was closed, a large specially prepared flat stone slab was lowered into the chamber to rest on four upright round stone pedestals. When the vault was ultimately raised and capped with several layers of flat stones, the top of the chamber rose above the floor of the building into which the chamber had been intruded. This protrusion required the construction of a low (ca. 30 cm) platform over the area to level the space. The surface of this platform was refurbished at least twice, and it appears to have started to weaken and sag even before Hunal was buried by subsequent construction. No evidence of activity (such as burning or caching) was noted on the surface of this platform, but there was the suggestion that the doorway into the central room might have been sealed.

The Hunal Tomb was used to inter the body of a mature male, laid on the stone slab, along with offerings placed both upon and below the slab (see Bell et al. and Buikstra et al., this volume). Although we do not know how soon after the chamber's completion this interment occurred, the provision of an access portal implies that it could have taken place some time after the chamber was completed. From inside the chamber it was noticed that the northernmost capstone was wider than the other capstones, and unlike its companions, was not set in and sealed around its edges by stucco mortar. Thus, it would have been relatively easy for this northern capstone to be removed, allowing the body to be lowered through the opening. The length of time Hunal Mo' remained open and used after the Hunal Tomb was sealed remains unknown, but there is evidence that, at a minimum, it remained accessible during the time the remains of the interred individual decomposed. This accessibility allowed for the re-entry of the tomb for what might have been ritual purposes. In fact, not only do certain objects and bones within the tomb appear to have been moved in antiquity, but cinnabar was also applied to the exposed bones. Therefore, access to the tomb for any post-mortem activity would probably have been via the northern capstone.

Taken as a whole, Hunal served during a period that saw K'ak, with a more restricted interior floor area, first renovated and subsequently replaced by the more spacious Mo' building. There are indications that Hunal's *talud-tablero* style substructure was refurbished at least twelve (if not as many as twenty) times with thin stucco coatings, some of which were tinted red. Accordingly, the total use period for the substructure could have been as short as ten to twelve years (based on a minimal number of stucco coatings marking annual refurbishments), or as long as two decades or more.

Throughout its existence, Hunal appears to have exhibited special distinction with its *talud-tablero* style, red paint on both exterior and interior, sub-floor chambers, and markers for sub-floor features (a platform over the Hunal Tomb, a red-painted possible shrine over Bac Chamber). It is likely that at least one of the building phases on Hunal had mural decoration, but it was totally demolished when the substructure was refurbished. If the thicker walls for Hunal K'ak did not support a vaulted structure, they might have been designed to support heavy stucco decoration.

Given that there are still unresolved questions regarding the status and function of the Bac Chamber, the original ritual function of Hunal K'ak remains less evident. Hunal Mo' clearly exhibits a mortuary function after the placement of the off-axis Hunal Tomb, although, strangely, ritual deposits (caches or other sign of ritual activity) that may have informed on Hunal's primary orientation (whether exclusively eastward, bi-directional, or even of radial configuration, see above), were not found.

Hunal was set to the north of a larger masonry entity named Wilin that had developed during this same stage on the southern half of Yune. Prior to Wilin a broad, low (ca. 30 cm high) expanse (of unknown extent) named Tatá that bore traces of at least one masonry building (Otot) seems to have evolved from the earlier construction (Mamá) over this locus (Figure 5.1). Evidently drainage toward the south was both a desired and necessary feature for this middle stage because an open stone-lined channel (Tatiana) led off in this direction, transecting Tatá. The observable southern portion of Tatiana extends under Wilin for an estimated 15–20 m and presumably is one indication of this structure's significant size.

Wilin is an extensive, ca. 1.5 m high, masonry platform built directly on Tatá. Much of our reconstruction of Wilin's size is based on the assumption that its eastern half was symmetrical with its westward extent, and that the observable length of the covered-over drain (Tatiana) and a pattern of later floor cracks over the area (caused by the compacting of differential depths of fill required to bury Wilin's substructure) relate to its over-all size. On Wilin's western end there was a secondary substructure, named Quej, which rose almost 1 m higher and supported a masonry building that probably faced east. Although its over-all size is not documented, Wilin may have been large enough to support additional structures. If so, hypothetical structures on its southern and eastern ends could have formed a triadic grouping open to the north. Regardless, the basal elevation of the building on Quej and any possible companion buildings would have been more than 1 m higher than the building on Hunal.

The Middle Yune stage seems to correspond to a period in Copan's history when a great many changes were under way (Fash et al., this volume; Traxler, this volume). The continued remodeling of earthen structures in and around Yune Platform suggests that local traditions and styles were maintained alongside new or foreign architectural traditions, such as those represented by Hunal (and Yax structure to the north of Yune; Fash, et al., this volume). Indeed, as mentioned, one earthen structure

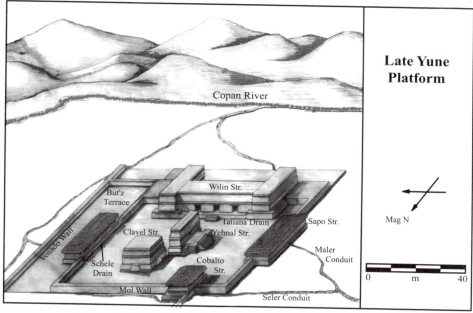

Figure 5.4 Hypothetical reconstruction of Late Yune Platform
(drawing by Fernando López).

built early in the central area, Uranio, was renovated, maintained, and used for a span
of more than a century, long after any remaining vestiges of Yune had been buried by
later construction.

Late Yune Platform Stage

The Late Yune stage (Figure 5.4) is recognized by expanded peripheral structures on
the north and west sides of the platform as well as the replacement of Hunal at the
central locus by a structure named Yehnal. Unlike Hunal before it, Yehnal was unam-
biguously oriented to the west, an orientation recognized for all succeeding structures
at this locus, including the latest, Structure 10L-16. This westward orientation for
Yehnal may reflect the initial organization of Yune, which prevailed during Cab's use-
life. If Hunal had been atypically oriented eastwards, Yehnal would indicate a 180° shift
in orientation, but given the possibility of Hunal's bi-directional focus (see above),
there might be more continuity in the orientation of Yune's central structure than once
thought.

Although Yehnal's orientation was to the west, it had ancillary staircases on
both the south and north. These secondary staircases may have been analogous to similarly situated stairs believed to have existed for Hunal. Seen as a whole, Yehnal may

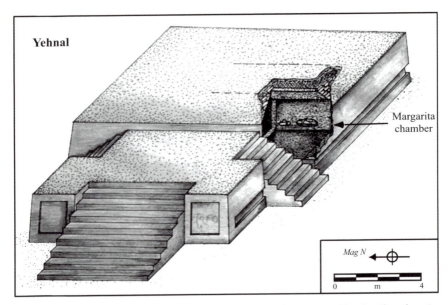

Figure 5.5 Reconstruction of Yehnal Structure and Margarita Tomb, Chamber 1
(drawing by Fernando López).

not be such a radical departure from the norm for this locus, but rather a functional change relating to the use of the building and surrounding court areas.

Yehnal was a red-painted masonry substructure exhibiting the fully developed Maya apron-molding style common to the central lowland Maya area in the Early Classic (Figure 5.5). On its main (west) façade decorated panels made of modeled stucco flanked an outset staircase (see Sedat 1997c:fig. 1). These panels depicted the solar deity K'inich Ajaw (possibly a reference to K'inich Yax K'uk' Mo';Taube, this volume), or an aspect of this god named K'inich Tajal Wayib' (Martin and Grube 2000:195). Recalling how the more clearly evident emblemic name of K'inich Yax K'uk' Mo' appears on Yehnal's successor, Margarita (see Sedat 1997c; Figure 5.1), Stuart has proposed that the Yehnal panel may be a large name glyph, and he has speculated that it refers to a celebrated ancestral figure during the reigns of the first rulers, possibly even naming an earlier historic figure associated with both Copan and Tikal (Stuart, this volume). Regardless, it is important to note that the first indisputable *in situ* reference to K'inich Yax K'uk' Mo' at this locus occurs on Yehnal's successor, Margarita Structure, contained in the central figure of the stucco-modeled panel on the western façade of its substructure (Sedat 1997e; Stuart 1997).

During the construction of Yehnal, an intrusion was made into Hunal Mo's central room, apparently encountering the Bac Chamber. The red paint and other indications over this feature may still have been present or remembered, giving the ancient excavators a direct indication of its location. Certainly this intrusion skirted the southern edge of the platform overlaying the Hunal Tomb immediately to the north. Apparently the Bac Chamber was smaller than desired because it appears that only the lower portions of the northwest corner of the original construction were reused by the builders of Yehnal as the base for a new chamber (Figure 5.5). When completed, the new Yehnal Chamber was an impressively large vaulted space (oriented north-south) measuring some 2.5 m by 1.7 m. Overall, this Yehnal Chamber would have been at least 3 m high from capstones to floor, effectively making it almost 1 m higher than the adjacent Hunal Tomb.

Although sealed by the summit floors of Yehnal, this new vaulted chamber incorporated a stepped access that led down to an entrance through its northern wall. At this time, this chamber probably did not include a raised stone burial slab, but may have had a ca. 70 cm wide bench (ca. 1.0 m high) on its west side. Preserved lower portions of the Yehnal Chamber exhibit a characteristic dark discoloration suggestive of smudging by frequent or intense smoke. Since this new chamber was significantly transformed and modified at least three more times after the termination of Yehnal (resulting in what we term the Margarita Tomb; see Sedat 1997e; Sharer, Fash, et al. 1999), it cannot yet be determined whether the Yehnal chamber at this stage was simply left empty, was used exclusively for subterranean rituals (conjecturally associated with the deceased in the nearby Hunal Tomb), or contained an interment during the use life of this substructure. Regardless, it is of interest to note that retrospective texts at Copan recall a smoke-related event associated with K'inich Yax K'uk' Mo' (Taube, this volume).

Also during the Late Yune stage, the north boundary wall (height unknown) was moved northwards by some 2 m. Along the outside (north) of this wall there was an open stone-lined channel for water. It is hypothesized that this water flowed eastwards and had its source from the same channel that led to the Maler conduit on Yune's west side. Earthen Uranio was superseded by a larger substructure of the same material designated Cobalto, which measured over 2 m high. Cobalto seems to have been situated on a northwest projection of Yune, possibly a new addition. Projecting to the north from Cobalto (for a distance unknown) was a wall, later reinforced by cobbles, that may have formed part of the newly extended defining boundary wall around Yune. Before Cobalto was replaced by an even larger earthen substructure, an extensive deposit of burned wood and broken jade was thrown off the north side of the substructure, perhaps as part of a termination ritual (Offering 93-1, see Bell 2003).

During the Late Yune stage, further construction seems to have taken place on Wilin, consisting of a wall added to the central area to the east of Quej. This wall either increased the covered space of the largely hypothetical building on Wilin's southern portion (suggested by smooth, unweathered flooring in this area) or blocked access in this direction. It seems to have been a prelude to a large secondary substructure (Ná) on the southern end of Wilin, apparently built during the terminal span of

Yune Platform. An anciently violated, refilled, and modified small masonry chamber (1.6 m by 0.7 m and 0.85 m in height) integral to Ná could have contained a burial or a cache deposit. This same chamber was later filled, leaving only the northwest corner open as a square masonry feature (ca. 40 cm square) slightly more than 1 m deep. The form of this later feature suggests that it could have contained an offering disturbed in antiquity (indeed several small broken pieces of jade were found), or the base of a tennoned upright sculpture. This final construction on Wilin foreshadows a later northward expansion that engulfed Yehnal as well as ultimately all the structures situated on the northern half of Yune Platform. This later expansion from the south created the Early Acropolis as a large-scale raised edifice (named Witik Platform), built over the original expanse of Yune Platform, with Margarita Structure covering the site where Yehnal had stood before.

The Dating of Yune Platform

There are at present no means of directly dating either the first construction or the introduction of stucco and stone masonry construction into the center of Yune Platform. The available radiocarbon dates for relevant levels of Yune Platform are generally too early to be reasonable, probably indicating that the samples used were from old-growth or re-used wood. In any case, radiocarbon dates from the early levels have a greater standard deviation than the probable use period of the entities we are attempting to date.

Based on a substantial series of absolute dates and related events supported by a variety of epigraphic, iconographic, and bioanthropological sources, there is an ongoing effort to connect the archaeological data derived from the early levels of Yune Platform to the historical record of Copan and the wider Maya world as it is now known (Sedat and Sharer 1997; Sharer 1997a, 1997d, this volume; Sharer, Fash, et al. 1999; Martin and Grube 2000). This conjunctive approach (Fash and Sharer 1991) has led to understanding the Structure 10L-16 locus as a focus of commemoration for the Copan dynastic founder (Agurcia F., this volume). While the association of the Structure 10L-16 locus with K'inich Yax K'uk Mo' most appreciably starts with the Margarita Structure (dated within the span of A.D. 440–470; Sharer, Traxter, et al. 1999) based on the indisputably *in situ* decorative panels, the identification of the Hunal Tomb as the most likely resting place of Copan's Classic Period founder has obliged us to consider the Middle Yune Stage as spanning the period of K'inich Yax K'uk Mo's "arrival" at Copan at the time of the dynastic founding (A.D. 426–427) until his death, most likely in A.D. 437. This manner of dating the Yune sequence suggests that the Early Yune stage dates to pre-dynastic times, but still within the Early Acbi phase (ca. A.D. 400–426), while Late Yune stages would be linked to the early years of Ruler 2's reign (after ca. A.D. 437) and Yehnal would be the first commemoration of the founder.

In a critical evaluation of the fit between the archaeological evidence derived from Yune Platform and the conjunctive evidence used to date its stages, it seems apparent that if all the known dates associated with K'inich Yax K'uk Mo' (spanning from ca. A.D. 416-437; Stuart, this volume) are associated with his life at Copan and Yune/Hunal, this ca. 20-year period would seem to coincide quite well with one estimated use span period for Hunal (see above). The assumption that K'inich Yax K'uk Mo' built and used this substructure would accordingly imply his "arrival" at Copan significantly preceded his founding of the new dynasty by some 10 years.

The Origins of Yune Platform

Two significant general observations can be offered concerning the early stages of the construction of Yune Platform. The first is that the initial earthen-cored construction appears to have been planned and executed utilizing local construction techniques and materials, similar to other Early Classic regional sites such as Los Achiotes (Canuto, this volume), and Cerro Chino (Fash and Fash 2000:447). The Yune plan featured a rather extensive open space of some 70 m square, which was surrounded by low structures and other delimiting features, with an important building situated toward the center of this interior area. The plan and prevailing earthen construction of Yune implies that the complex of structures that was to become the Early Acropolis was first built by local inhabitants in the early years of the Acbi phase (presently dated to ca. A.D. 400), following local traditions in construction and site planning that presumably date well back into the Preclassic (Canuto, this volume), although unlike these Late Preclassic valley centers, Yune's structures appear to be cardinally oriented throughout all three phases of construction. Early Yune might have been associated with a coalescing political organization in the valley center, but there are no clear indications that the initial residents were of royal status. The continuation of earthen construction on Yune Platform throughout all its stages suggests that local traditions and ideals continued to be followed in the development of activities at this locus.

A second general observation about the early stages of Yune Platform is that there are indications of a variety of contacts and interaction between Copan and other parts of the Maya world (Sharer, Traxler, et al. 1999). The potential Plaza Plan 2 pattern noted for Early Yune's center might reflect a degree of interaction with the Maya lowlands at even the very founding of Yune. During the Middle and Late Yune Stages, foreign architectural styles and construction techniques, including *talud-tablero* and apron-molding style masonry, stucco-polychrome relief decoration, and corbel vaulting, seem to have become accentuated on Yune, especially in the central temple-like structure. It may be that these innovations and stylistic changes were brought about during a relatively short span of time (ca. one decade) by the influence and associations of one individual, possibly even by military conquest (Sharer, Fash, et al. 1999). On the other hand, six retrospective texts at Copan recount events and early rulers as far back as A.D. 159 (Stuart, this volume). Therefore, either architectural development remained relatively static and focused on rather rudimentary earthen substructures with perishable buildings until the founding era, or early masonry construction at Copan has yet to be discovered.

The Margarita Tomb and Its Predecessors

As we have noted, the space that became the Margarita Tomb chamber underwent a number of transformations during the initial stages of Yune Platform, beginning very early in Yune's history. These transformations and the activities that must have accompanied them were centered at the core of the developing Early Acropolis and can be assumed to have played a vital role in the establishment of the new dynasty.

Disregarding ambiguous evidence relating to the early stages of the Bac Chamber, it is clear that on the termination of Hunal by Yehnal, that spot became the locus of a large vaulted masonry chamber whose form and architectural context has been detailed as follows: (1) chamber is constructed (Yehnal); (2) chamber is narrowed (Margarita); (3) chamber is made less deep (Margarita); and (4) new floor is laid together with the placement of a burial slab and the interment of a woman (Margarita Tomb). In sum, three distinct pre-Margarita Tomb stages have been detailed at this locus, but there is no evidence indicating they ever were used for interments or any other activity.

While we do not know the functions of the constructions that preceded the final Margarita Tomb, we offer three main options, granting that all are hypothetical based on the lack of conclusive evidence, and there is no evidence yet to directly evaluate, refute, or support any of the options outlined here.

1. The pre-Margarita chambers would have served for offerings, subterranean ritual, or other non-mortuary activity.

2. The pre-Margarita chambers may have been pre-planned burial chambers that remained empty before they were refurbished for a burial.

3. The pre-Margarita chambers may have been tombs. Hypothetically, the Bac Chamber may have served for the interment of Early Yune's founding ancestor. If so, any body once deposited within would have been disinterred when the chamber underwent its next refurbishment. Such a process of burial and disinterment would have been repeated several times before the space was used for the burial of the woman in the Margarita Tomb. In the future, sophisticated analyses of the several earlier chamber floors might look for proteins resulting from the decomposition of different corpses.

Conclusion

Efforts thus far to calibrate the archaeological data from Yune Platform with known historical individuals and events have led to the interpretation of Middle Yune as the center associated with K'inich Yax K'uk' Mo', who upon his death was interred in the Hunal Tomb. Consequently, the antecedent Early Yune stage would be pre-dynastic, but it is not known yet whether this early complex was laid out by earlier rulers and modified by the founder or if Yune was originally designed and built by a much younger K'inich Yax K'uk' Mo'. The resolution of questions such as these will continue to challenge investigators of early Copan history.

Acknowledgments

It is not possible to list everybody here who deserves credit. Nevertheless, we are indebted to the editors of this volume for allowing us the opportunity of floating this interim trial balloon for several ideas, in the hopes that our colleagues will continue to provide us with their insights and, above all, constructive criticisms.

6

ROSALILA, TEMPLE OF THE SUN-KING

Ricardo Agurcia Fasquelle

"Religion permeates all their public and private acts: their morality, science, education, language, clothing, literature, theatre, and the remaining artistic manifestations; their festivals, entertainments, and industries, their social institutions, politics, economics, and judicial system and, finally, all of their cultural corpus, is, to different degrees, a manifestation of their religious ideology"—Girard (1949:385)[*]

As all Americanist archaeologists well know, ethnology is the science that gives substance to the skeleton that is the archaeological record. In the present work, I shall emphasize the research conducted by Rafael Girard among the Ch'orti, a Maya group that occupies the same territory as ancient Copan, in order to illuminate my investigations in the Copan Acropolis.

Rosalila

Within Structure 10L-16, at the center of the Copan Acropolis, I discovered, on June 23, 1989, the predecessor of this building and gave it the field name "Rosalila" (Figures 6.1 and 6.2). This building is the best intact example of Copan's Early Classic architecture and monumental art uncovered to date. Unlike most of the buildings found in our excavations within the Acropolis, which were destroyed to increase the stability of the structures built above them, Rosalila was not systematically demolished. Not only was this building not destroyed, it was carefully interred with a great deal of ceremony: its

---

[*] All passages from Girard (1949) were translated by the editors.

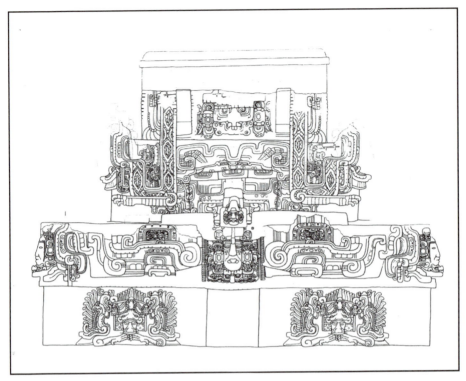

Figure 6.1 Reconstruction of the west façade of Rosalila
(drawing by Barbara W. Fash).

rooms, moldings, and niches were carefully filled with clay and rocks, while its enormous modeled stucco panels (which retain their original polychrome paint) were covered with a thick layer of white stucco before they were buried. This embalming of
the temple in white finds its counterpart in mortuary practices that remain in use
among the Ch'orti, who dress the death god in a white cloak, cover cadavers with a
similar sheet, and use white candles and flowers as decorations in funerary ceremonies
(Wisdom 1961:484).

Rosalila has three levels (or bodies) which together rise to 12.9 m. Its base
measures 18.5 m by 12.5 m, with the principal façade facing west. The building sits on
a small substructure called Azul. As is the case for all temples on this sacred axis, its
principal staircase faces west, the direction associated by the Ch'orti with the entrance
to the underworld, the world of the dead and the place where the sun dies daily
(Girard 1949:204, 641; Wisdom 1961:482). The stair consists of seven steps. The fifth
includes a carved hieroglyphic text with a Long Count date reconstructed as

9.6.17.3.2.3 Ik' 0 Kumk'u (21 February, A.D. 571). This date places it at the end of the reign of the tenth ruler of Copan, "Moon Jaguar," whose name also appears in the text (Martin and Grube 2000:198, but cf. Stuart, this volume).

The style of the façade decoration and the thick layers of stucco in which it is executed combine to indicate an early date for this structure. The ceramics found in the architectural fill of Rosalila strengthen this interpretation, given that they are part of the Acbi ceramic complex, which dates to Copan's Early Classic period (A.D. 400–600). The proximity of Rosalila to Stela P, erected by the eleventh ruler, Butz' Chan, in A.D. 623, and the similarity of their iconography, lead me to believe that the stela was originally placed in front of the structure and that it was the ruler's preferred sanctuary for venerating his ancestors.

Twelve radiocarbon dates support the ceramic and stratigraphic chronological assessment. These radiocarbon dates place the construction of Rosalila after A.D. 520 and its termination before A.D. 690, with the termination date most likely closer to A.D. 655. Consequently, the temple had a long history, being built by the tenth ruler,

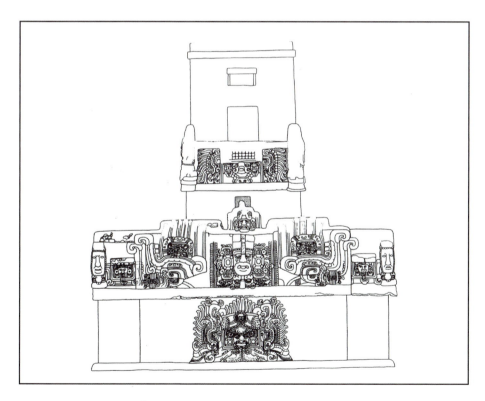

Figure 6.2 Reconstruction of the north face of Rosalila
(drawing by Barbara Fash).

Figure 6.3 Rosalila offerings: (a) ceramic censer found in the central room; (b) chert eccentric found in the west room (photographs by Reyna Flores).

used by the eleventh, and buried by the twelfth.

The interior walls of the temple are covered with soot from the ceremonial use of incense and the burning of torches to illuminate the dark interiors. Inside the temple we found a number of objects that reflect the practices and function of the building. Among them were seven ceramic incense burners with carbon in their interior. Two of these were located on carved stone jaguar pedestals. Additional offerings included chert knives (for sacrifices), chert eccentrics (used as ceremonial scepters), jade ornaments (worn as jewelry), sea shells, stingray spines (perforators used in auto-sacrifice), shark vertebrae, jaguar claws, and flowers (Figure 6.3).

Many of these remains remind us of religious practices that are still current among present-day Maya groups. For example, Girard (1949:404, 569, 593–594, 647, 651) indicates that (1) the interior of Ch'orti temples should be dark as "they are the representation of the subterranean world"; (2) in these "the most artistic and sacred objects are kept"; and (3) ritual paraphernalia include censers, foliage, flowers, feathers, and blood. Wisdom (1961:434, 437, 485) makes similar observations.

The Iconography of Rosalila and Azul

Rosalila has been the principal focus of my investigations since its discovery in 1989 (Agurcia F. 1997b, 1998; Agurcia F. and Fash 1991, 1992; Agurcia F. and Valdés 1994;

Figure 6.4 Sun god mask on Azul substructure
(photograph by Reyna Flores).

Agurcia F. et al. 1996). Nevertheless, though our investigation has been intensive and has produced a systematic and representative sample of the structure's art and architecture, at least half of the building remains unexcavated.

Azul, the Rosalila substructure, is rectangular and scarcely 3 m high. It measures 20.5 m along its long (north-south) axis and 14.2 m along its short (east-west) axis. Its principal stair is located on the west, while secondary access is provided on the south and east sides. This small substructure is known through excavations on three of its sides: the majority of its east (rear) side, half of its west (front) side, and a small portion of its south side have been exposed. Although ephemeral traces of modeled stucco remain on the east side, these are not sufficiently complete to permit valid interpretations of their design and iconography.

On the west side, the portion of the substructure north of the central stair has been excavated. It includes a magnificent polychrome painted, modeled stucco portrait of the Sun God (K'inich Ajaw, Ah K'in, or God G in the Schellhas nomenclature; Taube 1992b) placed in the center of a rectangular shield bordered by feathers (Figure 6.4). The mask is almost entirely red, although there are clear traces of green on the earflares. The face of this solar deity includes very large eyes which, as is typical, are marked with rectilinear incisions that give the god a crosseyed appearance. There are three small incised circles arranged in a triangular pattern on each cheek that may represent jaguar spots, recalling the nocturnal aspect of the same deity. Unfortunately, as the nose and mouth of this mask are very damaged, it cannot be determined if the depiction includes a "Roman" nose, nor if the teeth were filed into a *tau* or T-shape. Two scrolls form a mustache-like shape around the mouth.

The anthropomorphic face of this deity is ringed with beads, and elaborate Early Classic-style earflares are located on either side of the face. The headdress was only partially exposed, but it appears to represent a jawless zoomorph. The deteriorated remains of another crosseyed zoomorph are visible below the Sun God's rectangular beard. It is highly likely that this lower face represents a jaguar, as it does on other examples from the same time period at Copan, Tikal, and Kohunlich (A. Miller 1986:fig. 9; Segovía Pinto 1981:figs. 152–160; Sharer, Traxler, et al. 1999:fig. 6; Valdés 1991:figs. 4, 5).

Turning to the structure itself, atop Azul, we can say that, in general, the iconography of Rosalila is repeated on its four sides, particularly on its lower level (Plate 1b). There is a little more variation in the design on the two upper levels, which form the roof comb of the temple. The ornamental panels on Rosalila are polychrome painted, with red being the predominant color, although orange, green, yellow, and black paint have also been found.

The lower level of Rosalila, the largest of the three, measures 18.5 m north-south and 12.5 m east-west and rises to a height of 5.7 m. Its exterior walls are horizontally divided by a medial molding located just above the doors (2.6 m above the floor) and are vertically divided by the doors themselves. Seven identical panels are located below the moldings and between the doors. Two have been completely exposed to date: one on the west side of the building, south of the principal entrance, and another in the center of the north side.

The panels include a representation of the Sun God, K'inich Ajaw, as a celestial bird. The god faces forward with crossed eyes and three small circular depressions that form a triangle on each cheek. An enormous square earflare is located on either side of the face, while a quetzal (*k'uk'* in Maya) with the eyes of a macaw (*mo'*) is worn as a headdress. When combined, these elements form a reference to K'inich Yax K'uk' Mo', the founder of the Classic period ruling dynasty at Copan. It should be remembered that, on Altar Q, as in many texts at Copan, the name of this first dynast is composed, hieroglyphically, of the "K'inich" prefix followed by the head of a quetzal with a macaw's eye, just as is depicted on Rosalila. Alongside the face of the solar deity wings are personified as serpents with feathers in their jaws, with the talons of the celestial bird clearly visible below. We have here, then, albeit in a highly stylized form and at a very large scale, the personification of the name of the founder, K'inich Yax K'uk' Mo'.

Above the medial molding, the iconography of Rosalila is slightly more complicated. Most of the west side, like the north side, has been exposed, while the other two façades remain unexcavated. Based on current data, we can say that the central decorative elements on all four sides are similar, although there is variation along the edges, especially near the corners, with symmetry preserved only on opposite sides (that is, the north and south façades are identical, as are the east and west sides).

A large anthropomorphic mask is located at the center of the north façade. Here the Sun God is again present in a representation very similar to that on the Azul substructure. It is also possible that this central mask once had a headdress like that described above, which references K'inich Yax K'uk' Mo'. Unfortunately, with the exception of a stone hook, which may have served as the armature for the quetzal's beak, the evidence for this interpretation has disappeared.

Here this solar deity is also represented as a celestial bird. On both sides of the solar face, which visually dominates the iconography of the central portion of Rosalila, are found the wings of the celestial bird, represented as inverted feathered serpents. Small Sun God medallions emerge from the jaws of the serpents. These are worked in exquisite detail with incisions that clearly depict the solar face in profile, with its lock of hair, large "Roman" nose, crossed eye, trio of circles on the cheek, and filed teeth. To emphasize the meaning of this portrait, the sun glyph (*k'in*) was added to the rear portion of the mandible.

On the north side of Rosalila, the serpent-shaped wings include a number of elements that are not found on the west side. The principal missing element is the bundle of the personified perforator (or the Perforator God) which is located on the arms of the K'inich Ajaw and below the eyebrows of the feathered serpents. Another important difference is the use of the *ak'bal* or "darkness" glyph on the bundle located on the arm on the east side of the central panel, as opposed to the use of the "mirror" or

Figure 6.5 Face emerging from a niche on the north side of
Rosalila structure (photograph by Reyna Flores).

"brightness" symbol on the west side.

Beyond the wings of the solar deity, and forming the corners of the west side of the building, are found large-scale representations of serpent heads. The anthropomorphic face of a deity with protruding teeth surrounded by beads (very well preserved on the northeast corner) emerges from the partially open maw of each serpent. No other diagnostic elements are present, although it is certain that these must exist below the multiple layers of stucco typical of the building. In any case, this is probably another portrait of the Sun God, and the serpents most likely represent the bicephalic serpent bar commonly held by Copan rulers depicted on stelae.

On the north side, between the wings of the celestial bird and the corners of the building, anthropomorphic faces emerge from niches (Figure 6.5). These figures wear red turbans on their head and have a bowtie-shaped element over the mouth. Three circles forming a triangle similar to the divine markings found on solar deity masks are located below the nose and above the bowtie-shaped element covering the mouth.

The turban worn by these figures marks them as royal personages, as is the case for all of the rulers depicted on Altar Q. Furthermore, Hellmuth (1987:353) has linked the element over the mouth with auto-sacrifice. To this we may add that the niches from which these figures emerge are marked with scrolls and pendants that I interpret as the fangs of the vision serpent. Additionally, the sides of the niches are formed by slit windows that open into the interior rooms of the temple. Inside these rooms, my excavations revealed a substantial accumulation of soot, the residue of smoke from the incense burners used there. The smoke passing through the slits in the niches must have formed a dramatic backdrop for the ritual of auto-sacrifice performed by the ruler as he invoked his ancestors. Consequently, I consider these masks to be representations of an earlier ruler (possibly K'inich Yax K'uk' Mo') being called from the underworld, a ritual that may have been practiced inside Rosalila as it was inside Structure 10L-16.

The second level of Rosalila, which, together with the third level, forms the ornamental roof comb of the temple, is dominated by a mask of the Cauac or Witz monster, which identifies the building as a sacred mountain, as is the case with Structure 10L-22 (B. Fash et al. 1992; W. Fash 1991; M. Miller 1986a; Schele and Freidel 1990). Here again we find historical links to the Maya of today. Girard (1949:569) indicates that,"the sacred mountain of Quetzaltepeque, named Chan Witz (hill of the snake), has a door that provides access to the underworld"(Girard 1949:569) and goes on to clarify that this "is similar to archaeologically known doorways formed by a giant serpent's mouth that provide access to a chamber where rituals were performed" (Girard 1949:569).

The second level of the building rises 3.7 m above the first level and measures 11.5 m in plan. On the east side, the Witz monster mask is well preserved. Its eyes are large and rectangular, and include rectilinear incisions that give it the appearance of being crosseyed. Its brow is split, and scrolls that end cradling a young maize cob emerge from this cleft. This Mountain God has mirror symbols on his eyebrows and cheeks. Next to the mirror symbols on his cheeks are their dialectical counterparts, *ak'bal* symbols, which are carved into the profile of portraits of the same creature. These project to the north and south from the central figure, and each has teeth in its mouth marked by the *tun* or "stone" glyph. On the forehead and muzzle they also have elements known as "grape clusters" or *cauac* symbols.

A large number of these profile depictions of the Mountain God are covered by another iconographic element which descends from the upper level of Rosalila consisting of a serpent's body decorated with large trapezoids and quadrangular incisions. Below the body is found a reptilian limb with three digits which may identify the serpent as the Sky Monster that, as Freidel and Schele (1988:78) have suggested, shifts from a serpent in the Preclassic period to a caiman in the Classic period. It is possible that the example on Rosalila represents a transitional form between the two. The head of this serpent forms the corner of the building, as is the case on the first level of Rosalila. From its mouth also emerges a face whose identity cannot be determined due to its eroded condition. It is likely that the body of this reptile once formed an arc over the upper portion of the third level of Rosalila, creating a celestial arc like that found above the interior door of Structure 10L-22.

The third level of Rosalila is the least-well preserved of the three. This is due to the partial destruction of this level by the Maya to create space for the construction of Structure 10L-16-1st, whose central axis was shifted 13 m to the south. This shift required the destruction of the north side of the third level of Rosalila to make room for the Structure 10L-16-1st terraces.

The third level rises 3.5 m above the second and measures 8.2 x 4.3 m in plan. It originally included three small sections separated by two narrow passages. This arrangement must have produced an unusual noise as the wind whistled through the slit windows, as it must have done frequently given that, during its use life, the structure was the highest on the Acropolis and therefore completely exposed to the elements. The central decorative element consists of a macabre anthropomorphic face with spiral-shaped eye elements, large earflares, and a defleshed jaw. The slit windows are located on either side of the central face, with the body of a serpent that descends toward the lower portion of the roof comb located along the exterior edge of each window. Alongside the snake's body, reaching to the corners, we can identify elongated wings depicted as feathered serpents.

Karl Taube (1998a, 2000b, this volume) has convinced me that the zoomorphic masks on the third level of Rosalila represent incense burners. The building is thereby marked as a "house of smoke" or rather, a temple. This concurs with the archaeological remains found in the interior, especially the large number of stone and ceramic incense burners. The bodies of the serpents, therefore, symbolize the smoke that emerges from the building and descends to become the vision serpent. In any case, the cosmic and religious significance of this building is clear.

Conclusions

In summary, Rosalila was the principal religious temple at Copan in the late 6th century, and it is the only example of intact architecture dating to that period that has been discovered to date. Like the cover of a book, its façades are profusely decorated with a complex religious message. The theme is cosmological and it emphasizes the Sun God, K'inich Ajaw, divine patron of Copan rulers, and the spiritual coessence of the dynastic founder, K'inich Yax K'uk' Mo', whose name may literally translated as "Eye of the Resplendent Sun-Quetzal-Macaw." Additional cosmic themes combine with representations of the means used by the rulers to control them (sacrifice bundles, vision serpents, and bicephalic serpent bars). This extraordinary example of the religious architecture of the ancient Maya placed the Sun King of Copan at the center of the cosmos and all of Maya society. Its physical presence marked the center of the city and ordered the social, political, and ideological world about it. At the same time, the archaeologically recovered remains within this building emphasize the historical ties that bind the past to the present and remind us that the Maya of today are the guides to understanding the Maya of yesterday.

Rosalila was a living being, charged with spiritual force. Upon its death, it was treated as such: it was wrapped in a white mantle and buried with due ceremony and offerings of great value. In life it was a sacred mountain that provided access to the world of the dead, a showy religious precinct from which emanated colors, sounds, and odors as rich as those found today in the churches of highland Guatemala. Inside, copal burned continuously, flowers and pine needles carpeted the floor, and ritual chants reverberated from its walls, lending splendor to a millennial tradition in which "religion saturates all of their acts, public and private" (Girard 1949:385).

7

MEASURES OF POWER: THE ENERGETICS OF ROYAL CONSTRUCTION AT EARLY CLASSIC COPAN

Christine W. Carrelli

S ince the 1980s, we have seen a florescence in the number of pioneering methods employed by archaeologists and anthropologists to understand ancient Maya polities and the political, religious, and economic factors that molded and changed them. Among these methods are fresh approaches to the study of Maya cosmology, hieroglyphic decipherment, and the built environment, including settlement patterns, site layouts, and innovative ways of assessing architectural function and meaning.

This chapter outlines one of the newer techniques being developed to investigate the built environment—the study of "architectural energetics" (Abrams 1984)—and presents an update on how this energetics approach is being applied to analyze the emergence and development of royal power at the ancient Maya center of Copan, Honduras (Carrelli 1997, 1998, 1999).

For centuries, since Europeans first became aware of the marvelous architectural achievements of the ancient Maya, general differences in the quantity and quality of Maya monumental constructions have been used to evaluate the varying size and complexity of their polities (Landa 1938; Stephens 1963[1841]). Likewise, the status of individual members of Maya society and the power of specific kings often have been assessed by the location, elaboration, and size of the architecture produced during their reigns and the implied amount of labor at their command (Price 1978; Renfrew 1973; Trigger 1990; Webster 1998). Simply put, the rather vague hypothesis has been that architectural size and elaboration directly equate with power. Until recently, however, few scientific quantifications of the labor involved in monumental construction had been attempted. The study of architectural energetics is being developed in an effort to fill this gap in our knowledge.

Background of the Research

Architectural energetics studies in the Maya area began in Mexico in the 1960s with Erasmus's (1965) replication of ancient Maya earth carrying, stone excavating, and stone carrying tasks, and his quantification of the person-days of labor invested in those tasks. Erasmus applied his calculations to the Maya center of Uxmal and began the calculation of the labor involved in Uxmal's construction. While he made some scientific quantifications, he relied heavily on word-of-mouth time estimates for many tasks and made no real attempt at a detailed understanding of the construction techniques utilized or the sequence of construction events at Uxmal. Erasmus's work received only minimal attention at the time.

In the 1980s, Abrams (1984, 1994) conducted additional ethnographic and time-and-motion studies and refined many of Erasmus's formulae for calculating the labor necessary to complete various construction tasks. He also conducted additional ethnographic and time-and-motion studies of such tasks as quarrying, stone cutting, and materials transport. Using the Late Classic residential architecture of the Copan Valley as an example, Abrams applied his broadened approach to quantify the labor and materials involved in the construction of houses of various types and sizes. He produced the first effective, systematic means of reducing architectural constructions to the various materials and tasks involved and the number of person-days of labor required to build them. Abrams's work became a fountainhead from which has sprung a growing stream of innovative research.

Abrams's study concentrated on residential structures—from the simplest wattle-and-daub houses of the poorest Maya peasants to the ornately sculptured Structure 10L-22, believed to be the 8th century A.D. palace of Copan's thirteenth king, Waxaklajun U'baah K'awiil. He proposed three systems of labor organization at Copan and concluded that Classic Maya constructions, including the massive accumulation of architecture at the Copan Acropolis, required less energy investment and fewer specialists than might intuitively be expected. He extrapolated his findings to the more general conclusion that "the level of cultural complexity both caused by and reflected in the architecture of Copan was exceptionally limited and arguments suggesting a high level of complexity of the Mayan cultural system based on the volume and/or beauty of the architecture must be reconsidered" (1984:268). In short, Abrams's results suggested that only minimal numbers of construction personnel, working for only short periods of time, were needed to account for even the most visually elaborate structures at Copan.

Abrams's studies, along with the Copan settlement data, have been used by several other scholars (Webster and Freter 1990b; Webster et al. 1992) to support their vision of a relatively low population for the Copan Valley and a ranked or chiefdom-like sociopolitical structure, rather than a stratified or state-like complexity. Webster, Sanders, and van Rossum have argued that Copan "did not have the usual economic characteristics we associate with urbanization" (1992:193). They also have declared that the "population of the Copan Valley was comparatively small, even at its height" and that "construction of royal and sub-elite architecture would not have entailed onerous labor demands" (1992:196).

Conversely, Fash and Sharer (1991) and others (Canuto 2002; Sharer, et al. 1998) see the clear emergence of a state level of sociopolitical complexity at Copan. They argue that the use of a multidisciplinary approach, combining archaeological research at the urban core, settlement data, and epigraphic and iconographic analyses, reveals a more accurate picture of ancient Maya society than that revealed through settlement and energetics studies alone. They profess that "from the beginning of the 5th century, the Classic Copan polity was ruled by powerful kings who controlled large populations and, quite likely, an extensive territory" (Fash and Sharer 1991:166).

As this debate continues, current energetics research at Copan is producing significant new data to increase our understanding of the sociopolitical complexity achieved by the Copan polity and the varying amounts of human labor controlled by the succession of Copan kings. Although Abrams's landmark work made an excellent beginning to the study of architectural energetics at Copan, it dealt almost entirely with smaller houses and family shrines and was limited to the analysis of the labor costs for their construction. In fact, when calculating the energy costs for even the largest residence, Structure 10L-22, Abrams's limited his scope to the residence alone and excluded the greater volume of architecture comprising Structure 10L-22's enormous supporting platform and staircases.

Present research builds upon Abrams's synchronic investigation of residences by conducting an energetics analysis of the numerous and massive superimposed royal structures which form the Copan Acropolis. It takes advantage of the unusual opportunity provided by three interconnected tunneling programs (see Figure I.3, this volume). The excavations directed by Robert Sharer, tunneling in from the river cut to the east, have now united with the tunneling excavations of William Fash beneath Structure 10L-26 (Hieroglyphic Staircase), some 50 m to the northwest, and the excavations of Ricardo Agurcia F. beneath Structure 10L-16, approximately 50 m to the southwest. By combining the data from the three interrelated projects, it is possible to examine diachronic change in the form, function, and organization of the Acropolis architecture on a broad scale and at a level of detail previously impossible through more conventional clearing and trenching methods.

The Acropolis tunneling excavations have revealed numerous and extensive leveling, filling, and resurfacing events, constituting a magnitude of construction far beyond that represented by the construction of even the most elaborate single structure. By focusing on the entire construction process, thousands of square meters of construction have been added in an individual construction episode, with the result that large sustaining platforms might represent more person-days of labor than do the superstructures they support. The Acropolis tunneling excavations also make it quite evident that numerous construction, destruction, and modification projects were concurrent.

This unprecedented tunneling program at Copan provides an opportunity to move beyond Abram's single-structure approach for residences to an analysis of all Acropolis temples and palaces that were concurrently under construction, modification, or maintenance. This broader scope and greater time depth provides a clearer and more detailed panorama of royal construction projects at Copan's site core and of the labor involved in producing them.

Methodology

Having first presented this brief background on energetics research, this chapter will next address some of the methodological specifics of the present energetics study at Copan. It is hoped that an explanation of the methods utilized will aid others in their studies of royal construction and its relationship to royal power at other sites in the Maya area and beyond. It should be noted that this is a work in progress, given that, while field research at Copan was completed in 2000, analysis and interpretation are ongoing. Presented here is a brief overview of how that research has been conducted. The reader is referred to my forthcoming doctoral dissertation which will present further details of the methodology and energetics calculations (Carrelli n.d.).

The present research follows procedures developed by the Early Copan Acropolis Program (ECAP) adding and expanding recording systems to address my specific architectural research questions in greater depth. Current procedures for recording excavated architecture include drawings of excavation levels and architecture at varying scales and from varying views, photographs, video recordings, and descriptive field notes. ECAP maintains a computerized database for storing and manipulating all spatial, artifactual, and architectural information.

As part of the above program, my project has developed the Copan Architectural Catalog. This catalog provides a standardized system of field recording for descriptive architectural information which will ensure the collection of consistent, complete, and detailed data on construction materials, methods, and decoration for each structure. This computerized catalog codes for the spatial information, compositional description, and a summary discussion of each structure, and provides an index of all related documents such as drawings, photographs, and field notes.

Recording of architecture is accomplished using two standardized forms, a Unit Form and an Element Form. Structures exposed in excavation are divided into arbitrary but intuitive units of analysis defined by familiarity with Maya architecture; for example, individual walls, platform faces, or stair components, and basic descriptive architectural data are recorded on the Unit Form. Recorded details include the size and surfacing of cut-stone blocks, a description of the mortars and plasters, the number and thickness ranges of plaster resurfacings and layers of paint, thickness ranges of plaster floors and a description of their ballast, and the height and composition of walls and their fills. Specialized architectural details, such as curtain holders, drains, or inscriptions, are recorded on the Element Form. All descriptive terminology follows Loten and Pendergast (1984) to ensure the uniformity of nomenclature used.

The stratigraphic sequence of the Copan Acropolis consists of levels of construction which were partially destroyed, filled in, and buried before the construction of the succeeding architecture levels. Consequently, a portion of the stratigraphic sequence within the Acropolis is composed of demolition debris and imported fill used in the complete or partial burial of structures—materials other than those intended for actual architectural construction. Fill episodes vary in size and scope and may result from minor construction events, such as structural modifications, or major overhauls, such as the burial of an entire plaza complex. Numerous fill episodes may exist within a single Acropolis construction level. The Structural Fill Checklist is used for standardized recording of the location and composition of each fill episode and is supplemented by section drawings and photographs of each fill type. The detailed recording of demolition debris in the fill provides valuable information about razed structures and the quantity, or absence, of cut-block building stones within each fill episode—supplying data on the possible reuse of masonry salvaged from demolished buildings. Samples are taken of all construction materials, and the compositions of mortars and plasters are now being analyzed at the Architectural Conservation Laboratory of the University of Pennsylvania.

Calculating Energy Costs

With a clear picture of the assorted materials, tasks, and volumes of architecture and fill involved, labor input can then be calculated. Given that Abram's ethnographic and replicative work (1994) seems well conceived and logically conducted, his formulae for the procurement and transport of tuff, earth, cobbles, and lime, the manufacture of masonry blocks, the burning of lime, and the construction of walls and plaster surfaces have been retained for the purpose of this study. Individual calculations are made for each material involved in the construction process—quarried stone, river cobbles, lime and aggregates for plaster making, earth, etc. All calculations are made in person-days of labor—the number of workdays one person would require to complete each task.

Following Abrams, construction processes are divided into five separate stages, each with its own calculation based on ethnographic and replicative studies. The first is procurement of raw materials: for example, the amount of time and number of people needed to quarry stone for an individual platform or building. The second is transport: for example, the person-days of labor needed to carry stone from the quarry or water from the Copan River to the Acropolis. The third is production: such as the time required to transform rough-cut stones into dressed building blocks or raw limestone into plaster. The fourth is the actual construction time for each platform, superstructure, or fill episode. An effort is also being made to account for the necessary perishable materials and construction requirements which do not survive in the archaeological record, such as the procurement of wood and the time necessary to build scaffolding to reach the upper portions of buildings. Finally, the fifth stage is the maintenance cost, which is calculated from the known number of plaza and building resurfacings, modifications, additions, and repaintings.

Besides these general categories of energy and resource expenditure, a series of previously unrecognized costs has also been quantified and included. The first additional cost that is that of water transport. Abrams discounted water procurement as insignificant in his analyses of residential structures. He is quite correct that water transport add costs only a few negligible person-days to the construction of most superstructures, even a royal residence the size of Structure 10L-22. However, when we look at the series of extensive supporting platforms buried within the Copan Acropolis, water transport costs can become considerable. Each of these platforms is constructed of thousands of square meters of wet-laid fill. In fact, the wet-laying of nearly all of the Copan Acropolis fill, and its subsequent stability, is the very reason that tunneling excavations are possible at all. Observations of modern backfilling episodes have yielded a ratio of 100:1 of water consumed for every 3 m^3 of wet-laid fill and an output of 4 m^3 of wet-laid fill per person per day. Those figures have been added to my calculations and add an appreciable number of person-days of labor.

Water transport experiments were conducted using Honduran workers, who carried traditional-size 10L jugs of water from the Copan River where it passes just east of the Cementerio Group to a central point in the East Court of the Acropolis, where it was used in wet-laid backfilling operations. The distance traveled was 200 m in each direction. The average worker carried 560L per day, and this labor cost was added to the cost of laying fill.

The second additional cost relates to the lime required to make *argamasa*— the mortar of earth, sand, water, and burnt lime used in platform and masonry wall construction. *Argamasa* analyses are currently under way at the Architectural Conservation Laboratory of the University of Pennsylvania. For preliminary energetics calculation purposes, I have used the following simplified average for the *argamasa* components: three parts earth, two parts sand, and one part lime. As Abrams notes, lime production is the single most costly factor in masonry construction. One m^3 of lime produced by open-air burning requires 44 person-days to manufacture. Rather than the simple "mud mortar" encountered by Abrams in residential structures, *argamasa* was used in virtually all masonry Acropolis constructions to set and back walls, terrace faces, and floors to a depth of 1–2 m over the core of wet-laid earth fill. Some platforms contain fill made solely of *argamasa* and stone. The large quantity of lime contained in this mixture adds one of the most significant hidden costs in masonry construction at the Acropolis.

A third additional cost considered in the calculation of the energy investment in Acropolis architecture is the fact that numerous structures, especially superstructures, were demolished before their successor buildings were constructed. Many of these destroyed structures are known only from remaining low walls, floor scars, and demolition debris. We have sound archaeological evidence that the structures existed and, often, sound evidence of their composition. However, until recently, we have had no adequate means of recreating their full height. Agurcia F's excavations in and around Rosalila Structure (this volume) have yielded a wealth of information to aid in this endeavor. A three-story Early Classic structure, buried intact, Rosalila provides an unprecedented model on which we can base site-specific reconstructions of other Early Classic structures at Copan. During the 1995 field season, the details of Rosalila's construction were measured and recorded. Based on those data, reasonable reconstructions of the relative area covered by the demolished buildings have been created. Estimates have been developed for the construction of standardized vaulted and unvaulted rooms, with wall thickness used as an indication of vaulting. Although no building has been reconstructed with more than one story, many large structures undoubtedly incorporated multiple levels.

Some of the earliest constructions beneath the Acropolis have presented yet another energetics dilemma—they are not masonry at all, but rather are constructed of tamped, wet-laid clay, then "plastered" with a layer of red-pigmented clay. These clay structures are not small adobe or wattle-and-daub buildings, but massive terraced platforms. One example, called the Maravilla Structure, built in approximately A.D. 440, is 28 m wide by 12 m long and rises in three terraces to a height of over 4 m, all surfaced in red-pigmented clay. Important to the energy calculations is the fact that these large platforms are not constructed of simple river clays, but of a consistent and purposeful mix of fine clay with tuff, lime, and other tempers. My preliminary use of formulae for simple wet-laid fill most likely underestimates the person-days of energy required in their construction and, therefore, under represents the energy expended in the earliest levels where these platforms are found. Their very composition also poses the problem of roofing the platform for protection against the elements and the costs of maintenance. Post holes around Maravilla Structure indicate that the roof extended not only beyond the superstructure but beyond the edges of the entire platform. We have good evidence for clay superstructures atop these platforms, and I have used Nancy Gonlin's (1993) standard formula for wattle-and-daub constructions. However, I believe they may be inadequate for areas of this magnitude.

Finally, I have added the energy expended in the construction of elaborate, deep-relief plaster decoration found on numerous structures from the earliest levels through the end of the Early Classic period. These large animal and deity masks cover entire platforms and their superstructures. From an energetics standpoint, this deep-relief plaster decoration involves two types of calculations—one to quantify the large amount of labor-intensive plaster involved, and the second to calculate the construction time to complete the artistic representations. Since there are no living architects or artists, to my knowledge, who surface buildings with this type of deep-relief mod-

eled and incised decoration in plaster; it has been nearly impossible to quantify the
work involved with this activity.

During recent field seasons at Copan, the extraordinary new Copan Sculpture
Museum was under construction. The centerpiece of that museum is a full-size repli-
ca of the Rosalila Structure. In order to recreate the temple's exquisite facade masks,
experienced artists were brought in to fashion full-size duplicates in clay. Molds were
then fabricated and cast from the clay models. Personal observations and extensive
interviews with the artists have yielded competent figures for the completion of discrete areas of decoration. Areas differed in completion time, depending upon the intri-
cacy of the design and the depth of relief. The average completion time was 14.3 person-days of labor for one square meter of area. While some materials and methods utilized by the modern plaster sculptors differ from those used by the ancient Maya, I
believe this formulation, based on actual plaster mask construction for real-life purposes, provides the closest possible approximation of the original processes and time and
labor required.

It remains important to note that these calculations are still in progress and
are sometimes incomplete. For example, they do not yet incorporate several of the
newly identified very early stages of construction (Sedat and López, this volume). In
addition, they exclude all royal constructions beyond the Acropolis, among them, many
areas of the Great Plaza and the Northwest Platform (Fash et al., this volume).
Consequently, at this writing, these calculations consistently underestimate, rather than
overestimate, the labor involved.

Translation of Energy Costs to Power

The ultimate goal of this research is to tie the data on the construction—and destruction—sequence of the Acropolis to known historical events and to the Copan dynastic
sequence. By calculating the labor input into all Acropolis architecture commissioned
by a specific ruler, we create a window into the amount of power wielded by that
ruler. As an example, preliminary calculations of the labor commanded by Copan's two
earliest kings are set forth below.

The areally extensive and broad diachronic scope of this research, and the
much narrower scope of this chapter, preclude the inclusion here of the hundreds of
individual procurement, transport, manufacture, and construction calculations
required for the construction, refurbishment, and maintenance of every structure and
building episode in each Acropolis construction level attributed to these first two
rulers (see Carrelli nd for full calculations). In the interim, the reader is referred to
Abram's original formulae and my modifications to them, as set forth above.

Estimates of population in the Copan Valley during the 5th century A.D. follow Webster et al. (1992). Those estimates are 3,500 people for the first half of the century and 4,000 for the second half. Although probably underestimating population lev-

els (see Canuto, this volume), these estimates are used for illustrative purposes only. It is assumed that half the population consisted of children and that half of the adult population consisted of women, leaving one-quarter of the population as the adult male workforce. In tradition Maya society, men are usually the personnel involved in building construction. Of course, women and children undoubtedly contributed their time and efforts to certain chores, such as providing food for the workers; however, those energy investments are not considered here. In addition, many specialized tasks such as architectural design, ornate plaster facade decoration, stone sculpture, or mural painting would have required additional highly skilled experts not drawn from the general labor pool.

The hieroglyphic evidence indicates that K'inich Yax K'uk' Mo' established the Copan dynasty in A.D. 426–427 and ruled for the next decade. During his reign, the focus of his construction efforts appears to have been the Yune Platform (see Sedat and López, this volume). At this locus, he constructed or modified a series of clay surfaces supporting multiroomed adobe structures and built at least two large masonry structures. To the north of Yune Platform, K'inich Yax K'uk Mo' established Copan's first ballcourt and the first masonry temple at the important location which would grow through time into a series of superimposed structures culminating in Structure 10L-26, the Late Classic Hieroglyphic Stairway. Conservative preliminary energetics calculations yield a total of over 175,000 person-days of labor during K'inich Yax K'uk Mo's reign, or over 17,500 person-days per year. Every adult male in the Copan pocket (875 adult males) would have devoted about one month per year to these royal construction projects.

In approximately A.D. 437, Ruler 2 took power and launched a major building campaign at the site center. A half-dozen masonry temples and several new multitiered clay platforms were constructed. Prodigious amounts of lime plaster, the most costly material to produce and the least readily available at Copan, were consumed in the production of multiple ornate plaster-decorated building facades. Truly a master builder, Ruler 2 continually initiated new, larger, and more elaborate constructions, while modifying existing ones. In just the first five years of his reign, he commanded over 38,000 person-days of labor per year. Every adult male in the Copan pocket would have given more than a month and a half of labor each year in support of Ruler 2's royal building campaigns.

Of course, we have no archaeological evidence as to exactly which segments of the population devoted their time and efforts on the king's behalf. Perhaps only young men were pledged to toil for the ruler, but each devoted three months of his time. In addition, many variables must be considered, such as whether the workers approached their labor with a foot-dragging sense of drudgery or with the festive spirit of fulfilling important civic and religious responsibilities. The present calculations often include only the principal constructions in a building stage. Work on more detailed calculations for refurbishments, resurfacings, repaintings, and similar modifications is still in progress. These calculations also do not include the construction of the Great Plaza and its initial flanking structures dating to the reigns of K'inich Yax K'uk Mo' and Ruler 2 (Traxler, this volume). As research continues, more specific information on construction and destruction episodes will be added, and population estimates and energy calculations will be refined. Overall, however, the point is that evolving energetics research is attempting to move beyond vague generalizations to a more scientific approach that can begin to quantify the labor investment made in the royal built environment.

These two brief examples clearly illustrate the fact that even the earliest rulers at Copan required substantial labor investments from the surrounding populace. The construction complexity and ornate artistry of these royal structures, the kings' conspicuous consumption of the most costly materials, and this sizable labor investment all point to significant levels of task specialization, labor organization, and royal power at Early Classic Copan.

Table 7.1 Preliminary Calculations of Person-days of Labor by Structure

Construction Level 1: Time Period A.D. 425–435 (Yax K'uk Mo')

YUNE
70 x 70 x 1 meters.
Masonry, fill of earth, cobbles, tuff and argamasa, plaster surfacings (2).
Platform   **Total: 39,118 PD**

HUNAL
10 x 8.5 x .5 meters.
Masonry, fill of earth, cobbles, tuff and argamasa, plaster surfacing.

Substructure	725 PD
Superstructure #1	9,529 PD
Superstructure #2 (replaced #1)	9,689 PD
	Total: 19,943 PD

WILIN
6.5 x 8 x .5 meters.
Masonry, fill of earth, cobbles, tuff and argamasa, plaster surfacing.

Substructure	644 PD
Superstructure	6,628 PD
	Total: 7,272 PD

YAX
12 x 17.5 x 1 meters.
Masonry, fill of earth, cobbles, tuff and argamasa, plaster surfacing.

Substructure	3,008 PD
Superstructure (vaulted, 4 rooms)	15,272 PD
	Total: 18,280 PD

YEHNAL
11.25 x 12.5 x 3 meters + 5 x 1.75 x 3 meters.
Masonry, fill of earth, cobbles, tuff and argamasa, plaster surfacing, ornate plaster decoration.

Substructure	9,425 PD
Superstructure (vaulted, 2 stories, 3 rooms)	20,110 PD
	Total: 29,535 PD

KAR
7.5 x 13 x 1.4 meters.
Clay, fine clay surfacing, adobe superstructure

Substructure	182 PD
Superstructure	279 PD
	Total: 461 PD

(continued next page)

URANIO
7.75 x 14 x 1.05 meters.
Clay, fine clay surfacing, adobe superstructure.

Substructure	155 PD
Superstructure	114 PD
	Total: 269 PD

LAUREL
12 x 12 x 1.18 meters. Clay, fine clay surfacing, adobe superstructure.

Substructure	228 PD
Superstructure	272 PD
	Total: 500 PD

TARTAN
20 x 6 x .3 meters. Clay, fine clay surfacing, adobe superstructure.

Substructure	58 PD
Superstructure	206 PD
	Total: 264 PD

CURRY
8 x 10 x 1.8 meters.
Clay, fine clay surfacing, adobe superstructure.

Substructure	201 PD
Superstructure	162 PD
	Total: 363 PD

COMINOS
12.5 x 15.5 x 1.87 meters.
Clay, fine clay surfacing, adobe superstructure

Substructure	473 PD
Superstructure	407 PD
	Total: 880 PD

Newly discovered CAB and LANUH
Current estimate is that, together, they are roughly equivalent to Laurel in size
and construction (to be refined)   500 PD

MOTMOT
15 x 22 x 2 meters.
Masonry, fill of earth, cobbles, tuff and argamasa, plaster surfacing, ornate plaster decoration.

Substructure	13,815 PD
Superstructure (4 rooms, vaulted)	32,290 PD
	Total: 46,105 PD

BALLCOURT I
28 x 12 x 1.5 meters.
Masonry, fill of earth, cobbles, tuff and argamasa, plaster surfacing.

Ballcourt	**Total: 11,935 PD**

TOTAL PERSON-DAYS OF LABOR FOR LEVEL 1	**175,425 PD**

WITIK TEMPRANO

27 x 53 x 1.2 meters + 22 x 17.5 x 1.2 meters.
Masonry, fill of earth, cobbles, tuff and argamasa, plaster surfacing.

Platform	**Total: 46,706 PD**

SAPO

14 x 24 x 2.5 meters.
Clay, fine clay surfacing, adobe superstructure.

Substructure	1,080 PD
Superstructure	602 PD
	Total: 1,682 PD

COBALTO

12.5 x 8.5 x 2.2 meters.
Clay, fine clay surfacing, adobe superstructure.

Substructure	297 PD
Superstructure	181 PD
	Total: 478 PD

CLAVEL

11 x 12 x 2.1 meters + 8 x 3 x 2.1 meters.
Masonry, fill of earth, tuff and argamasa, plaster surfacing.

Substructure	6,988 PD
Superstructure (2 rooms, vaulted)	13,554 PD
	Total: 20,542 PD

NA

22 x 16 x 2.5 meters + 6 x 2 x 2.5 meters.
Masonry, fill of earth, cobbles, tuff and argamasa, plaster surfacing.

Substructure	43,969 PD
Superstructure (4 rooms, vaulted)	43,764 PD
	Total: 87,733 PD

WILIN

11.5 x 15.5 x 2.5 meters.
Masonry, fill of earth, cobbles, tuff and argamasa, plaster surfacing.

Substructure	16,780 PD
Superstructure (2 rooms, vaulted)	15,971 PD
	Total: 32,751 PD

TOTAL PERSON-DAYS OF LABOR FOR LEVEL 2	**189,892 PD**

WITIK TARDIO

56 x 60 x .65 meters + 20.9 x 16.4 x .65 meters.
Masonry, fill of earth, cobbles, tuff and argamasa, plaster surfacing.
Platform   **Total: 35,618 PD**

MARGARITA

10 x 16.36 x 3.5 meters + 5 X 12.27 X 3.5 meters + 5.45 x 6.82 x 3.5 meters.
Masonry, fill of earth, cobbles, tuff and argamasa, plaster surfacing, ornate plaster decoration
Substructure   18,975 PD
Superstructure (3 rooms, vaulted)   26,059 PD
                                                     Total: 45,034 PD

MARAVILLA

11.82 x 24.73 x .96 meters + 9.55 x 21.82 x 1.25 meters + 7.73 x 18.64 x 1.85 meters.
Clay, fine clay surfacing, adobe superstructure.
Substructure   1,027 PD
Superstructure   201 PD
                                                     Total: 1,228 PD

MARIPOSA

21.82 x 10.91 x 2.5 meters + 4.09 x 5.9 x 2.5 meters.
Masonry, fill of earth, cobbles, tuff and argamasa, plaster surfacing.
Substructure   7,942 PD
Superstructure (4 rooms, vaulted)   11,044 PD
                                                     Total: 18,986 PD

BOMBILIA/ZOPOTILLO

11.82 x .6 x 4 meters + 6.36 x 27.73 x 4 meters + 8.18 x 5.45 x 4 meters.
Masonry, fill of earth, cobbles,tuff and argamasa, plaster surfacing.
Substructure   37,398 PD
Superstructure (3 stories, vaulted rooms)   116,704 PD
                                                     Total: 154,102 PD

PAPAGAYO ————————————————————————————

13 x 9 meters.

Masonry, fill of earth, cobbles, tuff and argamasa, plaster surfacing.

Substructure   to be calculated

Superstructure (3 rooms, vaulted)   **Total: 16,160 PD**

TOTAL PERSON-DAYS OF LABOR FOR LEVEL 3	**271,128 PD**

Note: Due to the limited scope of this chapter, the reader is referred to my forthcoming dissertation for detailed measurements of individual structural components and for calculations for procurement, transport, manufacture, and construction costs for each building material by structure. This is a work in progress. These preliminary calculations are based on incomplete data and are subject to future refinement and change.

III EARLY CLASSIC TOMBS AT COPAN AND THEIR INVESTIGATION

8

TOMBS AND BURIALS
IN THE EARLY CLASSIC ACROPOLIS AT COPAN

Ellen E. Bell, Robert J. Sharer, Loa P. Traxler,
David W. Sedat, Christine W. Carrelli, and Lynn A. Grant

T unneling excavations within the Early Classic levels of the Copan Acropolis have revealed burials that inform our understanding of the early history of the Copan polity and those who ruled it. The majority of those known to have been interred within the Acropolis were members of the Copan nobility. Their burials indicate the prominence and wealth of the ruling elite, their strong ties to rulers of distant centers, and a continuing emphasis on the founder of the Classic period ruling dynasty, K'inich Yax K'uk' Mo'.

Others interred within the Acropolis were buried without the trappings of wealth or power, which may or may not reflect their status in life. While these individuals may have been retainers or captives sacrificed and interred for the benefit of the rulers, it is also possible that some were members of the nobility whose roles and statuses dictated a distinct mortuary treatment.

These burials also provide glimpses into the role of many early structures as funerary shrines that became the loci of dynastic power and ritual practice. The buildings established iconographic themes that continued throughout the entire construction sequence, and archaeological evidence of burning, offerings, and frequent architectural modification suggests that they were the site of recurrent ritual practice (Agurcia F., this volume).

As recent interpretations are based on the analysis of these interments and their contents, we offer the following descriptions to contextualize this information. We consider in depth only the nine Early Classic interments encountered within the lower levels of the southern and central portions of the Acropolis. All were excavated as part of the University of Pennsylvania Museum Early Copan Acropolis Program (Sharer, Traxler, et al. 1999), although we also briefly consider four additional burials located beneath Structure 10L-26 (Davis-Salazar and Bell 2000; Fash 2001; Fash and Fash 2000; Valdés and Cheek 1983; Viel and Cheek 1983; Williamson 1996, 1997).

Sub-Structure 10L-16 Burials

Interments located beneath the Late Classic Structure 10L-16 (Figure I.3), along with the elaborately decorated buildings that contained them, appear to have formed the core of the Copan Acropolis. By the end of the Late Classic period (ca. A.D. 822), Structure 10L-16, the highest point on the final version of the Acropolis, capped a sequence of structures whose iconography strongly associates them with the dynastic founder, K'inich Yax K'uk' Mo' (see Agurcia F., Taube, and Sedat and López, this volume).

The earliest structures at this locus date to the founding era (A.D. 400-450) and the interments within them, one of which (the Hunal Tomb) may contain the remains of K'inich Yax K'uk' Mo' himself, also emphasize strong connections to the founder. The Margarita Tomb holds the remains of a woman who appears to have been an important member of the royal house, possibly the wife of K'inich Yax K'uk' Mo', while Burial 95-1, positioned on the central axis of Margarita Structure, and Burial 94-1, located at the north end of the vaulted passage that leads to the Margarita Tomb, may have been placed during the construction of ancestral shrines. The fifth interment in this area, Burial 93-1, was placed within an earthen structure that formed part of an early architectural complex at this locus (Sedat and López, this volume). Objects included within these burials and the form and decoration of the structures that encase them emphasize both strong local ties and connections to foreign centers (Reents-Budet et al., this volume; Sharer 2003a, b).

Hunal Tomb (Burial 95-2)

The Hunal Tomb is a vaulted masonry burial chamber (2.5 x 1.5 x 1.7 m) that is part of an extensive funerary and offertory complex located below Structure 10L-16 in the earliest levels of the Acropolis. It contains the remains of an adult male on a stone funerary slab (Plate 3a) accompanied by extensive jade, shell, ceramic, and worked bone offerings (Plate 3b). Multiple lines of evidence (see below) suggest that the remains are those of the dynastic founder, K'inich Yax K'uk' Mo' (Sharer 1997b; Sharer, Fash, et al. 1999; Sharer, Traxler, et al. 1999).

Form, Location, and Architectural Context

The tomb lies within Hunal Structure, an early masonry building whose *talud-tablero* style is unusual at Copan (Figures 5.3, 14.1). The chamber was intruded below the north room of the second version of the superstructure, and, as the vault stones protruded above the floor level, they were capped by a low, stucco-surfaced bench.

The tomb and its contents appear to have been disturbed by human activity (reentry), water infiltration, and seismic events. The seismic events, along with more subtle structural pressures, caused most of the plastered wall surfaces to fall and provoked the partial collapse of the masonry walls and vault. The resultant debris covered the burial slab and the margins of the floor, while finer dust and silt coated the ceramic vessels sheltered below the slab. The skeletal remains appear to have been coated with red pigment (cinnabar) after the soft tissue disintegrated, suggesting that the chamber was reentered at least once.

Date

The stratigraphic, ceramic, and epigraphic data associated with the Hunal Tomb are consistent with an early Acbi date (ca. A.D. 400–450). The structure overlies one of the earliest buildings within the Acropolis (Sedat and López, this volume), and the names of the founder and Ruler 2 are associated with a short-hand reference to the 9.0.2.0.0 period ending (A.D. 437) on the Xukpi Stone, a carved monument reused in the slightly later Margarita Tomb (see below). Although two radiocarbon dates from samples of the southern vault beam provided earlier dates (A.D. 85–390, two sigma range calibrated at A.D. 235 and A.D. 85–415 calibrated at A.D. 245), they are inconsistent with the materials in the tomb, suggesting that the wood had been reused.

Skeletal Remains

The remains of an adult male, 5'6" tall and 55 to 70 years old when he died, were placed on the funerary slab in a supine position with the head to the south. The teeth were modified, and the skeleton bears evidence of multiple healed traumas (Buikstra et al., this volume). The bones were painted with cinnabar pigment, possibly as part of a ritual that involved reentering the tomb. Most of the bones remained on the slab, although some had been displaced varying distances from their original positions by falling masonry or human activity.

Associated Artifacts and Ecofacts

The burial slab was covered with residue from a textile or finely woven mat on which the body and numerous shell, jade, and bone adornments had been placed (Plate 3a). These objects include a cluster of stingray spines and cut bone awls (Figure 8.1a) near the left leg, an anklet of jaguar canines and small jade disks located near the right lower leg (Figure 8.1b), and several poorly preserved shells. Objects associated with the upper body include a polished jade bar pectoral, a jade bead carved with a mat motif, and a jade earflare associated with a perforated jade disk. An elaborate headdress or helmet composed of cut-*Spondylus sp.* shell "spangles" was placed near the cranium. This helmet is similar to the composite headdresses worn by figures on the sides of Tikal Stela 31 (Martin and Grube 2000, Taube 2000b) and cut-shell headdresses identified as war serpent representations at Teotihuacan and Lowland Maya sites by Karl Taube (Taube 2000b).

Additional objects and ceramic vessels were placed on the tomb floor (Plate 3b). Twenty-one pottery vessels (four with lids) were arranged in the center of the

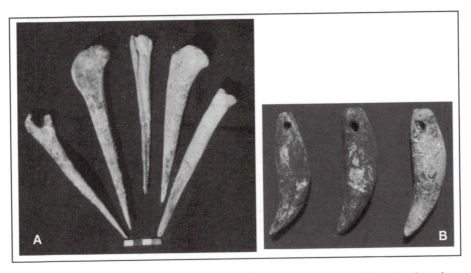

Figure 8.1 Objects associated with the lower leg bones of the adult male, thought to be K'inich Yax K'uk' Mo', interred in the Hunal Tomb. (a) Carved bone awls or perforators; (b) three of four jaguar canines located on the burial slab (photographs by Ellen E. Bell).

floor beneath the burial slab. All of the vessels date to the Early Acbi ceramic phase (A.D. 400–450), and analyses drawing on INAA and stylistic assessments indicate that the vessels were produced in workshops located in Copan, Tikal, highland Guatemala, and central Mexico (Reents-Budet et al., this volume). The central area of the floor also included concentrations of bird bones, a carved bone tube (Figure 8.2), and the remains of stuccoed, painted organic objects (most likely gourds).

Groupings of objects were also placed along the margins of the floor. A small cluster of three vessels was deposited in the northwest corner, while four vessels, including an extraordinary deer effigy, were located along the eastern wall. Shell and jade beads and mosaic earflares, possibly part of a large necklace or chest ornament, were placed just north of the deer effigy, near the remains of an armadillo hide bag or container. The southeast corner included five eccentric chert points associated with the remains of a painted organic object that may have been a wooden shield.

A collar-shaped shell pendant with Maya-style jade and pearl inlay was located north of the jade and shell necklace (Plate 4). Collar-shaped artifacts of this type are associated with both Teotihuacan and Kaminaljuyu in the Early Classic (Kidder, Jennings, and Shook 1946:149) and are widely distributed in later time periods. The Hunal shell is very similar to a disk found in Burial 92-3 (Plate 4e; see below), and both are manufactured from *Patella mexicana*, a Pacific coast mollusk species (Ekholm

Figure 8.2 Bone tube with the remains of an organic attachment located on the floor of the Hunal Tomb (photograph by Robert J. Sharer).

1961; Emery personal communication to E. Bell, 2000). Three cut-shell animal figures representing a jaguar with a water lily tail and two peccaries were found inside the Hunal shell (Plate 4a, c, d). According to a preliminary study by David Stuart (this volume), a short name-tag hieroglyphic text incised on the shell reads (*u*)*y-uh wi'te'* ("his necklace, tree root"), suggesting that the text includes two of the three components of the *Wi'-te'-naah* phrase closely associated with the dynastic founder throughout the Copan inscriptions.

Several objects appear to have fallen from the burial slab onto the tomb floor, including a second jade earflare and perforated disc, two concentrations of *Oliva* shell "tinklers," one of which was associated with the bones of the right arm, and shell "spangles" that may have formed part of the headdress.

Discussion

Although all the evidence cannot be reviewed here, the Hunal Tomb's stratigraphic position and contents suggest that it held the remains of K'inich Yax K'uk' Mo' (Bell et al. 1999; Sharer, Fash, et al. 1999, Sharer, Traxler, et al. 1999). The name-tagged shell pendant may provide a direct link to the founder, and other elements resonate with the depiction of K'inich Yax K'uk' Mo' on Altar Q. These include the large jade bar pectoral, the parry fracture of the right forearm, and the remains of a painted shield. Stable isotope ratio analyses of the bones suggest the interred man was not native to Copan and may have spent his early years in the Petén (Buikstra et al., this volume). Finally, Hunal Structure and its tomb clearly established a location at which K'inich Yax K'uk' Mo' was venerated for the remainder of the Classic period (Sharer 1997b, 2003a). The second temple built over Hunal, known as Margarita Structure, presents the founder's name on its western façade, and he is mentioned on the Xukpi Stone, an Early

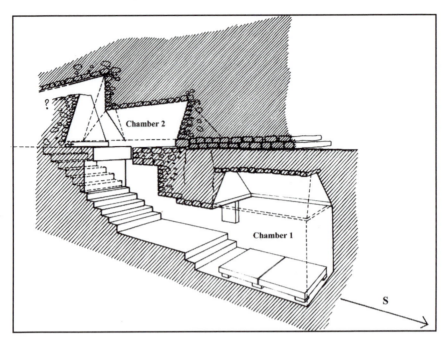

Figure 8.3 Schematic section of the Margarita Tomb. The burial chamber (Chamber 1) is separated from the offering chamber (Chamber 2) by a stone and earth stair. The body was placed in Chamber 1 on the stone funerary slab, which fractured in antiquity. Chamber 2 was filled with organic offerings, including three fiber-based baskets, and 18 ceramic vessels, many of which were elaborately painted (drawing by José Espinoza).

Classic monument found on the summit of Margarita (see Burial 93-2, below). Both the extraordinarily preserved Rosalila Structure and Structure 10L-16 are decorated with carved portraits and iconographic references to the founder (Agurcia F., this volume and Taube, this volume).

Margarita Tomb (Burial 93-2)

The Margarita Tomb consists of two masonry chambers—an upper offering chamber and a lower burial chamber—connected by a stone and earth stairway (Figure 8.3). The upper offering chamber is a vaulted, rectangular, masonry chamber that measures approximately 1.2 x 3.2 x 1.35 m and is oriented north-south. The interior surface of the chamber was plastered, and the south wall rests on a large, reset, carved monument nicknamed the Xukpi Stone (Figure 11.18; Sharer and

Sedat 1994; Stuart, this volume). The inscription appears to center on a funerary theme and mentions both K'inich Yax K'uk' Mo' and Ruler 2 (Stuart, this volume), before closing with a possible reference to Siyaj K'ak' (Martin and Grube 2000; Schele, et al. 1994), a Tikal warlord of probable central Mexican descent (Stuart 2000). This chamber contained no human remains, but rather an array of jade, shell, organic, and ceramic offerings (Plate 6a).

The lower mortuary chamber is a vaulted rectangular masonry chamber that measures 1.2 x 2.4 x 2.1 m and is also oriented north-south. Its walls were plastered and painted red, and it contained a large rectangular stone slab fractured in antiquity. The body of an adult woman was placed on the slab in a supine position with the head to the south. Offerings were positioned on the slab along with the body and on the floor below (Plate 6b).

Location and Architectural Context

The Margarita Tomb is located within the Yehnal and Margarita Structures, south and east of the Hunal Tomb. The Margarita lower chamber overlies an earlier masonry feature known as the Bac Feature (Sedat and López, this volume). The Margarita lower chamber was built on this foundation when the Yehnal structure was erected over Hunal. The lower chamber was subsequently modified to include a doorway and staircase when Yehnal was succeeded by Margarita. The upper offering chamber was added and a stone burial slab was placed in the lower chamber when the building on the summit of Margarita was demolished. The remains of an adult woman were then placed on the slab accompanied by elaborate, high-status offerings in both chambers. The first of several northern vaulted entrance passages was constructed to provide continued access to the tomb chambers with the building of Chilan Structure.

Skeletal Remains

The body of an adult woman, approximately 5' tall and between 50 and 60 years old at death (Buikstra et al. this volume), was extended in a supine position on the stone slab with the head to the south. The burial slab fractured in antiquity, separating the femurs from the pelvis. The skeleton was embedded in massive amounts of cinnabar, and the bones appear to have been painted with a cinnabar solution or slurry. Stable isotope ratio analyses suggest that the woman spent her early childhood near Copan and was in residence at the center by early adolescence, while marked "gestation pits" on the pelvis indicate that she bore at least one child, (Buikstra et al., this volume).

Artifacts and Ecofacts (Upper Offering Chamber)

The upper offering chamber contained jade ornaments, ceramic vessels, decorated perishable containers, and other organic offerings (Plate 6a). The floor of the chamber was lined with organic material, possibly the remains of a mat or pelt. Woven and twined straw containers with jade, slate, and pyrite objects interleaved among them were placed near the south end of the chamber.

Eighteen ceramic vessels and at least five painted organic containers were placed on top of the organic layers that carpeted the chamber floor. INAA data indicate that many of the vessels were produced outside the Copan Valley (Reents-Budet et al., this volume). A concentration of vessels placed in the southeastern corner of the chamber includes a brilliantly painted lidded cylinder tripod nicknamed "The Dazzler" (Plate 7a-c). This vessel and its lid are decorated with representations of a *talud-tablero* platform (similar to the Hunal structure) that supports an anthropomorphized temple with a goggle-eyed face and plumed arms. The INAA data indicate that the vessel was manufactured in central Mexico, but the Maya-style design may have been painted in Copan (Reents-Budet et al. this volume). The vessel may depict Hunal Structure and the fiery resurrection of K'inich Yax K'uk' Mo' (Sedat 1997b; Taube, this volume). Two ceramic vessels decorated with fish and flower motifs (Plate 7d) held thousands of polychrome-painted stucco flakes which are the remains of similarly shaped perishable vessels (Plate 7f-g). Some of the organic objects were painted with fine-line decoration, and one includes the depiction of a figure wearing a Teotihuacan-style tasseled headdress (Plate 7g). A ceramic vessel in the shape of a small squash, also stuccoed and painted, lay along the west wall (Plate 7e). Four vessels were located under canted paving stones, suggesting that they were added after the stones had been displaced.

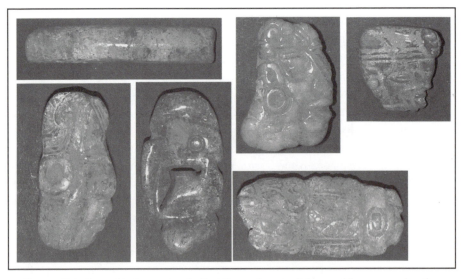

Figure 8.4 Carved jade pectorals that formed part of the necklace worn by the woman buried in the Margarita Tomb, Chamber 1
(photographs by Robert J. Sharer).

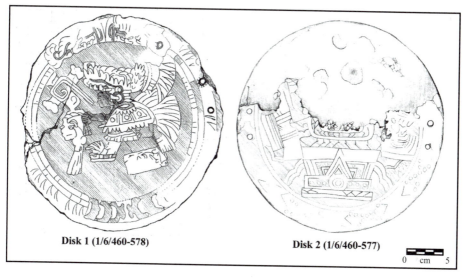

Disk 1 (1/6/460-578)   Disk 2 (1/6/460-577)

0   cm   5

Figure 8.5 Slate mirror backs, Margarita Tomb, Chamber 1. Two iron pyrite mirrors were found inside a basket with a stuccoed and painted lid. The slate backs of the two mirrors were also stuccoed and painted with Teotihuacan-style designs. Disk 1 includes a standing figure who wears a feathered headdress and cloak, holds a decorated object in his hand, and has a flower-studded speech scroll in front of his mouth. Disk 2 depicts an elaborate headdress inside a border decorated with stars and dots (drawings by Nelson Paredes).

Artifacts and Ecofacts (Lower Burial Chamber)

The burial slab was covered with a fiber-based mat on which the body and offerings were laid (Plate 6b). The feet were wrapped together within the remains of shell plate sandals or anklets and a band of large jade beads encircled each lower leg. Strands of jade beads were laid on the slab along the woman's lower right side, while more than 9,000 tiny jade beads were piled on top of a thick layer of red cinnabar on her left side.

The woman's upper body was adorned with a massive jade, shell, and pearl necklace. The necklace is asymmetrical, with long, curved shell beads on the east and globular shell beads on the west. Both sides included jade beads, flower-shaped shell ornaments, and tiny seed pearls. The innermost circle of the necklace was formed by a strand of carved jade pectorals, five of which were recovered in the course of excavation.[*] These include a jade tube, a vulture head, a monster-headed fish, and two anthropomorphic heads, one of which wears a tri-lobed headband (Figure 8.4). These jades may provide clues to the woman's identity, given that no royal women are men-

---

[*] The remainder of the shell and jade necklace, including the carved jade pectorals that remained *in situ*, was looted from the chamber on the night of February 28, 1998.

tioned in known Copan texts that refer to the Early Classic period. A large, solid jade earflare was located on either side of the head. The woman also wore double-strand arm bands made of large jade beads around her forearms and jade plate wristlets with small reflective pyrite elements. Her waist was encircled by a belt made of jade beads and earflares, shells, and bird heads. The entire upper body was coated in cinnabar, at least some of which appears to have been deposited as a liquid paint or slurry.

Additional offerings, including 16 ceramic vessels (Figure 9.12) and two pyrite mirrors (Figure 8.5), were placed on the floor beneath the burial slab. The majority of the objects on the floor were arranged in the north end of the chamber, consistent with the location of the entrance to the north, although a single ring-foot bowl was placed in the southwest corner.

The northern end of the floor contained six ceramic vessels, including two orange-slipped bowls, one of which held the remains of a small quail. A small bowl and potstand were located near the northeastern pedestal, and two miniature vessels placed nearby held cinnabar and small pink shell beads. A cluster of ceramic vessels along the western wall included a "cuspidor"-shaped Thin Orange vessel; four small red-on-orange basal flange dishes filled with fish remains; a red-on-orange bowl with a ring foot; and three cylinder tripods (two with lids).

The area adjacent to the vessels held a pair of jade and shell mosaic earflares with mother-of-pearl backs, and three painted gourds placed near the entrance held large quantities of cinnabar. A jade bead necklace that included nine crudely carved feline heads was coiled into a painted perishable container near the cinnabar-filled gourds. The eastern side of the tomb floor held two concentrations of green-stained bone needles bundled into organic wrappings.

The greatest concentration of objects was located in the central area of the tomb floor. This deposit included painted organic objects, two pyrite mirrors, *Oliva* shells, stingray spines, and a large concentration of small objects that were probably strung or woven together (Figure 8.6). These small objects include shell rings carved with small faces, tabbed jade and shell rings, a worked bone spatula and awl, and needles, beads, and spangles made of shell and jade. All of these objects seem to have been held by perishable containers, including netted, coiled, or woven baskets, bags, and painted gourds. The top layer of this deposit included a painted, stuccoed basket lid with fine-line polychrome design depicting a figure in profile wearing a decorated turban headdress similar to those seen on Altar Q and elsewhere at Copan (Bell et al. 2000).

The stuccoed basket lid lay on top of two disk-shaped slate and pyrite mirrors (Figure 8.5). These seem to have been wrapped in a finely woven textile and then bundled into a loosely twined container. Other objects, including carved shell rings and bone needles, were also bundled into the wrapping. The mirror backs are stuccoed and painted. One shows a winged Teotihuacan-style figure standing in profile and framed by a scaled serpent. A speech scroll emanates from the figure's mouth and an object dangles from his hand. The painting on the other disk depicts a large, central Mexican-style headdress, and the border is formed by yellow dots and stars similar to those on a jar from central Mexico found in the Hunal Tomb (Figure 9.8).

Figure 8.6 Concentrations of bone needles, shell and jade rings, jade beads, shell spangles and other objects bundled into organic containers beneath the burial slab in Chamber 1 of the Margarita Tomb (photograph by David W. Sedat).

Discussion

The complexity of the architecture and contents of this deposit, its location within the Early Acropolis, and the associated sculpture and modeled stucco façades indicate that the person buried within it was of very high rank. Although no royal woman is mentioned in Copan's known contemporary or retrospective texts, it has been suggested that the woman buried within the Margarita Tomb was an important member of the royal house, possibly the wife of K'inich Yax K'uk' Mo' and the mother of Ruler 2 (Sharer 2003a; Sharer, Traxler, et al. 1999).

The tomb artifacts fall within a variety of stylistic canons and suggest contact with people in highland Mexico (especially Teotihuacan), the central Petén (particularly Tikal), highland Guatemala (most likely Kaminaljuyu), and southeastern centers (sites in modern-day western Honduras and El Salvador). While the Teotihuacan-style imagery on the mirror backs and fine-line painted gourds is striking, there are forms

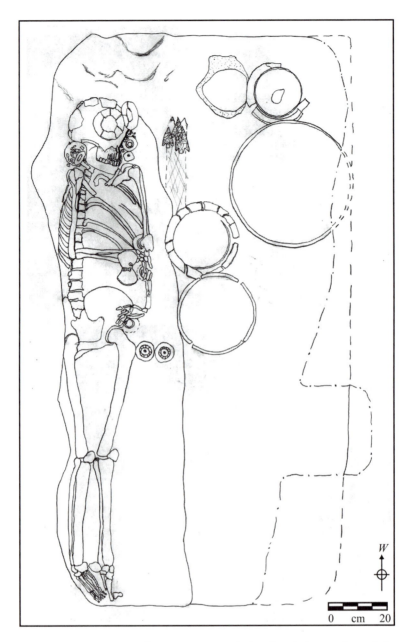

Figure 8.7 Burial 95-1. This interment includes the skeleton of an adult male accompanied by the weapons and regalia of a central Mexican warrior. Two shell ring "goggles" were placed on his forehead, five obsidian-tipped darts (traces of the wooden shafts were visible below the stone points) were located near his right shoulder, and three ceramic vessels, along with two painted organic objects, were deposited along his right side. The entire deposit was wrapped in a fiber-based mat whose traces were visible throughout (drawing by José Espinoza).

and designs that fit squarely within Maya traditions from the Petén and with those of the Copan Valley and the greater southeastern region (Reents-Budet et al, this volume).

Together with the Hunal Tomb and nearby offerings and burials, the Margarita Tomb came to form the core of a nascent Acropolis through which the legacy of the dynastic founder was incorporated and venerated. This emphasis on the founder continued through the construction of Rosalila (see Agurcia F., this volume) and Structure 10L-16, the last building above this locus (see Taube, this volume).

Burial 95-1

This burial consists of an unlined cist intruded below the floor of the platform that cancelled Margarita Structure. The burial lies along the central axis and 12 m west of Margarita Structure and was placed prior to the construction of the upper chamber of the Margarita Tomb. The grave measures 2 x 1 x 0.25 m and was lined with the remains of a woven grass mat. The body and offerings were placed on top of this mat, while a second, smaller (1.5 x 0.40 m) mat or bark-cloth covering was laid on top of and wrapped over the body and offerings (Figure 8.7).

Skeletal Material

The skeleton is that of an adult male at least 40 years of age at the time of death (Buikstra et al., this volume). The individual was approximately 5'3" to 5'6" tall, and signs of a poorly healed parry fracture are present on the lower left arm. The teeth are unmodified, and stable isotope ratio analyses indicate that the buried individual was not native to the Copan region. He appears to have spent his early life in an area to the north, perhaps in Petén or Yucatan (Buikstra et al., this volume).

The skeleton was placed in an extended position with the head to the west, with the right arm bent across the lower portion of the chest and the left hand curled inward over the pelvis. The right leg and foot were turned inward and the right side of the pelvis lay along the southern edge of the grave, as if the body had been turned onto its left side to fit into the grave while leaving space for the offerings placed to the north.

Artifacts and Ecofacts

The body was surrounded by offerings consistent with the weapons and adornments of a warrior arrayed in the tradition of central Mexico. These include two flat mother-of-pearl shell rings or "goggles" placed on the frontal bone above the eyes, five obsidian dart points associated with the wooden shafts to which they were hafted, and mosaic disks located at the ears, waist, and wrists. Additional adornments included a large jade bead placed in the mouth, a long tubular jade pectoral, a small jade macaw-head pendant placed beneath the cranium, and a small shell "wallet" that held a jade bead near the right wrist.

Figure 8.8 Cylinder tripod and lid from Burial 95-1
(photograph by Robert J. Sharer).

Three ceramic vessels and two painted gourds were placed to the north of the body. The ceramic vessels include a large mammiform tetrapod dish, a basal-flange polychrome bowl, and a stuccoed cylinder tripod with a figurine-handled lid (Figure 8.8). The basal-flange polychrome bowl is very similar to vessels in the Margarita Tomb, Tikal Burial 10 (Culbert 1993:fig. 18a), and Esperanza phase tombs at Kamilajuyu (Kidder, Jennings, and Shook 1946:178–179, figs. 182a–e, 183a–d, 184b, 207d). It includes a design in the center of the vessel interior that may be a stylized fish or heart (Kidder, Jennings, and Shook 1946:178–179). The cylinder tripod includes appliquéd anthropomorphic heads that look toward a seated figure on the lid who emerges from a tortoise shell. Two stuccoed, painted organic objects were placed near the ceramic vessels. One appears to have been a stuccoed gourd painted blue-green with a red rim band, while the other may have been a stuccoed, polychrome-painted shield, tray, or lidded container.

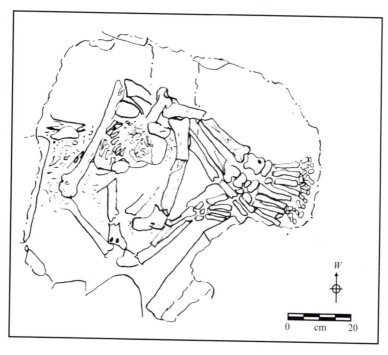

Figure 8.9 Burial 94-1. This burial includes the very robust skeleton of an adult male who was tightly flexed and interred in a seated position near the entrance to the final extension of the vault that provided access to the Margarita Tomb. No offerings were associated with the individual (drawing by José Espinoza).

Burial 94-1

This burial was placed at the north end of the series of vaulted passageways that extended and preserved access to the Margarita Tomb as the Acropolis grew up around it. The robust, seated male appears to have been left as a final offering within an intrusion made into the Mitzil Platform after this construction had buried the entrance to the Margarita passageway. The burial appears to have been placed in a simple pit, and there were no associated offerings (Figure 8.9).

The burial pit contained a large male who had been interred in a tightly flexed, seated position. The skull and spine collapsed in one direction and the legs slumped on each other in another direction, suggesting that the burial pit had been left

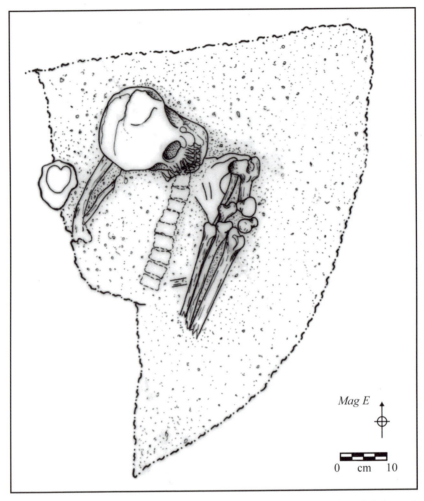

Figure 8.10 Burial 93-1. This interment contains the remains of an adult buried in a flexed position. Many of the anterior teeth include jade inlays (drawing by José Espinoza).

open, or that it had been lined and capped with some now perished material, such as wood. The feet remained together, and the fact that the toes were reflected up over the metatarsals suggests that they had been bound. The left arm seems to have been placed around and in front of the legs, while the right arm rested palm down. The central incisors show heavy wear, while the molars show only faceting, placing the age of the individual between 30 and 40 years at the time of death (Buikstra et al. this volume). The bones are very robust and are clearly male.

Burial 93-1

This burial was located inside the clay fill of Cobalto and Uranio Structures, two buildings on Early Yune Platform that formed part of the Early Acropolis (Figures 5.1 and 5.2; Sedat and López, this volume). The burial was located near a series of burnt and cracked jade offerings. There are no other offerings directly associated with this interment (Figure 8.10).

The burial consists of the skeleton of an adult (probably male) seated in a flexed position facing west. There are no traces of a formalized burial crypt of any kind. Several of the upper teeth included jade inlays, although detailed assessment of the remains has yet to be completed (Buikstra 1996).

Early Acropolis Burials Beyond the Sub-Structure 10L-16 Axis

Interments located along the eastern and northern margins of the Early Acropolis suggest that the emphasis on royal ancestry and ritual extended beyond the sub-Structure 10L-16 axis. Unlike the tombs placed on the central axis, however, royal burials located on the margins of the Early Acropolis appear to have been vulnerable to later disturbance and desecration. Skeletal remains and objects in Burial 92-3, which may have been the tomb of an Early Classic ruler, were partially destroyed when the interment was re-opened in the mid-6th century. Sharer (this volume) has suggested that this may have been part of a larger program of desecration in A.D. 550-560.

The interment of a dismembered adult male (Burial 92-1) at the base of the northern terrace of the Early Acropolis extends the practice of placing individuals without grave goods in association with architectural features (e.g., Burial 94-1) beyond the central axis of the Acropolis. The arrangement of the remains (see below) suggests that the individual may have been interred as a votive offering.

Burial 92-3

This burial contains the remains of an adult male placed in a supine, extended position (head to the north) on a layer of coarse sand in an unlined pit intruded into Chirmol Structure (Figure 8.11). Chirmol was located on the central axis of the stairway that provided secondary access from the Copan River to the eastern summit of the Early Acropolis. The burial dates to the mid-6th century.

Skeletal Remains

The skeleton appears to have been articulated and was extended in a supine position. While the skull was crushed beneath a large rock, the size and robustness of the mastoid process suggest that the individual was male, and dental wear indicates that he was middle aged at the time of death (Buikstra 1996). Cinnabar pigment was found in

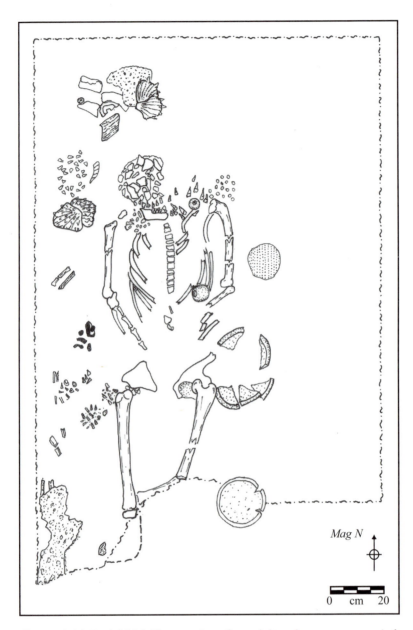

Mag N

0 cm 20

Figure 8.11 Burial 92-3. The remains of an adult male are accompanied by a number of shell and jade offerings, including a large jade bead, placed in the mouth and a shell disk inlaid with jade and shell mosaic pieces (Plate 4e) similar to a shell disk found in the Hunal Tomb (drawing by Christine W. Carrelli).

the burial, and it is likely that the bones or body were painted with it, as was the case in the Hunal and Margarita Tombs.

Artifacts and Ecofacts

The burial contained a number of objects, including two ceramic vessels, one of which contained red pigment. A small carved jade was placed in the mouth of the deceased. Shell and jade mosaic earflares, shell and jade beads, and three different varieties of pierced shell pendants accompanied the body, as did obsidian blades, a *Spondylus sp.* shell, and an unidentified material that may be black coral. The burial also included a stuccoed, painted gourd and the remains of fibrous organic material that may have been part of a woven bag or backing associated with hundreds of tiny shell beads.

The most notable item recovered from this burial was a large univalve shell (*Patella mexicana*) modified to form an ovoid disk and inlaid on its interior, concave surface with shell and jade to form an elaborate avian representation, probably Itzamnah, the Principal Bird Deity (Plate 4e). This large shell was associated with the tiny shell beads and may have formed some sort of pectoral. The shell is pierced on either side for suspension. This object is very similar to the inlaid shell disk found in the Hunal Tomb (Plate 4a).

Discussion

In light of the later disturbance, the circumstances surrounding the deposition of Burial 92-3 remain unclear, as does its attribution. The articulated bones are consistent with a primary burial, although the fragmentary nature of the remains and lack of a formal burial chamber suggest the possibility that the interment was redeposited. The objects in the burial, including the large shell and jade inlaid *Patella mexicana* shell, are similar to those present in the Margarita and Hunal Tombs and are consistent with the identification of the interred individual as an Early Classic ruler. Sharer (this volume) has suggested that the disturbance of this royal burial may have been part of a larger program of plunder and desecration that included the destruction of accessible monuments around A.D. 550-600.

Burial 92-1

This disarticulated burial (Figure 8.12) is located at the base of Teal Platform, between the northern façade of the Early Acropolis and the southern edge of the Northeast Court Group. Around A.D. 450, the bones of an individual (probably male), aged 18–25 years at the time of death (Buikstra 1996), were placed in a simple, unlined pit dug into structural fill below the Patio 5B court floor.

The interred individual appears to have been dismembered prior to burial, with the disarticulated long bones of the legs stacked above the cranium and

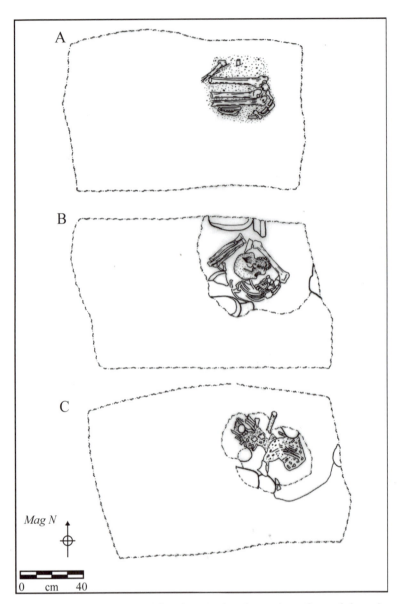

Figure 8.12 Burial 92-1. The disarticulated remains of an adult male were placed in a pit at the base of the Teal Platform, a large platform that formed part of the Early Acropolis. The long bones (a) were piled on top of the skull and ribs (b) which rested on the feet (c). The only objects associated with the body were scattered potsherds (drawing by José Espinoza).

mandible, which were placed upside down on top of the jumbled bones of the upper body. The pelvis was located on top of the articulated feet, which had been placed in anatomical position at the base of the pit. Some of the cervical vertebrae remained articulated, suggesting that the bones had not been completely defleshed prior to burial. The right arm was also completely articulated (including the bones of the hand), although the bones of the left arm were scattered. The mandible had been separated from the cranium and placed upside down above it, while portions of the rib cage and vertebral column were scattered throughout the second and third levels of the burial. Although the skeleton is fragmentary, the teeth remained in excellent condition, with little general wear. The skeleton is probably that of a male (Buikstra 1996). The only artifacts associated with this burial are snail shells and sherds mixed into the fill of the pit in which it was placed. There were no associated mortuary offerings.

The disarticulated remains present the possibility that the individual was sacrificed, dismembered, and buried in the Early Acropolis, presumably as an offering. The body may even have served the same function as offerings of burnt, cracked jade found elsewhere at the base of this platform (Bell 2003).

Northeast Court Burials

The area north of the Early Acropolis includes a series of court groups that appear to have served as residences or royal palaces throughout the early years of the Copan polity (Traxler 1996, 2001, 2003, this volume). While interments are often associated with residential structures in the Maya area (e.g., Haviland 1988), only one, Burial 91-1, has been found to date associated with a Northeast Court building. This interment is located below Chorlito Structure in the fill of Platform Purple and did not include grave goods. Burial 91-1 appears to be a secondary interment of long bones wrapped in bark cloth laid within the platform fill during construction.

The use of space in this area appears to have shifted subsequently (Sharer et al. 1992), and in the mid-6th century a royal interment, the Sub-Jaguar Tomb, was placed on the western margin of Court 2B opposite Ante Structure, a large decorated temple. This tomb is thought to contain the remains of Ruler 8 (see below) and is the earliest known royal interment outside the central axis beneath Structure 10L-16.

Sub-Jaguar Tomb (Burial 92-2)

This tomb contains the remains of an adult male laid supine on a raised funerary platform (Plate 8a). It lies below a structure that formed the western side of the penultimate version of the East Court. While this interment was initially thought to hold the remains of Ruler 7 (Sharer, Traxler, et al. 1999; Stuart 1997; Traxler 1994), current evidence suggests that its occupant was Ruler 8, a mid-6th century king about whom little was known before recent research by Stuart (see below).

Location and Architectural Context

The tomb lies on the west side of Court 2B, below and west of the later East Court Jaguar Stairs. It was placed on the east-west axis of the Ante Structure which formed the eastern side of this early version of the East Court. Constructed within a pit intruded beneath the Court 2B floor, the tomb is a rectangular masonry chamber measuring approximately 3 x 1.2 x 1.5 m. The walls are constructed of roughly shaped blocks set in irregular courses with mud mortar. The hurried appearance of the wall construction was concealed behind a thick layer of coarse plaster, finished with a vivid red paint. The west wall of the chamber includes a central niche or alcove (0.7 x 0.5 m) that probably provided access to the chamber floor. The floor was finished with the same plaster and red paint that covered the walls.

The chamber was sealed by eight large capstones, set lintel-fashion, on the upper courses of the east and west walls. The center capstone supported a masonry box that contained an offering of two *Spondylus sp.* shells, cinnabar, and four pieces of jade. A carved blackware cylinder tripod was placed on its side in the fill next to the west side of the offering box. The pit was filled, and a final offering of burned *Spondylus sp.* shell was made above the location of the offering box before the construction of an east-facing shrine structure over the burial. This structure was later burned and dismantled before its successor, a larger platform with apron-moldings similar to the Ante Structure across the court, was built.

Date

The ceramic vessels in the Sub-Jaguar Tomb have been assigned a date of ca. A.D. 550 based on their form and typological affiliation (René Viel, personal communication to L. Traxler, 1992). The architectural stratigraphy indicates that the tomb postdates the construction of Ante Structure but predates two superimposed structures and the final paving of Court 2B. The inscription on the Ante stairway provides two dates recently reinterpreted by Stuart (1992;, personal communication to R. Sharer 2001). The inscription begins with an initial series date of 9.5.7.?.2 (A.D. 541 or 542) which falls during the reign of Ruler 8, Wil Ohl K'inich. Stuart has identified the second date in the text, a problematic calendar round which he suggests corresponds to 9.4.18.6.12 (A.D. 532), as the accession date of Ruler 8.

Initial interpretation of the Ante Step inscription (Morales et al. 1990; Sharer et al. 1992) suggested that Ante Structure was built during the reign of Ruler 7, Balam Nehn (also known as Waterlily Jaguar), and that years later it was rededicated by his son, Ruler 10 (also known as Moon Jaguar). The revised dating of the step inscription and its attribution to Ruler 8 shortens the list of possible royal occupants of the Sub-Jaguar Tomb. Based on the ceramic assemblage and the historical succession of Rulers 7 through 10, as reconstructed by Stuart (1992, personal communication to R. Sharer, 2001), it is probable that the Sub-Jaguar Tomb held the remains of either Ruler 8 or Ruler 9 (who reigned from A.D. 551 to 553). Given the tomb's location on the central axis of Ante Structure, it seems most likely that it was built to hold the body of Ruler 8, who is named prominently on the outset stairway.

Skeletal Remains

The bones are those of an adult male at least 35 years of age (and probably much older) at the time of death (Buikstra et al., this volume). The remains are poorly preserved due to water infiltration, and although the pelvis was too disintegrated for examination, all other features suggest that the individual was male. No teeth were lost ante mortem, and extreme calculus developments are present on the anterior teeth. The postcranial skeleton is also poorly preserved, and red pigment present on the burial slab appears to have been transferred onto the bones. It is unlikely that the bones were painted with red pigment as is the case in the Hunal and Margarita Tombs.

Associated Artifacts and Ecofacts

The burial chamber contained a funerary slab formed by two large stones supported by six stone pedestals. The slab was covered by cinnabar pigment and a thin layer of magnetite. A finely woven mat was placed on the red and black surface of the burial platform, followed by 27 *Spondylus sp.* shells arranged in a rectangular pattern around the location of the body. At least one shell near the body's left shoulder covered the remains of a bird. It seems likely that other perishable items or animal remains were placed beneath other shells, but the infiltration of water over time makes this difficult to establish. The body was laid supine on this prepared platform in an extended position with the head to the north. The limbs were positioned so that the arms, hands, and feet rested on the shells, and a large jade bead was placed in the mouth. There is no indication that the body was bundled or wrapped.

      The man wore several items of adornment, including bracelets and anklets of shell and jade beads. Remains of feathers were found with the left anklet, and the close articulation of the foot bones suggests that he wore foot gear of some kind. A pearl and shell bead necklace hung around the neck. At the waist was a large jade pendant, and two obsidian disks (part of a belt or loin cloth decoration) were found near the thighs. A pair of intricate mosaic earflares was worn either on the body or attached to a headdress. A very poorly preserved organic headdress seems to have been placed above the head.

      Other costume pieces were clearly placed on the body after it was laid on the platform. An elaborate multi-strand necklace of large, carved shell beads was positioned across the chest so that its ends draped over the shoulders. Some type of perishable mask or decorated fabric also seems to have been placed over the necklace, but all that remains of this object are two sets of shell eyes. A large shell was placed near the head, while another was placed over the jade pendant at the waist. A wooden object was left near the right hand along with an obsidian blade. A cluster of small polished wood pieces and seeds was also located in this area. These may have been inside a perishable bag, used as counters or divination pieces, or they might have been rattles inside the disintegrated wooden object.

A thick layer of magnetite was spread on the tomb floor before objects, including 28 ceramic vessels, were placed underneath and around three sides of the funerary platform. Twelve of the ceramic vessels are stuccoed and painted, and several include serpent images that relate to vessels from Kaminaljuyu Burials A-VI and B-II (Kidder, Jennings, and Shook 1946) and Tikal Burials 10 and 48 (Culbert 1993). The objects directly below the platform may represent the personal effects of the deceased. They include an *Oliva* shell necklace with a jaguar-claw pendant, the remains of a *Spondylus sp.* shell "spangle" headdress or mask, a stuccoed-and-painted ceramic cup and bowl, a pair of shell rings, a painted wooden box, and other painted-and-stuccoed perishable containers. A group of nine objects was placed beneath the south end of the burial platform after the more personal items had been arranged. This group includes seven stuccoed and painted vessels and two stuccoed and painted perishable objects (Plate 8b). Around the north and west sides of the chamber floor were placed 13 ceramic bowls and three everted-rim ceramic basins. The remains of an organic container or bundle on the floor of the chamber contained nine small stingray spines. The final group of objects left in the tomb includes three ceramic vessels—a jar, a stuccoed-and-painted cup, and large cylinder tripod—placed along the west wall in front of the access niche. Analyses of 26 vessels by INAA indicate that the majority were produced in workshops located in or near Quirigua, Guatemala, while five were produced locally and the origins of another five remain undetermined (Reents-Budet et al., this volume).

Discussion

The identity of the Sub-Jaguar interment is not certain. However, the Acropolis location of the burial chamber, the axial relationship of the chamber to Ante Structure, a prominent building bearing the name of Ruler 8, and the imagery on the lavish funerary goods strongly suggest that the man was a ruler of Copan. While this interment was initially thought to hold the remains of Ruler 7 (Sharer, Traxler, et al. 1999; Stuart 1997; Traxler 1994), current evidence suggests that the best candidate may be Ruler 8, a mid-6th century king about whom much remains to be learned.

Structure 10L-26-Sub Burials

In addition to the nine burials found within the southeastern portion of the Acropolis discussed above, excavations below Structure 10L-26 by William L. Fash and his colleagues (Davis-Salazar and Bell 2000; Fash 2001; Fash and Fash 2000; Fash et al., this volume; Williamson 1996, 1997) revealed at least three elite burials that date to the Early Classic period (Burials 37-1, 37-2, and the Motmot Tomb). A fourth Early Classic elite burial (Burial V-6) was found just north of Structure 10L-26 by Juan Antonio Valdés and Charles Cheek (Fash 2001; Valdés and Cheek 1983; Viel and Cheek 1983).

In many ways, these four interments complement the Early Classic burials located elsewhere in the Acropolis. Like the Margarita Tomb, the Motmot Tomb contains the remains of a woman, in this case, seated on a reed mat in a circular chamber capped by an inscribed circular marker (Figure 4.3; Fash et al., this volume). One of the ceramic vessels in the Motmot Tomb included carved jade, shell, and pyrite offerings nearly identical to those found in an offering box northwest of the Margarita Tomb, both of which were associated with liquid mercury (David-Salazar and Bell 2000; Bell 2003). The occupant of Burial V-6, an adult male, was also interred in a seated position accompanied by extensive grave goods. Many of these offerings, including a slate-backed pyrite mirror, a shell plate necklace, sheets of gold-colored mica, two large shell rings, and small *Oliva* shell "tinklers," are similar to objects found within the Hunal and Margarita Tombs. Like the Hunal and Margarita Tombs, this burial included ceramics that appear to have been imported from central Mexico and Kaminaljuyu. It also contained a large jade pectoral carved with a mat design that is reminiscent of a smaller pectoral found in the Hunal Tomb and very similar to a pectoral found in PIC-PAC Burial 36, an elite Early Classic interment located west of the Main Group (Nakamura 2000; Sharer, this volume). Burial 37-1 was located beneath a large polychrome stucco façade on the east side of a substructure east of Papagayo (Fash et al., this volume). While it contained the remains of an adult male, the associated offerings included two bone needles similar to those found in the Margarita Tomb, as well as a polychrome vessel decorated with carved quetzal and macaw motifs that echo the representation of K'inich Yax K'uk' Mo's name on the Margarita façade. The robustness of the male skeleton interred in Burial 37-2, located to the east of Burial 37-1, recalls that of the individual in Burial 94-1.

Conclusions

The Early Classic burials within the Acropolis expand our understanding of this dynamic period in the polity's history. Taken together, the interments indicate the prominence and wealth of the ruling elite, the strong ties they enjoyed with their counterparts in the Maya Lowlands, the Maya Highlands, the Southeast, and central Mexico, and a continuing emphasis on the founder of the Classic period ruling dynasty, K'inich Yax K'uk' Mo'.

The interments and their associated structures served as ancestral shrines dedicated to the maintenance of the royal house and its authority. The Acropolis—the material manifestation of the polity—was therefore built on and with the remains of its rulers, intimately linking them to the past, present, and future of the center. Their remains mingle with the structures built to encase and commemorate them to form the core from which political power at Copan was wielded throughout the Classic period.

Many objects placed within these burials served as costumes, signaling both the elite status of the people with whom they were interred and identifying the interred with temporal and divine roles and statuses. The large amounts of prestigious goods placed in these tombs also demonstrate the wealth, status, and power of the interred and those responsible for their burial. In addition to providing a measure of wealth, the objects represent access to the source of exotics (jade, shell, feathers, cinnabar, mercury, and foodstuffs), the power and connections required to procure them, and the ability to acquire the labor and talent necessary to recover, process, transport, and craft them into exquisite works of art. Their presence represents control not only over precious materials, but over human labor and talent. It also demonstrates the status level for which the possession of such goods was appropriate and necessary. Spanish chroniclers report that sumptuary laws were in place at the time of contact (Sahagun 1969; Tozzer 1941), and similar restrictions may have been enforced in the Classic period.

While most of those interred within the Acropolis were buried with objects that signaled wealth, power, and prestige, others were not. Although their presence within the central architectural monument of the Copan polity suggests connections with the ruling elite, the individuals interred in Burials 92-1 and 94-1 may have held very different roles and statuses, possibly ending their lives as sacrificial victims; their bodies left to sanctify a building or to guard the entrance to a royal tomb.

The burials also tell a more personal story. The skeletal remains inform on the biography of the interred individual, reflecting instances of physical stress caused by illness or injury, repeated postures or practices, aesthetic modifications (dental inlay, filing and notching, or cranial modification), nutrition, and even residence location throughout life (Buikstra et al., this volume). This evidence provides glimpses into the personal experience of the interred which can be compared with the personage created through the arrangement, furnishing, and commemoration of the tomb.

The Acropolis interments, especially those located on the axis below the Late Classic Structure 10L-16, combined with the structures that encased them to serve as focal points for the veneration of K'inich Yax K'uk' Mo'. This veneration played a substantial role in strategies of royal legitimation throughout the Classic period.

Acknowledgments

The research and interpretations presented here are the outgrowth of years of close collaboration among all members of the University of Pennsylvania Museum Early Copan Acropolis Program, past and present, and our colleagues in the Instituto Hondureño de Antropología e Historia and other institutions working at Copan. While we are indebted to all members of the research team for the ideas outlined above, all errors, mistakes, and misrepresentations remain our own.

ECAP's work at Copan has been made possible by support from the University of Pennsylvania Museum (Boyer and Shoemaker Chair Research Funds and the Kolb Society), the University of Pennsylvania Research Foundation, the IIE Fulbright Program, the National Science Foundation, the Foundation for the Advancement of Mesoamerican Studies, the Maya Workshop Foundation, the Kislak Foundation, the Selz Foundation, the Holt Family Foundation, the Segy Foundation, and numerous private donors.

The authors would like to thank the people responsible for discovering, documenting, and excavating the burials described herein for their generous collaboration: Harriet F. Beaubien, José Bringuez, Jane E. Buikstra, Marcello A. Canuto, Eleanor Coates, Hernando Guerra, Ramón Guerra, Rudy V. Larios, Fernando López, Cameron McNeil, Rufino Membraño, Christopher Powell, Nelson Paredes, Dorie Reents-Budet, Julie Trosper, and E. Christian Wells.

9

EARLY CLASSIC CERAMIC OFFERINGS AT COPAN: A COMPARISON OF THE HUNAL, MARGARITA, AND SUB-JAGUAR TOMBS

Dorie Reents-Budet, Ellen E. Bell, Loa P. Traxler, and Ronald L. Bishop

B urials comprise a narrative relating to person, place, politics, and religion. In this chapter we examine pottery from the Hunal, Margarita, and Sub-Jaguar Tombs, three high-status burials discovered in the Early Classic levels (A.D. 400–550) of the Copan Acropolis, excavated by the Early Copan Acropolis Program of the University of Pennsylvania Museum of Archaeology and Anthropology (ECAP) and the Instituto Hondureño de Antropología e Historia (IHAH). The Hunal and Margarita Tombs are located in an early complex of ceremonial buildings below Structure 10L-16, a large temple pyramid that forms the core of the last version of the Acropolis (Agurcia F., this volume; Sedat 1996; Sedat and López this volume; Sharer, Fash, et al. 1999; Sharer, Traxler, et al. 1999; Taube this volume), while the Sub-Jaguar Tomb lies to the north, beneath the stairs that form the western boundary of the last version of the East Court (Traxler 1994; Sharer, Traxler, et al. 1999).

All three deposits contained the remains of high status members of the Copan elite accompanied by extensive offerings. The adult male buried in the Hunal Tomb may have been the Early Classic dynastic founder K'inich Yax K'uk' Mo' (Sharer 1997b; Sharer, Traxler, et al. 1999), while the adult female interred in the Margarita Tomb appears to have been an important member of the royal house, possibly the wife of the founder. While the mid-6th century Sub-Jaguar Tomb was initially thought to hold the remains of Ruler 7 (Sharer, Traxler, et al. 1999; Stuart 1997), current evidence points to the interment being that of Ruler 8, a mid-6th century king about whom little is known (Bell, et al., this volume).

The three tombs' occupants were buried with numerous shell, jade, and painted perishable objects (Bell et al. this volume) and a variety of decorated and undecorated ceramic vessels. Most of the vessels were made locally, indicating a thriving

native ceramic industry during Early Classic times. Each tomb also contained imported vessels, their "foreign" origins indicated by formal stylistic features shared with pottery found in similar contexts in the Maya area and highland Mexico. The apparent origins of these vessels may emphasize the role of foreign connections in the construction of royal power and prestige by and for the rulers of Copan (Helms 1979, 1993).
Ties to these distant centers are also suggested by similar styles among the tombs' associated non-ceramic artifacts, their surrounding architecture, and contemporaneous accounts
in the hieroglyphic texts of both Copan and other Maya centers (Sharer 2003a,b).

To determine whether the stylistic features of the ceramics in the tombs represent local wares, local imitations of foreign pottery, or vessels imported from distant
ceramic workshops, we combine stylistic investigations with trace elemental chemical
analysis of ceramic pastes. This multidisciplinary approach allows us to assess the
degree of intra-group stylistic and chemical similarity (or dissimilarity) and the simili-
tude of the sampled tomb vessels with pottery produced in other Maya and non Maya
regions and even within specific Maya centers. These data can indicate the likely
locales of ceramic production and the directionality of trade. They also may reveal
other cultural, historical, and geographic relationships among the ancient producers
and users of the pottery.

Instrumental Neutron Activation Analysis (INAA)

The chemical data used in this study are derived from neutron activation analysis
(INAA; Bishop et al. 1982; Glascock 1992; Neff 2000) and are a product of the Maya
Ceramics Project of the Smithsonian Center for Materials Research and Education.[*]
The project was created to investigate Classic Maya painted pottery production, combining chemical and art historical analyses to identify individual styles of Classic period painted ceramics and to suggest locations for the communities and/or workshops
where they were produced (see Rands and Bishop 1980; Reents-Budet et al. 1994;
Reents-Budet et al. 2000; Reents-Budet et al. in press). When used as one of many lines
of evidence of contact among social groups and residents of distant centers, INAA is a

---

[*] The Maya Polychrome Ceramics Project follows the established INAA analytical procedures discussed in the following publications: Blackman (1986), Bishop, Harbottle, and Sayre
(1982), Perlman and Asaro (1969). The Maya Polychrome Ceramics Project began under the auspices of the Department of Chemistry, Brookhaven National Laboratory, with support from the
Museum of Fine Arts Boston, and moved in 1982 to the Smithsonian Center for Materials Research
and Education (SCMRE, formerly the Conservation Analytical Laboratory), Museum Support
Center, Smithsonian Institution, Washington, DC. Analyses of additional samples have been carried
out at the SCMRE facilities operating at the National Institute of Standards and Technology (NIST,
formerly the National Bureau of Standards), under the direction of Dr. James Blackman. The elemental concentrations used for inferring chemical similarities among the analyzed samples' ceramic pastes include Rb, Cs, Ba, Sc, La, Ce, Eu, Lu, Hf, Th, Ta, Cr, Fe, Co, Sm, Yb, and Ca.

powerful tool to discern patterns of interaction that may inform on questions concerning political and economic history, craft production and exchange, and the use of foreign symbols to solidify and maintain political power.[*]

Data Analysis

In the present study, we investigate the ceramic offerings in three Early Classic royal tombs at Copan to propose hypotheses about their historical and cultural meanings. We seek to determine whether those vessels with stylistic similarities to ceramics found in central Mexico, Kaminaljuyu, Tikal, and regions of western Honduras represent imported wares or locally manufactured imitations of foreign styles. Initial research indicates that all four regions are represented in the tombs' ceramics. The chemical compositional data from those vessels believed to have been produced in central Mexico were further investigated by Dr. Hector Neff at the Missouri Research Reactor (MURR) facility of the University of Missouri. The MURR program has generated an extensive database focusing on the chemical composition of central Mexican ceramics, and Neff quickly identified four of the Copan samples as matching one of the major Thin Orange ware compositional groups from southern Puebla, Mexico, thereby verifying our initial findings. Some tomb samples were similar to other MURR determined central Mexican data but do not necessarily belonging to any of Neff's well characterized groups. Neff's ongoing investigations of central Mexican ceramics promise

---

[*] There are many presentations of the numerical procedures by which archaeologically interpretable patterns can be found in compositional data (e.g., Harbottle 1976, Bishop and Neff 1989, Glasscock 1992, Neff 2000). Such analyses, however, involve a series of different conceptual steps including: (1) visual assessment of the raw data, (2) application of numerical procedures, (3) initial impression of numerical/chemical patterning in the data, (4) convincing oneself that patterning exists, and (5) consideration of the means by which one will attempt to convince others that patterning is present. While steps 1–4 can be carried out in relative leisure, that luxury does not exist in step 5 when presenting analytical findings in a summary format such as that of this chapter. Synopsis presentation of a seemingly straight road is thus required without description of all of the dead ends or recitation of even most of the caveats. This can give a false and unfortunate impression of absolute certainty about the methodology. In this chapter, we give only a brief discussion of the compositional data and analytical processes that underlie our research, presenting the general manner in which the numerical synthesis was carried out. We indicate those attributions that appear firm, those that are probable (likely), and those for which we have insufficient compositional data to indicate a source of production. This means that our attribution of samples will be non-exhaustive, with several vessels assigned to that ever-present category of specimens that "will be considered in the future" as our database continues to expand. Interpretation, of course, will proceed from patterning that is perceived in the attributed ceramic vessels. A fuller discussion of the data set and relative statistical analysis will be forthcoming with the completion of a large set of new samples from the Copan Valley which are currently undergoing neutron activation analysis.

to provide new data that may indicate the specific production locations of these other vessels.[*]

The broadly constituted geographic groups represented by all of the vessels may be more correctly considered as composite entities comprising separate groups that have been merged to form a reference unit with a regional or subregional focus. Several "natural" groups are similarly present in the other reference units, with relatively strong geographical patterning to their respective compositional variation (Figure 9.1a). Using only the concentrations of chromium (Cr) and scandium (Sc), the data for vessels made at Quirigua are clearly separate from the other groups. This is an important finding because if one group can be observably and statistically separated from all other groups in any single elemental concentration space, that group also will be separable from the others in multivariate space. Other combinations of elements then can be used in this analytical context. For example, a greater tendency for the western Honduras samples to separate from those of the Guatemala–El Salvador highlands can be seen in Figure 9.1b where the data are shown for the logged concentrations of antimony (Sb) and iron (Fe).

A simple form of attribution is presented in Figure 9.2, where the data for the tomb pottery are shown relative to the Cr-Sc concentration space of Figure 9.1. While some of the tomb data clearly fall within the compositional and geographic space enclosed by the ellipsoid, any firm attribution is lost because the tomb pottery could deviate from the data of the reference groups when other elements are considered. Multivariate evaluation, therefore, is necessary not only to distinguish groups that

---

[*] The reference groups for western Honduras, central Mexico, and the other regions mentioned here are composite entities consisting of "natural" or homogeneous subgroups as well as other samples that might not be good group members in a statistically refined sense. Based on their cluster patterns on the dendrogram, they show relative internal homogeneity as compared to the other similarly selected groups. The central Mexican group, for example, consists of a broad range of ceramic types including Thin Orange Ware. The latter, attributable to several different compositional groups, was manufactured in the general region of southern Puebla (Rattray and Harbottle 1992).

For the better characterized units, such as that of Quirigua, the probabilities of the vessels' group memberships could be calculated. Using the Quirigua reference unit, the probability of the sampled vessel being a member of the group was determined using the sample's Mahalanobis distance from the multivariate group centroid. All attributed tomb specimens fell within an 80% or closer confidence interval.

It would have been preferable to treat all of the reference units as well-characterized reference groups so that robust probabilities of group membership for the tomb pottery could have been obtained. We did not proceed in this manner, however, because of the conflated and imposed multigroup nature of the reference units. Instead, for the present chapter we rely on (1) sample-to-sample comparison within a Euclidean space, (2) associations within an average linkage dendrogram, (3) patterns of tomb vessel co-variation within a principal components space, (4) calculation of the likelihood of membership in a reference unit when reasonable, and (5) close inspection of the raw chemical concentration data. Ongoing work continues to supplement available ceramic compositional data for the Tikal region, the Copan Valley, west-central Honduras, and Kaminaljuyu. The new data likely will provide a more solid statistical basis for some of the attributions proposed in this chapter.

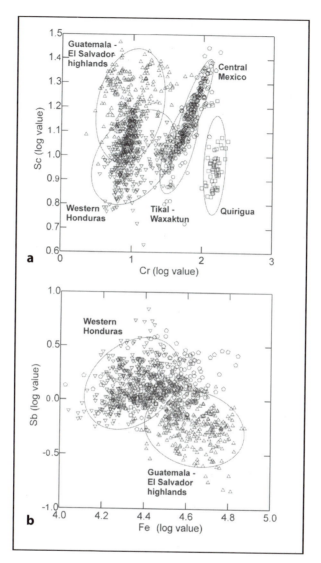

Figure 9.1 Log concentrations for referenced geographic regions. Loosely constituted "macro" units with specific geographic focus are based on the major structural breaks observed using an average-linking dendrogram, which was derived from a Euclidean distance matrix of logged elemental concentrations. All units contained one or more clustered Copan tomb samples. Ellipses represent 90% confidence levels, heuristically used here to focus attention on areas of geographic concentration in the plot. (a) Chromium and scandium log concentration plot. Note the extensive overlap of the samples from the Guatemala-El Salvador highlands with those from western Honduras. (b) Iron and antimony log concentration plot. When plotted relative to these two variables the overlap of the samples from the Guatemala-El Salvador highlands, as seen in Plot 1 (top) is greatly diminished.

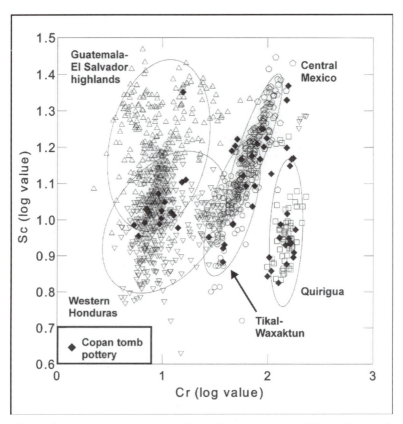

Figure 9.2 Log concentrations for referenced geographic regions and Copan tomb vessels. Data for the Copan tomb specimens have been added to the plot described in Figure 9.1a (top). Attention is called to the location of the tomb specimens within the probability ellipse for the Guatemala–El Salvador highlands. When Mahalanobis distances are used to evaluate the likelihood of a sample's membership in the macro units, no tomb specimen is a member of this unit.

might not be found to separate in any one dimension, but also to insure that groups are actually similar in many dimensions.

As an aid to understanding the basis for the chemical separation of the geographically focused reference units, the data were submitted to a linear discriminant analysis, which formed new axes to maximally separate the groups (Figure 9.3). This technique provides a spatially economical means by which to present summary information about groupings and any associated pottery. The elemental contributions to the discriminant axes are given in Table 9.1, and the projection of the tomb pottery onto the derived discriminant axes is shown in Figure 9.4. Several of the grouped samples

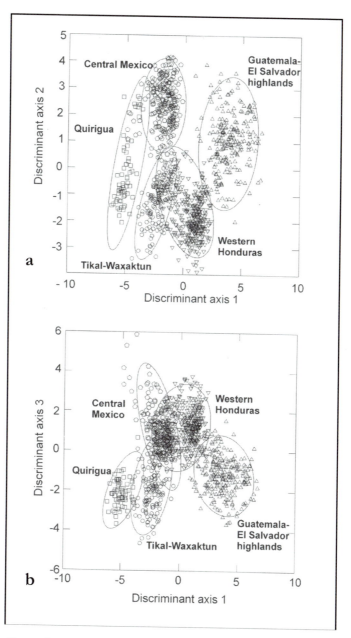

Figure 9.3 Discriminant analysis plot for referenced geographic regions with projection of Copan tomb specimens. The loosely constituted "macro" units with specific geographic focus, as described in Figure 9.1, are shown relative to Discriminant axes 1 and 2 (top, Figure 9.3a) and 1 and 3 (bottom, Figure 9.3b). Ellipses represent 90% confidence levels.

Table 9.1 Canonical Discriminant Functions (standardized by within variances)

	Df 1	Df 2	Df 3	Df 4
Sc	0.121	0.319	0.277	0.623
Cr	-1.002	0.247	-0.367	-0.329
Fe	0.457	0.303	0.513	-0.189
Rb	0.122	0.371	-0.076	0.679
Sb	-0.266	-0.433	0.346	0.213
Cs	0.048	0.380	0.521	-0.581
Ba	-0.110	-0.195	-0.143	-0.180
La	-0.037	0.256	0.667	-0.285
Ce	-0.067	0.079	-0.057	0.517
Eu	0.333	-0.003	0.063	0.119
Lu	-0.120	0.053	-0.204	-0.728
Hf	0.196	0.037	0.090	0.488
Ta	-0.204	-0.088	0.482	-0.006
Th	-0.196	-0.535	-0.845	0.343

Table 9.2 Principal Component Loadings (tomb vessels only)

	PCA 1	PCA 2	PCA 3
Sc	0.482	-0.693	-0.398
Cr	-0.171	0.262	-0.830
Fe	0.199	-0.475	-0.745
Rb	0.628	0.382	-0.402
Sb	0.507	0.277	0.287
Cs	0.653	0.450	-0.197
Ba	0.105	0.018	0.422
La	0.891	-0.315	0.100
Ce	0.875	-0.368	0.136
Eu	0.587	-0.776	0.079
Lu	0.791	-0.163	0.289
Hf	0.493	0.397	0.050
Ta	0.649	0.534	-0.234
Th	0.623	0.708	0.054

Variance Explained by Components

4.97	3.01	2.04

Percent of Total Variance Explained

35.52	21.47	14.59

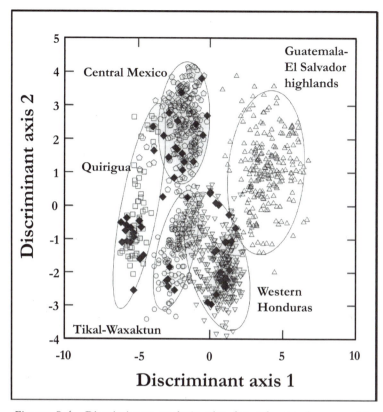

Figure 9.4 Discriminant analysis plot for referenced geographic regions with projection of Copan tomb specimens. The Copan tomb specimens are shown projected onto the reference axes 1 and 2 defined by a discriminant analysis of the referenced geographic regions of Plot 3 (Figure 9.3).

had sufficiently large distances from any of the groups' multivariate centroids to suggest that they had little similarity to any of these represented groups. In this chapter, then, we must designate these samples as "unassigned" as to group and geographic affiliation.

The bivariate plots of Figure 9.5 are obtained from a principal components analysis of only the tomb pottery (component loadings are given in Table 9.2). Using the first three principal components, Figure 9.5a shows greater intra-group compositional similarity among vessels from the Sub-Jaguar and Margarita Tombs than is evident in the Hunal Tomb. Using the same reference axes, the attribution of the tomb pottery is shown in Figure 9.5b.

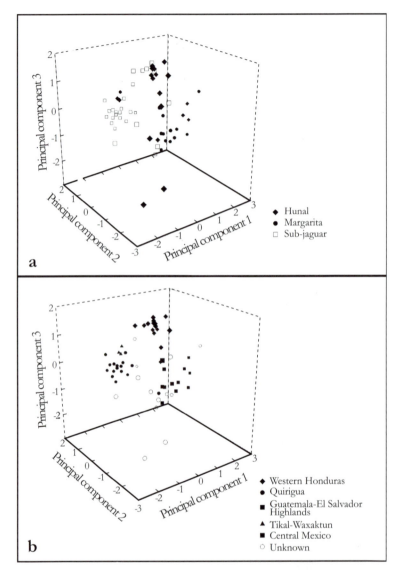

Figure 9.5 Principal component plots of analyzed Copan tomb vessels. The Copan tomb ceramics are shown relative to their position on the first three extracted principal components obtained from a correlation matrix of logged elemental concentrations. (a) Data points are labeled to reflect their tomb provenience; (b) data points are labeled according to their suggested geographic source attribution.

Hunal Tomb

The Hunal Tomb is a vaulted masonry chamber that contained the remains of an adult male accompanied by high-status burial goods, including carved jade, shell, and bone objects, 21 ceramic vessels, and 4 ceramic lids (Plate 3; Bell et al. this volume). Many of the objects in the tomb have counterparts at Teotihuacan, Kaminaljuyu, and Tikal, and strontium isotope ratio analysis suggests that the occupant was not native to the Copan Valley (Buikstra et al. this volume). The evidence suggests that the skeletal remains may be those of K'inich Yax K'uk' Mo' (Fash and Fash 2000; Martin and Grube 2000; Sharer, Traxler, et al. 1999).

Trace elemental analysis of the ceramic pastes of 20 vessels and 4 lids from the Hunal Tomb may shed light on the origin and life history of the interred man. The data indicate that 10 vessels and 2 lids are of Honduran manufacture (Figure 9.6), two come from the vicinity of Quirigua (Figure 9.7), one may be from the southern highlands of Guatemala or the adjacent region of the Pacific Coast (Plate 5a), two vessels and one lid were made in the central Petén lowlands of Guatemala (Plate 5b), three are from different locations in the central highlands of Mexico (Figure 9.8), and three cannot be assigned to any geographic area at this time (Table 9.3). Together, the 20 vessels and 4 lids sampled comprise an "international" assemblage of ceramics that may reflect the sociopolitical associations for the tomb's occupant.

Figure 9.6 Hunal Tomb vessels made in or near the Copan Valley. *Front row*, left to right: Vessel 11 (1/6/381-10, MSC346), Vessel 12 (1/6/381-9, MSC349), Vessel 18 (1/6/381-35, MSC343), and Vessel 5 (1/6/381-410, MSC381); *back row*, left to right: Vessel 13 (1/6/381-8, MSC348), Vessel 21 (1/6/381-98, MSC347), Vessel 20 (1/6/381-63, MSC351), Vessel 6 (1/6/381-4), Vessel 14 (1/6/381-36, MSC352), and Vessel 17 (1/6/381-39, MSC353) (photograph by Robert J. Sharer).

Figure 9.7 Hunal Tomb vessels made in or near Quirigua. (a) Vessel 8 (1/6/381-6, MSC344); (b) Vessel 15 (1/6/381-37, MSC382) (photographs by Robert J. Sharer).

Ten vessels and two lids from the Hunal Tomb represent local wares, including Copan Valley versions of a Thin Orange ware semi-hemispherical ring-foot bowl (Vessel 18, MSC343), four mammiform tripod or tetrapod dishes with Usulután resist decoration (Vessels 11, 12, 13, and 21; MSC346, MSC349, MSC347, and MSC348), one monochrome black tripod vessel (Vessel 6, MSC345), one monochrome black Z-angle bowl (Vessel 5, MSC381), two lidded cylinder tripods with spherical rattle appliqués (Vessels 14 and 17; MSC352 and MSC353 and their corresponding lids, MSC384 and MSC383), and one neckless jar (tecomate) with a ring-stand support (Vessel 20, MSC351).

Table 9.3 Hunal Tomb INAA Attributions

MS #	Vessel #	Operation #	NAA Attribution
MSC340	Vessel 7	1/6/381-5	Mexican highlands
MSC342	Vessel 3	1/6/381-7	Mexican highlands
MSC343	Vessel 18	1/6/381-35	Copan region
MSC344	Vessel 8	1/6/381-6	Lower Motagua Valley/ Quirigua
MSC345	Vessel 6	1/6/381-4	Copan region
MSC346	Vessel 11	1/6/381-10	Copan region
MSC347	Vessel 21	1/6/381-98	Copan region
MSC348	Vessel 13	1/6/381-8	Copan region
MSC349	Vessel 12	1/6/381-9	Copan region
MSC350	Vessel 9	1/6/381-11	Indeterminate
MSC351	Vessel 20	1/6/381-63	Copan region
MSC352	Vessel 14	1/6/381-36	Copan region
MSC353	Vessel 17	1/6/381-39	Copan region
MSC354	Vessel 10	1/6/381-13	Mexican highlands
MSC355	Lid 4	1/6/381-62	Petén
MSC356	Lid 3	1/6/381-41	Petén
MSC357	Vessel 4	1/6/381-137	Indeterminate
MSC366	Vessel 1	1/6/381-138	Guatemalan highlands
MSC367	Vessel 16	1/6/381-38	Indeterminate
MSC381	Vessel 5	1/6/381-410	Copan region
MSC382	Vessel 15	1/6/381-37	Quirigua sherds only similar
MSC383	Lid 2	1/6/381-40	Copan region
MSC384	Lid 1	1/6/381-34	Copan region
MSC388	Vessel 19	1/6/381-42	Petén

Indeterminate...................3
Local.............................12
Motagua/Quirigua..........2
Guatemalan highlands......1
Petén...............................3
Mexican highlands...........3

N = 24

Figure 9.8 Hunal Tomb vessels manufactured in highland central Mexico. *Left*, Hunal Tomb Vessel 3 (1/6/381-7, MSC342). *Center*, Hunal Tomb Vessel 10 (1/6/381-13, MSC354). *Right*, Hunal Tomb Vessel 7 (1/6/381-5, MSC340) (photograph by Robert J. Sharer).

Although the paste chemistry of the tecomate jar (Vessel 20) is slightly aberrant, it more closely resembles the aggregate Copan ceramics compositional profile, which indicates it was made locally. However, its form is not typical of any vessels in the corpus of contemporaneous Honduras pottery. Specifically, the shape of its ring foot (an unbroken concave arc) is more similar to pottery found at Kaminaljuyu (Kidder et al. 1946:82, figs. 182h, 206g) than those known from Honduras, the Petén lowlands, and western Belize (e.g., Merwin and Vallaint 1932:plates 19, 26, 27). The data suggest that the Copan tecomate jar reflects a broad southern Maya ceramic tradition locally interpreted by Copanec potters.

The Hunal Tomb contained two vessels imported from the southern Maya region. Two vessels come from the vicinity of Quirigua (Vessels 8 and 15; MSC344 and MSC382), while another may have been manufactured in the southern highlands or along the Pacific Coast of Guatemala (Vessel 1, MSC366). Vessel 8 is a monochrome black bowl that was found inside a black cylinder tripod made in the Copan Valley (Vessel 6, MSC345). Vessel 15 is a Quirigua-area version of a Thin Orange semi-hemispherical ring-foot bowl. And Vessel 1, a large deer effigy, is the most unusual ceramic object in the Hunal Tomb. Its paste chemistry is reminiscent of pottery from the southern highlands and Pacific Coast of Guatemala, although the match is not particularly strong. In general form, aesthetic concept, and construction technique, Vessel 1 recalls contemporaneous ceramic effigies from Burial 10 at Tikal, which Patrick Culbert believes were imported to the site (Culbert 1993:figs. 14, 18). Culbert also notes that effigy vessels of this general form are common in both the pre- and post-Esperanza phase tombs at Kaminaljuyu and along the Pacific Coast of Guatemala (Culbert personal communication to D. Reents-Budet, 1999).[*] The Kaminaljuyu examples recall Thin Orange ware zoomorphic and anthropomorphic effigy vessels from highland Mexico. Therefore, these effigy vessels from Copan, Kaminaljuyu, and Tikal may represent a southern Maya highlands ceramic tradition of notable antiquity into which similar Mexican ceramic forms were integrated during the earlier centuries of the Early Classic period.

Based on assays of paste samples taken from their lids, two tripod vessels from the Hunal Tomb were imported from the Petén lowlands of Guatemala (Lid 4 of Vessel 2, MSC355, and Vessel 19 and its lid, MSC356 and MSC388). Vessel 19 and its lid are decorated with elaborately carved, red-painted cartouches and volutes in typical Early Classic Petén style, while Vessel 2 is an unusual composite-silhouette tripod dish whose lid is topped with a modeled turtle knob. Their paste chemistry suggests that both were made in the central Petén lowlands, recalling the composition of pottery from the Mundo Perdido Complex at Tikal. However, their chemical composition also recalls that of pottery from the Naranjo area, including cylinder vases and plates painted in the Holmul-style (Zacatal Cream polychrome) and unprovenienced Saxche Orange polychrome vessels similar to pottery excavated at Yaxha (based on the Reent-Budet's assessment of type collections at Museo Nacional de Antropologia e Historia, Guatemala). The chemical data suggest that these vessels and four compositionally similar sherds (MSC133, MSC178, MSC247, MSC249) found in Group 10L-2, the Late Classic elite residential group south of the Copan Acropolis (Andrews and Fash 1992, Inomata and Houston 2000:3-11), were made in the Naranjo-Tikal-Yaxha triangle, with Tikal being the most likely candidate (Reents-Budet 2000). These findings coincide with John Longyear's initial identification of ceramic connections between Copan and the Petén (Longyear 1952:56-58, 64, 73-74) and with shared architectural similarities noted later (Sharer, Fash, et al. 1999; Sharer, Traxler, et al. 1999).

The three Hunal Tomb vessels imported from highland Mexico include two Thin Orange ring-foot bowls with incised geometric motifs (Vessel 7, MSC340 and Vessel 3, MSC342). The paste color, shape, and decoration of Vessel 3 recall a bowl from Palacio 3 at Teotihuacan (Sempowski 1992:fig. 9). Both Hunal bowls are chemically similar to Thin Orange pottery made in the Valley of Puebla (Neff 2000; Rattray et al. 1992) located southeast of Teotihuacan in highland Mexico and to the stuccoed and painted jar Vessel 10 (MSC354), the third highland Mexico vessel found in the Hunal Tomb.

---

[*] The deer effigy from the Hunal Tomb (Vessel 1, MSC366) is stylistically similar to a slightly smaller modeled deer vessel in the collection of the Museo de Vidrio, Antigua, Guatemala. The museum's records state that this vessel came from the slopes of the piedmont of the Pacific Coastal region of southwestern Guatemala.

Vessel 10 (MSC354) is a typical Teotihuacan-style jar with a tall, out-flaring neck. It is covered with post-fire stucco decorated in yellow, black, and white paint on a red ground, an artistic technique and palette particularly associated with Teotihuacan (Séjourné 1966). The imagery is Teotihuacan in iconographic content and style. The reproduction of the pictorial program twice on opposing sides of the jar also is characteristic of Teotihuacan ceramic decoration (Anton et al. 1979:38; Parsons 1988:214). Interestingly, discoloration on the surface of the vase follows the decoration on the overlying stucco, allowing partial reconstruction of the design in damaged areas. The imagery features a male humanoid figure with out-stretched arms. He holds what may be a round, feathered shield and spear-thrower darts in his left hand and grasps a spear thrower decorated with small white circles in his right hand. The figure either wears a large feathered headdress or emerges from a feathered cartouche which may represent a mirror (Taube 1992a:171). The neck of the jar is embellished with four large star motifs, and its base is encircled by curled elements that symbolize water and clouds in Teotihuacan art (e.g., the "Paradise Mural" at Tepantitla (Cabrera Castro 1992:116, 122; Pasztory 1976). As noted, the jar's paste chemistry recalls that of the Thin Orange ware bowls (Vessels 3 and 7) from the Hunal Tomb and Thin Orange pottery made in the Valley of Puebla.

At this time, three of the Hunal Tomb vessels cannot be assigned to a ceramic production area because they are not chemically similar to any other samples in the database. These include two unslipped cylinder tripods (Vessel 9, MSC350, and Vessel 16, MSC367), and one stuccoed basin (Vessel 4, MSC357). Each of the cylinder tripods has a double row of nubbin appliqués around its base and hollow-slab tripod feet with geometric cutouts. Both share slight chemical similarities with pottery from the Naco Valley, Honduras, but the correlation is weak, and they are unlike most pottery produced in that area (Urban 1993). The third unassigned vessel, Vessel 4 (MSC357), is a thin-walled, stuccoed, and painted basin decorated with at least one owl and several feathered oval cartouches that may represent mirrors (Taube 1992a:171; but see Langley 1992:figs. 6, 8, for counter examples). The vessel's form and decoration recall both incised and stuccoed-and-painted vessels found at Teotihuacan (e.g., Kubler 1976:figs. 29, 30, 36). While the basin's paste chemistry does not provide a secure provenience attribution, the stylistic data suggest an origin in highland Mexico.

Margarita Tomb

Located south and east of the Hunal Tomb, the Margarita Tomb continues the ritual complex established by the earlier interment. The tomb consists of an upper offering chamber (Chamber 2; Plate 6a) connected by a vaulted stairway to a lower burial chamber (Chamber 1; Plate 6b) that contained the remains of an adult woman. Both chambers were filled with elaborate, high-status offerings that likely were deposited at different times during the mid- to late 5th century A.D. The deceased woman was

Table 9.4 Margarita Tomb, Chamber 2 INAA Attributions

MS #	Vessel #	Operation #	NAA Attribution
MSC325	Vessel 17	1/6/214-4	Copan region
MSC326	Vessel 1	1/6/208-1	Mexican highlands
MSC327	Vessel 13	1/6/214-6	Mexican highlands
MSC328	Vessel 16	1/6/214-2	Southern Guatemalan highlands
MSC329	Vessel 14	1/6/214-5	Petén
MSC330	Vessel 15	1/6/214-1	Copan region
MSC331	Vessel 3	1/6/208-1	Indeterminate
MSC332	Vessel 5	1/6/208-6	Indeterminate
MSC335	Vessel 11	1/6/209-2	Indeterminate
MSC336	Vessel 12	1/6/209-3	Indeterminate
MSC363	Vessel 6	1/6/215-3	Copan region
MSC364	Vessel 9	1/6/210-1	Indeterminate
MSC368	Vessel 7	1/6/215-1	Copan region
MSC371	Lid 2	1/6/208-8	Copan region
MSC377	Vessel 18	1/6/214-3	Mexican highlands
MSC378	Vessel 2	1/6/208-3	Honduras

```
Indeterminate.................5
Local............................6
Motagua/Quirigua.........0
Guatemalan highlands....1
Petén............................1
Mexican highlands.........3

        N = 16
```

dressed in a sumptuous burial costume that includes a massive jade and shell necklace, shell-covered sandals, and more than 9,000 small jade beads. Her elite status and possible ritual office are emphasized by the offerings found below the burial slab, including two slate-backed iron pyrite mirrors with Teotihuacan-style decoration, small jade, shell and bone objects in painted basketry containers, and 16 ceramic vessels (Bell et al. this volume), 12 of which were sampled for neutron activation analysis.

Chamber 2 contained a few jade objects and the extensive remains of decorated perishable organic items (Bell et al. this volume) which probably were deposited at different times after the interment of the tomb's occupant in Chamber 1. The most numerous durable offerings in Chamber 2 were 18 ceramic vessels and 2 lids, of

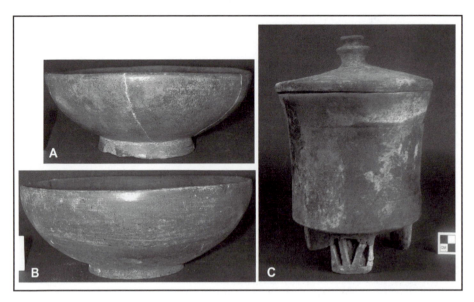

Figure 9.9 Selection of Margarita Tomb Chamber 2 vessels made in or near the Copan Valley: (a) Vessel 17 (1/6/214-1, MSC325), (b) Vessel 6 (1/6/215-3, MSC363), and (c) Vessel 15 (1/6/214-1, MSC330) (photographs by Robert J. Sharer).

which 15 vessels and 1 lid were sampled for neutron activation analysis (Table 9.4). The chemical data reveal that at least five vessels and one lid are of local manufacture including a small ring-foot dish (Figure 9.9a, Vessel 17, MSC325), a lidded cylinder tripod (Figure 9.9c, Vessel 6, MSC363) whose lid (Lid 2, MSC371) may have been made from a different local paste recipe, and three ring-foot bowls (Vessels 17, 7, and 15; MSC325, MSC368, and MSC330, Figure 9.9b) whose form and color imitate Thin Orange ware bowls from highland Mexico.

  Chamber 2 held two vessels imported from other regions in the Maya area, including a basal-flanged dish from the southern highlands of Guatemala (Figure 9.10a; Vessel 16, MSC328) and a second basal-flanged dish made in the central Petén lowlands (Figure 9.10b; Vessel 14, MSC329). Three vessels came from workshops in the central Mexican highlands, including two Thin Orange ware ring-foot bowls (Figure 9.11; Vessels 13 and 18; MSC327 and MSC377) and a stuccoed-and-painted lidded tripod (Plate 7a-c; Vessel 1, MSC326). The source of five vessels currently cannot be identified because their compositional patterns are intermediate between those of central Mexico and western Honduras.

  Chamber 2 contained seven ring-foot bowls (Vessels 2, 7, 13, 15, 17, and 18; MSC378, MSC368, MSC327, MSC330, MSC325, and MSC377, as well as Vessel 4, which remains to be sampled) whose form and monochrome orange surface color recall Thin

Figure 9.10 (a) Margarita Tomb Chamber 2: Vessel 16 (1/6/214-2, MSC328) manufactured in the southern highlands of Guatemala; (b) Vessel 14 (1/6/214-5, MSC329) manufactured in the Tikal region, Petén, Guatemala (photographs by Robert J. Sharer).

Orange ware ring-based dishes from highland Mexico. The chemical composition of four bowls, Vessels 17, 15, 7 and 2 (MSC325, MSC330, MCS368, and MSC378), establish them as locally produced dishes, likely imitations of their highland Mexican counterparts (Vessels 13 and 18; MSC327 and MSC377).

Chamber 2 contained two basal-flanged polychrome dishes, one from the Guatemalan lowlands (Vessel 14, MSC329) and one from the highlands (Vessel 16, MSC328). The paste chemistry of Vessel 14 is similar to that of vessels from Tikal's Mundo Perdido complex, suggesting that it was made in a workshop near Tikal. Its painted geometric decoration recalls a dish from Tikal Burial 177 (Culbert 1993:fig. 37), although the Copan vessel's erect walls more closely approximate monochrome dishes from Holmul (Merwin and Vallaint 1937:plates 22, 23, 26) and polychrome dishes from Uaxactun (Smith 1955:fig. 25a). Vessel 14 also is chemically similar to the

Figure 9.11 Margarita Tomb Chamber 2 vessels made in central Mexico: (a) Vessel 13 (1/6/214-6, MSC327); (b) Vessel 18 (1/6/214-3, MSC377). Vessel 1 (1/6/208-1, MSC 326) is shown in Plate 7a-c (photographs by Robert J. Sharer).

Hunal Tomb's carved lidded tripod imported from the Tikal region (Vessel 19 and Lid 3, MSC356 and MSC388; see above).

The paste chemistry of the second basal-flanged polychrome dish, Vessel 16 (MSC328), exhibits some resemblance to pottery made in the southern highlands of Guatemala, including the Alta Verapaz and the Kaminaljuyu area. At the present time, however, the chemical database contains insufficient samples from the southern Guatemala highlands to differentiate ceramic production in this region. Vessel 16's form and painting style closely recall Polychrome A dishes from Kaminaljuyu tombs A-III, A-VI, and B-I (Kidder et al. 1946:178–179, figs. 182a–e, 183a–d, 184b, 207d). Interestingly, a similar dish was found in Yax Nuun Ayiin's tomb at Tikal (Burial 10), which Patrick Culbert notes is a rare type at Tikal and a likely import, perhaps from Kaminaljuyu (Culbert 1993:fig. 18a).

The most remarkable imported vessel from Chamber 2 is Vessel 1 (MSC326), a large, lidded, post-fire-painted cylinder tripod. Nicknamed the "Dazzler" because of its

Table 9.5 Margarita Tomb, Chamber 1 INAA Attributions

MS #	Vessel #	Operation #	NAA Attribution
MSC365	Vessel 7	1/6/419-7	Indeterminate
MSC369	Vessel 5	1/6/418-10	Honduras
MSC370	Vessel 4	1/6/421-6	Honduras
MSC372	Vessel 1	1/6/422-1	Indeterminate
MSC373	Lid 1	1/6/420-3	Copan region
MSC374	Lid 2	1/6/420-4	Copan region
MSC375	Vessel 8	1/6/421-7	Central highland Mexico
MSC376	Vessel 14	1/6/420-2	Copan region
MSC385	Vessel 13	1/6/460-3	Copan region
MSC386	Vessel 9	1/6/420-8	Honduras
MSC387	Vessel 12	1/6/420-5	Honduras
MSC389	Vessel 11	1/6/420-9	Honduras

> *Indeterminate*....................2
> *Local*............................9
> *Mexican highlands*..........1
>
> N = 12

exceptionally fine painting, its imagery is an unusual blend of highland Mexican and Maya technical and artistic traits. The vessel's proportions and the shape of its lid and knob recall cylinder tripods from Teotihuacan and Kaminaljuyu, while the manipulation of the iconography is more Maya in style. The decoration includes an anthropomorphized temple whose feathered arms grasp objects associated with both Copan's dynastic founder and Teotihuacan. The temple's form and iconography link it to the *talud-tablero* Hunal structure and the modeled stucco façades on the building encasing the Margarita Tomb (Sharer, Fash, et al. 1999; Sharer, Traxler, et al. 1999; Sedat and López, this volume).

The chemical composition of the "Dazzler" is no less enigmatic. It is not statistically similar to any of the samples in the Maya Survey chemical database, although it does exhibit a low probability of chemical similarity to two sherds from Veracruz and one from Teotihuacan. While these results allow us to hypothesize that the vessel was made in highland Mexico, analysis of the decorative style suggests that the painter was schooled in Maya pictorial and hieroglyphic conventions. Together, the data prompt our hypothesis that the undecorated vessel was manufactured in highland Mexico and

Figure 9.12 Margarita Tomb Chamber 2 vessels (photograph by Robert J. Sharer).

then came to Copan where it was painted by a master artist. Although we cannot identify the painter's ethnicity, we can say that the artist was well versed in both Maya and Central Mexican pictorial canons.

Two cylinder tripods, one with a lid, came from Chamber 2 (Vessels 6 and 9; MSC363 and its lid MSC3271, and MSC364). The geometric cutouts on their tripod supports and post-fire decoration recall highland Mexican pottery, although similar cutout motifs are found on locally produced tripod vessels from the Hunal Tomb. Their paste chemistry does not match closely any other samples in the database, although Vessel 6 may be a local product. Interestingly, the lid's chemical profile does not match that of its vessel (Vessel 6, MSC363). It is not known if this represents two paste recipes from one workshop, the products of two different workshops, or the pairing of base and lid at the time the vessel was deposited in Chamber 2. And last, the origin of a monochrome orange bowl (Vessel 3, MSC331) and a stuccoed-and-painted orange-paste bowl (Plate 7d; Vessel 12, MSC336) from Chamber 2 cannot be determined at this time. The exterior of Vessel 12 is decorated with a row of fish that recall piscine representations in the murals of Caxaxtla, Mexico. Any further provenience attributions must await future chemical characterization for Copan and highland Mexican ceramic production.

Chamber 1, the funerary chamber, contained 16 ceramic vessels (Figure 9.12), of which 10 vessels and 2 lids have been sampled for neutron activation analysis (Table 9.5). Most likely they were deposited at the same time as was the tomb's occupant.

Nine are local products, one jar came from highland Mexico, and two cannot be attributed to any source at this time.

The local vessels include a monochrome orange ring-based bowl (Vessel 11, MSC389), two small cup-like vessels (Vessels 4 and 5; MSC370 and MSC369), and two lidded tripods with the remains of pigment on their exterior surface (Vessels 13 and 14, MSC385 and MSC376; Lids 1 and 2, MSC373 and MSC374). Due to the collapse of the burial slab, it is uncertain which lid went with which vessel. The lids' chemical profiles are slightly different from those of the tripods, rendering their paste chemistry useless for recovering the original vessel-lid pairings. The disparate chemical compositions also suggest that the lids may have been made from slightly different clay resources or paste recipes, which is reflected in their coarser texture than the pastes of the cylinder tripods. The chemical compositions of the two small vessels, a tiny tecomate with a single loop handle (Vessel 5, MSC369), and a tiny jar with two loop handles (Vessel 4, MSC370), deviate from the norm for Copan. They may represent local products made from different clay resources and/or divergent paste recipes.

Other locally produced vessels from Chamber 1 are two bichrome basal-flanged dishes (Vessels 9 and 12; MSC386 and MSC387). Their nearly equivalent chemical compositions indicate they were made in the same workshop, perhaps as a pair.

The one certainly imported vessel from Chamber 1 is a tall-necked (cuspidor) jar that was made in highland Mexico (Vessel 8, MSC375). Two vessels cannot be attributed to any region: a monochrome orange ring-based bowl (Vessel 1, MSC372) and a ring-stand with the remains of painted stucco decoration (Vessel 7, MSC365). Its chemical profile has vague chemical similarities to samples from the central Veracruz coast of Mexico and the Jonuta area of Tabasco.

Sub-Jaguar Tomb

The Sub-Jaguar Tomb is an unvaulted masonry chamber found beneath the Jaguar Stairs of the East Plaza, located on the north side of the Early Acropolis that encases the Hunal and Margarita Tombs (Traxler 1994). The chamber contained the remains of an adult male thought to be a mid-6th century ruler of Copan, most likely Ruler 8. Among his tomb offerings are large amounts of shell and an array of ceramic vessels, all of which connote the high-status of a paramount ruler. His burial costume includes an elaborate necklace of massive carved shell beads. His body was surrounded by *Spondylus sp.* shells imported from the Caribbean Sea and Pacific Ocean. A concentration of shell spangles found on the floor is believed to be the remains of a shell headdress similar to that found in the Hunal Tomb (Bell at al., this volume).

Arranged around the chamber were 28 ceramic vessels (two with lids). Twenty-six of the vessels and one of the lids were sampled for neutron activation analysis (Table 9.6). The data indicate that five were manufactured locally (Figure 9.13,

Table 9.6 Sub-Jaguar Tomb INAA Attributions

MS #	Vessel #	Operation #	NAA Attribution
MSC300	Vessel 18	1/7/290-22	Indeterminate
MSC301	Vessel 23	1/7/290-12	Copan region
MSC302	Vessel 14	1/7/290-14	Copan region
MSC303	Vessel 21	1/7/400-7	Copan region
MSC304	Vessel 12	1/7/290-13	Copan region
MSC305	Vessel 24	1/7/290-17	Copan region
MSC306	Vessel 27	1/7/290-28	Quirigua
MSC307	Vessel 17	1/7/290-23	Quirigua
MSC308	Vessel 8	1/7/290-3	Indeterminate
MSC309	Vessel 26	1/7/290-26	Indeterminate
MSC310	Vessel 10	1/7/290-6	Quirigua
MSC311	Vessel 28	1/7/290-29	Quirigua
MSC312	Vessel 15	1/7/290-18	Weak Quirigua
MSC313	Vessel 1	1/7/290-16	Quirigua
MSC314	Vessel 4	1/7/290-15	Quirigua
MSC315	Vessel 22	1/7/290-8	Weak Quirigua
MSC316	Vessel 6	1/7/290-9	Quirigua
MSC317	Vessel 2	1/7/290-19	Quirigua
MSC318	Vessel 16	1/7/290-21	Weak Quirigua
MSC319	Vessel 7	1/07/290-2	Quirigua
MSC334	Vessel 13	1/7/290-11	Indeterminate
MSC358	Vessel 9	1/7/290-4	Indeterminate
MSC359	Vessel 19	1/7/290-24	Weak Quirigua
MSC360	Vessel 20	1/7/290-27	Quirigua
MSC361	Vessel 11	1/7/290-7	Quirigua
MSC379	Vessel 5	1/7/290-10	Weak Quirigua
MSC380	Lid 2	1/6/290-1	Quirigua

Indeterminate..................5
Local............................5
Motagua/Quirigua........17
Petén..........................0
Mexican highlands...........0

N = 27

Figure 9.13 Sub-Jaguar Tomb vessels manufactured in or near the Copan Valley. *Front row*, left to right: Vessel 24 (1/7/290-13, MSC304), Vessel 23 (1/7/290-12, MSC301), Vessel 21 (1/7/400-7, MSC303); *back row*, left to right: Vessel 12 (1/7/290-13, MSC304), Vessel 14 (1/7/290-14, MSC302) (photograph by Robert J. Sharer).

Vessels 23, 14, 21, 12, and 24; MSC301, MSC302, MSC303, MSC304, and MSC305), five are of undetermined origin (Vessels 18, 8, 26, 13, and 9; MSC300, MSC308, MSC309, MSC334, and MSC358), and 16 vessels and one lid were made in the lower Motagua Valley, most likely near the site of Quirigua (Vessels 27, 17, 10, 28, 15, 1, 4, 22, 6, 2, 16, 7, 19, 20, 11, 5, and Lid 2 of Vessel 6; MSC306, MSC307, MSC310 through MSC319, MSC319, MSC359, MSC360, MSC361, MSC379 and MSC380; see Plate 7b for a selection of the above vessels).[*]

---

[*] Results are pending for Vessel 3 (1/7/290-99), Lid 1 (1/7/290-20) was not sampled, and Vessel 25 (1/7/290-25) could not be sampled without damaging its stucco-and-paint decoration. The stylistic similarity of these vessels to the other post-fire-painted vessels, however, strongly suggests that they were also made near Quirigua, bringing the total number of vessels in the tomb produced in a Quirigua workshop to 18.

The five locally manufactured vessels (Vessels 12, 14, 21, 23, and 24; MSC301, MSC302, MSC303, MSC304, and MSC305) are ring-footed semi-hemispherical red-on-orange bowls with negative curvilinear resist decoration similar to that on Usulután ceramics, identified as the archaeological type Chilanga in the Copan ceramic typology (Bill 1997; Viel 1993a:96-98). All are similar in form to monochrome orange bowls from the Hunal Tomb (Vessel 18) and the Margarita Tomb Chamber 2 (Vessel 15), although the chemical composition and decoration of these bowls differ slightly from those of the Sub-Jaguar vessels. Such variation implies that they were made from different paste recipes, perhaps reflecting utilitarian pottery manufacturing adjustments at local workshops over time.

Other possible local vessels include a monochrome red jar (Vessel 18, MSC300) and three tall, unslipped basins or *apastes* (Bill 1997:16) with wide everted rims (Vessels 8, 13, and 9; MSC308, MSC334, and MSC358). The walls of these coarse-ware vessels are lumpy, uneven, fire-clouded, and haphazardly burnished. The paste chemical profile of Vessel 8 matches that of domestic pottery made at Copan (Bishop and Beaudry 1994), and its shape and surface treatment recall the local ceramic type Titichón Red-and-Brown (Bill 1997:93-95; Viel 1993a:114-115; Willey 1994:82-84). Although Vessels 9 and 13 have no matches in the chemical database, their form and surface treatment recall Vessel 8, implying that they too are local products. The monochrome red jar (Vessel 18, MSC300) is decorated with incised lines on its whitewashed neck. It likely represents the archaeological ceramic type Ricardo Composite, a local Early Classic type (Bill 1997:127-129).

Surprisingly, most of the Sub-Jaguar Tomb vessels come from the lower Motagua Valley in Guatemala (17 of the 27 sampled vessels and one lid). Ten share paste chemical profiles with sherds excavated at Quirigua, indicating their origin in workshops at the site. Among these are 6 basal-flanged plates (Vessels 27, 17, 19, 20, 11, and 10; MSC306, MSC307, MS310, MSC359, MSC360, and MSC361) decorated with orange slip and red-and-black-on-orange geometric motifs. The near chemical equivalency of 4 of the plates (Vessels 11, 17, 20, and 27) strongly suggests they were made in the same workshop.

Three of the plates (Vessels 17, 20, and 27) have a small, trough-like spout in their rim. Two plates lack spouts (Vessels 10 and 11; MSC310 and MSC361). They also have a stylized fish painted in the center of their interiors, recalling in form and decoration vessels from northern Belize (e.g., La Milpa tomb Op. B-11), the central Petén (e.g., Tikal Burial 10; Culbert 1991:fig. 18), and the southern highlands (e.g., Kaminaljuyu Burials A-III, A-IV and B-I; Kidder et al. 1946:figs. 183, 184).[*] Interestingly, one of these plates, Vessel 11, shares a 99.9% probability of chemical similarity with Vessel 17, a plate that does not include the fish motif. The 6th plate (Vessel 19) differs

---

[*] The Tikal plate is identified by T. Patrick Culbert as a rare type at the site whose paste is unlike anything else from Tikal (Culbert 1991:fig. 18). It is likely that the Burial 10 plate was imported to Tikal, possibly from the Motagua Valley.

slightly from the others in form (no basal break), surface decoration (non-representational and more carefully executed geometric designs), and paste chemistry (slightly divergent from the Quirigua aggregate signature). In spite of these variations, the overarching stylistic features and chemical similarities support a Lower Motagua Valley source for all six plates.

Ten of the 12 stuccoed-and-painted vessels and one of the two stuccoed-and-painted lids found in the Sub-Jaguar Tomb were chemically sampled. The chemical data indicate that at least 6 vessels and one lid were likely made in workshops at or near Quirigua (Vessels 1, 2, 4, 6, 7, and 28; MSC313, MSC317, MSC314, MSC316, MSC319, MSC311), while 4 have less chemical similarity to Quirigua ceramics (Vessels 5, 15, 16, and 22; MSC379, MSC312, MSC318, and MSC315), implying they were made using different paste recipes and/or clay resources. This could indicate the presence of different yet concurrent paste traditions at Quirigua or the vessels were manufactured elsewhere in the lower Motagua Valley.

Figure 9.14 Sub-Jaguar Tomb: (a) Vessel 2 (1/7/290-19, MSC317) and Lid 1 (1/7/290-20); (b) Vessel 6 (1/7/290-9, MSC316) and Lid 2 (1/7/290-1, MSC 380) (photographs by Robert J. Sharer).

In spite of the chemical variation within the two groups discussed above, the vessels are notably uniform in shape and decorative style, many with slip-painted and/or carved decoration underneath their post-fire-painted stucco surfaces. These include 5 small cylinder cups (Vessels 1, 3, 5, 15, and 22), one tripod dish with an appliqued human effigy face (Vessel 28), a sub-hemispherical bowl (Vessel 25), 2 large cylinder tripods (Vessels 7 and 16), and 3 small cylinder tripods with solid slab supports (Vessel 4 and lidded Vessels 2 and 6).

The two stylistically similar tripods with human effigy head knobs on their lids (Figure 9.14; Vessels 2 and 6) have nearly identical chemical profiles (a 99.4% probability of similarity). The tripods' exterior walls initially were embellished with comparable carved-incised designs accented with deep red and black slip paint. Their subsequent post-fire-painted decoration features a Teotihuacan-style zoomorphic icon surrounded by red motifs that symbolize liquid. Yet the tripods' lids are painted with an Early Classic Maya saurian and have knobs sculpted in the form of Maya-style human head effigies. The Teotihuacan-style icons include elements that are more typical of Maya imagery, however, including the small feathers at the corners of the zoomorph's eyes and the more rounded nature of the imagery overall. Created as a pair from the same paste mixture in a workshop near Quirigua, Vessels 2 and 6 exemplify the incorporation of Teotihuacan artistic techniques and pictorial canons by ceramists working in the Maya lowlands during the Early Classic period.

The paste and carved decoration of Vessels 2 and 6 recall ceramics found in Tikal Burials 35 and 48 that Patrick Culbert believes were imported to Tikal (Culbert 1991:figs. 27c1,3 and 30). Although chemical data for the Tikal vessels are not available, their similarities to the Sub-Jaguar pottery may indicate they too were manufactured near Quirigua.

Vessel 4, the third small cylinder tripod, was placed in the tomb without a lid. It is decorated with three painted-stucco cartouches containing poorly executed renderings of a Maya-style saurian. This long-snouted zoomorph is unlike any saurian image in the known corpus of Early Classic Maya art. The chemical profile of Vessel 4 is similar to those of Vessels 2 and 6 and sherds excavated at Quirigua, suggesting the site's vicinity as their location of manufacture.[*]

The paste chemistry of the two large stuccoed-and-painted cylinder tripod vessels (Vessels 16 and 7; MSC318, MSC319) points to their manufacture in the vicinity of Quirigua. Their congruent size, shape, and paste chemistry suggest they, like their small counterparts Vessels 2 and 6, were made as a pair. Unlike the smaller pair, however, Vessels 16 and 7 are decorated with two different iconographic systems, one Maya, the other central Mexican. Vessel 16 presents three renderings of a feather-encircled star motif with liquid motif issuing from its lower edge. Vessel 7 is decorated with

---

[*] Of note is the 99.1% probability of chemical similarity of Sub-Jaguar Tomb Vessel 4 (MSC314), likely produced in a workshop located in the vicinity of Quirigua, to MSW015, a sherd excavated at San Agustín Acasaguastlan, indicating that it too was imported to San Agustín Acasaguastlan from the Quirigua area.

Figure 9.15 Three views of Sub-Jaguar Tomb Vessel 5 (1/7/290-10, MSC379). All 6 glyphs are illustrated (photographs by Robert J. Sharer).

four Maya-style cartouches, each featuring the profile head of a different saurian being.[*] The two tripods' pictorial programs may be complementary in form and content, the vessels having been made as a set to convey interrelated concepts.

The size and shape of the five small cylinder vases (Vessels 15, 1, 22, 5, and 3; MSC312, MSC313, MSC315, MSC379) suggest they were personal drinking vessels. All are decorated with post-fire-painted stucco images executed in Maya style on top of a red-on-cream slip-painted surface. Vessel 1 is ornamented with two profile saurian heads embellished with water curls. Vessel 15 features three oval cartouches containing a *k'inich ajaw* glyphic icon and two zoomorphic heads rendered upside down. Vessel 5 (Figure 9.15) and Vessel 22 (Figure 9.16) carry three columns of two Maya hieroglyphs each, separated by vertical bands. The glyphs on Vessel 22 may relate to maize, the sun (*k'in*), and the sky (*chan*). David Stuart has suggested that they may be toponyms (personal communication to E. Bell, 1999). The surface of Vessel 3 is poorly preserved, but it appears to be painted with two elaborate glyph blocks on each side. The paste chemistry of Vessels 1, 15, and 22 suggest that they were manufactured near Quirigua,[†] Vessel 5 has weaker links to Quirigua, while results are not yet available for Vessel 3.

---

[*] One has the central Mexican iconographic element denoting dripping liquid falling from its upper jaw line, one is feathered, and the body of one terminates in a serpent. The markings on the serpent recall those of a boa constrictor, although the bulbous form at the end of its tail may depict the rattles of a rattlesnake.

[†] Although the chemical profiles of Vessels 15 and 22 are less like those of other pottery made in the vicinity of Quirigua, their compositions are consonant with the aggregate profile of Quirigua-produced pottery.

Figure 9.16 Three views of Sub-Jaguar Tomb Vessel 22 (1/7/290-8, MSC315). All 6 glyphs are illustrated (photographs by Robert J. Sharer).

Vessel 28 (MSC311) is a wide tripod dish with solid supports, whose exterior is decorated with appliquéd Teotihuacan-like human faces separated by an incised zigzag line. The post-fire-painted stucco decoration on the upper part of the exterior wall includes a Maya-style saurian head and feathered wing rendered in profile and water symbols like those on Vessel 1. The chemical profile of Vessel 28 is remarkably similar to Vessels 2 and 27, which may indicate that all were made from the same paste recipe, perhaps in the same workshop, at Quirigua.

Discussion

Pottery vessels from the Early Classic period Hunal, Margarita, and Sub-Jaguar Tombs provide data pertinent to the sociopolitical history of Copan, which help us address important research questions. Two of these concern the geopolitical origins of K'inich Yax K'uk' Mo', and the nature and extent of interaction among members of the Copan polity and other Maya and Mesoamerican centers during this dynamic time in the polity's history.

Hieroglyphic texts at Copan (most notably the Altar Q inscription) suggest that K'inich Yax K'uk' Mo' arrived at the center after taking power elsewhere, possibly at Teotihuacan (see Stuart, this volume). His Teotihuacan-like depictions on stone monuments and ceramic vessels support this central Mexican connection. A growing body of new evidence, however, indicates ties to groups in the Maya lowlands. For example, other buildings within the Early Acropolis feature Petén-style architectural forms and decoration, including apron moldings and modeled stucco façades.

Given these conflicting clues, the foremost historical question about K'inich Yax K'uk' Mo' centers on his origins. Was he a local man with far-flung connections or an interloper from Teotihuacan, Tikal, Kaminaljuyu, or some other polity?

Stable isotope ratio analyses of skeletal remains from the Hunal Tomb show that the occupant spent his early childhood in the central Maya Lowlands (Buikstra, this volume). The ceramics from the tomb, however, indicate connections with all of these regions. A strong local focus (12 of the 24 sampled vessels and lids) is complemented by foreign connections indicated by those vessels made in the vicinity of Kaminaljuyu, Quirigua, Tikal, and Teotihuacan. Although the pottery from the Hunal Tomb provides no absolute indication of its occupant's origins, the ceramic data are consonant with osteological, epigraphic, and art historical evidence that suggests K'inich Yax K'uk' Mo' came to Copan from the central Maya Lowlands, and that he had ties to Teotihuacan in central Mexico and also to the southern highlands of Guatemala.

The Margarita Tomb contains the remains of a royal woman who likely figured prominently in the early history of the dynasty. Unfortunately, no women are mentioned in the contemporaneous hieroglyphic accounts, so her identity remains unknown. She may have spent her early childhood outside the Copan area, but she appears to have been in residence at Copan by early adolescence (Buikstra, this volume). The majority of the pottery from the mortuary chamber (Chamber 1) is from local workshops (9 of 12). Only two of the Chamber 1 vessels were imported to Copan, a cuspidor jar from highland Mexico and a ring stand of undetermined origin.

The pottery offerings found in Chamber 2 exhibit a pan-regional perspective similar to that of the Hunal Tomb assemblage. Of the 16 sampled vessels and lids, at least 6 (and perhaps as many as 11) are of local manufacture. The remainder came from the southern highlands of Guatemala (1 bowl), the central Petén lowlands (1 bowl), and highland Mexico (2 ring-foot bowls and a lidded cylinder tripod). The lidded tripod from highland Mexico stands out because of its exceptional artistry and apparently two-part production history. The vessel is Thin Orange ware made in the Valley of Puebla in highland Mexico (see Rattray and Harbottle 1992, Neff 2000). The post-fire-painted stucco decoration features Maya canons of pictorial representation, implying its painting at Copan by an artist trained in the Maya pictorial system.

The Sub-Jaguar Tomb contains the remains of an adult male who may be one of the mid-6th century kings of Copan, perhaps Ruler 8. In contrast to the other two burials, the majority of the Sub-Jaguar Tomb ceramics came from outside Copan. Seventeen of the 27 sampled vessels and one lid were made in workshops in or near Quirigua, Guatemala. Although many are decorated with post-fire-painted stucco, an artistic technique associated with highland Mexico, the iconographic and hieroglyphic imagery is almost exclusively Maya. Five of the 27 sampled vessels and lids are of local Copan manufacture, and the five non-attributed vessels also may have been made in local workshops. The ceramic evidence from the Sub-Jaguar Tomb, then, points to a notable elite-level relationship between Copan and Quirigua in the mid-6th century A.D. and fewer connections outside the region.

Our multidisciplinary analysis of the pottery from the three royal tombs demonstrates that ceramic vessels can reveal far more historical information than simply chronological data. By combining INAA compositional analysis with stylistic, iconographic, and epigraphic investigations, the pottery from primary deposits in the Acropolis provides a wealth of details concerning Copan's Early Classic social history. The vessels point to interaction among the ruling elite of Copan, Tikal, the southern highlands of Guatemala, and Teotihuacan in the early 5th century A.D. Some of this contact may have been on a face-to-face basis and perhaps even included the forceful incursion into the Maya Lowlands of individuals with ties to Teotihuacan. K'inich Yax K'uk' Mo' appears to have been living in Tikal during Teotihuacan's initial influence and perhaps physical presence in the Petén Lowlands. He also may have had some special relation with Teotihuacan foreigners and their Maya supporters at Kaminaljuyu and elsewhere in the Petén prior to his taking power at Copan.

Interestingly, the ceramic evidence does not reveal extensive interaction between Copan and sites in the southern Guatemalan highlands, especially Kaminaljuyu as posited by earlier researchers (e.g., Kidder et al. 1946). We hope that future research will investigate the role played by Kaminaljuyu in the sociopolitical power structures and international relationships during the dynamic Early Classic period (see Valdés and Wright, this volume).

Acknowledgments

The Maya Ceramics Project was initiated through the cooperation of the Research Laboratory, Museum of Fine Arts, Boston, and the Department of Chemistry, Brookhaven National Laboratory. Work at the latter institution was under the auspices of the U.S. Department of Energy with funding provided by Mr. Landon T. Clay of Boston. The project now is part of the research programs of the Smithsonian Center for Materials Research and Education (formerly the Conservation Analytical Laboratory), Museum Support Center, Smithsonian Institution. Dr. James Blackman's unfailing assistance with the activation of thousands of pottery samples at the National Institute of Standards and Technology is gratefully acknowledged. The project's success is based on the exceptional cooperation of numerous Mayanist colleagues, Maya culture aficionados, museums and national institutions in the United States, Guatemala, Belize, Honduras, Mexico, Canada, and England.

We are especially grateful to Dr. Hector Neff for his assistance in differentiating between the INAA signatures for pottery made in central Mexico and western Honduras. Many of the attributions presented above would not have been possible without his generous collaboration.

10

Tombs from the Copan Acropolis: A Life-History Approach

Jane E. Buikstra, T. Douglas Price, Lori E. Wright, James A. Burton

L ife-history approaches have become prominent in recent bioarchaeological investigations. An emphasis upon detailed accounts of individual human lives develops naturally from the confluence of two trends. One of these is increased archaeological attention to historical contexts; the other is the development of intricate and precise bioarchaeological techniques for documenting a person's history from birth until death. Prominent among the latter are chemical signals of health, diet, and residence that are literally crystallized within the body's tissues.

In the Americas, life-history approaches are most commonly applied at sites that post-date European contact. The ancient Maya are a singular exception, as hieroglyphic texts and iconography narrate histories and document identities. Life-history approaches have, for example, figured prominently in Saul's Maya "osteobiographic" investigations that span nearly three decades, beginning with his pioneering study of skeletal remains from Altar de Sacrificios (1972). Heavily influenced by Angel's "social biology," Saul has consistently emphasized the "total interaction" of biological and cultural elements to reconstruct Maya lifeways (Saul and Saul 1989). The research reported here continues Saul's holistic perspective, extending it to include not only the reconstruction of Early Classic lifeways but also an emphasis upon a historically known individual, K'inich Yax K'uk' Mo', the founder of the Classic period Copan dynasty.

K'inich Yax K'uk' Mo', whose skeletal remains are among those tentatively identified and investigated here, is said to have arrived and consolidated political power within the Copan Valley in A.D. 426 (Schele 1990c; Sharer 1997b; Sharer, Traxler, et al. 1999; Stuart, this volume; Stuart and Schele 1986b). Contemporary Early Classic Copan Acropolis structures provide evidence of architectural links to other well-known Mesoamerican regions: the central Petén, the Valley of Guatemala, and even the Valley of Mexico (Sharer 1997b; Sharer, Traxler, et al. 1999). Hieroglyphic texts associate K'inich Yax K'uk' Mo' with the site of Tikal prior to his arrival at Copan (Sharer, Traxler, et al. 1999). Are such statements in stone an accurate reflection of Copan's Early Classic connections? What of the founder's history and exploits prior to his A.D. 426 arrival? How embellished might these texts be, given the political, ideological and economic complexities of the early Classic Maya world?

A life-history approach complements and expands our perspective on K'inich Yax K'uk' Mo' and others interred within the Copan Acropolis. The significance of these bioarchaeological data should not be underestimated. We know, for example, that the correct attribution of sex to a set of remains can have a profound impact upon the interpretation of both architectural features and historical figures. At Copan, inscriptions and tomb elaboration led excavators to assume that the occupant of the Margarita Tomb was a male, perhaps Ruler 2, the son of K'inich Yax K'uk Mo' (Sedat and Sharer 1997; Sharer 1997b). Osteological study indicates that these remains are clearly those of a female (Buikstra 1996).

In this chapter, a life-history approach will be applied to the skeletal remains of seven individuals excavated from within the Copan Acropolis. These interments vary from the elaborate burial crypt for the remains thought to be those of K'inich Yax K'uk' Mo' (Sedat and Sharer 1997; Sharer 1997b; Sharer, Traxler, et al. 1999), to the simple entombment of a sentinel at the entrance to the final passageway leading into the Margarita sepulchre. We begin with physical and contextual descriptions for the remains, emphasizing age-at-death, sex, cultural modifications of physical features, and pathology, especially pre-mortem trauma. We then focus upon the residential histories as revealed by strontium and oxygen isotopic analysis. Also included here is a preliminary aggregate comparison between health-related features of this admittedly small and nonrandom sample of Early Classic remains with the Late Classic materials from Copan reported by Storey (1985, 1992, 1997, 1999) and Whittington (1989, 1991, 1992, 1999; Whittington and Reed 1997).

Burial Descriptions

Hunal Tomb (Burial 95-2)

The Hunal Tomb is the earliest considered in this analysis. It contained a single set of partially disarticulated remains from an adult male. The tomb's architectural and artifactual associations support the hypothesis that this is the final resting place for K'inich Yax K'uk' Mo' (Plate 3a; Bell, et al., this volume; Sedat and Sharer 1997; Sharer 1997b; Sharer, Traxler, et al. 1999). This association will be accepted here, recognizing that such attributions can be incorrect due to the Maya practice of reentry and the placement of multiple individuals within tombs (Gillespie 2001a). Reuse of the Hunal Tomb might be supported by the fact that the labial portion of a right permanent

Figure 10.1 Upper dentition of the Hunal Tomb remains
illustrating dental modifications.

upper central incisor from a second individual, a juvenile or young adult, was recovered from the tomb floor, although this tooth may have been in secondary context.

Standard osteological methods for estimating age-at-death from structures of the pelvis, including the pubic symphyses and the auricular surfaces support an age-at-death in advance of 50 years (Buikstra and Ubelaker 1994; Lovejoy et al. 1985; Suchey and Katz 1986; Suchey et al. 1984; Todd 1921a, 1921b, 1921c). To refine this estimate, we have employed "transition analysis," using standards for the pubic symphysis and auricular surface newly developed by George Milner and Jesper Boldsen (Boldsen 1997; Milner, Boldsen, and Usher 1997; Boldsen et al. 2002; Milner, Boldsen, and Wood 2000). The advantage of the Milner-Boldsen method is that it facilitates estimates for advanced adult years. While we cannot precisely estimate age-at-death for these remains because the age-at-death distribution for the Classic Maya is unknown, standards derived from 17th century Danish parish records suggest that K'inich Yax K'uk' Mo's life may have extended well into his second half-century (Milner and Boldsen n.d.). Maya texts indicate that only the final ten or eleven of these were at Copan (Sharer, Traxler, et al. 1999).

As illustrated in Figure 10.1, the Hunal individual's dentition was decorated both with jadeite inlays and through filing. The central incisors present single spherical inlays and were notched distally, Romero Molina's Type G-3 (Romero Molina 1986a). The lateral incisors, also inlaid, were notched mesially, again Romero Molina's Type G-3. Although the incisal edges of the lateral incisors had broken away during life, the notch pattern is well defined. Spherical jadeite inlays were seen in all anterior maxillary teeth, excepting the upper right central incisor, extending from the left lateral incisor through the right 1st premolar. The inlay had been lost from the upper right central incisor prior to archaeological recovery.

As a type of dental decoration, filing begins at Copan during the Middle Preclassic, with a diversity of forms observed during the Classic period. Inlays are limited to the Classic period, as they are throughout the Maya world, with the exception of Tikal and Nakbe (Mata Amado and Hansen 1992; Romero Molina 1986b; Tiesler Blos 1999).

Other Early to Middle Classic Maya sites where a similar notching pattern but without inlays (Romero Molina's B-5) has been observed include Mirador, Jaina, Jiquipilas, and Kaminaljuyu (Agrinier 1963; Cifuentes Aguirre 1963; Romero Molina 1986b; Tiesler Blos 1999). The Preclassic component of Uaxactun also contained individuals with B-5 notching (López Olivares 1997; Tiesler Blos 1999). Jade inlays were observed in remains from the Early to Middle Classic components of Jaina and Tikal (Romero Molina 1986b; Tiesler Blos 1999).

Romero Molina (1958) argues that there is no clear association between filed teeth and social status. In a review of materials from other contexts at Copan, Tiesler Blos (1999) reports that while filed teeth are somewhat more prevalent among males and at smaller residential contexts distant to the center of Copan, the presence of inlays appears to be associated with elite status. She also notes that at Copan inlays are more common on the right side than on the left, if asymmetry is present. Filing, observed on more than half the dentitions—52/87 (59.6%) or 52/78 (62%) if infants are excluded (Tiesler Blos 1999:185)—seems to signal horizontal rather than vertical status distinctions. As filing appears to be initiated only during or after late adolescence, an age grade effect may also influence this type of dental modification (Tiesler Blos 1999). The filing form present in the Hunal remains is therefore not unique among the Copan materials and is similar to that for several other Classic period sites. We may infer, however, that the inlays apparently signal elite status. As noted later, the only other remains from the Acropolis analyzed here that present evidence of dental modification are those from the Margarita Tomb.[*]

Slight fronto-occipital artificial deformation is present in the Hunal cranium (Figure 10.2), as it is also in the nearby Margarita remains. Pressure on the Hunal frontal bone was mediated by two pads placed on either side of the midline. The

---

[*] Although not part of this study, Burial 93-1 from the Acropolis also shows jadeite inlays in the central incisors, the right upper canine and the right upper 1st premolar (see Bell et al., this volume). Although the remains are still embedded in matrix, it appears that the incisors and canine conform to Romero's type E-3; the single inlay in the premolar, E-1 (Romero 1986). The remains appear to be those of an adolescent.

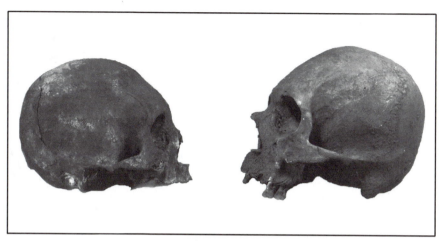

Figure 10.2 Crania from two Early Classic Copan royal tombs:
Margarita Tomb (left); Hunal Tomb (possibly K'inich Yax K'uk' Mo', right).

Margarita frontal shows evidence of only one pad, centrally located. In both cases, the posterior portion of the skull was deformed by pressure slightly above lambda, thus conforming to the "classic" tabular erect definition (Dembo and Imbelloni 1938; Imbelloni 1925; Tiesler Blos 1998, 1999). Overall, the percentage of individuals showing cranial deformation at Copan (~70%) is less than that for an aggregated Maya sample (~85%) reported by Tiesler Blos (1999). Tiesler Blos (1999) also reports that the tabular erect form dominates at Copan within the "ceremonial complex." Even though tabular oblique deformation appears to be the preferred elite deformation form in mural representations (Romano 1987; Tiesler Blos 1999), tabular erect deformation dominates Early Classic elite tombs from the Copan Acropolis.

Stature estimates, based upon an average of measurements from both femora, are presented in Table 10.1, along with those for other individuals considered in this study. These estimates have been generated through the standard Trotter (1970; Trotter and Gleser 1958) and Genovés (1967) methods. Figures derived from a recent modification of the Genovés formula by Del Angel and Cisneros (Tiesler Blos 1999) are also reported. Ranges are developed using the statistical procedures outlined by Giles and Klepinger (1988). As indicated in Table 10.1, height for the Hunal remains, and by inference, K'inich Yax K'uk' Mo', is estimated to have been between approximately 162 and 176 cm. Comparisons with published figures place the lower limits of the 95% confidence interval for Hunal above the mean of 159.47 cm Tiesler Blos (1999:273) reports for other Copan males. Tiesler Blos's sample, however, is small (n = 8) and may be dominated by Late Classic materials. Similarly, Danforth (1999:109) reports mean stature

Table 10.1 Estimated Stature of Early Acropolis Individuals

	Individual Genoves (1967)[1]	Trotter-Gleser (1958)[2]	Tiesler Blos (1999)
Hunal Tomb			
Femur	168.08 ± 7.32 cm	169.21 ± 7.40 cm	165.68 cm
	5' 6" ± 2.88"	5' 6" ± 2.79"	5'5"
Margarita Tomb			
Tibia	148.65 ± 8.06 cm	155.86 ± 7.08 cm	146.15 cm
	4' 10" ± 3.17"	5' 1" ± 2.79"	4'9"
Motmot Tomb			
Femur	153.98 ± 7.89 cm	159.11 ± 6.98 cm	151.41 cm
	5' 0.5" ± 3.1"	5' 2" ± 2.7"	4' 10"
Tibia	155.04 ± 7.96 cm	161.72 ± 6.78 cm	152.55 cm
	5' 1" ± 3.13"	5' 3" ± 2.67"	5' 0"
Burial 95-1			
Femur	164.24 ± 7.28	165.50 ± 7.45	161.83cm
	5' 4" ± 2.87"	5' 5" ± 2.93"	5' 3"

[1] ± indicates a 95% CI after Giles and Klepinger (1988).
[2] Trotter-Gleser stature estimates based on Mongoloid male reference sample.

for Maya males from the Early Classic Maya Southern Lowlands as 162.14 cm. K'inich Yax K'uk' Mo' therefore appears to have been tall for an Early Classic Maya male.

The most striking physical evidence of lifestyle for the Hunal individual derives from an analysis of blunt-force trauma that had been sustained during his adulthood but long before death (Buikstra et al. 2000). As did two other of the seven individuals described here, he had suffered a "parry" or "nightstick" fracture at the midpoint of the right forearm (Figure 10.3). Such fractures may result from either a fall or a direct blow to the forearm when the arm is pronated and raised to shield the face or by a fall (Galloway 1999; Merbs 1989; Perry et al. 1995). In this case, the fracture had not been reduced and the radius had healed with significant shortening. The broken ulna did not heal, thus forming a pseudarthrosis or false joint. Although there is arthritic lipping throughout the elbow, wrist, and hand, there is no indication of disuse atrophy. The right 5th metacarpal also presents evidence of a healed fracture and minor deformity, another possible defensive wound (Galloway 1999).

The inferior third of the sternal body or gladiolus is thinned to the left of a distorted sternal foramen, the apparent result of blunt force trauma to this region (Figure 10.4). The blow causing this fracture apparently depressed the caudal portion

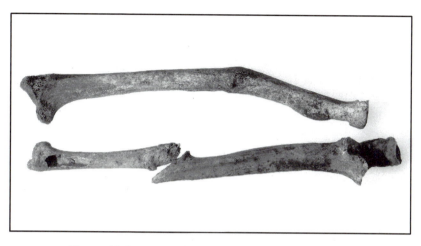

Figure 10.3 Fractured ulna and radius (right forearm)
of Hunal Tomb interment.

of the body (gladiolus) while compensatorily causing the superior portion to project
ventrally. The articulation between the body and the manubrium sternum had been displaced to the dorsal surface of the body. In association with this restructuring of the
thorax, the articulations between the manubrium and the clavicles were displaced laterally, forming new articular facets. While many other activities could be implicated, it
is tempting to suggest that the force that caused such extreme restructuring occurred
in the course of the ballgame. If the Early Classic rubber ball was as massive as that
recorded at the time of Conquest (3 kg), a blow to an unprotected portion of the body
could have caused considerable physical damage. The 16th century writer Diego
Durán (reported in Leyenaar 1978:38), who had personally witnessed ball games,
wrote that "the game could be fatal if a player who had become too tired received it
in the abdominal region."

The most unusual example of blunt force trauma involved the left shoulder.
As a result, the superior third of the glenoid fossa and the coracoid process of the
scapula had separated from the remainder of the bone (Figure 10.5). This fracture
never healed. Arthritic change at the shoulder was profound, including marked lipping
of the humerus and eburnation (bone-on-bone polish) on the inferior third of the
humeral head. While this fracture could have disrupted the shoulder's neurovascular
structures, thus leading to degenerative changes and paralysis, there is no evidence of
disuse atrophy in the left upper limb. Generalized moderate arthritis in the elbow,
wrist, and hand suggest that the limb continued to be used, however painful this may
have been.

Figure 10.4 Dorsal (posterior) aspect of sternum,
Hunal Tomb interment.

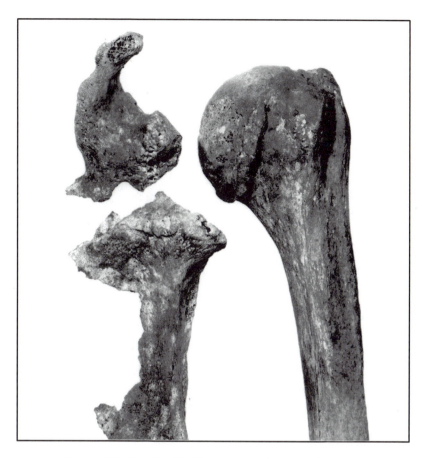

Figure 10.5 Proximal left humerus and scapula fragments,
Hunal Tomb interment.

Modern medical references emphasize that such fractures are rare and caused by high-energy forces (Galloway 1999; Goss 1992, 1996; Ideberg et al. 1995; Herscovici et al. 1992; Miller and Ada 1992; Neer and Rockwood 1984; Rogers 1982; Zuckerman, Koval, and Cuomo 1993). This scapular fracture most closely resembles Ideberg's Type III (Ideberg, Grevsten, and Larsson 1995; Zuckerman, Koval, and Cuomo 1993), which occurred in only one example of 338 cases recorded by Ideberg and colleagues in a Swedish clinical sample (Ideberg, Grevsten, and Larsson 1995: 395). Today, fractures of the scapula are said to comprise 3–5% of all shoulder fractures, 0.5–1% of bone fractures over-all (Herscovici et al. 1992; Zuckerman, Koval, and Cuomo 1993: 271). Of scapular fractures, glenoid cavities are involved approximately 10% of the time (Goss 1992: 299).

Today, automobile, pedestrian, and motorcycle accidents are commonly cited causes of Ideberg's Type III scapular fractures (Stephens et al. 1995: 440; Zuckerman, Koval, and Cuomo 1993: 271). Frequent associations between such shoulder trauma and rib and clavicle fractures are also reported (Goss 1992; Stephens et al. 1995; Zuckerman, Koval, and Cuomo 1993). These associations, however, may reflect exclusively modern risks and are not necessarily appropriate models for preindustrial contexts. Firearms-related recoil trauma termed "Trapshooter's Shoulder" is also cited as a cause of fractures to the coracoid process (Rogers 1982; Zuckerman, Koval, and Cuomo 1993).

Assuming that K'inich Yax K'uk' Mo' avoided vehicular trauma and did not engage in competitive or recreational shooting, there are three types of accidents that may have led to his scapular fracture. The first of these is a direct blow to the shoulder at its point or in the region of the coracoid process (DePalma 1983; Neer and Rockwood 1984). Goss (1995:270) associates fractures at the base of the coracoid with direct blows to the shoulder in the more violent "stick" sports such as lacrosse and hockey.

A second type of accident that could have led to Ideberg's Type III fracture would have involved a fall with the arm adducted, the shoulder striking the ground or other similarly hard surface. Goss (1992: 299) reports that "Type III fractures result when the force of the humeral head is directed somewhat superiorly, creating a transverse fracture of the fossa, which then exits along the superior border of the scapula, sometimes disrupting the superior suspensory complex of the shoulder. A fragment of variable size, which includes the coracoid process and the superior articular surface of the glenoid cavity, is displaced."

Thirdly, the Hunal individual could have fallen toward the left with his arm extended and his hand outstretched to break the impact. Rogers (1982) argues that falls rather than direct blows are the most common causes of Type III injuries. Whatever the fracture's etiology, the two scapular segments were sufficiently displaced that they never again united. This displacement was probably associated with torn ligaments, such as the coracohumeral, coracoacromial, and coracoclavicular ligaments, as well as the contraction of the biceps brachii, coracobrachialis, and pectoralis minor muscles. Thus, as the ligaments ceased to stabilize the joint, the muscles would have worked to keep the fractured edges from uniting.

In addition to these injuries, one and perhaps as many as three ribs present well-healed fractures. The posterior aspect of the right parietal displays evidence of a healed depressed fracture approximately 4 by 2.5 cm in diameter. Within the spinal column, the joint between the 7th cervical and 1st thoracic vertebra is very arthritic, with marked porosity and eburnation of the articular facets. Rib facets in the lower thoracic region are expanded and lipped. The 11th thoracic vertebra is wedged anteriorly due to a compression fracture, which effects a 30–45° kyphosis. Finally, there is a vertical fracture through the distal phalanx of the right great toe. The arthritic changes appear to be sequelae either of direct injury to the spine or secondary results of trauma to other regions of the trunk.

Neither the timing of these injuries nor their relationship to each other can be determined. In the absence of any epiphyseal dislocation due to trauma, including the medial clavicular epiphyses, it would appear that the major injuries to the thorax and upper limbs occurred during his adult life, probably after approximately 25 years of age, when all epiphyses are united. The fractures are either healed or have permanent non-union, and they are associated with well-developed arthritis. Therefore, we may conclude that these traumata are not recent and most likely predate or were coincident with K'inich Yax K'uk' Mo's arrival at Copan. While in today's world, it would appear that the deceased had survived an auto accident in which he had been thrown from the vehicle, ancient explanations that focus upon the ballgame or the battlefield appear more probable.

Margarita Tomb (Burial 93-2)

The remarkably resplendent Margarita Tomb, adjacent to the Hunal sepulchre (Plate 6; see Bell et al., this volume), contained human remains of a single skeleton whose pelvic structures include a wide sciatic notch and ischiopubic indicators consistent with a sex diagnosis of female (Buikstra and Ubelaker 1994). The left pubic bone is nearly complete, presenting deep "gestation pits" on its dorsal aspect and pubic symphysis morphology consistent with an age-at-death in advance of 50 years (Buikstra and Ubelaker 1994; Lovejoy et al. 1985; Suchey and Katz 1986; Suchey et al. 1984; Todd 1921a, 1921b, 1921c). The auricular surface also contains features indicative of advanced age (Lovejoy et al. 1985). An evaluation of these pelvic structures according to the Milner-Boldsen transition method suggests that her age-at-death was only slightly less advanced than that of the male from the Hunal Tomb. As noted above, the only form of dental modification for the Margarita Tomb remains was an inlay in the lower right canine, which had been lost by the time of archaeological recovery.

The 95% confidence interval for stature, 140.6–163.9 cm (Table 10.1) places her well within the range for Copan females estimated by Tiesler Blos (1999: 274) based upon a sample of 4. She appears relatively tall, when compared to Danforth's (1999: 109) Early Classic Maya female sample mean of 142.2 cm, but this estimate is also based upon a small sample size (n=6).

Although generalized osteoporosis and trabecular coarsening bear witness to advanced age, only her lower back and knees show extreme degenerative change. Especially pronounced are the osteophytes that extend laterally from the inferior aspect of the 5th lumbar body and the superior aspect of the 1st sacral unit. Both femora and tibiae present raised osteophytes surrounding significant portions of the articular faces.

Motmot Tomb (Burial 37-8)

Built to commemorate a major calendric event near the end of K'inich Yax K'uk' Mo's reign, the Motmot Tomb comprised an elaborate chamber covered by a circular marker. The initial deposit within this tomb included a primary interment and at least one "trophy skull." The tomb was revisited, with evidence for the use of fire and the addition of at least two more skulls, one of which was associated with cervical vertebrae[*] (Fash and Fash 1996, 2000; Sharer 1997b; Sharer, Traxler, et al. 1999; Williamson 1996). Cutmarks are visible on the ventral and lateral aspects of the 5th cervical vertebra from this skull (Buikstra 1996).

The primary interment within the Motmot Tomb was a young adult female. All diagnostic pelvic structures support a sex diagnosis as female, including positive Phenice characteristics and other ischiopubic indicators (Buikstra and Ubelaker 1994; Phenice 1969). The skeleton is gracile and there are septal apertures on both humeri. Maximum femoral head diameters are: left 39 mm, right 38.5 mm, with both vertical diameters of the humeri being 37 mm. These fall well within expected ranges for females (Buikstra and Mielke 1985). The supra-orbital region of the skull supports this diagnosis, although the bilateral chin, the supra-meatal crest, and to a lesser extent the mastoid processes appear robust and therefore masculine.

An age-at-death estimate of 22–29 years is based upon the morphology of the pubic symphysis which was scored to the following stages: Todd 3–4; Suchey-Brooks 2; Lovejoy 2 (Buikstra and Ubelaker 1994; Lovejoy et al. 1985; Suchey and Katz 1986; Suchey et al. 1984; Todd 1921a, 1921b, 1921c). The clavicular epiphyses are fused, and all tooth roots, including those of the 3rd molars, are complete. Epiphyseal lines are visible on most long bones. A previous diagnosis of this skeleton as male and aged between 35 and 50 (Williamson 1996:173) is not tenable in view of the skeletal characteristics described here.

As indicated in Table 10.1, the Motmot remains are estimated to have been between 146 and 168.5 cm in stature. This is slightly (but not significantly) taller than the Margarita Tomb female and the four females measured by Tiesler Blos (1999).

A healed midshaft fracture of the right ulna and perhaps of the proximal right humerus at the surgical neck are the only notable forms of skeletal pathology. Both fractures were either effectively reduced or were incomplete, as no shortening or significant distortion is present. A single example of occlusal surface caries is present on the distal half of the lower right second molar. Dental wear had exposed a slight amount of dentin on the incisors and the mesial cusps of the lower 1st molars.

In general, the post-cranial remains are quite gracile, with areas of muscle attachment only slightly developed, e.g., the deltoid tuberosities and the linea aspera. The vertebral border of the scapulae is straight to concave. The bones are not, however, thinned or osteoporotic as one might expect in the case of chronic illness. This sug-

---

[*] Williamson (1996:173) reports four cervical vertebrae. Five were present.

gests that the principal individual buried in the Motmot Tomb simply did not lead an active life.

As noted above, adult human skulls and neck vertebrae accompanied other offerings within the Motmot Tomb. One of the three skulls (37-10) presents evidence for cutmarks on the ventral and lateral aspects of the 5th cervical vertebrae. While other archaeological evidence suggests that rituals involving fire occurred within the Motmot Tomb (Fash et al., this volume), none of the remains conform to classic definitions of calcination or smoking, which occurs at approximate 800°C and 200–300°C, respectively (Buikstra and Swegle 1989; Shipman et al. 1984; van Vark 1974).

Burial 95-1

Interred at approximately the same time as the Margarita entombment, ca. A.D. 450, the individual in Burial 95-1 was buried with cut shell "goggles," and other artifacts that explicitly link him to central Mexico (Sharer 1997b; Sharer, Traxler, et al. 1999). These remains were observed *in situ*; the skull was removed for further study. The corpse had been interred in an extended position, laid on its back but shifted slightly onto its left side.

The Burial 95-1 remains are those of a robust male, apparently over 40 years of age. This age estimate should be considered tentative, as it is based upon the fact that the cranium did not fracture along the frontal, sagittal, or lambdoid suture lines. The teeth are only slightly worn, and an epiphyseal line persists on the right femur. The pelvic and cranial structures are unequivocally masculine, including a narrow greater sciatic notch, narrow sub-pubic angle, well-developed areas of muscle attachment on the skull, prominent mastoid processes and supra-orbital region. An estimate of the femur head diameter is 45 mm, which is well within the expected range for a male.

Although his mean stature estimate is less than that of K'inich Yax K'uk' Mo', there is considerable overlap of their ranges, as expressed by the 95% confidence interval (Table 10.1). His only marked skeletal pathology comprised an enlarged callus formation on the right ulna that indicates a healed parry fracture.

Burial 94-1

The individual in Burial 94-1 was interred adjacent to the ultimate entry to the Margarita Tomb, probably at the time that the "long-enduring entry into the Margarita Tomb was finally closed and sealed, about A.D. 465" (Sharer 1997b). The body had been interred seated, in a tightly flexed bundle. These remains were observed in the field.

The Burial 94-1 remains were those of a robust male, whose left femur head had a maximum diameter of at least 48 mm. The central incisors show heavy wear, although only enamel facets appear on the molars. He was probably at least 30–40 years of age at death. The absence of degenerative changes suggest that 40–50 years of age is an appropriate upper limit for an age-at-death estimate.

Burial 92-1 (Teal Burial)

The individual in Burial 92-1 was interred farther to the north of the royal tombs. He was placed at the base of a more recent early Acropolis facade, ca. A.D. 480 (Sharer 1997b). These remains are very fragmentary, except for the dentition, which is well preserved. The postcranial skeleton is quite rugose, with an estimated maximum femur head diameter of 47 mm, well within the male range (Buikstra and Mielke 1985).

The anterior teeth are more heavily worn than the posterior. All observable epiphyses appear to have been fused, although the 3rd molar root tips are not complete. An appropriate age-at-death estimate is 18–25 years, probably at the upper end of this range, given the apparent skeletal maturation.

Sub-Jaguar Tomb (Burial 92-2)

An elaborate tomb attributed to Ruler 8 (or possibly Ruler 9) was located within later construction episodes and to the north of the earlier royal tombs (Plate 8; Bell et al., this volume; Sharer et al. 1992, 1999b; Traxler 1994, 1997). Ruler 8 died in A.D. 551, with his immediate successor ruling for only two years (Bell et al., this volume)

The remains from the Sub-Jaguar Tomb were extremely fragmentary, even for the dentition. Tooth crowns had become separated from the roots. The skull is quite robust, with a bilateral chin, suggesting that the remains may represent a male. The skull did not break along any of the posterior vault sutures. Dental wear on the anterior teeth and extreme calculus formation support an estimated age-at-death in advance of 35 years.

Linear enamel defects on the upper central incisors and the upper left canine are consistent with childhood developmental stress at approximately 1.5 and 3.5 years of age (Rose et al. 1985). A series of hypoplastic bands on the canine indicates a series of stressful events between 3.6 and 6 years of age. There is a single example of occlusal surface caries on the distal half of the lower right 1st molar.

Comparative Analyses

While dental observations are not complete at this time, the preliminary data reported here for the Early Classic remains contrast with the Late Classic "commoner" materials reported by Whittington (1989). Only two caries were recorded, contrasting with Whittington's (1989:261) observation that 68.2% of his non-elite adults present evidence of caries. In addition, he reports that fully 37.7% of the molar teeth were carious among individuals who lived more than 35 years. The materials from the Acropolis are therefore distinctive in their lack of caries. Calculus formation, pronounced on the lingual aspect of the lower anterior teeth, is widespread in the Early Classic sample and is especially prominent in the Hunal, Burial 95-1, and Sub-Jaguar remains. With the exception of the relatively recent Sub-Jaguar interment, linear enamel hypoplasias (LEH) were not observed. By contrast, Whittington reports that among his sample, such defects were ubiquitous. Storey (1985, as cited by Whittington 1989) describes status-related differences within a single site, with the more elaborate interments presenting less evidence of LEH.

Dental wear seems relatively minor, even in the older adults. While systematic comparisons have yet to be made, the dental attributes observed here suggest that the Early Classic elites consumed a relatively soft diet with less cariogenic potential than that for later groups. Differences in food preparation as well as the foods themselves may be implicated, as could genetic differences. Further study is required to select the appropriate suite of causal agents for the apparent contrast.

These Early Classic remains also present no evidence of periostosis, with the exception of a minor amount seen on the distal tibiae of the Hunal skeleton. While observations were limited by taphonomic factors, a virtual absence of such changes contrasts with Whittington's (1989:325) observation that over 25% of his Late Classic materials presented evidence of periosteal remodeling. The presence of three "parry fractures" in the seven remains from the Acropolis also departs markedly from Whittington's (1989:363–365) observation that there was only one such fracture in his sample. He reports that only one other parry fracture has been reported for ancient Maya materials. Apparently the Early Classic elite enjoyed relatively good health, though they were at risk for certain forms of trauma.

Residential Histories

Ongoing archaeological controversy surrounds the degree to which Teotihuacan and the other Classic Maya centers influenced the development of the Classic period dynasty at Copan. "Influence" can, of course, take many direct and indirect forms and, archaeologically, is generally read in terms of architectural and artifactual similarities, and through epigraphy, and iconography (see Fash and Fash 2000; Stuart 2000 for recent discussions of this issue in reference to Copan).

For Early Classic Copan, there are clear architectural and artifactual links to the Valley of Mexico, with K'inich Yax K'uk' Mo's title "Lord of the West" providing confirmation of Ruler 1's probable origin at Teotihuacan for some scholars (Fash and Fash 2000). Yet the artifacts from the Hunal Tomb reflect much more dispersed stylistic associations, including ties to highland Mexico, the Central Petén, highland Guatemala, and even the southeastern Maya region (Bell et al. 2000). The movement of concepts and objects is therefore documented, while that of people is implied.

For example, the following scenarios for K'inich Yax K'uk' Mo' could be proposed:

1. He spent his childhood in the Valley of Mexico.
2. He spent his childhood elsewhere and "apprenticed" in the Valley of Mexico.

3. He spent his childhood elsewhere and emulated attributes characteristic of the Valley of Mexico upon arrival in Copan.
4. He spent his childhood within the Copan pocket and emulated attributes characteristic of the Valley of Mexico.

Each of these models holds different implications for the origins of the Copan dynasty and the nature of external political relationships. Thus, the residential histories of K'inich Yax K'uk' Mo' and others interred within the Copan Acropolis can provide insight crucial for interpreting the nature of external influence upon the early dynastic period. This is possible through bone chemistry: the study of stable strontium and oxygen isotope ratios within skeletal and dental tissues.

Ratios of stable strontium isotopes ^{87}Sr and ^{86}Sr in soils and ground water vary systematically according to the age and composition of bedrock. Animals fix these ratios in their tissues without fractionation, through the consumption of water and foods grown on local soils. Dental enamel that forms during childhood reflects signatures for residence during youth, while bone, which is remodeled throughout life, rep-

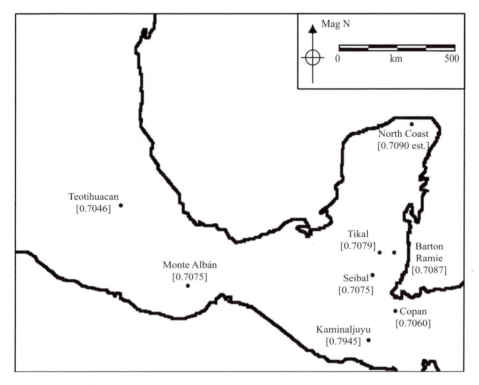

Figure 10.6 Map illustrating Strontium Isotope Ratios in Ancient Mesoamerica.

resents the final years of an individual's life (Ericson 1985; Price, Grupe, and Schrörter 1994, 1998; Price, Johnson, Ezzo, Ericson, and Burton 1994; Price et al. 2000; Sealy et al. 1991). The varied geological histories for the bedrock that anchored the ancient Maya world make this an ideal context for reconstructing individual and population mobility.

For example, as illustrated in Figure 10.6, previous research has isolated systematic differences in local $^{87}Sr/^{86}Sr$ signatures for remains from Copan, Seibal, Barton Ramie, Monte Alban, and the Valley of Mexico (Krueger 1985; Price et al. 2000). We also have unpublished data for Tikal and Kaminaljuyu and can estimate strontium isotope ratios for the northern Petén and Yucatan based upon bedrock age (Burke et al. 1982; Palmer and Elderfield 1985). $^{87}Sr/^{86}Sr$ values from the Petén and Oaxaca are higher than those from Copan; values for Kaminaljuyu and the Valley of Mexico are lower.

By contrast, the relative abundance of the stable isotopes of oxygen, designated as $\delta^{18}O$ ratios, are determined by rainfall patterns and climate. Skeletal tissues record the $\delta^{18}O$ of body water as they form and reflect the average $\delta^{18}O$ of all water sources imbibed at that time (Bryant and Froelich 1995; Longinelli 1984). After forming clouds over the oceans by evaporation, the first rain to fall as weather systems move over land is heavy with $\delta^{18}O$. Thus, the precipitation that falls on landlocked continental and rain shadow areas often has a lower $\delta^{18}O$ than that of coastal areas. The local $\delta^{18}O$ of water imbibed by the inhabitants of a given site depends on the cumulative effects of multiple weather systems that move across the landscape, as well as other climatic variables. Cultural practices, such as long-term water storage, cooking, diet, and breastfeeding, can also influence the $\delta^{18}O$ of human skeletal tissues (Bryant and Froelich 1996; Wright and Schwarcz 1998).

For Mesoamerica, stable oxygen isotope ratios have been measured for bone phosphate of skeletons from Teotihuacan and Monte Alban (White et al. 1998) and for enamel carbonate of skeletons from Tikal, Topoxte, and Kaminaljuyu (Wright and Schwarcz 1998, 1999; Valdés and Wright, this volume; Wright, unpublished data). Sites in the Maya lowlands, like Tikal, have the highest oxygen isotope ratios measured to date in Mesoamerica. As the prevailing weather systems come from the Caribbean, highland sites show lower $\delta^{18}O$. Values for enamel from Kaminaljuyu are somewhat lower than for the Petén and are followed by Teotihuacan and Monte Alban. Because oxygen isotopes in bone are determined by rainfall patterns and can be affected by climate change, we expect broad areas to share similar ratios. Regional variability in oxygen ratios for Mesoamerica has not yet been adequately mapped, but the limited data do help to constrain the origins of the Copan skeletons.

We have generated both $^{87}Sr/^{86}Sr$ and $\delta^{18}O$ values for teeth formed in early childhood (incisors or 1st molars) from five Copan skeletons (Table 10.2). These tissues reflect residence from birth to approximately 3-4 years of age (Hillson 1996). For the Margarita remains, we had to substitute a 1st premolar, which forms slightly later, at 2-6 years (Hillson 1996). We have not yet sampled an anterior tooth from the

Table 10.2 Stable Strontium and Oxygen Isotopic Composition of Bone and Enamel Samples from Copan

Skeleton	Sample	$^{87}Sr/^{86}Sr$	$\partial^{18}O$
Hunal Tomb(Burial 95-2)	L Fibula	0.70633	
Hunal Tomb(Burial 95-2)	L mandibular I2	0.70788	-3.2
Hunal Tomb(Burial 95-2)	L mandibular M1	0.70844	-3.4
Hunal Tomb(Burial 95-2)	R maxillary M3	0.70736	-4.0
Margarita Tomb (Burial 93-2)	L Tibia	0.70634	
Margarita Tomb (Burial 93-2)	R mandibular M3	0.70684	-5.0
Margarita Tomb (Burial 93-2)	L mandibular P3	0.70717	-4.5
MotMot Tomb (Burial 37-8)	L maxillary M3	0.70763	-1.6
Burial 95-1	R Ulna	0.70633	
Burial 95-1	L mandibular M1	0.70909	-2.2
Burial 95-1	L mandibular M3	0.70715	-2.7
Burial 94-1	Long bone	0.70630	
Burial 94-1	R maxillary I1	0.70711	-5.1
Burial 94-1	R mandibular M1	0.70686	-5.2
Burial 94-1	L mandibular M3	0.70685	-5.8
Burial 92-1	R Radius	0.70640	
Burial 92-1	R mandibular M1	0.70688	-3.3
Burial 92-1	R mandibular M3	0.70687	-4.0
Sub-Jaguar Tomb (Burial 92-2)	Rib	0.70683	
Sub-Jaguar Tomb (Burial 92-2)	R maxillary I1	0.70681	-1.0
Sub-Jaguar Tomb (Burial 92-2)	R maxillary M1	0.70688	-1.2
Sub-Jaguar Tomb (Burial 92-2)	L mandibular M3	0.70682	-6.0

Oxygen isotope ratios are in units permil PDB.

Motmot interment. For all seven skeletons, we report results from 3rd molar crowns, which form during late childhood and early adolescence, 9–12.5 years (Hillson 1996). For all individuals except the Motmot remains, we also report $^{87}Sr/^{86}Sr$ results from bone, which reflects relatively recent residence. We report $\delta^{18}O$ data for the enamel carbonate of 1st molars for five skeletons, the Margarita premolar, and 3rd molars for all seven skeletons. Analytical procedures for both strontium[*] and oxygen[†] isotope analyses are presented in the endnotes. Several significant results emerge from our summary data.

---

[*] The analytic procedures for strontium isotope analysis are as follows: each bone sample was mechanically abraded with a Dremel tool fitted with a sanding bit to remove any visible dirt and/or preservative. Tooth samples were drilled to remove the enamel layer from the underlying dentine. Samples were then placed in sterile plastic vials and sonicated in deionized (18 megaohm) water for 15 minutes. After rinsing, each vial was filled with 5% ultrapure acetic acid and placed in a drying oven at 80°C for approximately 24 hours. Dilute acetic acid dissolves not only the soluble carbonates but also that portion of the bone mineral that is most likely to have been contaminated by interaction with diagenetic fluids. After drying, samples were transferred to sterile silica glass tubes that have been soaked in hot ultrapure, concentrated nitric acid and were ashed in a muffle furnace at 825°C for 8 hours.

Bone and tooth enamel ash samples were then transferred to sterile savilex digestion vials and hot-digested in ultrapure concentrated nitric acid, dried in a sterile laminar flow drying box, and redissolved in ultrapure 2.5 N hydrochloric acid. This procedure may be repeated if there are any trace organics remaining in the sample. Strontium was then isolated using cation exchange chromatography with 2.5 N hydrochloric acid as the mobile phase.

Samples were mounted on zone-refined tantalum filaments, and strontium was analyzed using a thermal ionization multiple collector mass spectrometer (TIMS). $^{87}Sr/^{86}Sr$ ratios were corrected for mass fractionation in the instrument using the exponential mass fractionation law and $^{87}Sr/^{86}Sr$ - 0.1194. The samples were measured using a Micromass Sector 54 spectrometer. $^{87}Sr/^{86}Sr$ analyses (n = 40) of the NIST SRM strontium carbonate yielded a value of 0.710259±0.0003 (2 SE). Internal precision (standard error) for the samples analyzed ant UNC-CH is typically 0.000006 to 0.000010, based on 100 dynamic cycles of data collection.

[†] Stable oxygen isotope ratios were obtained from tooth enamel prepared as follows: samples of enamel approximately 2mm wide and spanning from cusp to cemento-enamel junction were removed from each tooth using a Foredom saw. Enamel sections were cleaned of surface contamination both mechanically and by rinsing with dilute HCl. First molar samples were then cut into three transverse sections, each 2 mm in height as measured along the dento-enamel junction. Data reported here correspond to the midcoronal section. Third molar and premolar samples were not divided into subsamples.

Enamel was ground using an agate mortar and pestle and passed through a 50 μm sieve. Organic components were removed by soaking the enamel overnight in 1 ml of 1.5% solution of sodium hypochlorite, after which the enamel was rinsed three times with distilled water. Diagenetic carbonates were removed by soaking the enamel in 1 ml of 1M acetic acid (pH4.5 sodium acetate buffer) for 1 hour, with periodic agitation. Enamel was then rinsed to neutrality with distilled water and dried at 70°C.

Stable isotope ratios were measured in the Department of Geology & Geophysics at TAMU. Enamel was reacted with orthophosphoric acid at 80°C for 12 minutes in individual reaction chambers of a Kiel II carbonate device, with sample gasses fed directly to a Finnegan MAT 251 mass spectrometer. Isotope ratios were corrected to PDB by comparison with aliquots of the carbonate standard NBS19 that were analyzed with each sample run.

First, all bone sampled present $^{87}Sr/^{86}Sr$ values near 0.7063 and indicate residence at Copan during the final years of each skeleton's life. Several of the dental values also suggest a local childhood, although tooth enamel is systematically offset from bone, near 0.7069. Specifically, both the strontium and oxygen indicate that the Burial 92-1 and Burial 94-1 individuals lived near Copan all their lives. The $\delta^{18}O$ values for the teeth from these individuals suggest a rainfall composition at Copan similar to that at Kaminaljuyu. For five skeletons, the 1st molar samples are about 0.7‰ higher in $\delta^{18}O$ than 3rd molars due to nursing during infancy (Wright and Schwarcz 1998).

As a child, the person interred in the Margarita Tomb may have lived away from the Copan Pocket, as suggested by her slightly higher $^{87}Sr/^{86}Sr$ value, although the $\delta^{18}O$ figure is consistent with Copan. By her adolescent years when the M3 formed, she was in residence near Copan. In contrast, the Sub-Jaguar interment shows equivalent $^{87}Sr/^{86}Sr$ values in M1 and M3, indicating a local residence throughout life. But his M1 $\delta^{18}O$ figure is dramatically higher than the M3. Since comparable values were obtained for the central incisor from this individual, the difference is not diagenetic and may indicate that this royal infant consumed water from a source distinct from other Copanecos.

The female interred in the Motmot Tomb shows a relatively high $^{87}Sr/^{86}Sr$ value in the M3, associated with a high $\delta^{18}O$ value. Both are consistent with preliminary data for Tikal and the Central Petén as well as Seibal.

The individual in Burial 95-1 was also raised at a distant site. Despite his characteristic goggles, his childhood $^{87}Sr/^{86}Sr$ value is not that of the Valley of Mexico but rather resembles that of Barton Ramie and the values that we expect for bedrock from Campeche and Yucatan, which underlie sites such as Calakmul and Dzbilchaltun. His $\delta^{18}O$ figures also support a Yucatec or Petén origin. He, too, had moved closer to Copan by adolescence.

The remains from the Hunal Tomb, attributed to K'inich Yax K'uk' Mo', present a childhood $^{87}Sr/^{86}Sr$ value (M1) slightly higher than local values from Tikal, Seibal, and Monte Alban and lower than the values for Campeche and Yucatan. The $\delta^{18}O$ of this tooth indicates that he spent his childhood in the central Maya Lowlands and that he could not have come from the Valley of Oaxaca (Monte Alban). He, too, apparently moved closer to Copan by adolescence. His M3 $^{87}Sr/^{86}Sr$ value might indicate either that he migrated at roughly 11 years of age when the M3 was forming or that he resided at a third location at this age.

Based on the identification of the Founder as the occupant of the Hunal Tomb, these results indicate that K'inich Yax K'uk' Mo' did not spend his youth in the Valley of Mexico, nor was he of local origin. Thus, we can dismiss scenarios 1 and 4 outlined above. With these data, we cannot ascertain whether or not he served a brief apprenticeship at Teotihuacan during a period not reflected in his isotope values. A second "foreigner" is clearly the individual in Burial 95-1, whose shell goggles and other artifacts belie years spent in the Petén or Yucatan, not Teotihuacan. Finally, the female skeleton in the Motmot Tomb also appears to have spent her childhood and adolescence in the Petén and perhaps provides evidence for long-distance exchange of royal marriage partners (Molloy and Rathje 1974). The identification of foreign elites within the Copan Acropolis contrasts with the pattern reported by White et al. (2000) and Valdés and Wright (this volume) for Kaminaljuyu. By comparing oxygen isotope ratios among skeletons, they identify key elite skeletons as those of local individuals who adopted foreign symbols. Foreign skeletons at Kaminaljuyu are primarily sacrificial victims. The situation at Copan is clearly different and more complex.

Conclusions

A bioarchaeological life-history or osteobiographic approach has enriched our knowledge of Early Classic Copan. Based on the identification of the remains in the Hunal Tomb, we have learned that Ruler 1, K'inich Yax K'uk' Mo', spent his formative years to the north, not the west, as interpretations of material culture, inscriptions, and monumental architecture might lead us to believe. Together with the chemistry of his boyhood home in the central Petén, his body had also absorbed abundant evidence of the combative politics which anchored the Early Classic Maya world. His long life included violent episodes, whose healed skeletal scars suggest wounds sustained upon the battlefield or perhaps the ballcourt. Dental evidence of elite status would have been obvious to those with whom he spoke or upon whom he smiled.

Also in apparent contradiction to written evidence, the remains recovered from the Margarita Tomb are those of a female who lived to an advanced age. Aside from minor arthritic change, she apparently led an active life and enjoyed good health. In addition to her elaborate grave and its abundant funerary artifacts, her dentition also bore evidence of elite status. While she may not have spent her childhood in the Copan Pocket, she apparently grew up nearby.

The female recovered from the Motmot Tomb, accompanied by the skulls of three male sacrifices, died during young adulthood. She, too, was not of local origin, nor had she led an active life. Her skeleton bore evidence of an earlier traumatic event, sustained during her youthful years and well healed by the time of her death.

While Burial 95-1 presents material evidence that would place him in the Valley of Mexico, his isotopic signatures link his childhood to the Yucatan or Petén. Dying during his later adult years, he had sustained a parry fracture that had healed by the time of his death.

Two of the more humble interments, Burial 94-1 and Burial 92-1 had apparently lived near Copan all their lives. Both these remains were extremely robust. The individual in Burial 94-1 died during his middle adult years, Burial 92-1, during young adulthood.

The most recent of the burials, recovered from the elaborate Sub-Jaguar Tomb, presents conflicting isotopic signatures. While his strontium isotope values would place him in Copan, the Sub-Jaguar interment's oxygen isotope signature suggest a distant water source. Only he, of all the remains studied here, shows evidence of ill health during his early childhood years. In this way, he more closely resembles later Classic "commoners" from more recent, dispersed Classic Copan communities. Even with such youthful stress, he lived to middle age.

We have in this chapter used skeletal evidence to examine the life histories of Early Classic Copan residents. The scars of battle have been exposed, as has evidence of youthful health status. Alternative models for residential histories link three "foreigners" with northern sites such as Tikal, Barton Ramie, Seibal, and even Calakmul and Dzibilchaltun. Apprenticeships at Kaminaljuyu, Monte Albán, or in the Valley of Mexico are not reflected in these bones. Our perspective on Early Copan's political, social, and economic history is thus enhanced, as we explore the humanity of its residents.

Acknowledgments

The research reported here has benefited from support by the National Geographic Society the National Science Foundation, and Texas A&M University. Permission for study has been granted by the Instituto Hondureño de Antropología y Historia and by Robert J. Sharer and William L. Fash of the Copan Acropolis Archaeological Project. The assistance of Ellen Bell, Marcello Canuto, Lynn Grant, Christopher Powell, David Sedat, and Loa Traxler has been essential to the success of the project.

IV The Epigraphy and Iconography of Early Classic Copan

11

THE BEGINNINGS OF THE COPAN DYNASTY: A REVIEW OF THE HIEROGLYPHIC AND HISTORICAL EVIDENCE

David Stuart

Until recently the study of Copan's early dynastic history was little more than a speculative exercise, due in large part to the poor condition of the inscriptions. Stone monuments from before the reign of Ruler 10 (inaugurated on 9.5.19.3.0, A.D. 553) tend to be incomplete and fragmented, having been intentionally broken in the Classic period and often reused as ancient construction material in the Principal Group as well as in the modern town. Only since 1987 have excavations revealed more complete and better-preserved inscriptions from the Early Classic, providing a far more workable documentary record from Copan's earliest years as a major political and ritual center. The results of these interdisciplinary efforts now provide key archaeological contexts and evidence for understanding Copan's historical development, as well as the varied stories of the rulers who oversaw its initial growth. In this chapter, I offer an overview of the early written record of Copan, extending, modifying, and building upon earlier discussions of the lives and works of Copan's first kings (Fash 1991; Martin and Grube 2000; Schele 1990b; Schele and Freidel 1990; Sharer, Traxler, et al. 1999; Stuart 1992, 2000; Stuart and Schele 1986b).

Although the scope of this chapter is ostensibly the earliest years of Copan's dynastic history, it is necessary to cover a far longer time span, beginning with the obscure "pre-dynastic" era. The pivotal figure in this history is of course K'inich Yax K'uk' Mo' ("Great Sun, Green Quetzal Macaw"), the celebrated "founder" of Copan's Classic period dynasty (Stuart and Schele 1986) who became the subject of an elaborate ancestral cult that seems to have dominated Copan's religious art and architecture for the rest of the Classic period. As the varied chapters in this volume demonstrate, his intriguing associations with Teotihuacan can be detected through epigraphy, iconography, and archaeology (but see Buikstra et al., this volume). We can fairly say that K'inich Yax K'uk' Mo' has emerged from such varied evidence as one of the most intriguing and unusual individuals in ancient Mesoamerican history. The present study proposes several new hieroglyphic readings and text translations critical to a better understanding of the rise of Copan's polity and the nature of its apparent central Mexican connections in the early 5th century.

The Pre-Dynastic Era

Copan's pre-dynastic era can be defined as the time prior to the accession of K'inich Yax K'uk' Mo' (on 8.19.10.10.17, or September 6, A.D. 426) and the ensuing political and cultural transformations his rule triggered. The individual events comprising this earlier history are highly scattered and difficult to connect, but they nonetheless indicate that Late Classic Copan kings and scribes had recollections of a local history of considerable time depth (Fash and Stuart 1991; Stuart 1992). Copan's archaeological record is certainly ancient enough to accommodate these recalled events, although it remains difficult to assign any prominent architectural remains in the valley to pre-dynastic times.

Historically, Copan's pre-dynastic period is defined by only six dates, all from Late Classic inscriptions:

7.1.13.15.0	9 Ajaw 13 Kumk'u	October 14, 321 B.C.
8.6.0.0.0	10 Ajaw 8 Ch'en	December 18, A.D. 159
8.6.0.10.8	10 Lamat 16 Pop	July 13, A.D. 160
8.10.10.10.16	9 Kib 4 Pax	April 6, A.D. 249
8.17.0.0.0	1 Ajaw 8 Ch'en	October 21, A.D. 376
8.19.0.0.0	10 Ajaw 13 K'ayab	March 25, A.D. 416

The first of these dates, from Altar I', immediately stands out as arguably too early to be considered part of Copan's pre-dynastic history. Curiously, no event phrase or name accompanies the isolated reference; it is stated simply as a "just-so" date, as if the reader of the text had previous knowledge of its significance (Stuart 1992). It is also very possible that "9 Ajaw 13 Cumk'u" held some cosmological or mythical meaning beyond the precocious local history of Copan.[*]

Two other dates, 8.6.0.0.0 and 8.6.0.10.8, fall several centuries later and could be considered the first historically grounded events from Copan's pre-dynastic period. The K'atun ending is recorded in two Late Classic inscriptions from the Main Plaza, Stelae I and 4, and seems to have been especially significant. The inscription on Stela 4 (see W. Fash 1991:fig. 41) is difficult to read in many respects, yet a few interesting terms and phrases stand out. After the record of the K'atun ending an unreadable verb at B3a is followed by 4-TE'-CHAN, *chan-te' chan*, "the four heavens," suggesting a topic

---

[*] It could well be significant that each of the numerical coefficients on 9 Ajaw 13 Kumk'u are five positions above the Calendar Round of the 13.0.0.0.0 creation date, 4 Ajaw 8 Kumk'u.

Figure 11.1 Passage from Copan Stela I, describing early events
(drawing by Barbara W. Fash).

Figure 11.2 Passage from Tikal Stela 31
(drawing by David Stuart).

of some cosmological importance.[*] Another verb phrase recorded at B4 is more readable as CH'AM-[?] IK'-HU'N, being the verb root *ch'am* "to take, receive" with an object *ik' hu'n*, possibly "black headband." This curious statement is followed, in turn, by a place name written chi-?-a (A5a), which specifies the location of the K'atun ending event.

Many of these same elements occur in a parallel citation of 8.6.0.0.0 on Stela I (Figure 11.1). The text on the right side of the monument states that on this day and at the same location mentioned in Stela 4, "6 K'atuns ended" and that it was governed by a ruler named K'INICH-ya-?-na. The inscription goes on to mention 8.6.0.10.8 10 Lamat 16 Pop, a date falling 208 days later. Sadly, the event of the next block is completely effaced, but in the final glyph we find the bat of the Copan Emblem Glyph followed by CHAN-CH'EEN, "sky and cave." This last portion is a frequent ending on place names in the Classic texts, as here, and I believe it carries the sense of "universe" through two opposed spaces—something along the lines of "the realms above and the realms below."

The bat of the Copan emblem glyph does not function here just as a place name. Rather, it serves to name a political or territorial unit, much like emblem glyphs of other important centers. It is important to note that very little space is available in the penultimate block for a verb phrase and a personal name; it could have held no more than "16 Pop" in the first half and a single verbal glyph in the second, without any personal subject. The fact that the Copan bat emblem remains is a strong indication that the effaced verb was some simply expressed action or event concerning the polity. Schele and I have felt that there is enough circumstantial evidence present to suggest that this passage recorded a key event in the advent of Copan's political identity, perhaps even a time of a formal "foundation" of the bat polity (Schele 1987b; Stuart 1992).[†]

The place glyph given on Stelae 4 and I with the 8.6.0.0.0 K'atun ending remains unidentified, but it seems to be a foreign locale, possibly in the central Petén region. We find the same place (hereafter referred to as the "Bent Kawak" glyph) cited on Tikal Stela 31 (Figure 11.2) where it appears near the end of a partially missing passage commemorating an unknown K'atun that occurred sometime before 8.14.0.0.0 (A.D. 317), recorded in the subsequent passage.

---

[*] The same verb phrase is repeated later in connection with the contemporary date 9.14.15.0.0—evidently to highlight some special repetitive quality shared between the two dates, separated by 1.18.5.0.0.

[†] Dates this early are of course extremely rare in Maya inscriptions. Stela 25 from Naranjo bears the Initial Series 8.5.18.4.0 7 Ajaw 3 K'ank'in, which came less than two years before the K'atun ending cited at Copan. This too may be some sort of "foundation" event for Naranjo, but the damaged text after the date prevents any more speculation on the matter. It is interesting that the Copan and Naranjo dates are contemporaneous with a fairly narrow cluster of dates found on several pre-Classic monuments from coastal Guatemala and Veracruz: Abaj Takalik Stela 5 (8.2.2.10.5 and 8.4.5.17.11), La Mojarra Stela 1 (8.5.3.3.5 and 8.5.16.9.7), the Tuxtla Statuette (8.6.2.4.17), and Chiapa de Corzo Stela 2 (8.7.3.2.13?).

Figure 11.3 Masonry blocks from Structure 10L-7 doorjamb
(drawing by David Stuart).

Several Period Endings are recorded on Stela 31, all associated with their own distinctive place glyphs (Stuart and Houston 1994:fig.58). Because Tikal rulers presided over these ceremonies, I have long assumed that the named locations, including the one cited at Copan, refer to communities, site areas, or temples in the vicinity of Tikal.[*]

Significantly, references to the "Bent Kawak" place at both Copan and Tikal accompany extremely early historical records. Another example, at Yaxchilan, occurs with the name of its local dynastic "founder," Yopaat Balam (Schele 1992). I find it fas-

---

[*] This may seem a rash assumption, for it is entirely possible that Stela 31 records its K'atun endings in a way similar to chronicles from Late Postclassic Yucatan, when the "seats" of the K'atuns shifted from town to town and over large distances. Much of the epigraphic evidence on this remains vague, due to the difficulty of identifying place glyphs with actual locales, but such an interpretation is well worth future consideration.

The Tikal ruler who oversaw this distant and obscure Period Ending is nicknamed "Foliated Jaguar" by Martin and Grube (2000:26). His name glyph shares the same "three-leaves Ajaw" found with the name of the early Stela I ruler at Copan, which seems suggestive of some connection between them.

Figure 11.4 Central medallion of the peccary skull
(drawing by Barbara W. Fash).

cinating that Copan's supposed "foundation" event on Stela I, whatever its nature, came 208 days after the Period Ending at a distant location. Might this span have represented some travel period from the "Bent Kawak" location to Copan? Little more can be said until the Bent Kawak place is better identified, but the evidence does at least indicate that the early ruler named on Stela I was not a Copan lord by origin. Copan's explicit historical connections to the Petén could have come as early as 8.6.0.0.0— nearly 280 years before the time of a far better-known political "outsider," K'inich Yax K'uk Mo'.

A previously unrecognized pre-dynastic date was inscribed on the doorjamb of Structure 10L-7 (Figure 11.3), a small building opposite Structure 10L-26 that faces east onto the court of the Hieroglyphic Stairway. This is a Late Classic construction but the doorjamb text cites the far earlier Long Count date 8.10.10.10.16 (the K'in glyph

Figure 11.5 Copan Stela 15, right side
(drawing by David Stuart).

is missing, but reconstructable), which corresponds to a day in A.D. 249. This inscription survives in only a few masonry blocks from the two doorjambs, and is therefore incomplete. No event or name appears on any of the remaining portions of the original text, but a Calendar Round cited elsewhere in the same inscription, 8 Ajaw 3 Zotz', surely corresponds to the accession date of Ruler 10, 9.5.19.3.0, also given on the Hieroglyphic Stairway. Presumably the other blocks of this important inscription await excavation near the front slope of Structure 10L-7.

One other possible reference to early Copan history comes from the famous peccary skull excavated from Tomb 1. Within the central medallion engraved on the skull (Figure 11.4), two lords face the representation of a stela and altar—one of a few such representations in all of Maya art. Four hieroglyphs above the monument begin with the date "1 Ajaw 8 Ch'en." The associated event—*k'altuun* (K'AL-TUUN-ni), "stone binding"—must be the K'atun ending 8.17.0.0.0 (the carving style on the peccary skull seems later, however). The fourth and last glyph is the "foliated ajaw" sign, by now familiar from the name of the very early ruler who oversaw the period Ending 8.6.0.0.0 cited on Stela I (despite the overlap in the names, the rulers are of course different individuals, overseeing K'atuns separated by 220 years).

The specific identities of the seated figures are probably given in their "glyphic" or "emblematic" headdresses. The man at right sits upon a jaguar cushion with his body facing the viewer, and is probably the higher ranking of the two. He wears a jaguar-like head as his headdress, atop the royal headband. The figure at left gestures directly at the monument and/or the enthroned ruler and wears a macaw head above his own royal headband. This approximates the pre-accession name of the founder: K'uk' Mo' Ajaw (Quetzal-Macaw Lord) as recorded on Altar Q. 8.17.0.0.0 would certainly be an early date for K'uk' Mo' Ajaw, falling about fifty years before his accession day, but not an impossibility, given that we have no record of his age at any point in history.

Aside from such speculations, there is good reason to believe that K'inich Yax K'uk' Mo' was indeed present at Copan before his supposed arrival and "inauguration" date. Stela 15 cites 8.19.0.0.0, a K'atun ending that predates the accession of K'inich Yax K'uk' Mo' by over a decade (Figure 11.5). The tantalizing reference is of great importance, for Stela 15 was carved on a much later Period Ending (9.4.10.0.0) during the reign of the seventh king, Balam Nehn (previously nicknamed "Waterlily Jaguar"). The text is incomplete, but it clearly lists several Period Endings leading up to the contemporary station, thereby emphasizing ritual continuity and a "like-and-kind" history that harkens back to pre-dynastic times. We will revisit the implications of the Stela 15 inscription below when we consider the question of K'inich Yax K'uk' Mo's ethnic identity and place of origin.

Finally, I would hazard to offer one other very speculative observation about Copan's pre-dynastic history. One of the earliest "glyphs" from Copan may exist as a stucco mask decorating the substructure of Yehnal (Figure 11.6a), an early structure

a

b

c

Figure 11.6 Examples of K'inich Taj Wayib name.
(a) Yehnal mask, (b) GIII name at Palenque,
(c) step from Copan Structure 10L-11-sub.

within the Acropolis constructed at roughly the time of K'inich Yax K'uk' Mo' (Sedat and López, this volume; Sharer, this volume). The well-preserved southern mask is essentially glyphic in its structure, showing the Sun God (K'INICH) wearing two hiero-glyphic signs on his head—an arrangement often found in emblematic names of K'inich Yax K'uk' Mo' and his son, Ruler 2. Above the Sun God is a large WAY sign flanked by a pair of torchlike devices (glyphic TAJ), components that quickly recall the name K'inich Taj Wayib (written K'INICH-TAJ-WAY-bi), cited on Palenque's Tablet of the Sun, where it refers to an aspect of the Triad deity GIII, known to be a Solar God (Figure 11.6b). A similar name also is cited on inscribed Early Classic cache vessels from the Tikal region, but the reference is not at all clear.

The Yehnal mask is a hieroglyphic name writ large, and as such it serves a role identical to the better-known emblematic names of K'inich Yax K'uk' Mo' adorning the later constructions of Margarita and Rosalila, built directly above. One might reasonably wonder, therefore, if there existed a deity or historical individual named K'inich Taj Way who was celebrated during the reigns of the first rulers—an "ancestor's ancestor." At Palenque the name clearly serves as a descriptive term for a deity, but it could easily be a historical name in other contexts (ruler names and deity names are often difficult to distinguish in Maya texts). This interpretation is quite speculative, but it is significant that a personal name glyph on the Early Classic inscribed step of Structure 10L-11-sub (Figure 11.6c) is K'INICH and WAY-bi. No known historical figure from Copan bears this name, but it seems closely related to the Yehnal mask and perhaps less directly to the cited examples mentioned from Palenque and Tikal (see also Taube, this volume).

To summarize Copan's very early history, we can only say that the extant sources are extremely fragmented, and what little information does exist comes from much later, retrospective texts. The dearth of information probably reflects the pro-found historical and cultural transformation that Copan experienced with the coming of K'inich Yax K'uk' Mo'. Upon his arrival and subsequent celebration of the Bak'tun ending, Copan emerged as a literate society in the Lowland Maya tradition, with novel emphases on stone monuments and the presentation of permanent written records. Perhaps the discovery of inscriptions that truly date to pre-dynastic times will change this scenario, but as the archaeological and epigraphic records clearly attest, his appearance at Copan represented a new and redefining phase in the political evolu-tion of an already extant and vibrant community.[*]

---

[*] One supposed pre-dynastic reference has gone unmentioned. Schele (1987b) suggest-ed that Stela E mentions K'inich Yax K'uk' Mo' as the "successor" of another ruler, presumably his predecessor in office. This interpretation is unlikely, however, since the second of the names strongly resembles that of Ruler 12, who may have erected the monument (Stuart 1992). Stela E's inscription remains one of the most baffling in all of Copan, and little of it is deciphered.

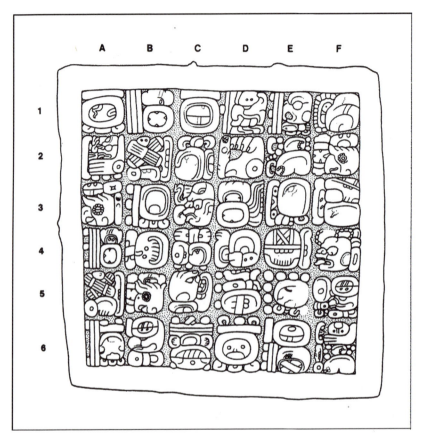

Figure 11.7 Upper text of Altar Q
(drawing by David Stuart).

Setting the Stage: The Epigraphic Discovery of K'inich Yax K'uk' Mo'

K'inich Yax K'uk' Mo's identity as an Early Classic ruler was first suggested in 1983, during my first studies of Copan's inscriptions.[*] The first telling clue of his dating came from Altar Q, where a Distance Number of "17 K'atuns" intervenes between the third and fourth dates of the inscription (Figure 11.7, Plate 1a). The latter of these dates, 9.17.5.0.0, is the dedication date for the altar, which is "owned" or dedicated to K'inich Yax K'uk' Mo'. Calculating 17 K'atuns back from the dedication one reaches the approximate beginning of the Bak'tun. This association of the much earlier date with the K'inich Yax K'uk' Mo' name seemed to be confirmed by the inscription on the back of Stela J, where it occurs in a section of the inscription concerned with events on or around 9.0.0.0.0.

Also in the 1980s, the understanding of Altar Q as a dynastic monument (Riese 1988) bearing sixteen royal portraits became clear. The first portrait of the Altar Q series initially remained problematic because the main figure did not sit upon a name glyph,

---

[*] The glyphs we now recognize as the name of K'inich Yax K'uk' Mo' have a complicated history in Maya epigraphic research. Morley (1920) seems to have made no mention of the distinctive parrot glyphs found on Altar Q or in other inscriptions, and it was perhaps Proskouriakoff (1993:129) who first made note of them in her over-all consideration of Maya history (Proskouriakoff's book was written long before its 1993 publication date). She never interpreted what she called "the parrot" as a personal name, however, preferring to see it merely associated with times of political instability at Copan and beyond. Proskouriakoff went so far as to say that these glyphs possibly referred to militant usurpers of the local government during the Late Classic, but clearly this has little to do with the historical reality as we today understand it. Pahl (1976) was perhaps the first to note that the "Yax Macaw" glyph served a role as a personal reference, and posited that it was a variant name for "New Sun at Horizon," the great Late Classic ruler now better known as "Yax Pac" or "Yax Pasaj." The recognition of the glyph as a personal name was certainly helped by the common presence of the then-called "mahk'ina" sign, which had recently before been cited by Mathews and Schele (1974) as a diagnostic marker of sorts on royal names at Palenque. Today this is read K'INICH, an honorific prefix on many proper names that essentially equates the name-holder with the Sun God, K'inich Ajaw. Shortly after Pahl's identification, Lounsbury traced several more examples of the macaw name in Copan's texts, and recognized that it consistently included a quetzal and macaw, either fused or shown as separate entities.

Lounsbury did not publish his observations on the "Quetzal Macaw" name, but they were included within a lengthy series of letters he composed to William Fash in 1978. Some of his ideas from this time, especially regarding the variants of the name of the sixteenth king, Yax Pasaj Chan Yopaat, did eventually find their way into print in a modified form (Lounsbury 1989). Many of his conclusions can now be greatly refined, but Lounsbury's observations initiated the study of K'inich Yax K'uk' Mo' as a historical personage.

The confusion surrounding the chronological placement of the "Quetzal Macaw" stemmed from ambiguities in the inscription atop Altar Q. The name is repeated three times in this inscription, the last being associated directly with the Calendar Round 6 Ajaw 13 K'ayab, or 9.17.5.0.0. This date falls squarely within the reign of the sixteenth ruler Yax Pasaj, who is named as well in the same Altar Q passage. Lounsbury considered that the two names might refer to the same individual. Also confusing for many years were the Calendar Round dates of this inscription: before the 9.17.5.0.0 date three specific dates seem to float without any explicit and precise Distance Number linking them to the Period Ending.

Figure 11.8 Portrait of K'inich Yax K'uk' Mo'
on the west side of Altar Q.

unlike most of the others. Eventually, Linda Schele and I recognized that the figure instead "wears" his name (Stuart and Schele 1986), much in the fashion of other portraits in Early Classic Maya art (Figure 11.8, Plate 1a). The long-tailed quetzal has the eye markings of a macaw, and the YAX and K'IN(ICH) signs are clearly given at the front of the turban he wears. In fact, the glyph upon which K'inich Yax K'uk' Mo' sits is not a name, but simply states AJAW, "lord, ruler." When later kings are seated in office "as the *ajaw*," one gets the clear impression that K'inich Yax K'uk' Mo' served as a social and political role model for the position (Fash 1998).

The other remarkable clue provided by Altar Q was the clear "foreign" appearance of K'inich Yax K'uk' Mo' in his portrait on the side of the stone. As Coggins (1988) first stressed, only the dynastic founder is explicitly shown in the guise of a

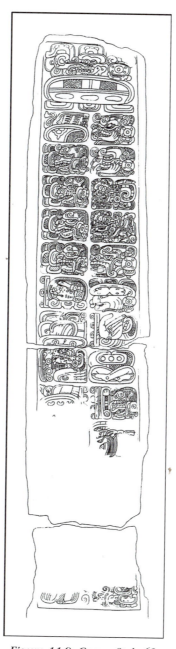

Figure 11.9 Copan Stela 63
(drawing by Barbara W. Fash).

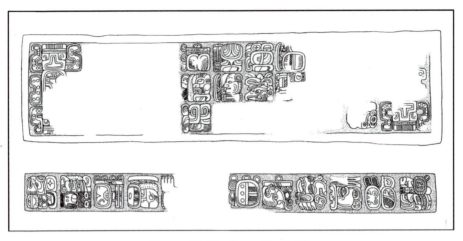

Figure 11.10 Altar of Stela 63
(drawings by David Stuart and George Stuart).

Teotihuacan warrior. This seemed consistent with the explicit Tlaloc iconography of
the altar's associated temple, Structure 10L-16. It also paralleled the relationship
reflected in the Mexican architectural symbolism of Structure 10L-26 and its
Hieroglyphic Stairway (B. Fash 1992). Indeed, this "Teotihuacan connection" has per-
vaded our interpretations of K'inich Yax K'uk' Mo' and early Copan history (Fash and
Fash 2000; Stuart 2000) and was eventually reinforced by the material remains uncovered in the excavations in the early levels of the Acropolis.

     Returning to our timeline, by the late 1980s the basic dynasty of Copan was
clearly worked out and cross-referenced among numerous written sources, chief
among them Altar Q and the Hieroglyphic Stairway inscription—both Late Classic
monuments. The few Early Classic inscriptions known in 1986 made it difficult to
determine if Copan's royal history ever held much internal consistency over time, but
it did appear significant that the name of K'inch Yax Kuk' Mo' was twice given on Stela
15 (9.4.10.0.0), one of the earliest monuments known since Morley's initial survey.

     The archaeological verification of K'inich Yax K'uk' Mo' and the dynastic his-
tory came with the discovery of the so-called Papagayo structure under Structure 10L-
26 and the inscribed monument within it, Stela 63 (Fash et al. 1992; Fash et al., this volume). This impressive sculpture (Figure 11.9) bears the Initial Series date 9.0.0.0.0,
with the name of K'inich Yax K'uk' Mo' inscribed on the front of the monument. One
portion of the side text names K'inich Yax Kuk' Mo' as the father of Ruler 2, establishing an important kin relationship between the first two dynasts.

The Papagayo shrine served as a place of veneration for well over two centuries (Fash et al., this volume). This is textually confirmed by the discovery of an inscribed altar or step in front of the stela (Figure 11.10) bearing the name of the fourth ruler, K'altuun Hix (formerly "Cu-Ix"). Evidence now suggests that Ruler 2 dedicated the Papagayo shrine and Stela 63 to the change of the 9th Bak'tun, but further excavations revealed that these were retrospective records as well.

The discovery of the Motmot building and its circular floor marker (Figure 11.11) revealed one of the earliest-known inscriptions from Copan, also bearing the date 9.0.0.0.0 (in Calendar Round form, as "8 Ajaw 14 Keh") and the names of the first two rulers. Unlike Stela 63, the Motmot Marker bears portraits of K'inich Yax K'uk' Mo' (on the left) and Ruler 2 on the right, clearly identified by the glyph names in their headdresses (the visual arrangement is not unlike that shown within the central cartouche of the peccary skull, discussed earlier). The Papagayo shrine was built directly atop Motmot as an elaboration of a sacred space devoted to the Bak'tun and the ruler, or rulers, who oversaw its passing (see Fash et al., this volume).

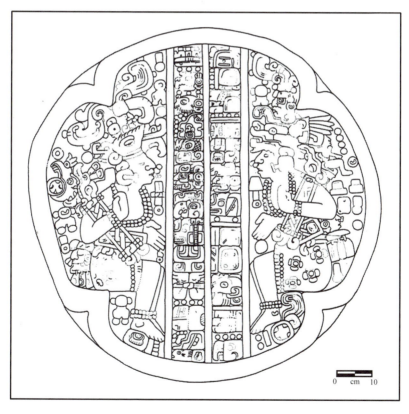

Figure 11.11 Motmot floor marker
(drawing by Barbara W. Fash).

Concurrent with these discoveries beneath Structure 10L-26 were the first ECAP excavations into the river cut and the meticulous excavations of the Rosalila structure by Ricardo Agurcia Fasquelle (this volume). These efforts resulted in another series of remarkable discoveries that provide more direct evidence of K'inich Yax K'uk' Mo' and his role as a political and religious figure venerated throughout the centuries of Copan's Late Classic period. The interred Rosalila Structure, probably built by Ruler 8,[*] was covered with the symbols of K'inich Yax K'uk' Mo' himself, whose large emblematic name glyphs graced the outer walls of the temple (Agurcia F., this volume; Taube, this volume). Beneath Rosalila was the edifice known as Margarita, likewise with at least one K'inich Yax K'uk' Mo' name glyph decorating its basal platform. Most recently, deeper excavations have unearthed Hunal Structure, with its remarkable Teotihuacan-style architectural features, and, most importantly, a tomb that may well be that of the founder himself (Bell et al., Buikstra et al.; and Sharer, this volume; Sharer, Traxler, et al. 1999).

One artifact interred in this important burial is an oval-shaped shell pectoral bearing an elaborate inlaid design and two small hieroglyphs (Plate 4b). These together read yu-ha WI'-TE', evidently a simple name-tag for the object composed of (u)y-uh, "the necklace of" and a curious name or personal reference wi'te', "tree root." This odd-sounding label is highly significant, for in later inscriptions we commonly find the term Wi'te'naah, "Tree Root House," the name of a ritual location that is intimately and exclusively associated with K'inich Yax K'uk' Mo'. This small textual clue presents support for Sharer's view that the Hunal Tomb is the founder's own interment.

A New Interpretation of Altar Q's Inscription

The sequential building phases in the southern area of the Acropolis, including Hunal, Yehnal, Margarita, and Rosalila, culminated in the Late Classic Structure 10L-16, with Altar Q placed on its front, or western, side. This remarkable table-altar is the most important historical source for studying K'inich Yax K'uk' Mo' and the establishment of the Copan ruling line, despite having been carved several centuries later during the reign of the final ruler. The upper inscription of Altar Q (Figure 11.7) records five dates, all written as Calendar Rounds:

Date A:	(8.19.10.10.17)	5 Kaban 15 Yaxk'in (6 September A.D. 426)
Date B:	(8.19.10.11.0)	8 Ajaw 18 Yaxk'in (9 September A.D. 426)
Date C:	(8.19.11.0.13)	5 Ben 11 Muwan (9 February A.D. 427)
Date D:	(9.17.5.0.0)	6 Ajaw 13 K'ayab (29 December A.D. 775)
Date E:	(9.17.5.3.4)	5 Kan 12 Uo (2 March A.D. 776)

---

[*] Rosalila has long been seen as the work of the tenth ruler ("Moon Jaguar"; e.g., Martin and Grube 2000:198-199), following Schele's study of the date inscribed on the badly eroded step from the west side of Rosalila's substructure. I doubt this is a very secure reading, however, and other interpretations certainly seem possible. My suggestion of an earlier Ruler 8 attribution must also remain tentative, but elements of his name glyph are visible in the text. Ruler 8 is now known to have ruled nearly twenty years, between 9.4.18.6.12 and 9.5.17.13.7.

The first passage (Date A) concerns an important ritual called *ch'am-K'awiil*, "*K'awiil* taking" (block A2), with the protagonist named as K'uk' Mo' Ajaw, "Quetzal Macaw Lord" (A3), evidently a pre-accession name for K'inich Yax K'uk' Mo'. Between the event and the name is a distinctive glyph (at B2) recognized by its "crossed bundles" main sign, suffixed by -TE'-NAAH. *Naah* means "house" or "structure," and the placement of the glyph after the verb suggests that it specifies the location of the ritual event.

"Taking the *K'awiil*" is a somewhat opaque description of an important ceremony strongly associated with royal accession. *K'awiil* is the ancient name of "God K" (Stuart 1987), the personification of royal ancestry and rulership itself. The expression occurs on Quirigua Stela E as a simple means of recording the inauguration of K'ak' Tiliw Chan Yopaat (the actual name of the noted ruler commonly known as "Cauac Sky") on 9.14.12.4.17 12 Kaban 5 K'ayab. Perhaps the most common examples of the phrase occur on a set of highly repetitive "codex style" vessels bearing a lengthy list of *ch'am K'awiil* rites by lords of Calakmul (Martin 1997). However, the interpretation of this term as "accession" is complicated by the text on Stela J of Quirigua, where we find it used to express K'ak' Tiliw Chan Yopaat's assumption of a new status on the very day of his noted defeat of the Copan king Waxaklajun Ubah K'awiil (Ruler 13), 9.15.6.14.6 6 Kimi 4 Tzek (Figure 11.12).

Ch'am K'awiil therefore cannot be a generic expression for inauguration, as is often supposed. Rather, it carries the sense of a more significant or pronounced political change, where a ruler receives new divine symbols or sacred charters associated with rulership. This sense is well attested at Quirigua, where the established ruler "takes the *K'awiil*" upon the capture of his Copan rival, and assumes also the mantle of the "14th successor" (Riese 1986). On Copan's Altar Q, the initial passage thus records how K'uk' Mo' Ajaw assumed some new, divinely sanctioned status—perhaps but not limited to his accession to rulership. The change of status is also clearly reflected in his name, given in the next passage in its conventional form K'inich Yax Kuk' Mo'.*

---

* The newly acquired name does away with Ajaw after the core K'uk' Mo' component and adds the prefix Yax, "green" or "new," as well as the important honorific prefix K'inich, meaning "Great Sun." When associated with royal names, K'inich serves to identify rulers as aspects or embodiments of the Sun God, or K'inich Ajaw. The common identity between ruler and solar deity is emphasized in the inscription of Stela 10 at Copan, where K'inich Yax Kuk' Mo' is somewhat redundantly dubbed K'inich Ajaw (K'INICH-K'IN-chi-AJAW-wa, at block F7). The addition of Yax is also noteworthy here, for it may have a literal meaning closer to "new" than to the color designation "green-blue," as it is customarily translated. Yax clearly means "new" in many Classic inscriptions, just as the word is defined in several modern Mayan languages. In such contexts yax typically describes the first of a set or series of actions or entities (for example, yax-k'altuun, "the new stone-binding"). In the royal name from Copan the role could well be similar, serving to mark his name as that of the "new" political order. As evidence for this, it is interesting to note that the apparent founder of the Tikal dynasty was named Yax Ehb' Xok or simply Ehb Xok (Stuart 1999; Martin and Grube 2000).

Figure 11.12 Passage from Quirigua, Stela J
(drawing by Annie Hunter).

Figure 11.13 The "house" title of K'inich Yax K'uk' Mo', from Copan Stela 12
(drawing by David Stuart).

Returning to the Altar Q inscription, we read that three days after the "*K'awiil* taking" another action of K'inich Yax K'uk' Mo' takes place at the very same "crossed bundles" location (Date B). The simple verb is spelled ta-li, spelling the intransitive form *tal*, "he comes." Although this has long been interpreted as K'inich Yax K'uk' Mo's "arrival" at Copan (Stuart 1992, 2000), there is now good reason to refine this translation. The word *tal* is found in many Lowland Mayan languages today as "come," but it specifically refers to one's arrival from a place away from the speaker. A better translation of *tal* would then be "he comes from there." When one wishes to specify someone's arrival toward the speaker, the verb *hul* is used, meaning "comes here." The difference between these two "arrive" terms is readily apparent in the following examples taken from the *Paxbolon Papers*, a 17th century document written in Acalan Chontal:

> tal-i Mexico
> "He came from Mexico" (Smailus 1975:58)
> hul-i ui ti cah Tixchel
> "He arrived here in the town of Tixchel" (Smailus 1975:100)

The first of these examples offers an exact parallel to the second passage from Altar Q, with "Mexico" occupying the same toponymic role as the building name. Evidently the Altar Q passage simply states that K'inich Yax K'uk' Mo' came from the "crossed bundles" house three days after assuming royal status at the same place.

What was this all-important "crossed bundles" location, where K'inich Yax K'uk' Mo's accession took place? The glyph is found throughout Copan's inscriptions, and it has a particularly close connection to K'inich Yax K'uk' Mo'. Significantly, Late

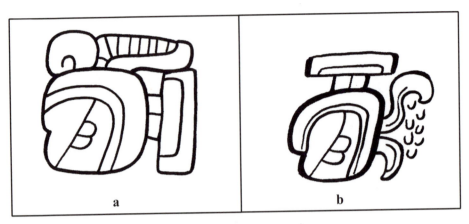

Figure 11.14 Early Classic examples of the Wi'te'naah glyph. (a) From Tikal, Stela 31, and (b) an Early Classic painted vessel (Kerr #1446).

Classic texts refer to the founder as "He of the 'crossed bundles House'" or as "The 'crossed bundles House' Lord" (Figure 11.13). When later kings bear numbered succession titles ("the fifteenth ordered one") the name of K'inich Yax K'uk' Mo' often follows (Schele 1992), and very often his name can be simply replaced by the "crossed bundles House" glyph. The identities of place and person are almost fused in such references, emphasizing the historical connection related on Altar Q.

It is interesting that the very same house name glyph occurs at several other sites, including Quirigua, Yaxchilan, and Machaquila. A variant form is cited in several Early Classic inscriptions from the central Petén (Figure 11.14), and is the more phonetically transparent spelling WI'-TE'-NAAH, analyzable as *Wi'te'naah*, or "Tree-root House."[*] We have already seen the use of *wi'te'* as a personal label on the Hunal shell pectoral ("it is the necklace of the 'Tree Root'"), where it may well refer to K'inich Yax K'uk' Mo' himself.

"Tree root" seems an odd name for a building or personal label, but the term *wi'* (proto-Mayan *wib*, "root") holds considerable religious and metaphorical mean-

---

[*] The connection between these posited early and late forms is as follows: both glyphs of course have the closing elements –TE' and –NAAH, but the early forms under discussion never make use of the "crossed bundles" logogram. However, their equivalence is strongly indicated by one especially revealing Late Classic example from Yaxchilan Lintel 25 where we find a wi- prefix on the form otherwise identical to the house name cited at Copan and elsewhere. If one opts for "tree-root house" as a literal reading of the name, it is difficult to analyze the "crossed bundles" itself. One might reasonably posit that it is a WI' "root" logogram, but this is countered by the fairly clear "root" visual origin of the wi syllable itself. The phonetic role of the "crossed bundles" remains unclear, but its iconographic connection to ritual fire may be a reason for its use here.

ing. For example, Wisdom, in his exhaustive lexicon of modern Ch'orti, notes that *wib* (cognate to *wi'* in other Ch'olan languages) means "source, origin, navel, umbilical cord, root" (Wisdom 1950). Although the presence of the -TE' ("tree") sign in the ancient building name specifically suggests "tree root," we cannot discount these extended meanings. A translation of the building name as "Origin House" would be particularly fitting, given the nature of the events we find recorded on Altar Q'.

Both early and late variants of the house name have strong associations with the imagery and symbolism derived from Teotihuacan (Stuart 2000). At Tikal, for example, it appears in text passages concerning the history of the ruler Nuun Yax Ayin (formerly known as "Curl Nose" or "Curl Snout"), who is consistently depicted as a highland Mexican warrior in his portraits. On Tres Islas, Stela 2, an Early Classic stela erected near 9.2.0.0.0, the portrait of a warrior in Teotihuacan-style dress is accompanied by a text caption with two examples of the WI'-TE'-NAAH collocation. Moreover, on

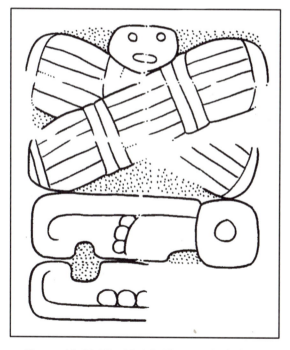

Figure 11.15 The "Origin House" glyph from
Structure 5 at Rio Amarillo
(drawing by David Stuart).

Yaxchilan Lintel 25, we find the later variant named in direct association with the image of the rearing Teotihuacan War Serpent.

The pattern of association with central Mexican imagery is striking, and it is reasonable to consider whether "Origin Houses" refer to conspicuous examples of Teotihuacan-inspired architecture at Maya sites, including the Copan region. The connection between the "Origin House" glyph and Teotihuacan symbolism is best made by looking at Structure 5 at Copan's satellite center Río Amarillo, a Late Classic building adorned on its outer walls with large "crossed bundles," TE', and NAAH signs, all grouped together as large glyphic labels for the edifice (Figure 11.15). Significantly, Mexican year signs and large warrior figures in Teotihuacan costume also adorned the exterior of Structure 5 (Saturno 2000).

Copan's Structure 10L-16, associated directly with Altar Q, is another prime example of a temple adorned with such foreign iconography (Taube, this volume), and the house named in the altar's text must somehow be related to this symbolism. Recalling that the *Wi'te'naah* was where K'inich Yax K'uk' Mo' "took the *K'awiil,*" one can easily see why "Origin House" seems a particularly fitting translation. That is, Structure 10L-16 seems to have been conceived as an explicit representation of this place of dynastic foundation, replete with the imagery of Teotihuacan, a culture distant in both time and space. The placement of an "Origin House" above earlier temples celebrating K'inich Yax K'uk' Mo', not to mention the Hunal Tomb itself, seems particularly appropriate.

The third passage of Altar Q relates yet another episode of K'inich Yax K'uk' Mo's story, and in some ways it is the most important portion of the inscription. A Distance Number of 7 Winals and 13 K'ins (totaling 153 days) takes the narrative forward to the date 5 Ben 11 Muwan (Date C). The event in the next two blocks is spelled hi-li o-ke, for *hil oke(l)*, literally "the leg-resting," probably in the sense of "the journey comes to an end."[*] The protagonist here is simply given as *K'awiil* and the "West Kalomte'," the latter being a title routinely found with K'inich Yax K'uk' Mo' in the inscriptions of Copan.

The passage ends with two glyphs that are the most important of the text. The first, a verb, is an odd form of the verb HUL-li, "he arrives here," for it is identical to an arrival glyph written on Stela M at Copan. The next glyph is 3-wi-ti-ki for *Uxwitik* ("Three *Witik*"), the ancient name of the Copan locality (Stuart and Houston 1994). Here, then, we have the counterpart to *tal,* much as we saw in the Acalan-Chontal text. In the earlier passage K'inich Yax K'uk' Mo' departs from the "Crossed Bundles House," and after about five months the *K'awiil* "rests the legs" and "arrives at *Uxwitik.*" *K'awiil* may well refer to the object acquired by K'inich Yax K'uk' Mo' in his *ch'am K'awiil* ceremony. Alternatively, it could also function as a descriptive term for the founder as a "royal ancestor."

---

[*] A text on a sarcophagus lid from Tortuguero, Chiapas, cites the same expression, possibly in a reference to the journey into the afterlife.

The inscription on Altar Q continues by carrying the narrative forward through "17 K'atuns" to the dedication date of the altar or its associate building, Structure 10L-16, on 9.17.5.0.0, under the authority of Yax Pasaj Chan Yopaat. Finally, 64 days later (9.17.5.3.4) another ceremony takes place, recorded at the end of the text, but it is difficult to interpret. The span of 64 days (4 x 4 x 4) might well relate to the four-part cosmological symmetry evident in the design of Altar Q itself. The rites associated with this final date may have also marked the end point of an extended ritual period concerned with the placement and activation of Altar Q and the veneration of K'inich Yax K'uk' Mo'.

By way of summary, the early history related on Altar Q records that K'inich Yax K'uk' Mo' "came from the Origin House" where he had received the divine charter of rulership (*K'awiil*) only three days before. Five months later, the *K'awiil* arrives at Copan, where we see the establishment of a new political and dynastic order lasting throughout the Classic period.

The question then becomes, where was this distant place, the "Origin House"? As noted earlier, the associations of this building name or location with Teotihuacan iconography are clear, but the label also probably refers to certain buildings at Maya sites, such as Copan's Structure 10L-16. I would venture to say that these were all conceived and designed as evocations of an "Origin House" that held direct symbolic meaning with highland Mexico. In the case of Altar Q, the "Origin House" was perhaps at Teotihuacan itself, which would account for the five months elapsed before the stated arrival at Copan. Alternatively, it is also possible that the *Wi'te'naah* location was at Tikal, where, after all, we find the earliest citation of the house name, on Stela 31 (Figure 11.14a).

This new assessment of Altar Q underscores our own (and perhaps the ancient) perception of K'inich Yax K'uk' Mo' as a political and cultural outsider when he arrived at Copan in the early 5th century. But the basic question remains: was K'inich Yax K'uk' Mo' an ethnic foreigner—perhaps even a non-Maya from highland Mexico? It is doubtful this is the case, despite his strong iconographic associations with Teotihuacan in Late Classic Copan art. The founder's earliest portrait on the Motmot Marker shows a "purely Maya" king, and it is probably significant that his is a decidedly Mayan name featuring two bird species that are native to the neo-tropical forests of southern Mesoamerica. Even Altar Q's inscription is ambiguous enough to allow several varied interpretations of the evidence. In the simple linear narrative it presents, K'inich Yax K'uk' Mo' "comes from" a ceremonial building—not a community or town—saying nothing of his previous life, wherever that took place. All in all, one can simply conclude from the earliest dynastic art and inscriptions that K'inich Yax K'uk' Mo' was a Maya king, but with important foreign contacts and associations.

Circumstantial evidence suggests that K'inich Yax K'uk' Mo' held some importance prior to his arrival. As mentioned, he may be portrayed on the Peccary Skull in connection with the 8.17.0.0.0 K'atun ending, a date falling five decades before his inauguration. This is obviously a large timespan, and perhaps too large for comfort. A more secure clue of the founder's early presence comes from Stela 15, where the K'atun ending 8.19.0.0.0 is recorded (a retrospective date) together with the name K'inich Yax K'uk' Mo' (Figure 11. 5). No place glyph accompanies the record, unfortunately, but this Period Ending falls only ten years before the supposed arrival. Stela 15's text raises the possibility that K'inich Yax K'uk' Mo' had an earlier political and ceremonial life, perhaps even at Copan.

By way of summary, we can say that the textual sources are in no way explicit about the ethnicity of K'inich Yax K'uk' Mo'. Yet if he were a Maya lord from Copan or elsewhere, as seems likely, he played a pivotal and direct role in bridging two important and very different Mesoamerican cultures, Copan and Teotihuacan. Copan's connections to highland Mexico in the Early Classic were historically real, and, even though the circumstances behind this connection are vague, I am inclined to think that the founder's motivation for political legitimization and ritual authority had much to do with it. By Late Classic times the ancestral cult centered on K'inich Yax K'uk' Mo' was, in its symbolic expression, equally a celebration of Teotihuacan's key importance as a place of pilgrimage and as a source of divine sanction for rulership.

Ruler 2 and the 9.0.0.0.0 Bak'tun Ending

Copan's inscriptions say little about K'inich Yax K'uk' Mo's life or accomplishments during the years following his arrival. The next major event came ten years later with the close of the Bak'tun on 9.0.0.0.0. The accounts of this event feature not only the founder, but also the king who has come to be known as Ruler 2 (his name remains undeciphered). As noted earlier, Stela 63's inscription states that Ruler 2 was the son of K'inich Yax K'uk' Mo', and he emerges from the texts of the period as a pivotal figure in his own right, who did much to establish the beginnings of a long-lasting dynastic succession.

Several inscriptions state that Ruler 2, perhaps together with his father, was a principal celebrant of the Bak'tun ending on 9.0.0.0.0. His portrait is the right-hand figure on the Motmot Marker, where he faces his father, seemingly as an equal. Given his adult look in this image (though this is by no means a certainty), Ruler 2 must have been born well before the pivotal foundation events recorded on Altar Q. Yet there is no way to know if he also "arrived" as an ethnic outsider in the company of his father, or if he was a local Copan lord by birth.

Five Copan inscriptions make reference to the 9.0.0.0.0 Bak'tun ending: Stelae J, 15, 28, 63, and the Motmot floor marker. Of these only the Motmot Marker is a truly contemporaneous record of the calendar station. All other monuments have either significantly later dedication dates (Stelae J, 15, and 28[?]) or can be stratigraphically associated with later phases of architectural construction (Stela 63).[*]

---

[*] It is remarkable that only two other Maya monuments offer contemporary records of this important Bak'tun ending: Xultun Stela 20 and El Zapote Stela 5 (see Mathews 1985).

An overview of the Motmot Marker's inscription (Figure 11.11) is therefore important, as it may be the earliest hieroglyphic text thus far unearthed at Copan. Although the central text is extremely difficult to read, the Calendar Round "8 Ajaw 14 Keh" (9.0.0.0.0) is very clear at B2 and B4, as are the personal name glyphs of each ruler (A6-7 and B6). Also, there are fairly legible references to the sacrifice of deer (A9-10) and a "fire-entering" ritual of architectural renewal (B5). Later in the Motmot text is a "4 sky" glyph (at A11) that surely must relate to the Motmot building itself, decorated on its substructure with four sky band decorations (Fash et al., this volume). These adornments leave little doubt that the Motmot Structure was designed as a cosmological model or microcosm, dedicated to the change of the Bak'tun. Integrated into this design, on the east side of the temple, was a poorly preserved stucco image that W. Fash et al. (this volume) suggest may have been an emblematic name of K'inich Yax K'uk' Mo.'

Near the end of the Motmot Marker's text we find a Distance Number (B8) of "7 days and 10 [unit?]," reckoning to a new date simply written at B9 as "5 (Day sign)." The verb in the next block is very hard to read, but the -*ya* suffix shows it is marked in the completive or past tense, making it clear that this second date is earlier than 9.0.0.0.0. Interestingly, the "7 days" of the DN indicates that the earlier date fell on the day Ben, also the day of the arrival of K'inich Yax K'uk' Mo' recorded on Altar Q (8.19.11.0.13 5 Ben 11 Muwan). In all probability that key historical date is the "5 Ben" near the end of the Motmot Marker text, connected to the Period Ending by a rounded Distance Number of "ten years, seven days."

Surprisingly, the Motmot stone and other inscriptions suggest that Ruler 2 had a more direct role than his father in overseeing the ceremonies of the Bak'tun ending. Earlier studies of Copan epigraphy and history (Fash and Stuart 1991; Stuart 1992; Stuart and Schele 1986) emphasized K'inich Yax K'uk' Mo' as the one ruler who reigned at the time, but this now seems an overly simplistic view. For example, in the Motmot text the son's name follows directly after the record of "8 Ajaw 14 Keh," whereas the father's name appears some distance away in the previous column of the text. The visual arrangement of the marker's portraits, showing Ruler 2 at right and K'inich Yax K'uk' Mo' at left, may also suggest the son's prominence during this ceremony. As with the similar double portrait on the Tomb 1 peccary skull, the placement of principal or higher ranking figures at the right of a scene, facing his or her subordinates, seems a pervasive convention of Classic Maya art, and it is especially prevalent in scenes painted on Classic Maya pottery (Houston 1998).

Stela 63, a later monument from the Papagayo Structure built directly above Motmot, also features the Bak'tun ending, written as an elaborate Initial Series on its front (Figure 11.9). The name of K'inich Yax K'uk' Mo' appears near the end of the severely damaged frontal inscription, but the glyphs on the side indicate that Ruler 2 was the stela's "owner" and actual protagonist. This is a retrospective or commemorative record, however, and Ruler 2 designed Papagayo as an elaboration of the ritual space still dedicated to the Bak'tun.

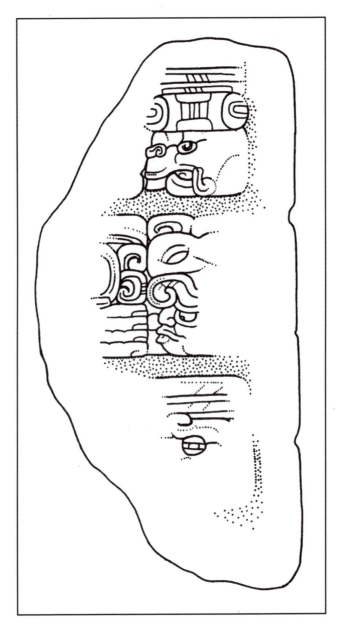

Figure 11.16 Copan Stela 28, side
(drawing by David Stuart).

Figure 11.17 Passage from Copan Stela J.

A later king, K'altuun Hix (Ruler 4), modified Papagayo's interior and dedicated a remarkable inscribed altar in front of Stela 63 (Figure 11.10). Its inscription cites the founder's name but in a highly unusual context: several of the surviving glyphs clearly have second-person pronouns ("your god" "you (are) his ancestor," "your kingdom"). Before the name of K'altuun Hix is a glyph reading *che'en*,[*] "so he says," leaving little doubt that the previous glyphs record an oration by the fourth Copan ruler, perhaps directed to K'inich Yax K'uk' Mo'.

One little-known early text fragment offers more explicit evidence for Ruler 2's direct association with the Bak'tun ending (Figure 11.16). Stela 28 was recovered in the early 1920s during construction near the plaza in the town of Copán Ruinas,[†] and only a few glyphs upon it are legible. Luckily, on the side of the surviving fragment three telling glyphs can be discerned:

pD1: 10+ Keh
pC2: u k'al-aw tuun, "he binds the stone"
pD2: K'inich ? (Ruler 2)

---

[*] Grube (1999) and the author (Stuart, Houston, and Robertson 1999) independently arrived at the reading of the che'en glyph (spelled che-e-na or che-he-na) and its role as a quotative particle.

[†] Stela 28 was not included in Morley's volume on Copan (1920), and the circumstances of its discovery in the town of Copan remain obscure. The Carnegie Institution of Washington took photographs of Stela 28 in the 1920s, when the monument was presumably numbered. Raul Pavón Abreu made images again in the 1940s. The stela fragment had suffered considerable wear and damage during the quarter century spanning these extant images. Its present location is unknown.

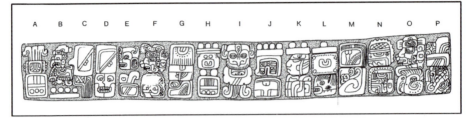

Figure 11.18 The Xukpi Stone (drawing by David Stuart).

The number above the month Keh is surely greater than 10. The accompanying phrase *u-k'al-aw tuun* marks Bak'tun and K'atun endings with fair regularity (Stuart 1996), and suggests a reconstruction of the fragmentary date as 9.0.0.0.0 8 Ajaw 13 Keh (11 December A.D. 435). Ruler 2 "binds the stone" on this day, clearly showing him to be the main celebrant.

Despite such indications, Copan's later history takes pains to remark on the strong links between K'inich Yax K'uk' Mo' and the Bak'tun ending, with little if any mention made of Ruler 2. It is as if during the Late Classic period, after much time had passed, the founder hero and the 9.0.0.0.0 date were somehow combined as paired elements within the local historical narrative. For example Stela J, a Late Classic monument (9.13.10.0.0), reckons back "13 K'atuns, 10 Haabs, and no days" to 9.0.0.0.0, when "K'inich Yax K'uk' Mo' took the *K'awiil*" (Figure 11.17). Of course this is precisely the same ritual expression initiating Altar Q's main text, where it describes the probable accession or sanctioning of K'inich Yax K'uk' Mo' as ruler. It seems likely that the time interval written on Stela J is one of several "rounded-off" distance numbers known from Copan's inscriptions. The calculation takes the reader to the beginning of the Bak'tun, but the "taking the *K'awiil*" actually took place a decade before. The Stela J passage is probably intended to orient the founder's accession to the general era of the Bak'tun ending.

The Xukpi Stone

Another significant inscription that dates from the time of the first two rulers is the so-called "Xukpi Stone" (Figure 11.18), discovered within the superstructure of Margarita (Sedat and Sharer 1993; Schele et al. 1994). Along with the Motmot Marker this may be one of the earliest inscriptions from Copan. The long rectangular format of the Xukpi Stone suggests it was originally a step, later torn out of its original setting and deposited within the upper temple. The pristine condition of the glyphs may further indicate that it was originally an interior step rather than built into an outer staircase.

The text of the Xukpi Stone is one of the most difficult and unusual of all Maya inscriptions.[*] No date is clearly expressed, and its internal structure and syntax

---

[*] This assessment is somewhat different from Stearns's (1997) comment that "almost all of the glyphs" "can be read as Maya words, and reasonable translations of them are possible."

are hard to discern (in this way it resembles the puzzling inscription on the Motmot Marker). The opening sentence follows an early form of the Initial Series Introducing Glyph (without an Initial Series), and it names a place or object—perhaps a tomb—associated with Ruler 2 ("*x* is the name of the *y* of Ruler 2"). Why a tomb? The glyph that records Ruler 2's "place" is based on a distinctive doubled skull sign that, although rare, is known from two other Maya inscriptions that probably marked royal burials.[*] After this statement we find a date written "13 Ajaw" and "2 Haabs," probably a short-hand form of the Period Ending 9.0.2.0.0 13 Ajaw 3 Keh (Schele et al. 1994; Stearns 1997). The remaining glyphs of the stone are far less readable, although they contain a very clear example of the name of K'inich Yax K'uk' Mo'.

Due to the ambiguities of the Xukpi inscription, I am hesitant to offer any firm conclusions about what it has to tell us of Early Classic Copan history. But it does appear that Ruler 2 is the protagonist, as his father's name appears far later near the end of the text, as if part of some secondary passage. I would agree with earlier analyses that suggest a funerary theme for the opening glyphs (Schele et al. 1994), and would venture to say that the step inscription originally served to mark the burial location of Ruler 2. If the 9.0.2.0.0 date (if interpreted correctly) approximates the time of Ruler 2's death, then there can be little doubt of his direct involvement in the Bak'tun ending a short two years earlier.

Like other early texts we have studied, the Xukpi Stone strongly suggests that Ruler 2 was established as a king before 9.0.0.0.0. But if so, are we to assume that his father was already dead by the Bak'tun ending? Not necessarily, for there is some evidence to suggest that the founder was alive when his son reigned. K'inich Yax K'uk' Mo's portrait on the Motmot Marker is decidedly unlike the deceased parental figures or ancestors shown on many early Classic monuments, who typically gaze from the heavens or stand behind kings' portraits on stelae. Moreover, the associations of K'inich Yax K'uk' Mo' with the Bak'tun ending, as presented on Stelae 63 and J, seem too strong to dismiss as indirect connections. Taken together, the evidence suggests that both the founder and his son played key roles on the celebration of the Period Ending.

K'inich Yax K'uk' Mo's role as a co-celebrant with his son is a strange arrangement, admittedly, but the unique status he held as founder may have involved the careful oversight of his son in order to ensure the stability of a new political arrangement. In many ways the relationship between K'inich Yax K'uk' Mo' and his son recalls elements of Tikal's Early Classic history, where Siyaj K'ak' may have arrived from Mexico to assure the accession of the young Nuun Yax Ayin, the probable son of a

---

[*] The "tomb" identification of the glyph suggested by Schele, Grube and Fahsen (1994) should remain tentative, for it is doubtful that the "doubled skull" sign is MUK, "bury, burial." It nevertheless seems to mean something very closely related to this. The other texts where the sign appears are Tamarindito Hieroglyphic Stairway 2 and a looted panel probably from the area of Cancuen, the location of which remains unknown. Although the doubled skull sign is still not deciphered, its contexts in these two inscriptions are suggestive of some funerary association.

Teotihuacan noble or ruler (Stuart 2000). Be that as it may, one gets the impression from these earliest texts that Copan's first two rulers operated very much as a pair, with one seldom being mentioned without reference to the other.

Conclusions

This chapter has put forward a series of observations on Copan's earliest dynastic history, based on the incomplete and sometimes superficial nature of the relevant texts. A meaningful integration of this information with the rich archaeological remains from the Early Classic is our ideal aim, but, as is often the case in Maya archaeology, only limited aspects of this written history can also be discerned in the material evidence. Yet the constant reinterpretation of the written evidence and the material record will continue well into the future, as inevitable refinements of both sets of data come into play. As of now, we can take heart in the fact that the written history of early Copan agrees well with the architectural and material evidence recovered thus far—a remarkable fact given that as recently as the mid-1980s, K'inich Yax K'uk' Mo's status as a real historical person was a matter of doubt.

The archaeological and historical records together demonstrate how the ritual and symbolic meanings of the two Late Classic temples dedicated to K'inich Yax K'uk' Mo' and his time—Structures 10L-16 and 10L-26—remained notably consistent over an extended period of time, despite continuous renovations and rebuilding episodes. But there are interesting contrasts between these two important ritual precincts. The southern sequence of temples—largely defined by Hunal, Margarita, Rosalila, and the final phase of Structure 10L-16—seem to be consistently focused on the persona of K'inich Yax K'uk' Mo', and arguably these were true ancestral shrines devoted to his veneration. To the north, the Motmot and later Papagayo buildings served for over two centuries as temples dedicated to the Bak'tun ending 9.0.0.0.0, and not as much to the persona of the founding dynast. This initial concern with the Bak'tun shifted over the centuries, and by the reign of Waxaklajun Ubah K'awiil (Ruler 13) the area that once focused on a particular station in time took on the significance of time itself and the history that defined the Bak'tun as it progressed through more than 260 years.

The destruction of Papagayo and the dedication of Ruler 12's tomb can be seen as a conscious recognition of this change, but Waxaklajun Ubah K'awil designed a stairway that became a detailed document of the Bak'tun and its historicity, recording the details of his ancestor's inaugurations and deaths, beginning with K'inich Yax Kuk' Mo' and ending with the demise of his own father. A later modification by Ruler 15, K'ak' Yipyaj Chan K'awiil, extended the representation of local history begun by the founder and carried it forward to include explicit mentions of Copan's own defeat by Quirigua. Significantly, both of the Late Classic rulers who contributed to the Hieroglyphic Stairway took pains to evoke the beginning of Copan's dynastic history—and by extension the Bak'tun ending itself—through the use of Teotihuacan symbolism, which by this time was used in Maya art as a marker of historical remoteness and antiquity (Stuart 2000).

One fertile area for future research centers on Copan's relations with the kingdoms of the central Petén during the Early Classic, and how these connections may have played a role in the history as presented here. Tikal has come up briefly in our discussion of the pre-dynastic period, and for many years it has been thought that K'inich Yax K'uk' Mo' himself had strong ties to the central Lowlands and Tikal in particular (Schele et al. 1994). Yet the evidence in the inscriptions of any direct links between Tikal and Copan remains weak: Tikal is never mentioned by name in an early Copan inscription, nor is K'inich Yax K'uk' Mo' ever clearly named at Tikal, despite some earlier proposals to the contrary.[*]

Even so, I do believe that the intensive interaction that Tikal and Copan each had with central Mexico during the Early Classic gives rise to natural comparisons between them and that historical connections may eventually find firmer support in the inscriptions. Perhaps the important "Origins House" glyph mentioned on Altar Q is one connection worthy of further consideration, given its earlier significance in Tikal's own local history as a place of royal accession.

It is probably no coincidence that K'inich Yax K'uk' Mo' and the new political order he established appeared on the scene shortly before 9.0.0.0.0 and the establishment of a new era in Maya history and cosmology. Four centuries later, Copan's royal history would come to an abrupt end a mere decade before the change of the next Bak'tun, on 10.0.0.0.0 7 Ajaw 18 Zip. Perhaps it is impossible to prove any intentional pattern in such bracketing of history, yet the influence of the calendar on Maya history and its perceived mechanisms was real and should not be underestimated (Puleston 1979; Farris 1987).

Altar Q presents the rulers of Copan in a perfectly symmetrical four-sided arrangement, and the sense of "closure" between K'inich Yax K'uk' Mo' and the 16th king seems to be one of the monument's many intended messages. Be that as it may, we can be confident that the passing of the 9.0.0.0.0 Bak'tun ending was the single most important event of Copan's earliest history. Perhaps it was even a motivation for the establishment of K'inich Yax K'uk' Mo' and the Classic dynasty that followed him.

---

[*] One of the oft-cited indicators of a Tikal-Copan connection comes from the so-called Hombre de Tikal monument, a headless statue of a seated man that bears an important early inscription on its back (Fahsen 1988). Two glyphs of the inscription, at E2 and F2, have been identified as the name of the Copan founder. These are, respectively, a k'u sign and an apparent macaw head, read MO', which have been interpreted as k'uk' mo', "quetzal macaw," approximating the Copan name K'uk' Mo' Ajaw or K'inich Yax K'uk' Mo'. The use of k'u for *k'uk'* is not unknown elsewhere, but it is highly unusual. The only instance known to me is the name of K'inich Yax K'uk' Mo' on Stela E at Copan, where we indeed find k'u used, but in combination with other syllabic elements (mo-o).

There are nonetheless problems with seeing these Tikal glyphs as the same we find at Copan. More significantly, the Tikal inscription is very incomplete above the two glyphs in question, and therefore no good context exists for understanding the "macaw" reference. We cannot even be sure that this is a personal name: k'u / K'U and MO' might arguably be used here to spell the thematically related words for "nest" and "macaw."

12

EARLY CLASSIC SCULPTURAL DEVELOPMENT AT COPAN

Barbara W. Fash

Although the Early Classic sculpture at Copan remains largely hidden from view, the monuments, fragments and sculptured façades that have come to light over the years allow us to follow early sculptural development at the site, which not only suggests inspirations from other regions, but a diversity of presentation. The well-known creative Copan style of the Late Classic period stems directly from these early innovations. Yet despite their creativity, Copan sculptors clung to certain archaisms throughout the Late Classic in an effort to define and maintain a connection to the past.

The earliest monuments at Copan show traces of evidence that support Coe's argument of contact, via the Pacific slopes and highlands across the Isthmus of Tehuantepec, with Olmec civilization during the Preclassic (Coe 1965; Sharer 1995). Boulder sculptures and early figural art (A.D. 100–400) share common traits with sculpture in these areas (Figure 12.1; Baudez 1994; Morley 1920:422). Yet by A.D. 426, and the onset of dynastic rule at Copan, those early highland traditions had merged with what we think of as the traditional Maya style, which had its strongest initial development in Lowland Petén, especially Tikal (Morley 1920). During the Preclassic, Highland art was primarily manifested in carved stone public monuments, while the Lowlanders emphasized massive public architecture. By the Early Classic, cultural exchange between the two regions is evident in the combining of these different formats for promotion of ritual and kingship (Schele and Miller 1986:109). This merging is evident early on at intermediary sites that maintained communication routes between the two zones, such as Polol near Nakbe (Hammond 1991:231).

This stylistic shift becomes apparent not only in the hieroglyphic monuments in the Lowlands, but also with the appearance of stepped pyramids displaying large stucco anthropomorphic masks flanking their central stairways throughout the Maya

Figure 12.1 Copan Preclassic boulder sculpture (photograph courtesy of the Peabody Museum, Harvard University, negative no. S13636 38-5-373).

region. Freidel and Schele (1988) argued that the prevalence of pyramids with stucco masks marks a move towards more "organized religion under the central control of the newly emerging elite class" (Willey and Mathews 1984:47). Arthur Miller (1986:74) saw the architectural sculpture as having a much broader meaning depicting an abstract visualization of time while emphasizing that political transitions necessitate increased use of texts to define the rules of succession with precision (1986:88). The architectural masks, often portraits of the sun god, equate the ruler buried in the temple to the sun and its cycle of rebirth, which directs and nurtures the social order (Miller 1986).

In this chapter I will explore some of the diversity of Copan's sculptural traditions, conventions, freestanding and architectural presentations and styles. I will also consider dimensions of monument classifications, foreign influences, and placement, use, and reuse.

Early Classic Copan Sculpture Traditions at Copan

At Copan, structures now buried at the heart of the Acropolis, such as Yehnal (see Sedat and López, this volume; Sharer, this volume), exemplify this period in Maya history. The ruler-as-the-sun theme, perpetuated through the Late Classic, is clearly visible in Early Classic stucco façades such as Rosalila (Agurcia F., this volume). Here the sun appears in its three diurnal phases: rising, zenith, and setting. The rising sun on the lower register personifies the first dynastic ruler, K'inich Yax K'uk' Mo', and cleverly embeds the attributes of his name in the depiction. Karl Taube first noticed the quetzal bird headdress and macaw beaks in the wings and connected them to the first ruler's name (Taube, this volume). At noontime, the overhead sun is at its most intense and therefore is depicted as ferocious and intimidating, complete with talons transformed into sacrificial knives. The setting or dying sun appears as a skeletal *incensario* head, as much equated with death as rebirth. The skeletal head rests atop a mountain or "*witz*" laden with elements of fertility and sustenance (maize kernels and cave water), all transformed by the curling cloud/smoke serpents.

By 1920, Morley, who has made the most comprehensive study of Early Classic monuments in Copan, had identified 22 stelae and altars falling within the Early Classic period that generally were *hotun* (five year) markers. Of these, more than half were

Figure 12.2 Broken stela in Group 9, Copan (photograph courtesy of the Peabody Museum, Harvard University, negative no. S13611 H-18-4).

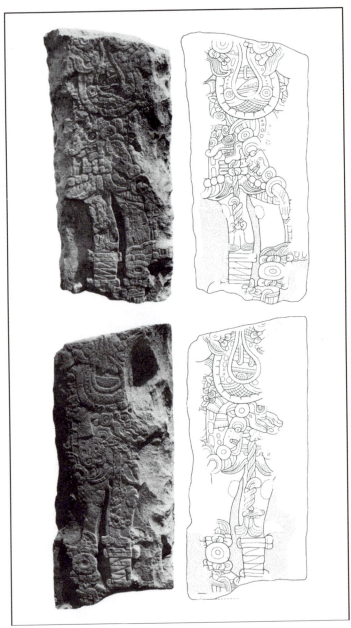

Figure 12.3 Copan Stela 35 (photographs courtesy of J. P. Couroau, PAC/IHAF; drawings by B. W. Fash).

broken fragments found in Group 9 (Figure 12.2), the site of the modern village, and other locales outside the Principal Group (1920). This distribution led Morley initially to believe that the village site was the capital and oldest in the valley. Thirteen more recently discovered Early Classic monuments and hosts of previously unknown modeled stucco façades, all from the Principal Group, have been expanding this list since 1980.

Due to the fragmentary nature or absence of texts, much of the dating of Early Classic monuments must be done on the basis of stylistic traits. Following Spinden's formal attributes of depth of relief and proportion (1913), Tatiana Proskouriakoff (1950) divided the Early Classic for the Maya area into four phases. She saw Highland characteristics in the Cycle 8 monuments of the Petén and reasoned that these early monuments would naturally reflect the peripheral ancestral styles that were their common source of inspiration, more so than the later monuments when Maya conventions had begun to crystallize (1950:104). This pattern holds true in broad outline at Copan as well.

Proskouriakoff was also insightful when she predicted that Early Classic stelae at Copan probably had figures in the style of the Leyden Plaque and Tikal Stelae 1 and 2 (1950:109). The Proyecto Arqueológico I (PAC I) excavations of Structure 10L-4 in 1979 uncovered Stelae 35 (Figure 12.3), possibly the earliest-known stela at Copan, carved on two sides with figures looking very much like the Leyden Plaque. In fact, it was originally suggested that the Leyden Plaque was left behind on a migration to Copan from northern Petén (Morley and Morley 1938). Since throughout Maya history the area now designated as Belize was actively involved in the cultural exchange flowing through the Highlands, Copan, and the Petén (Pendergast 1972; Reents-Budet et al. 1994:201), it is not surprising that the plaque was discovered along the Carribean coast of Guatemala, south of Belize. Baudez (1983) stylistically dates Stela 35 to about 9.0.0.0.0 (A.D. 435), and states that developmentally it starts the tradition of double figure stelae at Copan. Noting that the figures on both Stela 35 and the recently discovered Motmot Marker (Fash et al., this volume) wear jaguar pelts, carry serpent bars, and date to the same time period, I would suggest that both monuments represent images of K'inich Yax K'uk' Mo' and his son, Ruler 2. The mirror-image format on the marker is repeated on the stela with its back to back figures. These two rulers may be responsible for perpetuating and strengthening contacts with the Highlands and Lowlands while bringing the innovations of calendrical monuments and related religious beliefs to Copan.

Text–Image Conventions and Archaisms

The Copan monuments follow a diverse trajectory of conventions that have their beginnings in the Early Classic. Although Stela 35 portrays two figures in profile, it is

Figure 12.4 Copan Stela
(drawing by B.W. Fash).

Figure 12.5 (a) Copan Stela 5, broken (photograph negative no. C-45 Copan-Stela 5); (b) Copan Stela 5, restored (negative no. S13605 39-13-12; (c) Copan Stela C (photographs courtesy of the Peabody Museum, Harvard University and B.W. Fash).

the only known example of this style at Copan. This unique monument is followed by a dramatic innovation that lasted for almost 120 years: the radical shift to monuments with only glyphs and no figural representation. Then, spectacularly, the figural stelae reappear again around 9.6.0.0.0. (A.D. 554). These reemergent figures, quite different from the earlier, shallow-relief, profile figures, are carved in full frontal poses with flaccid serpent bars in a style closely identified with Copan (Figure 12.4). The earlier innovative mirror style of double figures is readopted in this second wave of ruler portraits by Ruler 12 (Stelae 3 and 5; Figure 12.5b) and continues into the Late Classic (Stelae C and N; Figure 12.5c). This development of figural poses coincides only in a general way with developments in the Petén, where profile figures with frontal shoulders change to full profile figures in the 5th and 6th centuries, then shift again in A.D. 600 (some years after Copan's shift) to the frontal figures with splayed feet (Kubler 1984), while never achieving the profound relief developed at Copan.

The first text we know of appears at Copan on the Motmot floor marker where it is combined with profile figure representation and a narrative scene closely resembling the Highland traditions at Abaj Takalik. Hieroglyphs appear next in the architectural format of steps leading to structures and soon after on stelae without figural representation. In a sense, Stela 63, placed as an interior, architectural monument, combines the latter two categories. These experiments with text and figures may reflect the cosmopolitan nature of Copan's Early Classic population. Perhaps early rulers attempting to engage enclaves from neighboring regions or forge trade relations with foreign cities enhanced their standing by erecting a monument that introduced or acclaimed a style from that area.

Proskouriakoff envisioned Copan's ancestral style diverging from the Petén tradition before 9.2.0.0.0 (A.D. 475), leading to an ornate, independent style, with traditional iconography that distinguished Copan from its contemporaries. Styles at Copan, she noted, remained deliberately archaic into the Late Classic period, when other sites had abandoned the Early Classic styles of costume. Stela P, from Ruler 11's reign, is one example. In fact, if we were to define the Early Classic at Copan based on stylistic traits of the freestanding monuments, we could extend it as late as A.D. 700. Not until the reign of Waxaklahun Ubah K'awiil (or 18 Rabbit, the 13th ruler) do higher relief and the characteristic flamboyant style emerge on the stelae. This archaism is what led Spinden to classify all monuments between 9.0.0.0.0 and 9.15.0.0.0 (A.D. 435–731) as Early Classic (Spinden 1913:165).

Freestanding Monument and Architectural Stylistic Development

I have emphasized elsewhere (B. Fash 1997b; Fash and Fash 1996) that the sculpted architectural façades evolved before the stelae and altars. By the end of the Early Classic, modeled stucco façades were already giving way to experimental styles of carved wall stones and were moving toward the full-fledged carved stone mosaic façades of the Late Classic period (Figure 12.6). Despite this innovation, Late Classic façades retain vestiges of lower register and substructure masks through the reign of Yax Pasah, the 16th ruler (e.g., Structures 9N-82, 10L-32, and 8N-66S), another archaic treatment at this late date particular to Copan.

The architectural façades served a purpose distinct from the freestanding stelae and altars. Not only did they create buildings that embodied deities and sacred space, but they portrayed religious and political messages for the public audience. Freestanding monuments commemorated the ruler and his embodiment of the passage of time. They were erected for ritual purposes and at specific points in the calendrical cycle. Indeed, the passage of time appears to have superseded the ruler in importance for the previously discussed 120-year interval, when the figural representations disappear from the monuments.

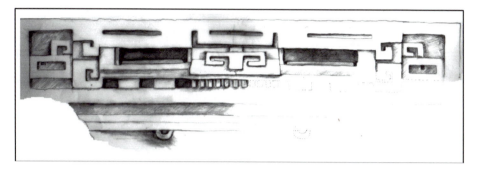

Figure 12.6 Indigo Structure façade, transition
from stucco to stone sculpture (drawing by B. W. Fash).

Carving Styles

Morley noted that the differences among Early Classic monuments were a result of the different periods in which they were executed and the varying skill of the sculptors (Morley 1920:52). Early Classic glyph delineation of very low, flat-relief, and irregular outlines of glyph blocks are found at Tikal and on the Leyden plaque. At Copan, while the relief is low and flat, the glyphs are more consistently rectangular.

Because sculptors varied in their use of extensive detail and glyphic spacing and outlines, I believe that there were many Early Classic sculptors at work and that we can possibly isolate some of these by their carving style. At a minimum, we may be able to define a school of carving followed by one or more sculptors over time. Based on some of these stylistic clues left by sculptors, we may be able to identify some of the individual fragments as actually being part of the same monument. Stela 52, for example, may be the base to Stelae 16 or 17 (Style Clusters include Stelae 16, 17, 32, and 52; Stelae 22, 24, 26, 49, 63 and the Papagayo Stone, with a tradition that persists on Stelae 2, 7, E and P; and Altars L', J' and Q'). If it proves possible to identify a sculptor's hand, then we might also be able to narrow the time frame for some of the undated monuments based on a sculptor's life span. I have always been intrigued by the variation among Initial Series Introductory glyphs, which have the potential to reveal much on this question.

Figure 12.7 Altar A', banded altar reused in the Hieroglyphic Stairway
(photograph courtesy of the Peabody Museum, Harvard University,
negative no. 315).

Monument Classifications

Copan's Early Classic sculpture can be grouped by a typology of form and decoration.
This includes Morley's stelae Types I–VI, separated into classes based on the number of
carved sides (1920:394). The classification, with my additions based on more recently
discovered monuments, is shown in Table 12.1.

  The style of banded altars predominated in the Early Classic (Figure 12.7),
with one example (an archaism, perhaps) from the Late Classic, Altar F' from Structure
10L-32. Thompson saw bound altars as equivalent to the Period Ending binding of
years, comparable to the *xiuhmolpilli* of the Aztec. Claude Baudez sees them as symbols of sacrifice, especially noting the knotted bands (Baudez 1994).

  There are several other monument types to include in an Early Classic survey.
Circular floor markers from Ballcourts I and II and Motmot Structure (Fash et al., this
volume), have their start at Copan in the Early Classic. Round markers continue at the
Ballcourt but are phased out by square markers with the final phase. Early floor mark-

Table 12.1 Early Classic Sculptural Development at Copán

Type	Characteristics and selected examples
Class I	1 carved side (Stelae 22, 25)
Class II	2 carved sides, all glyphs (Stelae 16, 17 24)
Class III	4 carved sides, all glyphs
	(Stelae 10, 12, 13, 15, 19, 20, 21, J)
Class IV	4 carved sides, 3 sides glyphs, one side figural
	(Stelae E, I, P, 1, 2, 7, 18, 23)
Class V	4 carved sides, two side glyphs, two sides figural
	(Stelae 3, 5, C, N)
Class VI	wraparound and other figure dominated formats
	(Stela D, F, H, M, 11)

Additions based on the more recently discovered stelae

Class VII	3 carved sides (Stela 63)
Class VIII	2 carved sides, both figural, no glyphs (Stela 35)

Altar styles and types include
Anthropomorphic potbellies—Preclassic
Banded table altars Altars J', K', L', M', P' Q', X, Y, A',
   and the Late Classic F'

er style and themes are closely related to Pacific Coast traditions. Similarities with Stelae 2 and 5 of Abaj Takalik and Kaminaljuyu altars (Proskouriakoff 1950:110, 178) are readily discernable. This marker tradition of two profile figures facing a central band of hieroglyphs is one of the merging traits apparent in the Highland/Lowland exchange during the Preclassic (Figure 12.8). A fragment found as far east of the Highlands as Polol dating to the 2nd century, as mentioned earlier (Hammond 1991), suggests a more widespread and earlier Highland influence in the Lowlands than that found in the Copan region in the Early Classic.

In situ hieroglyphic steps, commemorating building and stairway dedications for Early Classic Copan are found on Ante Structure (Figure 12.9), Rosalila Structure, and the Structure 10L-11-sub stairway. They all share a one-sided, double-line format also seen on the earlier Xukpi Stone (Sedat and Sharer 1994). The Xukpi Stone is probably a reused step, and if so, it is the earliest carved step known at Copan. The Xukpi Stone appears to be closely related to the carving style on Stela 31 from Tikal. Perhaps they were even monuments carved by the same sculptor. The interior of Papagayo

Figure 12.8 Comparisons of sculptures that include profile figures facing a central band of hieroglyphs. (a) Copan Motmot floor marker (photograph courtesy of B. W. Fash); (b) Kaminaljuyu Altar (photograph courtesy of the Peabody Museum, Harvard University); (c) Polol Altar 1 (photograph courtesy of the Peabody Museum, Harvard University); (d.) Abaj Takalik Stela 5 (photographs courtesy of R. J. Sharer).

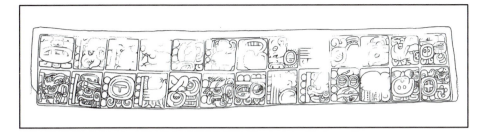

Figure 12.9 Drawing of Ante Step (drawing by B.W. Fash).

Structure yielded a monument that is an apparent combination of an altar and step (Fash et al., this volume). The Papagayo Stone has hieroglyphic carving across the top and sideways along the front side in an unusual configuration that has no other counterpart at the site. Similarities with the carving style on Stela 49 (Baudez 1983:fig. R10-11) some 60 years later provides another example of continuity of style.

Foreign Influences

The floor marker tradition reflects Pacific Coast and Highland Guatemalan affiliations at the same time that the hieroglyphic steps suggest an influence from the Petén. It would seem that, at Copan, the ballgame and religious ideology had spread early on from the Isthmian/Izapan Southeastern religious traditions, and the Early Classic hieroglyphic and (stucco) architectural styles evolved via contact with the transforming political and religious organization of the Lowlands.

Copan sculpture was also inspired by Teotihuacan art during Early Classic times, as is the case throughout the Lowlands (Fash and Fash 2000). The circular tomb under the Motmot floor marker (Fash et al., this volume), the *talud-tablero* Hunal Structure and murals (Sharer, this volume), and the modeled stucco feathered serpent from the Ballcourt I and II façade birds imply relations with or even the presence of elite Teotihuacanos. Ironically, the Teotihuacan artistic and theological tradition is much more visible in the art of Copan after the fall of the Central Mexican city than when it was in power.

Placement, Use, and Reuse

A study of the pattern of reuse and placement of the early sculptures tells us that there was a wide range of post-use treatment of the Early Classic monuments. Although incorporation into later monuments was common, no one type is reused the same way. Several locales seem to have been favored places for the reburial or abandonment of older monuments, such as the area around Structures 10L-2 and 10L-4 in the Great Plaza, or Mound 7 in the village. The circular markers and hieroglyphic steps are virtually the only types of Early Classic monuments left intact and *in situ*, with the single exception of the Xukpi Stone, which is used in the closure of the Margarita Tomb.

The careful placement of the largest fragment of Stela 63 between two columns inside Papagayo Structure along with the deposit of numerous Ballcourt I and II macaw head zone markers and numerous other examples imply ritual veneration and reuse of earlier monuments both at the Principal Group and throughout the Copan Valley. Other notable examples include the visible placement of Stelae 49, 50, and 52 in Structure 10L-4-3rd; the interment of the Stela 24 fragment beneath Stela 7; Altar A' reused in the Hieroglyphic Stairway; the burial of Stela 9 under Stela 8; the burial of Altars X and Y in the foundations of Stelae 5 and 4, respectively; and the reuse of Altars J' and K' (probably the same monument) in the foundation of Stela 10 (Morley 1920:418).

Other monuments were not broken but were reused in the foundations of newer stelae (e.g., Stela 9 or Altars X and Y). Some were broken and abandoned (e.g., Stelae 20, 23, 48, Altars L' and M'), left lying on the surface of floors (e.g., Stelae 32, 26, and 48) or merely reused as convenient building blocks (e.g., Altar A' and Fragment S'). Of those that seem to have been discarded altogether, as in the case of the scatter of fragments around the mound of Stela 7, much of this mutilation can be attributed to modern vandalism, as Morley long ago pointed out (1920:122). Later monuments such as Stelae 2, 3, and 5 (Figure 12.5a) were found in several pieces as well, possibly following this termination tradition or succumbing to the forces of earthquakes.

Arthur Miller (1986:55) considered the breaking of monuments and their resetting in architecture as both respectful and iconoclastic. It reflects the Maya dual attitude toward the past. The monument burial signals a break with the past and the initiation of a new era recalling the ever-present death–rebirth theme. Morley, who made the most comprehensive consideration of Copan's Early Classic monuments to date, held the opinion that "as the city grew, the earliest monuments probably passed out of fashion—became obsolete as it were—and thus having outlasted the purposes for which they were originally designed, and being in every case exceptionally good blocks of stone, they were occasionally reused in later constructions"(Morley 1920:55).

If we consider that termination rituals (Fash and Fash 1996) accompanied much of the destruction of early monuments and façades, this is in keeping with termination rituals as recorded by Landa at shrines where pottery vessels are destroyed in an effort to deactivate the vessel. With such destruction, the captured soul of the vessel or monument is released (Tozzer 1941). In at least two instances, Stelae 18 and 31, defacement by gouging regular holes into the monument can be noted.

Discussion and Conclusion

The widespread decommissioning of Early Classic monuments and façades reflects a consistent pattern of ritual dedication and reuse of old, sacred stones (see also Sharer, this volume). Thereafter, Copan sculptors and rulers sought a fresh start and architectural renovation on a large scale. The sculpture façades on buildings were evolving rapidly into higher relief, which the stelae and altar carving tradition was slower to attain. Sculptural façades at Copan, with an abundance of iconographic information, may have served a purpose similar to that of narrative monuments at sites such as Palenque and Piedras Negras, leaving the stelae free for ruler glorification and calendrical ritual. As time passed, new sculptors discarded old stelae styles and innovatively went on to more elaborate styles to complement and rival the transformations occurring on the temples.

The chief purpose of freestanding stelae, as elsewhere in the Maya region, was to represent the ruler and commemorate the passage of time (Proskouriakoff 1960; Marcus 1976; Kubler 1984; Pasztory 1998). The shifts from stelae with figural representations to those devoid of figures, with only text, may simply be an indication of the personal preferences of different rulers or sculptors, rather than signs of sweeping political movements or attempts to solidify associations. In fact, Kubler suggests that bands of professional sculptors moved from one site to the next (1984:247), which could account for similarities and continuities of style, rather than their being the results of intra-site political connections. It may be significant, however, that the dramatic transition from profile figures to those with frontal poses occurs in the Late Classic following the Early Classic hiatus. At Copan, where the figure disappears from the hieroglyphic monuments at roughly this time and then bursts back upon the scene, it may reflect a period when it was considered more important to continue to record the passage of time than to glorify the ruler. We can only ponder the reasons for this occurrence and speculate that it may have derived from an instability in early cultural ties between regions such as central Mexico, the Petén, and the Highlands or a weakened role of the ruler.

Even if stylistic similarities are the result of roving sculptors, they would presumably function within a regional area that maintained friendly relations and trade. If Copan were attempting to forge ties to Tikal, as is suggested by the stylistic similarity of carving on Copan's Xukpi Stone to Tikal's Stela 31, judging by the variety of stylistic traits and monument formats evident at Copan in the Early Classic, it seems to have been a one-time occurrence. This would tend to suggest that whatever the level of Petén influence may have been during the founding era, it was relatively short lived.

Copan residents seemed intent on individualizing their style, perhaps a result of having a diverse population and excelling in the sculptural arts. For example, "Tikal sculptors never investigated the possibilities of relief rounded in depth" but continued the Petén adherence to two-dimensional linear surfaces (Kubler 1984). Interestingly, when Copan does resurrect the early ties and its legitimization of power in the Late Classic, it does so with reference to central Mexico (Fash and Fash 2000; Stuart 2000).

Unlike the abundant Late Classic monuments and façade sculptures at Copan, the Early Classic sculptures, with a few exceptions, are generally less common and are partial and removed from their original context. This naturally presents a challenge for making broad stylistic connections with other sites, or tying shifts in presentation and conventions to particular rulers or political changes. What conclusions can be drawn from the above data is that traditions stemming from the Highlands, Lowlands, and central Mexico converged at Copan in the Early Classic, resulting in its own characteristic style. This regional Copan style in turn inspired sites such as Tonina and Quirigua in the Maya realm. The earliest dated monument from Copan, the Motmot floor marker (A.D. 435), with a narrative scene of profile figures accompanied by hieroglyphic text, provides evidence for a strong link to Highland Guatemala, a region that filtered Central Mexican styles and influenced early Petén carving as well.

Although the groundwork was being laid for it in the Early Classic, the preoccupation with individualized representation of the ruler combined with the virtuosity of the sculptor in increasingly elaborate carvings is not conspicuous prior to the Late Classic. Yet, for all the artistic brilliance and innovation evident in the Late Classic period, it appears that it was the Early Classic scribes, sculptors, and architects who invented and initiated the eclectic Copan style in a wide variety of media and formats.

Acknowledgments

I wish to thank the editors of this volume for the invitation to participate; William L. Fash and Norman Hammond, who read and commented on the initial paper; David Stuart, who shared ideas and engaged in insightful discussions during its preparation, and Jocelyn Pierce, who assisted in the final compilation of the text and figures.

13

STRUCTURE 10L-16 AND ITS EARLY CLASSIC ANTECEDENTS: FIRE AND THE EVOCATION AND RESURRECTION OF K'INICH YAX K'UK' MO'

Karl Taube

Since 1995 I have participated in the reconstruction and interpretation of the complex mosaic façades of Structure 10L-16, located in the center of the Copan Acropolis. With the assistance and guidance of Ricardo Agurcia Fasquelle and Barbara Fash, I have focused upon the various motifs encountered during the 1989 and 1990 excavations of this temple (Agurcia F. et al. 1989; Agurcia F. et al. 1996; Morales 1989; Stone and Kluth 1989;). Structure 10L-16 is the culmination of a complex series of underlying constructions encountered during excavations separately directed by Ricardo Agurcia Fasquelle and Robert Sharer (see Agurcia F. and Fash 1997; Sharer, Traxler, et al. 1999; D. Stuart 1997).

Beginning with the Early Classic Hunal Structure, this succession of buildings constitutes the Copan Axis, which for hundreds of years was the symbolic pivotal center of Copan and the place of the founder, K'inich Yax K'uk' Mo'. Although one of the last buildings constructed in the Copan Acropolis, Structure 10L-16 is filled with allusions to K'inich Yax K'uk' Mo' and the great Early Classic metropolis of Teotihuacan. In the Copan Axis series of constructions, allusions to the founder are related to fire rituals and offerings, an essential means of conjuring and communicating with gods and ancestors in both Teotihuacan and Classic Maya ritual (Taube 1998b, 2000b). It will be noted that Rosalila Structure constitutes a massive symbolic censer, a means of conjuring K'inich Yax K'uk' Mo' through fire ritual. For Structure 10L-16, nowhere are the allusions to fire, the founder, and Teotihuacan clearer and more profound than on the three massive sculptural façades projecting from the western stairway above Altar Q.

Structure 10L-16 and the Themes of Centrality and Fire

The placement, form, and sculptural motifs from Structure 10L-16 indicate that it was the symbolic hub and center of the Copan world: "Structure 16 is the heart of the Copan Acropolis which in turn is the center of the ancient kingdom of Copan and the seat of its social, political, economic and religious powers" (Agurcia F. and Fash 1997). It was also the tallest building in the Copan Acropolis and, at present, rises some 20 m above the West Court (Agurcia F. et al. 1996). The original foundations of the temple superstructure reveal that this building was originally even taller, as there were four massive piers, clearly designed to bear a great weight (Agurcia F. et al. 1989). For additional support, the central portion was subsequently filled, with a stairway in the northern doorway, indicating that the building was at least two stories high (Agrucia F. et al. 1989). With its four piers and interior stairway, the superstructure foundations recall the famous tower of Palenque adjacent to House E, the preeminent seat of power at the site (see Robertson 1985:fig. 385). Unfortunately, the Copan "tower" is far less well preserved. Given the intensely political nature of this building, it may have suffered intentional effacement during the Late Classic collapse of Copan.

Unlike other buildings of the Copan Acropolis, the four sides of the temple platform and superstructure have similar proportions, more closely resembling a square than a rectangle. This concern with radial symmetry is also reflected in the four piers and doorways of the temple, which form a cross oriented to the four directions. Leonardo López Luján (personal communication 1997) notes that the cross-plan of the foundations is very similar to the cruciform crypts under stelae at Copan (see Strömsvik 1941).

For both the Middle Preclassic Olmec and the Classic Maya, stelae served as models of the world axis (Freidel et al. 1993:134–135; Taube 2000a). Placed above the cruciform crypts, the Copan stelae are in the middle place, the axis of the four quarters. In a like manner, the radial symmetry reflected in the temple platform and superstructure mark Structure 10L-16 as the great axis of Copan. Both the stelae crypts and the temple plan evoke the Kan cross, which throughout ancient Mesoamerica represents the four world directions and corners, with a dot frequently marking and emphasizing the middle place. In Classic Maya iconography, the Kan cross can designate not only the center of the earth, but the sky as well (see Freidel et al. 1993:fig. 4.27c; Kerr 1990:196). It is surely no coincidence that by far the most developed presentations of the Kan cross at Copan are on Structure 10L-16, both alternating with "lazy eyes" in a twisted rope motif and as massive blocks some 40 cm wide (see Fash and Fash 2000:fig. 14.7b, f). Excavation and spacing suggest that there were at least forty of the large Kan cross blocks on the temple superstructure.

The quadripartite nature of Structure 10L-16 is replicated by its West Court monument, Altar Q, which is square in plan and stands on four circular pillars. In addition, Agurcia Fasquelle (personal communication 1998) notes that the altar and its sup-

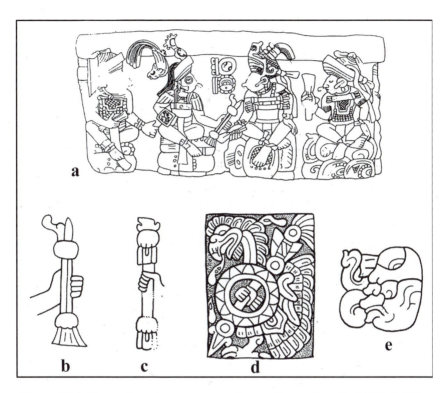

Figure 13.1 Fire and war imagery appearing on Copan Altar Q. (a) K'inich Yax K'uk' Mo' with shield and burning dart, note probable torches held in hands of other rulers, west side of Altar Q (drawing by Barbara W. Fash); (b) detail of dart held by K'inich Yax K'uk' Mo'; (c) dart from interior temple text of Structure 10L-26; (d) Thin Orange vessel portrayal of eagle with shield and dart (after von Winning 1987:I, chap. 7:fig. 6a); (e) K'awiil with cranial torch, Altar Q (after Stuart 1992:fig. 3).

ports resemble the burial slabs atop columns in the royal tombs of the Copan Axis. Along with explicit reference to the royal ancestors of the Copan dynasty, Altar Q is filled with allusions to fire ritual. The west side portrays the handing down of fire from the founder of the Copan dynasty, K'inich Yax K'uk' Mo', to the 16th and final king, Yax Pasaj Chan Yoaat (Taube 2000b:274).

The founder appears as a Teotihuacan warrior wielding a War Serpent shield and a burning dart (Figure 13.1a, Plate 1a). This feathered dart is virtually identical to examples known from Copan and Teotihuacan (Figure 13.1c-d). The concept of a burning dart is strongly militaristic and is quite consistent with David Stuart's scenario of a foreign, Teotihuacan take-over at both Tikal and Copan, the latter occurring with the arrival of K'inich Yax K'uk' Mo' (Stuart 2000). However, the symbolism of fire in relation to dynastic founding also recalls Late Postclassic highland Mexico, where the making of new fire marks the foundation of new polities (Boone 2000:160). In high-land Mexican scenes of fire making, a burning dart frequently constitutes the drill (Taube 2000b:294–295). Whereas K'inich Yax K'uk' Mo' wields a burning dart, Yax Pasaj Chan Yoaat and the other rulers on the sides of Altar Q hold a different object, quite probably a torch of bound paper (Figure 13.1a; see Taube 2000b:274). The ends of these devices resemble many depictions of the cranial torch of *K'awiil*, or God K, including an example from the Altar Q text (Figure 13.1e). Altar Q portrays K'inich Yax K'uk' Mo' and his 15 successors passing down the founding fire of the dynasty. The prominence of fire in association with dynastic descent concerns both political suc-cession and the importance of fire offerings for conjuring and communicating with the dead, a means of linking generations of the living and the deceased.

Although much attention has been paid to the *way* ("co-essence") spirit among the Classic Maya (Houston and Stuart 1989; Grube and Nahm 1994), another markedly different vitalizing force was the breath soul (Houston and Taube 2000:267). Commonly mentioned in Classic Maya death expressions, this spirit is personified by the floral god appearing as the head variant for the numeral three. In Mayan languages, terms for three, commonly *ox* or *ux*, also relate to words for breath, spirit, and aroma (Houston and Taube:272–273). Aromatic fire offerings constitute both the food and essence of the breath spirit. According to Prudence Rice (1999:41), Maya effigy censers are "living representations of the ancestors and conduits of divine inspiration." Among the most graphic expressions of this spiritual inspiration are Early Classic effi-gy censers with exit holes through open mouths (for Kaminaljuyu and Tikal examples, see Culbert 1993:fig. 14; Kidder et al. 1946:figs. 87, 201i, 207g; Martin and Grube 2000:7). The copal smoke truly is their breath, created by the "live" burning fire in the censer bowl. Quite probably, individuals in olfactory range were symbolically in the spiritual presence of the conjured being (Houston and Taube 2000:263).

At Copan, an impressive and elaborate series of 12 effigy censers stood around the exterior of Burial 37-4 in Chorcha Structure, an early phase of Structure 10L-26 corresponding closely to the reign of the 12th ruler, Smoke Imix God K (Fash 1991:fig. 66; W. Fash et al. 1992:111–112; W. Fash 1997:77–78; Rice 1999:39). The censers feature seated males atop the lids, including one example with Teotihuacan-style regalia tentatively identified as K'inich Yax K'uk' Mo' (see W. Fash et al. 1992:fig. 7, lower center). The probable portrayal of the founder, the number of effigy censers, and the presence of shared costume elements suggest that these braziers constitute an earlier version of the Altar Q king list (W. Fash et al. 1992:112; W. Fash 1997:78; Fash et al. 2001). It is especially noteworthy that censers form the Chorcha series, explicitly linking the royal sequence to fire ritual.

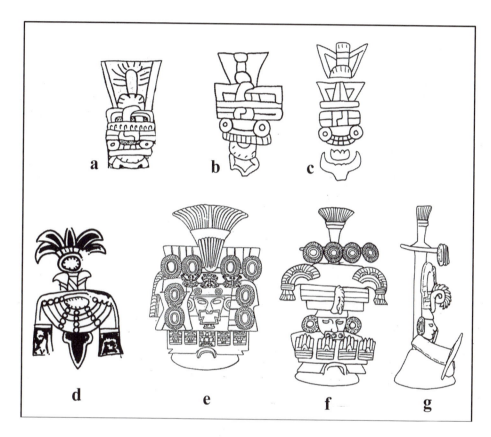

Figure 13.2 Glyphs appearing on Escuintla vessels and Teotihuacan theater censer imagery. (a, b) Similar glyphs of warrior bust and dart appearing on two Escuintla vessels (from Taube 2000c:figs. 16b, 14e); (c) glyph of warrior bust and dart from Escuintla vessel (drawn from photo in the Foundation for Latin American Research archive); (d) painting of dart and costume ornaments from Chalcatzingo Cave 19 (after Apostolides 1987:fig. 12.45); (e) Teotihuacan censer lid with probable feathered dart butt (from Séjourné 1964:fig. 17); (f) two schematic views of Teotihuacan theater censer illustrating dart chimney (after Linné 1942:figs. 316–317).

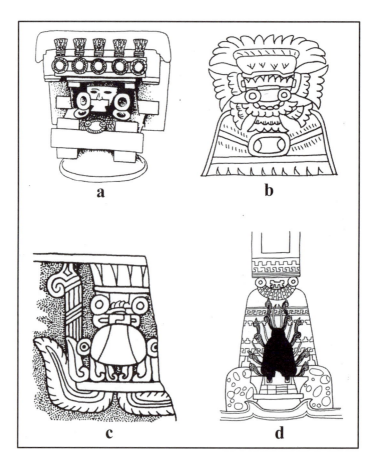

Figure 13.3 Teotihuacan style censers and mortuary bundles. (a) Theater censer from Escuintla region (from Taube 2000b:fig. 10.22b); (b) mortuary bundle portrayed on Teotihuacan vessel (after Séjourné 1976:fig. 48); (c) burning mortuary bundle, detail of plano-relief vessel (from Taube 2000b:fig. 10.22c); (d) mortuary bundle or censer lid atop burning brazier, detail of Temple of Agriculture murals (after Gamio 1922: I, pl. 33).

Although hollow human figures atop censer lids are rare in the Classic Maya Lowlands, they are a basic trait of Teotihuacan-style theater censers from the Valley of Mexico, as well as the Lake Amatitlán and Escuintla regions of Guatemala (Figure 13.2e–f; see Berlo 1984; Hellmuth 1983). Teotihuacan theater censers portray masked funerary bundles, a common motif in the iconography of Teotihuacan (Taube 2000b:306–309; for a discussion of Teotihuacan mortuary bundles, see Headrick 1999). The censer effigies frequently portray butterfly imagery, alluding to the souls of dead warriors, fire, and the Teotihuacan cult of war (Berlo 1983; Taube 2000b). Often faceless and static, the warrior bundles can also have basal flames and smoke (Figure 13.3). These burning bundles concern both theater censers and Teotihuacan funerary ritual. The placement of the effigy lid atop the smoking urn replicates the rite of placing the bundled dead atop a fire in the burial pit (Taube 2000b:307–309).

In a study concerning Teotihuacan writing, I noted an identical glyph on two different Early Classic Escuintla vessels, both apparently the name glyph of an historical figure (Figure 13.2a–b, Taube 2000c:21). Still another Escuintla-style vessel reveals its meaning, a faceless bust atop a downwardly pointing feathered dart (Figure 13.2c). The lower portion, which I previously misidentified as a pectoral, is the trefoil point which commonly appears in portrayals of Teotihuacan-style darts (Figures 13.1c–d, 13.2d). A very similar sign appears in a Teotihuacan-style painting from Chalcatzingo Cave 19 (Figure 13.2d). Although Alex Apostolides (1987:191–192) notes that this painting "resembles a human torso, neck and head," he also mentions that the upper and lower ends of this element are dart or spear-like. As in the case of the Escuintla examples, this mural portrays regalia on a vertical dart, much as if it were an effigy wearing a necklace and a piece of hanging cloth.

The Escuintla signs portray a faceless mortuary bundle with a vertical dart. Many Teotihuacan theater censers have a prominent central V-shaped feathered element at the top, immediately recalling the dart butt of the Escuintla and Chalcatzingo signs (Figure 13.2e). On one theater censer illustrated in a profile view by Sigvald Linné (1942), the long, hollow tube that supports the mask, headdress, and earspools of the censer assemblage is clearly a feather-butted dart (Figure 13.2f). When set afire, the censer would become a smoking dart in the image of a warrior bundle.

The Teotihuacan warrior bundle cult probably influenced later Aztec funerary ceremonies. Both warriors and kings were burned in bundles, with images of these mortuary bundles fashioned of bound *ocote*. Page 72 of the *Codex Magliabechiano* portrays the warrior bundle effigy with a prominent dart in the headdress. Diego Durán (1994:150, 284, 294, 385) mentions that Aztec mortuary bundles and the bundle images were identified with a structure known as the house of darts (*tlacochcalli* or *tlacochcalco*). Aside from dart chimneys, Teotihuacan theater censers are frequently marked with small dart bundles (Figure 13.3a). The burning dart held by K'inich Yax K'uk' Mo' on Altar Q could well refer to Teotihuacan warrior mortuary ritual and symbolism.

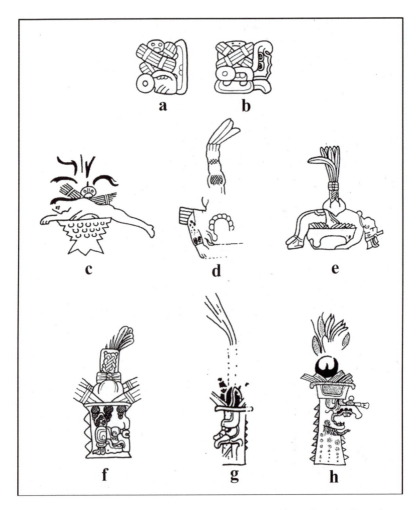

Figure 13.4 Crossed bundles fire sign. (a) Crossed bundles glyph with *te* and *na* affixes, Copan Altar Q (after Stuart 1992:fig. 3); (b) crossed bundles glyph with *wi*, *te* and *na* affixes, Yaxchilan Lintel 25 (after Graham and von Euw 1977:55); (c) victim in burning brazier with crossed bundles glyph, detail of mural from Tohcok, Campeche (from Taube 1994:fig. 10b); (d) victim with wood bundle, Piedras Negras Stela 14 (from Taube 1994:fig. 9c); (e) victim atop faggots, Piedras Negras Stela 11 (from Taube 1994:fig. 9b); (f) skeletal brazier containing four diagonally placed wood bundles, El Cayo Altar 1 (after drawing courtesy of Peter Mathews); (g) censer with *k'in* sign on brow (from Taube 1994:fig. 8e); (h) censer with diagonally placed firewood (from Taube 1994:fig. 8a).

The Altar Q text mentions K'inich Yax K'uk' Mo' in relation to the crossed bundles *te nah* sign, which could be glossed as "crossed bundles wood structure" (Figure 13.4a). Although Schele (1992:141–142) interpreted the crossed bundles as sprouts and, by extension, lineage, they are bound faggots of firewood. The same sign appears in a burning censer depiction from Tohcok, Campeche, complete with the schematic human face in the crux of the wood bundles (Figure 13.4c). Similar figures appear on Piedras Negras Stelae 11 and 14, although in this case the sticks lie below the victims (Figure 13.4d–e). The feathered element rising out of the abdomen is also found in censers with stick bundles, revealing that this form relates to fire offerings (Figure 13.4f–h). With their supine positions and open abdomens, the Piedras Negras figures recall the Aztec 52-year new fire rites, during which fire was drawn on the chest of a sacrificed captive (Sahagún 1950:82, bk. 7:25–26, 28). Of course, a prominent theme of the Aztec new fire rites, known as "the binding of the years" were *xiuhmolpil-li*, tied bundles of firewood.

Copan texts identify the crossed wood bundle structure with K'inich Yax K'uk' Mo' (Schele 1992; Stuart 2000:492). Copan Altar B' describes the founder as "he of" the crossed wood bundle structure (Morley 1920:plate 22a). At Copan and other sites, the wood bundle structure appears in Teotihuacan contexts, and the crossed bundles place sign may derive from Teotihuacan fire ritual. Stuart (2000:493) notes that one Tikal text mentions that Nuun Yax Ayiin, a king with particularly strong connections to Teotihuacan, performed a ritual at such a building. In addition, Stuart (2000) calls attention to the same crossed bundle glyph on Yaxchilan Lintel 25, a monument filled with imagery pertaining to Teotihuacan.

At Copan and nearby Río Amarillo, the crossed wood bundle sign appears with Teotihuacan motifs, including the Mexican year sign (Figure 13.5a–b). The south side of the recently reconstructed Structure 10L-26 temple text features a Teotihuacan-style bird with the crossed bundle sign in its headdress (for a view of the opposing north head, see Figure 13.14d). Copan Structure 10L-33 portrays the goggle eyes of Tlaloc with cloud scrolls atop the crossed wood bundles, recalling a Teotihuacan mural featuring the head of Tlaloc on four burning torch bundles (Figure 13.5a–b). A stela from San Miguel Totolpan, Guerrero, features Tlaloc holding a pair of such torches in his hands (Figure 13.5d). A Teotihuacan-style monument attributed to Veracruz portrays a goggled figure with another pair of burning torches (Figure 13.5e). The headdress contains another pair of hand-held torches, here below a temple roof motif. With this architectural element, the crossed torches are very similar to the crossed bundle house glyph of Classic Maya script.

The crossed wood bundle structure at Copan may refer to Structure 10L-16 and the veneration of K'inich Yax K'uk' Mo' (Taube 1997, 1998b; Stuart 2000:493). Aside from Altar Q, Structure 10L-16 has major axial stairway sculptures devoted to Teotihuacan and the fiery resurrection of K'inich Yax K'uk' Mo' as the sun god. One Classic Maya dedication glyph features a burning censer bowl marked with the solar

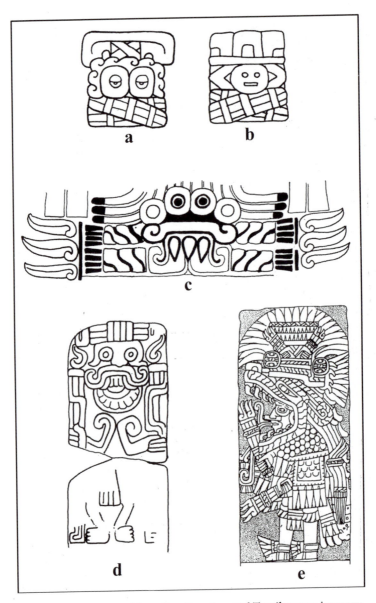

Figure 13.5 Crossed bundles fire sign and Teotihuacan imagery. (a) Crossed bundles sign with Tlaloc eyes and cloud scrolls, Structure 10L-33 (after B. Fash 1997:fig. 3); (b) crossed bundles sign rays and stylized Mexican year sign, Structure 10L-33 (after B. Fash 1997:fig. 3); (c) Tlaloc B with coyote tail headdress atop four burning torch bundles, San Sebastián, Teotihuacan (after Cabrera Castro, et al. 1996:pl. 2); (d) Tlaloc grasping pair of torches, stela from San Miguel Totolapan, Guerrero (after Reyna Robles and Rodriguez Betancourt 1990:230); (e) monument portraying figure with torches in hands and headdress (from Taube 2000c:fig. 35g).

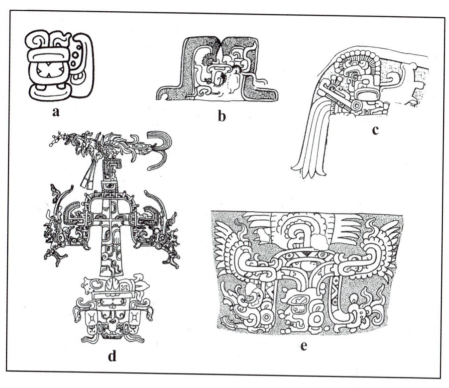

Figure 13.6 Classic Maya censers and solar imagery. (a) "House censing" glyph, Piedras Negras Panel 4 (after Stuart 1998:fig. 11a); (b) Quadripartite Badge brazier with flames (from Taube 1998:fig. 10e); (c) Quadripartite Badge with head of sun god, El Zapote Stela 5 (detail of drawing courtesy of James Porter); (d) world tree rising out of Quadripartite Badge censer, Sarcophagus Lid, Palenque (from Freidel et al. 1993:fig. 2:22); (e) world tree rising out of head of Maya sun god (drawing by Karl Taube from vessel in the Museo de Cultura Teotihuacana, Teotihuacan).

k'in sign, a glyph read as *el* (or *elel*) *nah* by Stephen Houston (personal communication 1992), meaning "structure burning." Given the presence of the censer sign, Stuart (1998:389–390) glosses this phrase as "house censing."

The so-called Quadripartite Badge is a censer glyph with offerings in the *k'in*-marked bowl (Figures 13.6b, d, 13.10a–b). At times, flames curl out of such censers (Figure 13.6b). In Early Classic Maya iconography, the head of the sun god, K'inich Ajaw, can substitute for the Quadripartite Badge, as can be seen on El Zapote Stela 5 (Figure 13.6c). The Sarcophagus Lid and the Temple of the Cross at Palenque depict

Figure 13.7 Mexican year sign headdresses, torches, and fire offerings in Classic Mesoamerica. (a) Maya sun god with Mexican year sign headdress with diagonal torches (after Sharer et al. 1999:fig. 6); (b) year sign headdress with pair of burning torches, detail of censer from Xico (Berlow 1984:pl. 45); (c) year sign headdress with probable torches, Xochicalco Stela 2; (d) Teotihuacan "manta" sign with upper portion composed of year sign with pair of vertical wood bundles (after von Winning 1987: II, chapt. 2, fig. 17c); (e) Tlaloc with vegetal material at side of headdress, detail of interior temple text, Structure 10L-26, Copan (after Stuart 2000:fig. 15.24); (f) year sign bundle of vegetal material in burning brazier, detail of interior temple text, Structure 10L-26, Copan (from Taube 2000b:fig. 10.5g).

serpents climbing the celestial branches of a world tree rising out of a brazier (Figure 13.6d). An Early Classic version appears on a carved Maya-style vessel from Teotihuacan. Rather than a skeletal censer, the sun god's head serves as the base of the world tree (Figure 13.6e). The Palenque and Early Classic vessel scenes concern the same theme, fiery resurrection out of a burning censer bowl.

In a recent discussion of censer ritual and symbolism, Prudence Rice describes some of the underlying meanings of fire offerings among Classic Maya elite: "As the rising smoke from the burning copal symbolizes the rising of the new sun from its 'death' in the Underworld, so too does it symbolize the (re)birth of the god-king" (Rice 1999:43). In a like manner, Laurette Séjourné (1964:173) interprets the Teotihuacan theater censers as the young sun rising out the dark underworld. Although the overlapping themes of fire, solar rebirth, and the conjuring of a deified ancestor are powerfully portrayed on the stairway of Structure 10L-16, they are also present in earlier buildings of the Copan Axis.

The Early Classic Antecedents to Structure 10L-16

One of the most striking traits of Structure 10L-16 and earlier buildings of the Copan Axis (Sedat and López, this volume) is the central importance of fire ritual. Hunal Structure, the first in the succession of structures, displays material evidence of burning and fire (Sedat 1997a; Sedat and López this volume). The western-facing Yehnal façade displays the Maya sun god, surely the apotheosized K'inich Yax K'uk' Mo' (see also Stuart, this volume), with a headdress of diagonal burning torches (Figure 13.7a). This headdress is a Mexican year sign with flanking diagonal torches, such as appears in the iconography of Teotihuacan and Xochicalco (Figure 13.7b–c).

One form of the Teotihuacan "*manta*" sign—a variant of the Mexican year sign—is supplied with a pair of vertical wood bundles (Figure 13.7d). On Mexican year sign headdresses worn by Tlaloc, the year signs often bind vegetal bundles, much as if they were torches or fire offerings (e.g., Copan Stela 6, Yaxchilan Lintel 25). The temple text from Structure 10L-26 portrays Tlaloc with vegetal material projecting from the side of his year sign headdress, with the same text featuring a similar year sign bundle atop a burning censer (Figure 13.7e–f). Although the Yehnal façades refer to the fiery apotheosis of K'inich Yax K'uk' Mo' as the Maya sun god, the year sign and torch headdresses pertain to Teotihuacan symbolism.

The Yehnal masks label this building as the place of K'inich Yax K'uk' Mo', as is surely also true for the magnificent façades of the subsequent Margarita Structure (Sharer, Traxler, et al. 1999:10). A sub-floor cache west of the Margarita Tomb bore clear evidence of burning, recalling both Maya and Teotihuacan fire ritual (Davis-Salazar and Bell 2000; Sharer personal communication 2001).

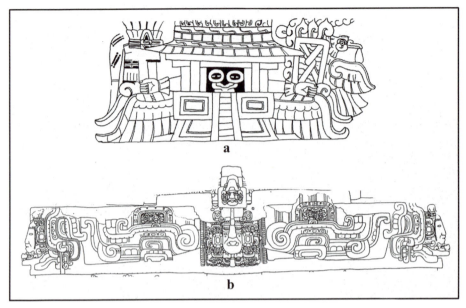

Figure 13.8 Early Classic imagery pertaining to K'inich Yax K'uk' Mo'. (a) Probable portrayal of K'inich Yax K'uk' Mo' as talud-tablero structure, detail of "Dazzler" vessel (after Stuart 1997:79); (b) Avian sun god on north cornice of Rosalila (detail of drawing by Barbara W. Fash from Agurcia F. 1997:fig. 7).

The fine, stucco-painted vessel discovered in the Margarita Tomb, commonly known as the "Dazzler,"[*] probably refers to the resting place and fiery resurrection of the founder (Figure 13.8a; Plate 7a-c). According to Sedat (1997b), the vessel portrays K'inich Yax K'uk' Mo' as a personified, winged form of his *talud-tablero* burial structure, Hunal. The temple roof or "headdress" is burning, designating it as a "fire-house." This flaming roof headdress recalls both the aforementioned Teotihuacan-style temple roof atop two torches and the Yehnal façades (Figures 13.5e, 13.7a). In contrast to the Yehnal and Margarita façades (Plate 2), the vessel is in strong Teotihuacan-style. The architectonic figure is very similar to Teotihuacan theater censers, which as their name implies, are also a merging of architectural and human components (Figures 13.3a, 13.2e–f).

---

[*] Margarita Tomb Chamber 2 Vessel 1 (1/6/208-1, MSC326) see Bell et al. and Reents-Budet et al., this volume.

As in the case of the Copan example, Escuintla Teotihuacan-style censer figures often have wings, although usually of butterflies rather than birds (see Berlo 1984:pl. 106–115, 130–131; Hellmuth 1975:pl. 26–27, 30–33). Nonetheless, whether they are of bird or butterfly, the wings allude to the celestial resurrection of the soul. In addition, theater censer figures commonly hold paper banners and other objects in their outstretched hands, quite like the banner and other items grasped by the Dazzler figure (Figures 13.2e, 13.8a). For the Dazzler scene, the *talud-tablero* platform corresponds to the censer bowl, with the burning structure representing the smoking lid. If the painted vessel portrays the Hunal Structure, the censer comparison is especially apt, as the inside of the flaming bowl would correspond to the interior Hunal Tomb, precisely the relation previously noted for censer bowls and burial pits at Teotihuacan.

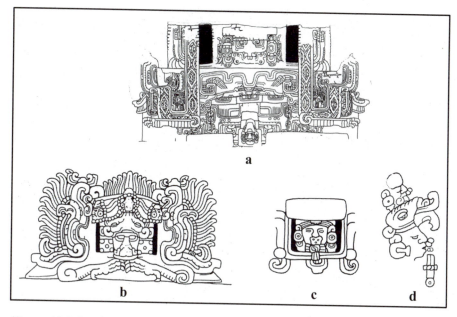

Figure 13.9 Smoke vents appearing on Rosalila. (a) Uppermost portion of north side with probable censer skull with flanking vent-like niches (detail of drawing by Barbara W. Fash from Agurcia Fasquelle 1997:fig. 7); (b) K'inich Yax K'uk' Mo' with head in bowl element supplied with pair of vents (detail of drawing by Barbara W. Fash from Agurcia F. 1997:fig. 7); (c) ancestor face in vessel cartouche with smoke vents (detail of drawing by Barbara W. Fash in Agurcia Fasquelle 1997:fig. 7); (d) K'inich Yax K'uk' Mo' with knotted element before face, Motmot floor marker (detail from drawing by Barbara W. Fash after Fash and Fash 1996:fig. 2).

The later Rosalila Structure (Plate 1b; Agurcia F., this volume) is another "fire-house" with strong references to K'inich Yax K'uk' Mo'. The lower walls depict the founder as an avian sun god with a quetzal bird headdress and open macaw beaks in his outstretched serpent wings (Figure 13.9b). The cornices immediately above portray massive images of the founder apotheosized as an avian sun god (Figure 13.8b). With their wings extended across almost the entire width of the temple cornices, these figures are in many ways a later form of the avian building on the "Dazzler" vessel (Figure 13.8a).

The interior of Rosalila is filled with smudging from fires, and at the time of excavation, it contained numerous censers (Agurcia F. 1997c:34–35, Agurcia F. and Fash 1997:16). I have suggested that the large skulls on the uppermost preserved portions of the north and south sides of Rosalila portray massive censers (Figure 13.9a; Taube 1998a).

In Classic Maya iconography, braziers are frequently skeletalized heads, and a censer fashioned from an actual human skull was discovered in the Cenote of Sacrifice at Chichen Itza (Figures 13.5f, 13.6d; see Coggins and Shane 1984:no. 199). The descending snakes on either side of the Rosalila censer may relate to serpents rising out of censer bowls in Classic Maya art (see Schele and Miller 1986b:pl. 63, 65, 74). However, the downward position of their heads strongly resembles the portrayal of snakes in the branches of world trees (Figure 13.6d–e). As in the case of the Sarcophagus Lid and Temple of the Cross scenes at Palenque, the Rosalila serpents may have hung from a tree rising out of the skeletal censer. Situated atop a zoomorphic mountain at the uppermost portion of Rosalila, the censers and serpents label this structure as a place of fire and resurrection.

The sides of the Rosalila skull have vertical niches, recalling niche windows or ventilators flanking the heads of the aforementioned K'inich Yax K'uk' Mo' figures on the lower walls of the structure (Figure 13.9b). Similar niches also border human heads in four cartouches on the east and west sides of the building (Figure 13.9c). Agurcia F. (1998:351) notes that these heads may represent "a dead ruler emerging from the underworld," and indeed the knotted element over the mouth commonly denotes death in Classic Maya iconography. It also appears with the possibly posthumous image of K'inich Yax K'uk' Mo' on the Motmot floor marker (Figure 13.9d).

The four Rosalila cartouches probably also portray the deceased K'inich Yax K'uk' Mo'. Their form is identical to Early Classic portrayals of censer bowls, although here with the interior k'in sign personified by the head of the founding "sun king" (Figure 13.10a–b). A series of Early Classic stucco reliefs from Yaxchilan Structure 6 display a very similar series of niched cartouches, in this case containing the head of the Maya sun god (Figure 13.10d). Other Early Classic niched cartouches appear on

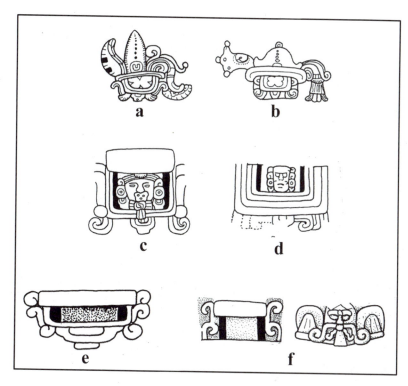

Figure 13.10 Censers and cartouches appearing on Early Classic Maya structures. (a, b) Early Classic censer bowls with interior k'in sign (after Hellmuth 1986:figs. 138, 108); (c) ancestor head in bowl cartouche, Rosalila (after Agurcia Fasquelle 1997:fig. 7); (d) head of sun god in bowl cartouche, Yaxchilan Structure 6 (after Tate 1992:fig. 53); (e) bowl cartouche, Building B of Group II, Holmul (after Merwin and Vaillant 1932:fig. 16); (f) cartouche with smoke volutes and sun god head, details from cornice of Structure 5D-82-1,Tikal (after Laporte and Fialko 1995:fig. 21).

the exterior of Building B of Group II at Holmul (Figure 13.10e). This building served as a sort of elite mausoleum, as some 22 individuals along with rich burial goods were interred in this building (Merwin and Vaillant 1932:404). The recessed niches lack sculpted faces, and it is conceivable that they held human skulls similar to the skull censer atop Rosalila. Recent excavations of the Castillo platform at Late Postclassic Mayapan revealed wall niches containing the remains of human skulls (Peraza Lope 1999:53).

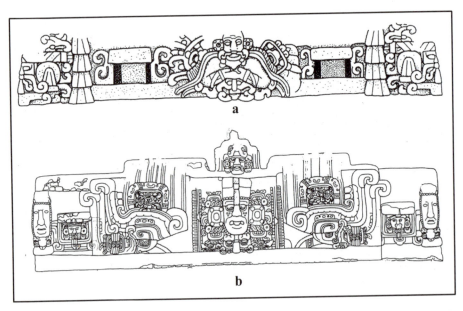

Figure 13.11 Comparison of Mundo Perdido frieze with west cornice of Rosalila. (a) Reconstructed cornice of 5D-82-1, from Mundo Perdido, Tikal (after Laporte and Fialko 1995:fig. 21); (b) west cornice from first story of Rosalila (detail of drawing by Barbara W. Fash from Agurcia F. 1997:fig. 7).

One of the earliest examples of cartouches with pairs of vertical niches occurs on the cornice of Structure 5D-82-1 from the Mundo Perdido at Tikal, dating to approximately A.D. 200–300 (Figure 13.11a; Laporte and Fialko 1995:54–55). In this case the vertical niches are flanked by pairs of scrolls, probably alluding to smoke (Figures 13.10f, 13.11a). As in the case of the Holmul examples, the cartouche interior is devoid of sculpture. However, the cornice corners portray anthropomorphic faces with knotted cloth or paper over their mouths, recalling the images in the four Rosalila cartouches as well as the large ancestral head at the corners of the building (Figure 13.11a–b). In addition, the Tikal cornice also bears the probable image of a winged sun god between the cartouches, very much like the avian sun gods flanked by cartouches on the east and west Rosalila friezes (Figure 13.11a–b). The folded arm position of the Tikal winged figure immediately recalls the K'inich Yax K'uk' Mo' images from the lower portion of Rosalila (Figure 13.9b). Although certainly a reference to the Copan founder, the cornices from the first story of Rosalila display many traits present in earlier dynastic imagery from Tikal. The similarity of the Rosalila façade to the earlier Mundo Perdido structure suggests that K'inich Yax K'uk' Mo' may have had strong political and cultural ties to Early Classic Tikal (see Sharer, this volume).

The smoke or cloud volutes flanking the Mundo Perdido cartouches reveal the symbolic function of the vertical niches. Ricardo Agurcia Fasquelle (personal communication 1997) notes that the Rosalila niches are smoke ventilators. These appear on the large portrayals of K'inich Yax K'uk' Mo' on the lowest portion of the temple, with the four cartouches on the first floor cornices, and in giant form flanking the skull atop Rosalila. Just as ancestral heads appear in the four censer bowls of the first story cornices, the heads of the large images of K'inich Yax K'uk' Mo' on the lowest portion of the building are also within bowl-like enclosures with vertical ventilators (Figure 13.9b; for clearer view of enclosure rim, see Agurcia F. 1997a:fig. 9).

Clearly enough, the flanking vents are giant, architectonic versions of the mouth vents of the Early Classic effigy censers, that is, the smoke pouring out of these vents constitutes the breath essence of the sculpted heads. If this be the case, what is the censer? Quite probably it is the Hunal Tomb deep in the foundations of the Copan Axis. During Classic Maya fire rites of conjuring, censers became focused, miniature forms of temples, the symbolic place of the ancestor or god (Taube 1998b:448). However, in terms of what Stephen Houston (1998:348) has called a "reciprocal metaphor," the opposite also holds true. Rosalila is a temple but also a huge symbolic censer, with the Hunal Tomb constituting the offering bowl. The smoke pouring symbolically out of the tomb of K'inich Yax K'uk' Mo' and actually out of Rosalila embodies the spirit and essence of the founder, which must have permeated the Acropolis with its pungent aroma.

The Stairway Sculptures of Structure 10L-16

Three massive, axially oriented altars projected from the western stairway of Structure 10L-16. Along with serving as platforms for performance and ritual, these stairway altars provided vertical surfaces for elaborate façades, among the largest and most impressive sculptural programs in the Acropolis. In their lexicon of Maya architecture, Stanley Loten and David Pendergast (1984:13) term this type of architectural feature a "stair block," which they define as: "A type of platform or bench-like unit, set in or on a stair or landing, usually athwart the primary axis."

In this study, the three units of Structure 10L-16 will be referred to as Stair Blocks I, II, and III, beginning with the lowest and most western and ending with Stairway Block III, located near the summit of the stairway (for a reconstruction see G. Stuart 1997:86–87). During 1995 and 1996, Barbara Fash and I reconstructed the three stair block façades of Structure 10L-16 for the newly created Copan Sculpture Museum. The following discussion is a direct result of this collaborate investigation, and was only possible with the active participation and assistance of Barbara Fash.

Figure 13.12 Stair Block I of Structure 10L-16 with skull and Tlaloc imagery from the Copan region. (a) Stair Block I, skeletal Tlaloc head with thirty human skulls (from Agurcia F. 1997:fig. 5); (b) detail of Tlaloc face (drawing by Karl Taube); (c) stone Tlaloc head censer in form of water jar, Structure 10L-16 (drawing by Karl Taube); (d) head from large seated Tlaloc, Structure 10L-16 (drawing by Karl Taube); (e) massive Tlaloc head with skeletalized maxillae, El Puente (drawing by Karl Taube); (f) massive skull in center of lowest stair block of Structure 10L-26 (drawing by Karl Taube).

Stair Block I

The largest of the three stairway façades, the vertical face of Stair Block I, consists of three units: a roughly square central surface and two flanking, recessed smaller elements (Figure 13.12a). In plan, the upper surface of this stair block resembles the Maya T-shaped *ik'* sign, signifying wind, with the lower portion of the "T" oriented to Altar Q.

The sculptural façade of Stair Block I is a tableau of death. The central composition features the head of Tlaloc with Kan Cross earspools, a trait found with Tlaloc heads from Structure 10L-16 and other Late Classic monuments at Copan (Figure 13.12b-d). Tlaloc appears as a massive skull with a hollow nasal cavity and a fleshless upper jaw. A trefoil element, probably representing a lolling tongue flanked by spiraling gouts of blood, replaces the missing mandible. Other examples of Tlaloc skulls displaying maxillae with outpouring blood are known from Copan Structures 10L-16, 10L-21, and 10L-26, as well as Lintel 25 at Yaxchilan (Figures 13.7f, 13.12d; see Fash and Fash 2000:figs. 14.7c, 14.8, 14.9e; Graham and von Euw 1977:55). A particularly large example with fleshless upper gums derives from the nearby region of El Puente, Honduras, quite possibly a local copy of the Stair Block I skull (Figure 13.12e). Flanking Tlaloc skulls with outpouring blood appear on the lowest stair block of Structure 10L-26 (see Freidel et al. 1993:fig. 8.24). Between this pair, in the central axis of the stair block, there is a massive skull (Figure 13.12f). However, due to its heavily eroded condition, it cannot be discerned whether this central skull had Tlaloc attributes.

The skeletal and jawless Tlaloc figures allude to war, sacrifice, and human trophies. Diego de Landa (Tozzer 1941:123) records that among the contact period Yucatec Maya, jaws were removed from vanquished warriors as trophies of war. This custom also recalls the effigy jawbone collars from the mass burials in the Temple of Quetzalcoatl at Teotihuacan, although the one example of actual human bone was of maxillae, not mandibles (Cabrera Castro 1993:100).

At Teotihuacan, an aspect of the rain god known as Tlaloc B displays a pair of bifurcated scrolls instead of a lower jaw, quite possibly an allusion to blood. According to von Winning (1987, I:94), this being principally concerns war and human sacrifice. The thirty human skulls surrounding the Stair Block I Tlaloc head reiterate the themes of militarism and sacrifice (Figure 13.12a). The skulls are pierced in the parietal region, immediately recalling a *tzompantli* skull rack. However, a figure in Teotihuacan-style military dress on Structure 10L-26 wears a similarly pierced skull as a belt piece (see Fash and Fash 2000:fig. 14.8), and such modified skulls may primarily denote trophies.

Eighteen skulls surround the Tlaloc head on the primary central façade. At Teotihuacan, 18 is a highly significant number commonly denoting war and sacrifice. Among the Classic Maya, the Teotihuacan War Serpent was commonly termed *waxaklahun u-bah chan*, a phrase meaning "18 its head (or image) serpent" (Freidel et al. 1993:308–310; Stuart 2000:494). In reconstructions of the Temple of Quetzalcoatl at Teotihuacan, 18 effigy War Serpent helmets flank either side of the stairway. In addition, three excavated mass burials from this structure contained 18 individuals with Teotihuacan war costume and weaponry (Taube 2000b:281). A pit containing the skulls of 18 children was discovered in the North Platform at Monte Albán (Martínez López et al. 1995:151) The excavators compared this offering to a mass burial of 18 infants in the region of Xolalpan, Teotihuacan (Martínez López et al. 1995:162; Jarquín Pacheco and Martínez Vargas 1991). More recently, excavations at the Pyramid of the Moon recovered 18 animal skulls in Burial 3, an offering oriented to the principal axis of the structure (Sugiyama and Cabrera 1999). The central image of Stair Block I probably signifies "18 its skull Tlaloc," a concept directly related to Teotihuacan numerical symbolism of war and sacrifice.

Stair Block I was surely the place of massive fire offerings. Among the Classic Maya, stair blocks served as central loci for temple fire ritual (Taube 1998b:449–452). In one Late Classic temple scene, a skull supports the censer, immediately recalling Stair Block I and the lowest stair block of Structure 10L-26 (see Taube 1998b:fig. 13a). Mention has been made of skull braziers, a probable allusion to ancestor worship. In addition, Tlaloc head censers are very common in Postclassic highland Mexico, including massive examples from the Aztec Templo Mayor (see Matos Moctezuma 1988:figs. 54, 77). One such brazier, in the form of a Tlaloc-faced water jar, may have been atop Stair Block I (Figure 13.11c). For the Aztec, Tlaloc was a being of ancient and remote antiquity and can be portrayed in sculptural genres alluding to earlier Tula and Teotihuacan (López Austin 1987:figs. 2, 5). According to López Austin, the Aztec Tlaloc embodied the deathly underworld, the place of repose before the fiery resurrection into the sky (López Austin 1987:279). Similarly, Stair Block I alludes to both ancient Teotihuacan and the underworld, and more specifically the burial crypt of K'inich Yax K'uk' Mo'.

Stair Block II

Above the Tlaloc and human skull façade stands Stairway Block II, an image of K'inich Yax K'uk' Mo' as the sun god in a great solar sign (Figure 13.13a). The bird headdress of the figure displays a beaded macaw eye and a quetzal crest, identifying him as the founder apotheosized as the sun deity. This portrayal is clearly related to the solar ancestor cartouches at Palenque, Yaxchilan, and other sites (Figure 13.13e–f; see Robertson 1985:figs. 112–138, 358–362; Tate 1992:figs. 22–23). On Yaxchilan Stela 11 and a number of Tikal monuments, this solar device is worn in the small of the back, thereby identifying it as a Classic form of the later Toltec back mirror (Taube 1992a:193–194).

As with Early Postclassic Toltec mirrors, the Stair Block 2 sculpture and other Classic Maya examples have four serpentine creatures on the rim. However, the Maya entity is skeletal, and due to an epigraphic reading by Nikolai Grube and Werner Nahm (1994:702), it can be identified as a centipede, or *chapat*, a creature closely identified with death and the underworld (Figure 13.13a, e–f).

The appearance of the skeletal centipede with solar imagery denotes the sun within or freshly rising from the underworld. One elaborately incised, Late Classic vessel portrays the Bearded Dragon, or "Vision Serpent" emerging out of the mouth of the earth crocodile. Whereas the upper body is ornamented with fret-nosed snake heads, the portion closest to the earth maw has five centipede heads marked with the sign for darkness (see Schele and Miller 1986:pl. 20). Along with the skeletal centipede heads, the rim of the Stair Block II solar motif displays pairs of *yax* sign elements, sure-

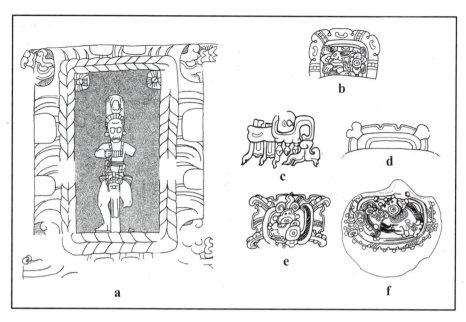

Figure 13.13 Stair Block II with solar and skeletal imagery. (a) Stair Block II, K'inich Yax K'uk' Mo' performing war dance in solar cartouche with four skeletal centipede heads at corners (drawing by Karl Taube primarily based on field drawing by Barbara W. Fash); (b) sun god head within crenellated yax sign with U-shaped bone elements, Rosalila (after Agurcia F. 1997:fig. 7); (c) mandible with U-shaped bone elements, Structure 10L-26 (see Figure 13.14d); (d) Initial Series Introductory Sign pertaining to Yaxk'in with projecting bones, Tikal Stela 4 (after Jones and Satterthwaite 1982:fig. 5); (e) ancestral cartouche with sun and moon imagery and four hook-nosed centipede heads, detail of Early Classic plano-relief vessel (after Kerr 2000:972); (f) Early Classic shell pendant with ancestor in solar cartouche with small centipede heads on rim (after Musée Rath 1998:no. 249).

ly denoting the newly born sun, or *yax k'in*. An earlier version of the *yax k'in* sign appears on Rosalila, here with the face of the sun god in the spoked form of the *yax* sign (Figures 13.8b, 13.13b). The U-shaped elements on the Rosalila cartouche are bone motifs, as commonly appear on mandibles and other bones at Copan (Figure 13.13c). The Initial Series introductory sign corresponding to the month Yaxk'in can display projecting bones with the solar cartouche (Figure 13.13d). Clearly, Yaxk'in embodies the eastern sun emerging out the deathly underworld, just as K'uk' Yax K'uk' Mo' rises out of his tomb on Stair Block II.

Stair Block II is both a rectangular shield and a solar mirror. Whereas most Classic Maya solar signs tend to be circular or square with rounded corners, Stair Block II is rectangular, with a thick woven band lining its interior rim. Rectangular War Serpent shields with similar woven rims occur at the nearby site of Rio Amarillo (see Taube 1992c:fig. 7f). Within this solar mirror shield, K'inich Yax K'uk' Mo' performs a victory war dance, with the left leg slightly raised and his feet turned sharply out from the central axis of his body. Perhaps the most graphic three-dimensional portrayal of dance known for the ancient Maya, this sculpture reveals that the outwardly splayed leg position in frontal portrayals of dance is not a problem of perspective, but rather constitutes a true dance pose.

The founder wears a pectoral of bound material resembling not only the torches on Altar Q, but the headdresses of large Tlaloc figures from the Structure 10L-16 superstructure (Figure 13.14a, cf. Figures 13.1a, 13.12d). Strands of rope fall from this fragmentary pectoral, with additional rope serving as a belt. A similar costume appears on jambs from nearby Structure 10L-18, the probable burial place of Yax Pasaj Chan Yoaat, who almost surely commissioned the Stair Block II sculpture. In one scene, Yax Pasaj Chan Yoaat wears a knotted rope pectoral while performing a war dance (Figure 13.14d). A text from an accompanying scene labels the war dance *kach*, a term signifying "to tie." According to Grube (1992:213), this term may refer to many the ropes and knots appearing in the war dance costumes of Structure 10L-18.

A warrior figure with another bound rope pectoral appears on the stairway of Structure 10L-26. The form of this example is notably similar to the pectoral appearing on Stair Block II (see Baudez 1994:fig. 109a). The Stair Block II image has also been compared to the façades of Structure 66C of Group 8N-11, which feature solar niches containing portrayals of the sun god wearing a thick knotted rope pectoral (Webster et al. 1998:331–332).

Rattles, rather than centipede or serpent heads, occupy the niche corners, again alluding to dance and performance. Aside from Copan, the knotted pectoral appears in the Terminal Classic murals from Structure A at Cacaxtla (Figure 13.14b). The eagle and jaguar warriors flanking the doorway and the figure upon the south jamb wear the knotted pectoral, with the two latter figures displaying obvious dance poses.

Both the Cacaxtla jaguar warrior and the south jamb individual have triple-knotted loincloths, denoting penitential bloodletting among the Classic Maya. The dancing K'inich Yax K'uk' Mo' wears the inverted head of the "Perforator God" atop his loincloth, a clear reference to penis perforation (Figure 13.13a). References to penitential bloodletting also occur on the east and west cornices of Rosalila, with the founder's hands replaced with Perforator God lancets (Figure 13.11b). The remains of downwardly curving cloth or paper elements project out from the loins of the Stair Block II figure. A very similar article appears on Yaxchilan Stela 9, which also portrays Bird Jaguar IV wearing the triple knot motif on his bracelets and anklets and a horizon-

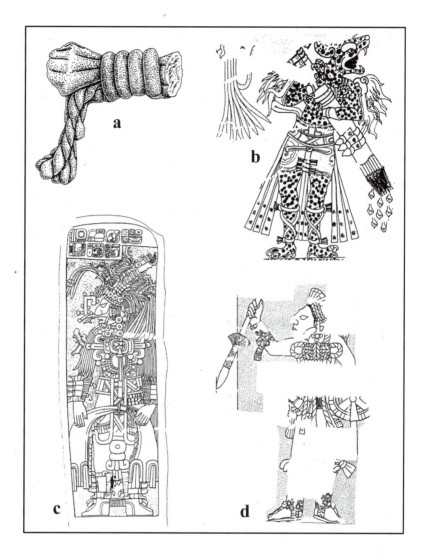

Figure 13.14 War and bloodletting dances in Late Classic Mesoamerica. (a) Fragmentary pectoral worn by K'inich Yax K'uk' Mo' on Stair Block II (drawing by Karl Taube); (b) jaguar warrior with rope pectoral (note triple-knotted loincloth) north panel of Structure A, Cacaxtla (from Foncerrada de Molina 1980:fig. 2); (c) Bird Jaguar IV wearing bloodletting regalia and fan item passing through loincloth, Yaxchilan Stela 9 (drawing courtesy of James Porter); (d) Yax Pasaj performing war dance with knotted pectoral, northeast jamb of Structure 10L-18 (detail of drawing by Anne Dowd from Baudez 1994:fig. 95b).

tal perforator in his headdress (Figure 13.14c). The curving, fan-like element passes directly through a portion of the loincloth, and it is clearly the same item of the well-known bloodletting fan dances appearing in a Late Classic vessel scene and Room 3 of Bonampak Structure 1 (Schele and Miller 1986:pl. 71; M. Miller 1986b:pl. 3).

The Bonampak scene is filled with allusions to war and sacrifice, with the principal figures brandishing axes above a probable victim. Galindo Trejo and Ruiz Gallut (1998:139) note that the frontal faces in the upper vault region portray the sun god, immediately recalling the Stair Block II image of K'inich Yax K'uk' Mo'. Diego de Landa mentions that war dances and bloodletting were performed during the *Muluk* new year rites in honor of the sun god, *K'inich Ajaw* (Tozzer 1941:144).

The fan dance of Bonampak Room 3 and Stair Block II clearly concerns the sun, bloodletting, and warfare. However, the fan dance probably is but a dramatization of the bloodletting act. One lintel from the Yaxchilan area portrays a dancing Bird Jaguar IV and a companion passing large writhing snakes through their loincloths, just as the fan passes through the pierced loincloth on Yaxchilan Stela 9 (see Grube 1992:fig. 150. Clearly, live snakes are not pulled through perforated phalli in this scene, and a similar case can be made for the massive fan elements, which could well have been directly supported by the loincloth. Rather than a rite of penitence, the blood-letting war dance is a celebration of male virility and bravery. Stair Block II portrays the founder as a solar war god performing a dance of victory as he rises skyward out of the dark realm of the dead.

Stair Block III

The highest and most eastern of the series, Stair Block III features a huge zoomorphic maw rimmed with cloud or smoke scrolls (Figure 13.15a). Although the mouth may have originally had an upper face, it has yet to be identified. Quite probably, the fanged maw refers to an open serpent mouth, an extremely widespread theme in Classic Maya iconography. Scrolls rim the upper and lower teeth, with a still larger series on the lower jaw. In Teotihuacan iconography, such scrolls denote clouds or smoke, and as such also appear in Teotihuacan-style Maya art (Figures 13.5a, 13.8a, 13.15c–d). With the cloud scrolls, the zoomorphic image may well be a Classic Maya form of the Aztec *Mixcoatl*, or "cloud serpent."

This interpretation finds further support in the pair of elements emanating from the lower corners of the mouth (Figure 13.15b). A pair of Teotihuacan-style rain drops fall from the curving tips of the mouth emanations. This drop motif appears not only at Teotihuacan, but also at later Cacaxtla and in Teotihuacan-style art from the Maya Lowlands (Figures 13.14b, 13.15c–d, 13.16c–e). At Copan and other Late Classic Maya sites, the rain drops fall from mouth emanations displaying the Teotihuacan scroll cloud sign, with the mouths breathing out rain clouds (Figure 13.15c–d). The Stair Block III sculpture portrays a celestial cloud serpent exhaling clouds of rain from its mouth.

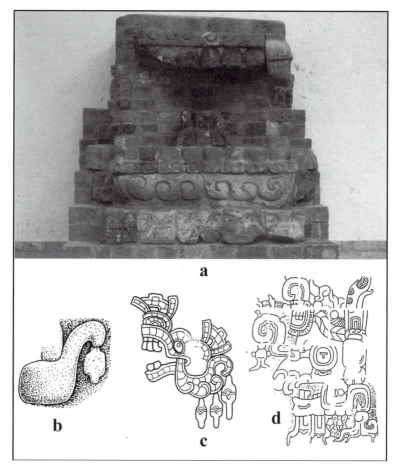

Figure 13.15 Stair Block III and Teotihuacan-derived cloud and rain imagery in Late Classic Maya art. (a) Stair Block III, featuring open mouth lined with cloud scrolls atop frieze of truncated triangles (photo by Karl Taube); (b) detail of cloud and rain emanation from right side of Stair Block III mouth (drawing by Karl Taube); (c) War Serpent with cloud and rain signs emerging from the mouth, Lintel 2 of Tikal Temple I (after Jones and Satterthwaite 1982:fig. 69); (d) skeletal head breathing out raining cloud scroll, detail of north side of Structure 10L-26 temple text (from Stuart 2000:fig. 15.24).

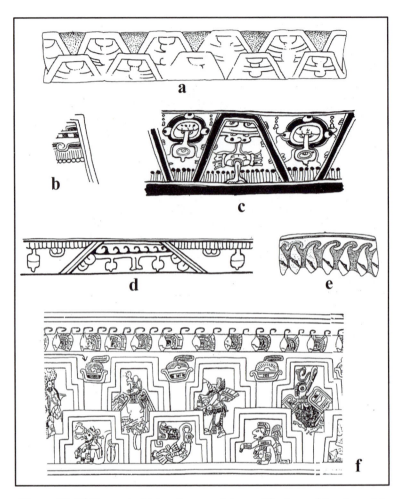

Figure 13.16 Truncated triangle mountain motif, rain, and *pu* signs. (a) Lower frieze of Stair Block III featuring mountains with *pu* signs (drawing by Karl Taube); (b) Mountain sign with infixed *pu* element, detail of panel from Palenque region (after Stuart 2000:fig. 15.29); (c) mountain signs with infixed *pu* elements and flanking Teotihuacan and Maya-style rain drops, detail of Late Classic codex-style vessel (after Kerr 1992:422); (d) mountain sign flanked by Teotihuacan-style rain elements, drawing by author from field photograph of Tomb 4 of Calakmul Structure II (after Carrasco Vargas 1999:30); (e) Teotihuacan-style cloud scroll with rain, ceramic plaque from Tomb 6 of Calakmul Structure II (after Carrasco Vargas 1999:31); (f) portion of Early Classic frieze with stepped mountains and pu signs below raining cloud scrolls, Acanceh Structure 1 (detail from Seler 1902-23: V, 400).

Along with the cloud serpent maw, Stairway Block III had a register of truncated triangle elements (Figures 13.15a, 13.16a). This register closely corresponds to
the maw width, making it likely it constitutes part of the stairway block. In addition, a
pre-excavation photograph demonstrates that these blocks were from the upper portion of the stairway, in the general vicinity of the serpent mouth (Barbara Fash, personal communication 1997). The placement of this frieze immediately below the cloud
serpent is confirmed by Classic Maya scenes, which portray the aforementioned drop
sign falling upon these very elements (Figure 13.16c, d, f). This register is notably similar to a Late Classic Codex-style vase, which has the same truncated triangles containing horizontal looped devices along with the stylized drops (Figure 13.16c). The more
conventional Classic Maya sign for rain, a vertical line of beads, flanks the large
Teotihuacan-style drops. At Calakmul, Tomb 4 of Structure II contained two vessels displaying versions of the same truncated triangle (see Carrasco Vargas 2000:30). In the
case of the bowl, drops fall from cloud scrolls (Figure 13.16d). Another Structure II
tomb contained a ceramic plaque depicting the same Teotihuacan motif of rain falling
from clouds (Figure 13.16f).

The lower frieze of Stair Block III probably had a toponymic significance, as
basal registers commonly allude to place names in Classic Maya art (see Stuart and
Houston 1994). The same truncated triangle appears on a carved panel from the
region of Palenque, here labeling a complex form shedding Teotihuacan-style drops
(see Stuart 2000:fig. 15.29). The interior of this motif contains the same looped element appearing on the Stair Block III examples (Figure 13.16b). David Stuart
(2000:503) identifies the carved panel example as a sign read phonetically as *pu*, a
term for cattail rushes in Mayan languages. According to Stuart, this term refers to the
legendary central Mexicoican Tollan, or "place of rushes," which. for Classic
Mesoamerica would be the massive center of Teotihuacan. The Copan frieze recalls the
Early Classic façade at Acanceh, Yucatan, which is filled with references to Teotihuacan,
including cloud scrolls with falling rain and the cattail *pu* sign (Figure 13.16f). In the
case of the Acanceh façade, the overlapping elements are stepped and quite probably
portray hills (Miller 1991:31). Similarly, the Stair Block III elements are stylized mountains marked with *pu* signs (Taube 2000c:26). Both the Acanceh scene and Stair Block
III portray clouds showering rain upon the mountains of Tollan.

Summary and Conclusions

Structure 10L-16 is the culmination of a long history of successive buildings dedicated
to the founding ancestor. From its location and very form, this building marks the pivotal axis of the Acropolis and the Copan world. The themes of fire and the evocation
of K'inich Yax K'uk' Mo' also appear with such earlier buildings as Hunal, Yehnal,
Margarita and Rosalila. In all of these structures the imagery and symbolism of
Teotihuacan is subtly or blatantly interwoven. It is likely that all of these successive

buildings were the crossed bundle *te na* structure, the lineage "fire house" of the Copan dynasty. The founding event of this dynastic fire is apparently represented on the west face of Altar Q, where K'inich Yax K'uk' Mo' is portrayed as a Teotihuacan warrior king wielding a burning dart.

Altar Q and the stairway of Structure 10L-16 concern the evocation of K'inich Yax K'uk' Mo' through fire ritual strongly couched in terms of Teotihuacan war and funerary symbolism. Passing from west to east, the three stair blocks portray the celestial resurrection of the founder. In mortuary rites of central Mexico, fire was of transcendental importance for casting off the mortal coil and the transformation of dead warriors into celestial beings of brilliance and beauty. In Aztec myth, this is expressed by the sacrificial pyre at Teotihuacan and triumphant resurrection of Tonatiuh, the sun god whose charge were the bird and butterfly warrior souls that followed him in celestial paradise (Taube 2000b).

Stair Block II portrays the victorious warrior king rising into such a solar paradise, a scene that also recalls the Tikal Stela 31 portrayal of Nuun Yax Ayiin floating as the sun god above Siyaj Chan K'awiil on Tikal Stela 31. Although the theme of solar resurrection does relate to central Mexican symbolism, it is also of considerable antiquity in the Maya region. Thus the Stela 31 portrayal of Nuun Yax Ayiin is extremely similar to the solar being appearing at top of Abaj Takalik Stela 2, a monument dating to the 1st century B.C. (Taube 1992b:55).

Referring to the levels of the underworld, earth, and sky, the three stair block sculptures of Structure 10L-16 are wonderfully graphic portrayals of the ritual process of fire offerings. Whereas Stair Block I refers to the tomb and the watery underworld, Stair Block II portrays the dawning sun rising from the fire, and Stair Block III the celestial clouds of smoke returning as falling rain. As Prudence Rice (1999:28) notes, rainmaking constitutes one of the most basic functions of censer ritual, with the smoke symbolizing clouds of rain. On Altar Q, Yax Pasaj Chan Yoaat wears the headdress of Chaak, referring to his ritual role as rain maker (Figure 13.1a). Just as the ancestors rise in flames and smoke, they return again as life-giving rain.

Acknowledgments

I wish to thank Ricardo Agurcia Fasquelle and William and Barbara Fash for their kind hospitality and logistic support during my field research at Copan. I am also indebted to Oscar Cruz Melgar, of the Instituto Hondureño de Antropología e Historia, for providing access to material pertaining to Structure 10L-16. Ricardo Agurcia Fasquelle, William and Barbara Fash, Robert J. Sharer and David Stuart generously provided me with unpublished as well as published manuscripts pertaining to their research at Copan. I am also very grateful to Charles Bouscaren and

Nina Delu for directly assisting me in reconstructing the façades of Structure 10L-16. My field research at Copan has been partly supported by Academic Senate Research Grants of the University of California at Riverside. Finally, I wish to thank Ellen Bell, Marcello Canuto, and Robert Sharer for their editorial comments concerning an earlier version of this chapter.

V EARLY CLASSIC COPAN FROM A REGIONAL PERSPECTIVE

14

EXTERNAL INTERACTION AT EARLY CLASSIC COPAN

Robert J. Sharer

This chapter addresses interaction between Copan and the external Maya world during the Early Classic era. It represents a microcosm of a much broader issue in the development of Maya civilization, namely the role of interregional interactions in this process.[*] Early Classic Copan manifests numerous examples of contact with other regions of Mesoamerica which undoubtedly influenced its course of development (Sharer 1997c, 2003a). The following discussion will examine two such episodes of contact with other regions of Mesoamerica. The first involves a specific external connection and what this interaction reveals about the dynastic founding, clearly the most important event in Copan's Early Classic history. The second concerns the possible role of external events in one or more apparent destructive episodes within central Copan that seem to have escaped recognition until now.

The External Impetus for Copan's Dynastic Founding

A long-recognized historical event at Tikal in A.D. 378 is now seen as a pivotal episode for interaction between central Mexico and the Maya Lowlands (Coggins 1975; Proskouriakoff 1993). Recent text decipherments indicate that in A.D. 378

---

[*] Concern with this issue has been especially noteworthy since the 1960s when evidence for external contacts recovered at Tikal reopened the debate on highland-lowland contact and its role in the development of Maya civilization (Kidder 1940; Miller 1983; Sharer and Sedat 1987). The Tikal interaction focused on the major Maya Highland center of Kaminaljuyu (Ball 1983; Coggins 1975), and further afield, Teotihuacan (Coggins 1979; Culbert 1991; Laporte and Fialko 1990; Marcus 1983a; Proskouriakoff 1993; Sabloff 1990; Sanders and Price 1968; Willey 1974, 1980, among others). Recent decipherments have turned most attention to Teotihuacan (Braswell 2003; Fash and Fash 2000; Martin and Grube 2000:29–31; Marcus 2003; Stuart 2000, this volume).

the Tikal dynasty was usurped by a foreign incursion, quite possibly from Teotihuacan, led by Siyaj K'ak' or "Smoking Frog" (Martin and Grube 2000:29–31; Stuart 2000:478–490). Following this event, which may have resulted in the defeat and death of the reigning Tikal king, a new ruler, Yax Nuun Ayiin (A.D. 379–404?) or "Curl Nose," was installed on the throne (Stuart 2000:481). Thereafter, promoting its ties to central Mexico, Tikal appears to have expanded its power over a wide area by military conquest and royal marriage alliances (Marcus 1976, 1992b; Martin and Grube 2000:35). Tikal's expansion served both political and economic purposes (Jones and Sharer 1980), but also may have had an ideological motive to reshape the destiny of the new Bak'tun that began in A.D. 435 (Sharer 2003a; cf. Puleston 1979).

In A.D. 426/427, just before the important arrival of the ninth Bak'tun, there was a dynastic shift at Copan (Stuart and Schele 1986b) with events that parallel some of those seen at Tikal a generation before (Martin and Grube 2000:193; Sharer 2003b; Stuart 2000:491). It is generally recognized that a new dynasty was founded at Copan with the arrival of K'inich Yax K'uk' Mo' in A.D. 427, as recorded on Altar Q (Schele 1989; Schele and Grube 1992; Stuart and Schele 1986b). There is clear evidence of interaction with central Mexico during the reign of Copan's dynastic founder, K'inich Yax K'uk' Mo' (ca. A.D. 426–437), including explicit artifactual, architectural, and iconographic links with Teotihuacan (Fash and Fash 2000:441–449; Stuart 2000:490–494, this volume; Sharer 2003b). These links reflect either direct contacts with central Mexico or indirect involvement through an intermediary such as Tikal or Kaminaljuyu. An evaluation of the current evidence leads me to conclude that K'inich Yax K'uk' Mo' is most directly linked to Tikal, although close ties to Teotihuacan and Kaminaljuyu are apparent as well (Sharer 2003a, b).

If we assume that Tikal was responsible for the founding of the K'inich Yax K'uk' Mo' dynasty at Copan, as the evidence strongly suggests (Sharer 2003a), how might the Teotihuacan ties seen at Copan during this time be explained? The answer may lie in the fact that links with central Mexico were clearly established at several key Maya sites during the Early Classic, including Tikal. The Teotihuacan presence at Tikal predates the Copan founding (Laporte and Fialko 1990; Stuart 2000). Thus, if K'inich Yax K'uk' Mo' did in fact come to Copan from Tikal, in all probability he would have brought with him an entourage of followers, military and ritual paraphernalia, and symbols of political power, with links to Teotihuacan.

It is possible that K'inich Yax K'uk' Mo' took the Copan throne by military conquest, although direct evidence for this is lacking. Most retrospective portraits of K'inich Yax K'uk' Mo' show him as a Teotihuacan-style warrior, as on Altar Q with his goggles and shield (Coggins 1988). Of course these associations are usually seen as connections to the great city of Teotihuacan, but as indicated above, they may just as likely reflect ties to Tikal and its close links to central Mexico. At the same time as the Copan founding, Tikal's expansion into the southeastern Maya Lowlands also apparently established a subordinate center at Quirigua (Jones and Sharer 1980; Martin and

Grube 2000:420; Proskouriakoff 1993; Schele 1990b). Quirigua's founding suggests that a major motivation for Tikal's expansion into this region may have been control over the Motagua jade and obsidian routes (Jones and Sharer 1980; Sharer 1988). A Copan connection also could have provided Tikal with better access to the markets and resources of Central America (Sharer 1988). These economic motives were undoubtedly reinforced by the increased political power and ideological prestige Tikal gained by expanding its power and influence into the southeastern Maya area.

The evidence for Tikal's expansion into the southeastern Maya area comes from the conjunction of data furnished by archaeology (Sharer 2003a), epigraphy (Fahsen et al. 1995; Grube et al. 1995; Schele et al. 1993), and bioanthropology (Buikstra 1997, Buikstra et al., this volume). One possible indication that K'inich Yax K'uk' Mo' was originally from Tikal comes from epigraphy—a reference to an individual named K'uk' Mo' in the text on the Early Classic Hombre de Tikal statue (Fahsen 1988; Martin and Grube 2000:32-33), dating some 20 years before the Copan dynastic founding (but see Stuart, this volume). Of course the "startling parallel" (Stuart 2000:491) between the arrival account at Copan recorded on Altar Q (see below) with the earlier Siyaj K'ak' episode at Tikal may also suggest a Tikal connection for K'inich Yax K'uk' Mo'. Among the many epigraphic connections between Copan and Tikal (Fahsen et al. 1995), several are directly associated with K'inich Yax K'uk' Mo'. For example, K'inich Yax K'uk' Mo' is the only Copan ruler who held the "Lord of the West" title (*Ochk'in Kalomte*) carried by several Tikal kings after its original use by Siyaj K'ak' (Schele and Grube 1992; Stuart 2000:493). Stuart (2000:503-504) also points out that the "cattail glyph" (*pu*) is present in the name phrases of K'inich Yax K'uk' Mo' (on Copan Stela 11) and Yax Nuun Ayiin (on Tikal Stela 31).

The archaeological evidence shows that at the time of the founding a variety of foreign elements appear at Copan. Prior to this time the patterns of settlement, architecture, and artifacts in the Copan Valley were allied to general southeastern traditions (Canuto, this volume; Sharer 2000b; Sharer, Traxler, et al. 1999; Traxler, this volume). Beginning with the founding a number of Lowland (Petén) Maya elements appear in Copan architecture, artifacts, and monuments. No Lowland Maya portrait monuments are known at Copan before the founding era; Copan's earlier stone sculptures belong to the southeastern tradition (Fash 2001:74). The first known portrait of K'inich Yax K'uk' Mo' appears on the Motmot Marker (Figure 11.11; Fash 1998:fig. 1) which Stuart (this volume) dates to the founder's reign. The Motmot Marker is a Maya Lowland monument both in its sculptural style and material (limestone). While some founding-era buildings at Copan were constructed in the local adobe tradition, the architecture of several of the earliest masonry buildings beneath the Acropolis reflects Early Classic Maya Lowland canons, including the structures nicknamed Motmot (Fash 1998:230), Yehnal, and its successor, Margarita (Sedat 1996; Sharer 1996; Sharer, Fash, et al. 1999; Sharer, Traxler, et al. 1999).

The same Lowland Maya ties appear in the artifacts associated with this era, including an assemblage of pottery vessels from both the Hunal and Margarita Tombs (Bell et al., this volume), several of which were manufactured in the Tikal region (Reents-Budet et al., this volume). At the same time distinctly central Mexican elements can be seen in both the architecture of Hunal Structure (discussed below) and artifacts, including warfare paraphernalia and Teotihuacan-style pottery vessels, several of which originated in central Mexico (Bell et al. and Reents-Budet et al., this volume). This synthesis of Maya and Teotihuacan elements seen at Copan parallels the situation at Tikal during the reign of Siyaj Chan K'awiil (A.D. 411–456) or "Stormy Sky" (Coggins 1975)—the presumed sponsor of K'inich Yax K'uk' Mo's move to Copan—which dates to this same era (Sharer 1997c, 2003a, b).

The initial mention of the founder in the retrospective text on Copan Altar Q refers to him simply as K'uk' Mo' Ajaw (Schele 1989), the same name used in the Hombre de Tikal text (Fahsen 1988; Martin and Grube 2000:32–33). The decipherment of the Altar Q text (see Stuart, this volume) records that on September 6, A.D. 426, K'uk' Mo' Ajaw took the *K'awiil* scepter. Three days later, his new status as king and founder was recognized by his being called K'inich Yax K'uk' Mo' ("Great Sun, First Quetzal Macaw"), the royal name that is most often used in Copan's texts. Altar Q records that on this day he came to (*ta-li*) the *Wi'te'naah* or "root tree house." We are not told where both these events took place, although some scholars have assumed they refer to Copan. The final event recorded on Altar Q took place 153 days later, when K'inich Yax K'uk' Mo' arrived at *Uxwitik* ("three mountain place"), a name for Copan. The reference to arrival at *Uxwitik* for this final event could imply that the two earlier episodes were not at Copan, but happened at a place 153-day journey away—perhaps at Tikal or, alternatively, at Teotihuacan as Martin and Grube (2000:193) and Stuart (2000; this volume) have suggested.

The *Wi'te'naah* glyph associated with the taking of the *K'awiil* scepter by K'inich Yax K'uk' Mo' is found in the Tikal inscriptions, including a reference to an action taken by Yax Nuun Ayiin (Stuart 2000:493). The *Wi'te'naah* glyph is also found at several other sites, including Quirigua, Yaxchilan, and Machaquila (Stuart 2000). The location of this important building remains unknown. While Stuart (2000:492–493) presents the Teotihuacan associations for this glyph, it is possible that Copan and other sites that used the *Wi'te'naah* in their texts did so to recall an especially important place at Tikal associated with the Teotihuacan-sponsored Siyaj K'ak' episode (see Stuart, this volume). It is equally possible that versions of buildings bearing this name were constructed at other Lowland sites for important royal events associated with the Teotihuacan heritage.

Altar Q dates to some 350 years after the founding. The inscription on the Xukpi Stone, revealed in our Acropolis tunnels, dates to only a little over a decade after the founding (Sedat and Sharer 1994). The Xukpi text appears to record the dedication of a tomb or funerary shrine by K'inich Yax K'uk' Mo's son, Ruler 2, on November

Nothern
Doorway

Tablero

Talud

Figure 14.1 Hunal Structure *talud-tablero* façade (photograph by David W. Sedat).

30, A.D. 437 (Schele et al. 1994). The text closes with the name of K'inich Yax K'uk'
Mo', a possible relationship glyph, and what has been identified as the name Siyaj K'ak'
or "Smoking Frog" (Schele et al. 1994). This could refer to the same individual whose
arrival at Tikal in A.D. 378 sparked the profound political changes at that site and
beyond. If so, this passage is obviously critical to understanding the Tikal–Copan relationship during the founding era.

The Xukpi Stone was reset on the summit of Margarita Structure, part of the
expanded royal center built by the founder's son and successor, Ruler 2 (Sedat and Sharer
1997; Sedat and López, this volume). However, the origins of this Early Classic royal center lie with an earlier complex of buildings dated to the reign of K'inich Yax K'uk' Mo'
(Sharer, Traxler, et al. 1999; Traxler 2001, this volume). As mentioned earlier, much of this
early dynastic architecture was a fusion of local traditions based on earthen constructions and Tikal-style masonry adorned by apron-moldings (Sharer 2003a; Traxler, this volume). But one building, nicknamed Hunal and built over a demolished earthen structure
(Sedat and López, this volume), is an exception. Hunal, a low masonry substructure with
an undecorated *talud-tablero* façade recalls the well-known central Mexican style
(Figure 14.1; Sedat and Sharer 1996; Sedat 1997a). Its proportions seem most similar to
those from Teotihuacan (Sharer 2003b), although its masonry construction technique
seems more closely allied to the Maya Lowlands (Traxler, this volume).

Hunal's summit building was subsequently rebuilt, and this later stage was almost completely demolished when Hunal was succeeded by a new structure (Yehnal). But enough of Hunal's superstructure survives to determine that it had at least three transverse rooms, the northernmost two being connected by a single doorway offset to the east. The northern room had a north-facing doorway that opened onto an outset stairway, and the remains of a balustraded stairway are on the east side (Sedat and López, this volume). Debris indicates that its interior walls were probably originally decorated with brilliantly painted murals, again recalling similar customs at Teotihuacan.

Prior to the structure's final termination, a vaulted tomb was intruded beneath the eastern half of Hunal's north room (Plate 3; see Bell et al., this volume). This chamber held the remains of a male more than 55 years old at death (Buikstra 1997; Buikstra et al., this volume) laid supine on a monolithic slab resting on four large stone drum-shaped supports. After an initial period of re-entry and veneration, the tomb was sealed by a series of increasingly larger and more elaborate temples built over Hunal by Ruler 2 and his successors. These subsequent temples formed the core of the evolving Acropolis which testify to the central importance of this location for the Copan dynasty (Sharer, Traxler, et al. 1999). The first two structures built directly over Hunal (Yehnal and Margarita) have Petén-style façades with apron moldings and elaborate stucco façades with motifs that implicitly (Yehnal) or explicitly (Margarita) refer to K'inich Yax K'uk' Mo', as do several of the best-preserved later buildings constructed at this same location (Plate 2; Taube, this volume).

A variety of evidence provides consistent clues that identify the burial in the Hunal Tomb as that of K'inich Yax K'uk' Mo' (Sharer 1996, 1997c). As mentioned previously, a number of later portraits of K'inich Yax K'uk' Mo' depict him as a Teotihuacan-style warrior. The Hunal interment wore a Teotihuacan-style shell platelet helmet (Stone 1989:156) that appears to be similar to that worn by Yax Nuun Ayiin in one of his Teotihuacan warrior portraits on Tikal Stela 31 (left side, see Jones and Satterthwaite 1982:fig. 51a). One of the offerings found on the floor of the Hunal Tomb is a collar-shaped shell pendant decorated with a jade mosaic (Plate 4). Although incompletely preserved, the mosaic depicts a bird which may be a full-figure version of the founder's name. The shell collar is inscribed with a short hieroglyphic "name tag" that identifies the owner of the object. The glyphs have been read as *yu-uh wi-te*, or "his necklace, root tree" by David Stuart (this volume). Interestingly, *wi te* is a title used exclusively to refer to the founder in later times at Copan (Plate 4b). The shell pendant is of the same species (*Patella mexicana*) and shape as undecorated "horse collar" shells found in Early Classic tombs at Kaminaljuyu (Kidder et al. 1946:149).

The bones in the Hunal Tomb also furnish clues that point to their being the remains of K'inich Yax K'uk' Mo'. These bones suggest that the man in the Hunal Tomb was a warrior, as they show evidence of injuries, such as a severe right forearm parry fracture (indicating he was left-handed), of a kind often resulting from hand-to-hand combat, all of which had partially mended years before death (Buikstra 1997; Buikstra et al., this volume). While it may be coincidence, on Altar Q, K'inich Yax K'uk' Mo' is portrayed as being left-handed, since he wears a shield on his right forearm. Consistent with the historical clues identifying K'inich Yax K'uk' Mo' with Tikal before his arrival in Copan, strontium isotope analyses of the Hunal bones indicate that this individual was not native to Copan, but probably spent his younger days in the Petén region of the Maya Lowlands (Buikstra et al., this volume)—an area which, of course, includes Tikal itself.

While lacking any textual support, it has been proposed that after K'inich Yax K'uk' Mo' became Copan's new king he legitimized his right to rule by marrying a royal woman from Copan's old ruling family (Sharer, Fash, et al. 1999); in other words, the takeover was accomplished by combining conquest and royal marriage, a common Lowland Maya pattern (Marcus 1992b:249-255). As a hypothesis, we have suggested that the richly adorned elderly lady in the adjacent Margarita Tomb, who was born and raised in the northern portion of the Copan region, according to strontium isotope evidence (Buikstra et al. this volume), was in fact K'inich Yax K'uk' Mo's queen and mother of Copan's second ruler (Sedat and Sharer 1997; Sharer, Traxler, et al. 1999).

There is more concrete evidence that the founder's son and successor emphasized Maya traditions in his monuments and buildings, again recalling trends at Tikal seen in the years following the arrival of *Siyaj K'ak'* (Coggins 1975; Sharer 2003a). Beginning with the reign of Ruler 2, and for almost 400 years thereafter, K'inich Yax K'uk' Mo' was recognized as the dynastic founder by the 15 kings who followed him to the throne. It should also be noted that several of Copan's Late Classic kings retrospectively emphasized links between K'inich Yax K'uk' Mo' and Teotihuacan, but did so after the decline and fall of this great city (Fash and Fash 2000:452; Sharer 1997c, 2003b; Stuart 2000:495-498).

Early Classic Destructive Events at Copan

The dynastic founding by K'inich Yax K'uk' Mo' seems to have forged a close alliance between Tikal and Copan. This undoubtedly brought economic and political benefits to Copan's new dynasty. But recent evidence suggests Tikal suffered the first in a series of disastrous defeats at the hands of the Calakmul alliance in A.D. 562 (Harrison 1999:119-124; Martin and Grube 1995, 2000:39-40). Until now scholars have assumed that Copan, insulated by its distance from the Petén, escaped the turmoil of Tikal's defeat and its dark age that followed. But an examination of Copan's corpus of dated dynastic monuments reveals evidence of both widespread desecration of these important symbols of royal power and a hiatus in their dedication (see Table 14.1). In addition, excavations have identified other possible destructive events in the Copan Acropolis and Great Plaza dating to the same period as the monument destruction. Thus, while there is no evidence of a further dynastic change or major political disrup-

Table 14.1 Patterns of Early Classic Monument Destruction at Copan

Date	Fragments	Complete	Intact	Ruler
820			Stela 11	Ruler 16
783			Stela 8	Ruler 16
761			Stela N	Ruler 15
756		Stela M		Ruler 15
738-756				Hiatus (Defeat by Quirigua)
736			Stela D	Ruler 13
731			Stela H	Ruler 13
731			Stela A	Ruler 13
731			Stela B	Ruler 13
726		Stela 4		Ruler 13
721			Stela F	Ruler 13
711		Stela 5		Ruler 13
711		Stela C		Ruler 13
702			Stela J	Ruler 13
682			Stela 6	Ruler 12
677			Stela I	Ruler 12
667		Stela 1		Ruler 12
652			Stela 10	Ruler 12
652		Stela 19		Ruler 12
652			Stela 13	Ruler 12
652		Stela 12		Ruler 12
652			Stela 2	Ruler 12
652		Stela 3		Ruler 12
623-652				Hiatus (Cause unknown)
623			Stela P	Ruler 11
616			Stela E	?
613			Stela 7	Ruler 11
573		Ante Step		Ruler 10; Sealed by construction
571		Rosalila Step		Ruler 10; Sealed by construction
564			Stela 9	Ruler 10
554-564				Transition from fragmentary to complete monuments
554	Stela 21			Ruler 10?
554	Stela 17			Ruler 10
524	Stela 15			Ruler 7
524	Altar Q'			Ruler 7?
(514-613)	Altar Y			?
(514-554)	Stela 18			?
(514-554)	Altar L'			?
(514-554)	Altar M			?
(495-593)	Altar X			?
(495-573)	Altar A'			?
(495-534)	Stela 22			?
485		Papagayo Altar		Ruler 4; Sealed by construction
485	Stela 24			Ruler 4?
485	Stela 25			Ruler 4?
472	Stela 16			Ruler 3 or 4
465	Stela 20			Ruler 2
442		Stela 63		Ruler 2; Sealed by construction
437			Xucpi Stone	Ruler 2; Sealed by construction
435			Motmot Marker	Ruler 2; Sealed by construction
(435-554)	V'1-13			?
(435-534)	Altar P'			?
(435-534)	Altar J'			?
(435-534)	Altar K'			?
?	Stela 60			?
?	Stela 35			Ruler 1?

KEY

FRAGMENT: Portion of incomplete monument
COMPLETE: Broken but complete monument
INTACT: Unbroken monument (minor damage)

Note: Sample from Morley (1920) with additions;
Late Classic Altars not listed;
Stela 63 and Papagayo Altar dates are approximate.

tion during Copan's Early Classic period, there is evidence of an apparent flurry of destruction, recalling a similar pattern seen in Tikal's Early Classic monuments and several royal tombs (Jones 1991; Schele and Freidel 1990).

The evidence for destruction at Copan comes from both monuments and architecture. The evidence for the deliberate destruction of Copan's monuments is both plentiful and widespread (Figures 12.2 and 12.3). As in the case of Tikal (Jones 1991), it seems reasonable to interpret widespread monument destruction as the result of foreign incursions, since these (along with royal buildings and tombs) were the most important symbols of the continuity of power maintained by the local ruling dynasty. But at the same time, locally inspired destructive activity cannot be ruled out. Regardless of cause, the end of the destruction of Copan's Early Classic monuments can be defined by a clear-cut transition between smashed and complete monuments, dating to the decade between 9.6.0.0.0 and 9.6.10.0.0 (A.D. 554–564). All but four of 23 Copan monuments dated between ca. A.D. 435 and 554 are smashed and incomplete (see Table 14.1),[*] while 26 stelae dedicated after A.D. 564 are complete (18 are intact and 8 are broken but complete), and none shows the pattern of apparent deliberate destruction seen in the pre-A.D. 564 monuments.

This evidence could well mean that Copan's Early Classic monuments were smashed during a single episode of destruction sometime between A.D. 554 and 564. Alternatively, this evidence could also indicate that if there was more than one such destructive episode, these events ceased after A.D. 564.[†]

The four exceptions to the pattern of Early Classic monument destruction require some explanation. Two Early Classic texts were found intact and undamaged in the Acropolis tunnel excavations (Sharer, Traxler, et al. 1999). These were buried long *before* the critical A.D. 554–564 decade and would have been inaccessible to anyone bent on monument destruction during the A.D. 554–564 decade. Two other recently excavated texts carved before A.D. 564 are complete, although both are broken and show signs of battering and breakage. Both of these are located inside a very important dynastic building, Papagayo Structure, and thereby remained protected but accessible during most of the Early Classic era (Fash 2001:85–86; Fash et al., this vol-

---

[*] A possible exception is Stela E, an intact Main Group monument often dated to 9.5.10.0.0 (A.D. 544), and assigned to Ruler 7 (Schele et al. 1995). But its text is notoriously difficult to read, and its dedication date and royal sponsor are by no means settled. Morley (1920:107) originally dated Stela E to 9.9.2.17.0 (A.D. 616), while Martin and Grube (2000:201) assign Stela E slightly later to the reign of Ruler 12 (628-95). The sample used here is based on Morley (1920) with additions from recent research, but does not include all Copan monuments and monument fragments.

[†] Morley (1920:129) also noted a later gap of some 30 years in the Copan monument sequence, with no dated stelae between Stela P at 9.9.10.0.0 (A.D. 623) and Stela 10 at 9.10.19.13.0 (A.D. 652). We now recognize that this hiatus came during the final years of the reign of Ruler 11, Butz Chan (A.D. 578-628), and during the early years of the reign of Ruler 12, Smoke Imix (A.D. 628-695). This break in the monument sequence (see Table 14.1) could signal a second disruption at Copan, although it is not associated with evidence of monument destruction.

ume). Stela 63, set inside Papagayo by Ruler 2 (Figure 14.2; Fash 2001:85; Stuart et al. 1989), was broken into three pieces and its lower text was erased, although its upper text is little damaged (Figure 14.1; Fash 2001:fig. 38). The lower portion of the monument also shows signs of burning.

In the same building, most of the text of a later carved altar dedicated by Ruler 4 was erased by battering (Figure 11:10; Fash 2001:89). Fash and Stuart (personal communication, 2000) conclude that both of these texts were damaged by Late Classic termination rituals (involving fire) just prior to the burial of Papagayo under a new and larger building. This explanation remains entirely feasible.

But it is also possible that there could have been more than one destructive event that created the damage seen today. Under this scenario, both Stela 63 and the Papagayo Altar could have been desecrated during the same A.D. 554-564 decade that appears to date the destruction of Copan's other extant monuments. If the Papagayo texts were damaged at this time, further destruction could have occurred during the later termination rituals which might have masked some of the evidence of earlier deliberate destruction. Some, but not all, of the destruction seen on both Stela 63 and the Papagayo Altar seems selective—certain glyph blocks appear to have been deliberately erased, while others are generally undamaged (Figures 11.10, 14.2). For example, the Long Count glyphs of the Stela 63 text are not damaged, except by one of the breaks in the monument. In contrast, the five rows of glyphs following the Long Count are almost completely erased (Figure 14.2; Fash 2001:fig.38), which may point to deliberate destruction bent on removing specific references to royal events or persons. In any case, it is clear that both Papagayo texts were terminated and sealed when the building that sheltered them was buried under new construction over a century later at the onset of Ruler 13's reign (Fash 2001:139), and well *after* the critical A.D. 554-564 decade.

There is evidence that the postulated A.D. 554-564 destructive episode extended beyond monuments. There are at least two unusually thorough building demolitions that date to this same era. The first is the destruction of the initial shrine constructed above the Sub-Jaguar Tomb, dated to ca.A.D. 550 based on stratigraphy and ceramics (Traxler 1994). Before this funerary shrine was later replaced by a larger structure, it was almost totally demolished. Only a remnant of its burned floor remained after its summit building and even the façade of its substructure were completely destroyed (Traxler 1994). The evidence for burning and the thoroughness of this destruction goes far beyond the normal pattern of partial demolition seen in dozens of building terminations in the Acropolis sequence. The second example is Structure 10L-2-3rd, located at the north end of the Great Plaza. This structure also reflects evidence of burning dated archaeomagnetically to A.D. 555-589 (Cheek 1983:108; see also Traxler, this volume). This date is suspiciously coincident with the A.D. 554-564 interval that seems to date the destruction of Copan's extant monuments and, therefore, may have been part of the same widespread violent event.

Figure 14.2 Copan Stela 63 (drawing by Barbara W. Fash, photograph by Robert J. Sharer).

It is possible that royal burials were also involved in this mid-6th century destructive episode.[*] There are two apparent royal burials that date to this period, and the unusual circumstances surrounding both may relate them to the same episode of destruction. The first is a disturbed and possibly redeposited interment without evidence of tomb architecture, Burial 92-3 (Bell et al., this volume), but its Acropolis location and associated artifacts suggest it may derive from a now-destroyed royal tomb. Found with the remains of a single human burial were two vessels, residue from a stucco-painted organic vessel, remnants of textiles or other organic materials, two jade and shell mosaic earflares, jade beads (one carved) and thousands of shells. While several of these items recall offerings from Copan's royal tombs (Bell et al., this volume), one item from Burial 92-3 stands out as especially important—a spectacular shell collar inlaid with a jade and shell mosaic (Plate 4e). The only similar jade mosaic shell collar at Copan comes from the Hunal Tomb (Plate 4a-b; discussed above). Burial 92-3 appears to date to ca. A.D. 550-600 based on stratigraphy—it is associated with the filling of Acropolis Court 2B, an episode that followed the destruction of the Sub-Jaguar Tomb shrine.

The second unusual royal burial was recently discovered within a masonry chamber under the now-demolished Structure 10J-45 during salvage excavations west of the Principal Group. The burial is unusual as the interment within the chamber may be the secondary reburial of a Copan ruler, according to its excavator, Seiichi Nakamura (personal communication 2000). Pottery vessels found in the Structure 10J-45 chamber date the burial to about the mid-6th century. If it is the tomb of a Copan ruler, as indicated by two large jade bar pectorals, one carved with an elaborate mat design, it would be the first such royal burial found outside of the Acropolis. It may be that destructive events within the Principal Group explain both its location and status as a secondary burial dating from this same general era.

Early Classic Destruction: Internal vs. External Origins

The pattern of smashed Early Classic monuments and the other examples of mid-6th century disruptions at Copan would seem to have two plausible explanations. Either they are the result of destruction wrought by outside intruders or they are the result of violence or ritual destruction rendered by the Copan residents themselves. If we accept the first explanation, it seems most likely that the destruction took place during one or more outside interventions, dated at ca. A.D. 554–564, resulting in the smashing of Copan's extant (and accessible) monuments, along with the burning of at least two buildings, and perhaps even the destruction of one or more royal tombs. If we

---

[*] Our tunnels beneath the Acropolis have found several deep pits intruded into the earliest construction levels. These intrusions were later filled in by the Maya. The dates and motives for these intrusions are unclear, but they may represent attempts to locate and pillage royal tombs.

accept the internal violence explanation, the destruction could have taken place either periodically or during a single destructive event which, in either case, dated before A.D. 564. Given the intact or complete status of later monuments (Table 14.1), it would appear that Copan suffered no comparable monument destruction events of either external or internal origin after A.D. 564.

Internally Motivated Destruction

The destruction considered here could be the result of a variety of internally induced events that represent several different motives, either singly or in combination. These can be summarized under a single hypothesis: that the A.D. 554-564 destruction at Copan was the result of internal events, such as political upheaval, or ritualized demolition sponsored by rulers to mark calendrical cycles or sever connections with their predecessors (see also B. Flash, this volume).

It is certainly possible that an internal revolt—perhaps during a period of political instability such as that postulated at Yaxchilan during the interregnum of A.D. 742-752 (Martin and Grube 2000:127)—could have produced the observed destruction at Copan during the A.D. 554-564 decade. Of course, an episode of internally generated violence would be difficult or impossible to distinguish from that caused by external agency, such as a foreign incursion. If we accept the possibility of an internal revolt dated to A.D. 554-564, it would have occurred in the first part of the reign of Copan's 10th ruler, Moon Jaguar (A.D. 553-578). While this king's initial Stela 17 is the last in the series of smashed Principal Group monuments (Morley 1920:89), another of Ruler 10's monuments, Stela 9, was found intact by Morley (1920:93) just west of Group 9 (the site under the modern town of Copán Ruinas). Thus, if there was a violent revolt during his reign, Moon Jaguar not only survived this event but went on to dedicate Stela 9 and become one of Copan's most successful kings (Fash 2001:98-100).

There are also a number of reasonable scenarios involving ritualized destruction that could account for the shattering of Copan's Early Classic monuments. The intent of such destruction could have been to disassociate a living king from his predecessors. One such scenario would postulate that before ca. A.D. 554-564 Copan's rulers followed a regular practice of ritual monument destruction—a custom which apparently paralleled the documented practice of ritualized destruction of buildings, including the placement of termination caches prior to the construction of new structures. One suggested motive for these practices was the need to destroy the inherent power in both monuments and buildings associated with recently deceased kings by their successors, much like the scenario proposed by Grove (1981) to account for the mutilation of Preclassic Olmec monuments. Of course if this was a regular practice followed by the Early Classic kings of Copan, a culture change would also have to be postulated to account for the lack of monument destruction after ca. A.D. 554-564. In other words, the postulated custom of monument destruction must have been abandoned by Copan's Late Classic kings.

This fact exposes several weaknesses in such a scenario. Something as profound as a shift away from a long-standing practice of ritual monument destruction might be expected to have occurred at the onset of a new reign, rather than, as the extant evidence indicates, in the midst of the reign of Moon Jaguar. Another potential problem is apparent in the contrast between the patterns of monument and architectural destruction. If monuments were ritually destroyed periodically (to negate a dead king's power) it might be expected that important royal buildings, especially those with clear associations with individual kings, would follow the same pattern. But there are direct examples of important Early Classic buildings that survived long after the death of the king who sponsored them, most notably the already-mentioned Papagayo Structure (Fash 2001:86). On the other hand, ritualized building termination and destruction occurred both before and after the A.D. 554–564 destructive episode seen in monuments. The evidence indicates that deliberate building demolition, accompanied by ritual, followed a consistent pattern throughout Copan's Classic period. Thus, the pattern of building destruction departs from that observed for monument destruction, and there is no evidence for a shift away from ritualized architectural destruction to support the idea of a cultural change that ended an Early Classic pattern of such ritualized monument destruction.

A variation on the ritualized destruction scenario would propose that monument smashing might have been motivated by calendrical prophecy, rather than the succession of kings. There appears to be some justification for this proposition in the most important of Maya calendrical-based prophecies (as seen among the Postclassic Maya of Yucatan), those based on the *u k'ahlay k'atunob* or cycle of 13 K'atuns that repeated every 256 years (260 years of 360 days; each K'atun being 20 of these 360-day years). Assuming that similar prophecies based on the K'atun cycle operated in the Classic Maya Lowlands—and there is evidence to support this possibility (Coggins 1979)—it is possible that events at Copan and other Maya cities were shaped by the prophecies generated by these cycles. In fact, Puleston (1979:70) proposed that the timing of the Classic collapse was linked "to very specific and deeply rooted assumptions that the Maya had about the nature of time." As a result, the belief in the cyclical course of historical events, especially as revealed in the *u k'ahlay k'atunob*, "became a self-validating myth, and ultimately a positive feedback mechanism of awesome compass." Seen in this light, therefore, perhaps the A.D. 554–564 episode of monument destruction at Copan was linked to the K'atun cycle and its prophecies.

A K'atun-based scenario has the advantage of not requiring a mid-Classic cultural change to explain the observed pattern of monument destruction. Instead, this destruction could be a response to a specific K'atun prophecy. The K'atun cycle that had begun in A.D. 278 ended in A.D. 534. The first K'atun of the new cycle, which extended over the next 256 years, or until A.D. 790, was K'atun 11 Ajaw (A.D. 534–554), an especially inauspicious period (Roys 1967:186). In Postclassic Yucatan, K'atun 11 Ajaw was associated with war and destruction: "Bring down fire; Bring down the rope; Bring down stones and trees; Then came the pounding of sticks and stones" (Edmunson 1982:46). It seems plausible, therefore, that the destruction seen at Copan and dated to A.D. 554–564 could have been sparked by the completion of K'atun 11 Ajaw (A.D. 554). This K'atun completion fell a year after Moon Jaguar took the throne. By this scenario, once a flurry of monument destruction had marked the end of K'atun 11 Ajaw, the remainder of Moon Jaguar's reign may have been characterized by renewal and a new era for Copan, beginning with the erection of Stela 9 in A.D. 564.

Another possible scenario for ritualized destruction has been raised in a recent study of the Early to Late Classic transition at Piedras Negras. Golden (2002) has proposed that destructive events seen in the royal Acropolis of Piedras Negras were motivated, at least in part, by the desire of Ruler 1 to disconnect his reign from a disastrous defeat suffered by his predecessor. Early in the reign of Ruler 1, the area of the Acropolis in use at the time of the defeat appears to have been destroyed, buried, and completely abandoned for a period of time. Ruler 1 chose an adjacent area associated with the origins of the dynasty to begin the rebuilding of the Piedras Negras Acropolis. As interpreted by Golden (2002), the motivation for this shift in location was to symbolically associate Ruler 1 and the renewal of the Piedras Negras dynasty with the more distant glorious past, while at the same time both were disassociated from the more recent defeat suffered by his predecessor.

Of course this kind of motivation for destructive disassociation need not exclude a calendrical prophecy scenario. In fact, actions undertaken to manipulate history such as proposed for Piedras Negras Ruler 1 would probably be more successful if they were timed to coincide with auspicious events such as K'atun prophecies. Applying such a scenario to Copan, Moon Jaguar's motives for the destruction of monuments, and perhaps selected structures in the Main Group, could be seen as an attempt to disassociate his reign from any link with his predecessor, the short-lived Ruler 9. In fact, Ruler 9's unusually short reign (551–553; Martin and Grube 2000:197–198) suggests his life ended unexpectedly, if not violently. A decade later, Moon Jaguar dedicated the first monument after the postulated time of destruction, Stela 9. But instead of placing this monument in the Main group, it was dedicated in Group 9. While the origins of Group 9 have been obscured by the town of Copán Ruinas, there are indications that it predates the Main Group (Fash 2001:88; Fash and Sharer 1991; see also Canuto this volume). Thus Stela 9 could have been dedicated in Group 9 to symbolically link Moon Jaguar's reign to the more distant past and the origins of the Copan polity at the same time as it disassociated his reign with the recent past and the destruction in the Main Group (Golden 2002).

Despite some similarities in the pattern of monument destruction and renewal between Piedras Negras and Copan, there is one significant difference. At Piedras Negras, the destructive event preceded the reign of the agent of renewal (Ruler 1). At

Copan, the destructive event appears to have occurred *during* the reign of the agent of renewal (Moon Jaguar). Thus if Moon Jaguar was the agent of monument destruction at Copan, he must have ordered his own monument, Stela 17, to be smashed. Although this cannot be ruled out entirely, it seems unlikely, even if Stela 17 was somehow associated with events to be disavowed later on (such as a previous K'atun). However, this difficulty could be removed by a scenario that calls for external agency as the explanation for monument destruction.

Externally Motivated Destruction

An alternative explanation would hold that violence wrought by outsiders produced the observed pattern of destruction at Copan, dated at ca. A.D. 554-564. This explanation is bolstered by the fact that destructive actions originating outside of Copan removes the already mentioned weaknesses apparent in the internally motivated scenarios. One such internal scenario depends on a postulated cultural change that abandoned an Early Classic custom of the destruction of a dead king's monuments every time a new king took the throne, for which there is no supporting evidence. Internal scenarios, including those based on fulfillment of K'atun prophecies or attempts by rulers to disassociate themselves from previous reigns, also run afoul of the apparent timing of Copan's monument and building demolition in the midst of Moon Jaguar's reign. The fact that this ruler's first stela was smashed, while his later stela was not, makes it unlikely that Moon Jaguar was the agent of this destruction.

As also mentioned, the destruction could be explained by a local revolt, an event that would be difficult to distinguish from violence that stemmed from external intrusion. But in this case there is an additional fact which may point to external agency as the most likely cause. The pattern of destruction seen at Copan seems to echo similar events at about the same time at several other Lowland Maya sites (Houston 2000:165), including the destruction of monuments at Tikal (Jones 1991). But while at least some of these other destructive episodes may have been the result of warfare (Freidel et al. 1998), the specific cause of the apparent destruction at Copan remains unknown. There are no known textual references that support warfare against Copan until almost two hundred years later in the Late Classic.

Nonetheless, the timing of the apparent destruction at Copan, dated to A.D. 554-564, clearly brackets the initial confrontation between Tikal and Calakmul. That conflict began with Tikal's defeat of Calakmul's ally, Caracol, in A.D. 556 and culminated in Tikal's defeat in A.D. 562 (Martin and Grube 1995; 2000:39-40). Other than Quirigua, pure coincidence, this suggests the possibility that about the same time as its defeat of Tikal, Calakmul also intervened at Copan, an event which could have produced the observed destruction of monuments and other features. Alternatively one of Calakmut's allies such as Caracol* could be proposed as the agent for this event. Given Copan's historic connections to Tikal, the logical motivation for such a proposed destructive incursion would be to strike a blow at Tikal's economic and political power by neutralizing one of its most prominent trading partners and allies.

Given the lack of supporting epigraphic evidence, any postulated destructive incursion at Copan must remain a hypothesis. The best means for testing such a proposition would be securing further well-dated archaeological evidence or new decipherments of texts referring to events dating to the A.D. 554-564 span. The previously mentioned indication that the reign of Copan's Ruler 9 may have been cut short in A.D. 553 might suggest that the opening round of an external intervention directed against Copan resulted in the death of this king.

In any case, if we assume an external incursion occurred at Copan, it would seem that the consequent destruction happened during the early years of Moon Jaguar's reign. The primary target must have been the Principal Group and its symbols of Copan's dynastic power. The destruction in the Main Group apparently included the smashing of Moon Jaguar's initial monument, Stela 17, along with an array of earlier monuments and several buildings, such as the probable funerary shrine of Ruler 8 which had been erected only a few years previously. Moon Jaguar survived these events to reassert Copan's power by raising Stela 9, choosing an ancient and apparently undefiled location, Group 9, for this expression of Copan's dynastic renewal.[†] This suggests similarity with the renewal events at Piedras Negras which took place at one of the most ancient areas of that center's Acropolis, avoiding areas associated with that center's defeat by Pomona (Golden 2002). This also raises the possibility that both outside intervention and attempts by Moon Jaguar to renew the dynasty could be responsible for the observed pattern of Early Classic destruction at Copan.

Nonetheless, it would seem that the consequences of these events were short lived. During the reigns of its next three kings, Rulers 11-13 (A.D. 578-738), Copan reached its apex of power and prestige (Fash 2001:101-114). It was not until well into the Late Classic that Copan suffered a well-documented setback with the capture and sacrifice of its 13th ruler, Waxaklahun Ubah K'awiil ("18 Rabbit") by Quirigua. And in light of the possible earlier destructive episode proposed here, it may be significant that in this later case there is textual evidence suggesting an external power, Calakmul, was behind this episode, Copan's greatest and most profound defeat (Looper 1999).

---

[*] Other than Quirigua, Caracol is the only site known to record a Copan king in its texts after the dynastic founder, K'inich Yax K'uk' Mo'. Copan Ruler 7, Waterlily Jaguar (ca. A.D. 504-544), is mentioned on Caracol Stela 16 dated to A.D. 534 (Grube 1990) at a time just prior to the Calakmul-Tikal confrontation, when Caracol was apparently still an ally of Tikal.

[†] Note that the previously mentioned tomb recently excavated by Seiichi Nakamura west of the Copan Main Group dates to this same era. If this tomb does represent a royal burial (or reburial), its location outside the Main Group might be a reflection of the same motivation— namely a desire to avoid the recently defiled Main Group.

Final Thoughts

This chapter has proposed that Copan was the recipient of an Early Classic incursion from Tikal that resulted in the founding of a new dynasty by K'inich Yax K'uk' Mo'. This event was initiated during the reign of the Tikal king Siyaj Chan K'awiil in A.D. 426/427. This foreign-sponsored dynastic founding at Copan may have been but one event in a process that saw the establishment of a new political order in the Maya Lowlands promoted by Tikal (and allied with the power of Teotihuacan in central Mexico). Thereafter it appears that Copan prospered under its alliance with Tikal, the greatest Lowland Maya power in the Early Classic Maya world.

More than a century later, between A.D. 554 and 564, nearly all of Copan's royal monuments, the most visible political legacy of K'inich Yax K'uk' Mo', seem to have been smashed, along with the destruction of at least two buildings and other likely disruptions during this same time span. Two general hypotheses can be advanced to account for the A.D. 554-564 destruction seen at Copan. The first is that this was due to internal events, including local political upheaval, periodic ritualized destruction, or a destructive event spawned by calendrical prophecy or an attempt to rewrite history. The second hypothesis would seem to remove most of the inconsistencies arising from the internally induced scenarios. This would see the destruction as being due to an outside incursion, most likely carried out directly or indirectly by Calakmul, the victor in a major confrontation with Tikal at this very same time. Following this episode, Copan's 10th ruler, Moon Jaguar, succeeded in renewing Copan's dynastic fortunes by dedicating a new monument in the ancient precinct of Group 9.

The testing of these propositions with newly acquired evidence—archaeological and epigraphic—will allow us to better define this destruction at Copan and pinpoint a cause. Of course someday the record may show that the invasion and K'atun cycle scenarios are related and together provide the best explanation for the destruction seen at Copan. For within the arena of Maya history as understood by the Maya themselves, the triumph of Calakmul over Tikal in A.D. 556-562 would have been seen as the fulfillment of prophecies foretold and retold by the K'atun chronicles. Thus with the arrival of a new K'atun cycle, the Maya may have believed it was destined for Tikal's dominance of the Maya Lowlands to end and be succeeded by Calakmul's ascendancy. Under such circumstances, it would be expected that events at Copan, whether created by external invasion or internal actions, would also reflect the profound changes brought by the new era.

As mentioned, it now appears that the effects of the changes brought by the new K'atun cycle did not end with the events of A.D. 554-564, for it is likely that the persistence of Tikal's greatest enemy, Calakmul, lay behind the far more serious blow struck against Copan by Quirigua in A.D. 738 (Looper 1999). This event, together with the possible causes of the earlier A.D. 554-564 destruction, make it clear that from the time of the founding of the K'inich Yax K'uk' Mo' dynasty in A.D. 426/427, Copan was fully drawn into the events and destinies of the larger Maya world.

Acknowledgments

I am very grateful for the institutional and funding support that made this research possible (see the Preface to this volume). This chapter was made possible by many colleagues, beginning with David Sedat for his work supervising the excavations that have revealed the earliest levels of the Copan Acropolis—including Hunal Structure and its tomb. The evidence from the Hunal Tomb was documented and conserved by the efforts of many people, chief among them Ellen Bell, Jane Buikstra, Bill Casselman, Bunny Coates, Lynn Grant, Fernando López, Chris Powell, David Sedat, and Loa Traxler. I am also grateful to my colleagues for their comments on an earlier version of this chapter. While there are different views as to the causes for the destruction of Copan's Early Classic monuments, discussions with Barbara Fash, William Fash, Charles Golden, Stephen Houston, Simon Martin, and David Stuart on this and related issues are very much appreciated.

Plate 1 (a) Copan Altar Q (photograph by Ellen E. Bell). (b) Full-scale reconstruction of Rosalila Structure in the Copan Sculpture Museum (photograph by Eleanor Coates).

Plate 2 (a) West façade of Yehnal Structure. (b) Photographic composite of west façade of Margarita Structure (photographs courtesy of David W. Sedat).

Plate 3 (a) Hunal Tomb burial slab after clearing fallen debris (b) Hunal Tomb floor. (photographs by David W. Sedat).

Plate 4 (a,b) Hunal Tomb shell disk with two glyphs (photographs courtesy of Kenneth Garrett). The disk was associated with three zoomorphic shell figures (a, c, d), and a similar disk (e) was found in Burial 92-3 (photographs c, d, and e by Robert J. Sharer).

Plate 5 (a) Hunal Tomb deer effigy vessel. (b) Hunal Tomb vessels manufactured in the Tikal region (photographs by Robert J. Sharer).

Plate 6 (a) Margarita Tomb, Chamber 2 (photograph courtesy of Kenneth Garrett). (b) Margarita Tomb, Chamber 1 (photograph by David W. Sedat).

Plate 7 Post-fire-painted ceramic (a–g) and organic (f, g) vessels in Margarita Tomb, Chamber 2 (photographs by Robert J. Sharer).

Plate 8 (a) Sub-Jaguar Tomb burial slab (photograph by Loa P. Traxler).. (b) Sub-Jaguar ceramic vessels (photograph by Robert J. Sharer).

15

MARCHING OUT OF STEP:
EARLY CLASSIC COPAN AND ITS HONDURAN NEIGHBORS

Edward M. Schortman and Patricia A. Urban

This chapter compares Early Classic political and cultural developments at Copan with those that transpired elsewhere in western and central Honduras. Since the Copan sequence is often so divergent from what is known about events and processes in the neighboring region, we originally found ourselves simply reciting a list of all the things not found, or that did not happen, outside of Copan. In the course of contemplating this lackluster prospect, however, it occurred to us that there was something intriguing about these discrepancies. To what extent were Copan and other Honduran societies marching to different drummers and what led to the choice of rhythms?

But differences are assessed in a variety of ways, only a subset of which can be discerned in the available data. The domains we have chosen for examination are political centralization, the extent to which power is concentrated or dispersed (Balandier 1970; de Montmollin 1989; Roscoe 1993), and degrees of intersocietal contact. Power, the capacity to direct the actions of others (Balandier 1970; Bourdieu 1977), is crudely estimated here by elite ability to harness community labor in constructing monumental edifices (platforms at least 1.5 m high) and other public works (see Carrelli, this volume, for a more sophisticated approach to quantifying architectural measures of power). Political success should also be reflected in paramount strategies to aggregate supporters around their capitals, thereby enhancing direct control over subordinate labor and loyalty while denying both to potential usurpers (de Montmollin 1989; Roscoe 1993). The more effectively power is centralized, the more pronounced should be intra-polity discrepancies in site sizes and the dimensions of their component edifices. A primate distribution, in which one center clearly outdistances its contemporaries in both dimensions, signifies a high degree of political centralization, whereas the absence of monumental architecture and general homogeneity in site sizes imply a wide dispersal of power.

Power, however, is not a monolithic phenomenon. It is made up of, and based on, control over military, economic, social, and ideological components not all of which may be monopolized by a single faction. The more of these processes emergent leaders co-opt, the more effectively they undermine the capacity of followers to sustain and reproduce their social units, and the more secure and enduring is their rule (Earle 1997; de Marrais et al. 1996; Mann 1986; Runciman 1982; Yoffee 1991). It is of some interest, therefore, to investigate the outcomes of factional contests over power sources, determining which political variables paramounts could and could not capture and the long-term effects of different strategies (e.g., Brumfiel and Fox 1994). Unfortunately, it is usually far easier to identify political centralization than to know how it was achieved. We will advance some speculative hypotheses, more to spur further research than with any hope that they can be effectively tested by extant data.

Interaction intensity is measured here by the spread of material styles, primarily in ceramics, across western and central Honduras. This assessment is based on the assumption that the closer the contacts maintained between residents of two polities, the more their artifact inventories will share similar designs and motifs. The above is, to be sure, a crude approximation of ancient reality and should be tested and amplified by recourse to other lines of evidence, including the nature and sources of imports. We are confronted by limitations on the kinds of materials with which we can work. While ceramics are fairly well and consistently described for the area in question (see Henderson and Beaudry-Corbett 1993 for a good example of such systematization), other data categories are still in the process of being analyzed and published. Exotics are discussed to such a varying degree by researchers, it is difficult to use them in assessing arguments for the nature and intensity of inter-polity transactions.

Complicating the matter even further, we must acknowledge that people, not societies, interact (Renfrew 1972, 1986). Cross-border transactions may be narrowly channeled through the initiatives of a few individuals; they may be open to all; or they may fall somewhere along the continuum defined by these extremes. Similarly, concepts and goods derived from afar might be limited to a privileged few, available to all polity residents, or restricted in some cases and accessible more broadly in others. Such distinctions have important implications for understanding the impact of inter-polity interaction on local developmental processes (e.g., Friedman and Rowlands 1978) but can be difficult to infer from mute material remains. Although we examine the data with such concerns in mind, we cannot yet speak to these issues with any certainty.

Why have we chosen to base our comparisons on these variables? In part, because we can. There is sufficient information relating to political centralization and interaction processes for enough Honduran regions during the Early Classic to permit comparison with each other and Copan. In part, because consideration of the above factors casts some light on the ways in which denizens of the Copan Valley were both embroiled with and distancing themselves from members of other Honduran polities during the period in question. We must begin this account, however, by looking at events leading up to the Early Classic. It is only by placing the latter interval within this context that we can appreciate just how discordant Copan's developmental trajectory was from that of its Honduran neighbors.

Late Preclassic Political Centralization and Intersocietal Contacts

The gradually expanding corpus of data on Late Preclassic (200 B.C.–A.D. 250) developments in Honduras suggests that elites able to command corvée labor were emerging in a number of investigated areas (see Figure 15.1 for the location of sites discussed). Yarumela, Los Naranjos, and the Baide Site appear as primate centers dominating the Comayagua Valley, Lake Yojoa's north shore, and the middle Ulua drainage during this interval (Baudez 1966; Baudez and Becquelin 1973; Benyo and Melchionne 1987; Canby 1949, 1951; Dixon 1991; Dixon et al. 1994; Joesink-Mandeville 1987). Santo Domingo seems to have been the capital of the Naco Valley by late in the span, whereas centers such as Río Pelo and La Guacamaya occupied the pinnacle of, at least, two-tiered settlement hierarchies in the Sula Plain (Urban 1986a, 1986b; Wonderley 1991). In general, these early capitals were organized following a similar plan in which large earthen platforms are ranged orthogonally around long, linear plazas (Schortman and Urban 1991). Usually, a single, massive conical or rectilinear edifice physically dominates the center. This pattern bears a generic resemblance to the organization of monumental edifices at such Maya Highland centers as Kaminaljuyu (Michels 1979: 141–142, 145; Sanders 1974:98–99; Shook and Proskouriakoff 1956:97) and El Portón (Sharer and Sedat 1987) as well as Chalchuapa in western El Salvador, where Structure E3-1 looms above a long, open plaza (Sharer 1978c:73–82; 1978e:121). Such commonalities tentatively imply a shared cosmology whose principles were expressed through the arrangement of large-scale constructions (Ashmore 1991; Schortman and Urban 1991). Insofar as these buildings were commissioned by and raised under the direction of social leaders, this ideology has an elite cast.

As physically salient as the above centers are, it is unclear how large their populations were. This results in part from difficulties experienced in identifying residences that were often built directly on ground surface and mantled by thick natural and cultural deposits (Reynolds 1979). It may also be the case, however, that Late Preclassic Honduran centers were not foci of marked population nucleation. Where there is sufficient evidence on which to advance an interpretation, it appears that Late Preclassic Honduran populations were widely dispersed in small aggregates around the monumental centers they helped create. This situation contrasts with the more densely nucleated settlement surrounding coeval centers such as Chalchuapa and Kaminaljuyu to the south and west (Michels 1979b:138; Sanders 1974:100; Sharer 1978b:210).

Figure 15.1 Location of Late Preclassic sites mentioned in the text.

What was going at Late Preclassic Copan? People were apparently flocking to the area south and west of what would become the Copan Acropolis, though they declined to invest their labor in raising monumental edifices there (Fash 1983c; 1991:71; Hall and Viel, this volume; Sedat and López, this volume). Such concentration of people on the floodplain is all the more surprising given the area's vulnerability to inundation (Hall and Viel, this volume). Elsewhere in the Copan Valley the situation is reversed: monumental architecture, whose form and arrangement generally parallel what is seen in other parts of Honduras at this time, is found at Los Achiotes and Cerro Chino but without clear signs of population nucleation (Canuto, this volume). The Copan Valley, therefore, presents us with a paradox in which our two measures of power, monumental construction and population nucleation, do not coincide at a single capital. This discrepancy suggests that several distinct strategies of political centralization were being used by valley magnates yielding different material results. The schemes employed by Los Achiotes' and Cerro Chino's rulers were seemingly in line with those used by aspiring leaders in other Honduran locales, while developments on the Copan floodplain hint at the existence of novel political processes.

The extensive distribution of similar ceramic motifs suggests a diffuse pattern of intersocietal contact in which interaction was not restricted within specific portions of Honduras (Schortman and Urban 1991). Orange- or red-slipped monochrome vessels are commonly represented in most collections along with burnished unslipped and zone-decorated containers, the latter embellished with painted, incised, or modeled designs set off in panels from unmodified portions of a vessel's surface (see especially descriptions in Henderson and Beaudry-Corbett 1993). Though it is certainly not true that if you have seen one Honduran Late Preclassic assemblage you have seen them all, these collections share enough attributes to suggest that their manufacturers were drawing inspiration from a similar design repertoire. The suite of shared motifs was most likely maintained through persistent intersocietal contacts, innovations spreading and being selectively adopted by people living throughout the region. Such generic resemblances imply that political boundaries were not being overtly expressed through ceramic styles, nor were intersocietal transactions limited to a privileged few.

Two other features of Late Preclassic ceramics are of importance here: the extensive spread of Usulutan pottery and the paucity of elaborately decorated containers. Resemblances among locally fashioned ceramic vessels are accentuated by the widespread distribution of negatively painted wares within the Usulutan tradition. Characterized by a distinctive fine, hard, tan paste, vessels in this system are slipped orange and decorated with negative-painted groups of parallel lines. Motifs are relatively abstract, tending toward geometric figures. Though forms vary considerably, the prevalent flaring-walled bowls supported by three or four nubbin feet are ideal food-serving containers. Chemical mineralogical assays coupled with the long history of *in situ* development of Usulutan technology in western El Salvador suggest that vessels sharing the above-noted features were traded from that area into Honduras (Demarest and Sharer 1982, 1986).

Whether there was one or multiple sources of Usulutan pottery, however, its sweeping distribution and formal similarities hint at: the existence of a widespread exchange network; links, however indirect, with Chalchuapa and the Maya Highlands where Usulutan ceramics are common components of Late Preclassic assemblages (Demarest and Sharer 1986); and shared patterns of behavior utilizing similar paraphernalia, probably having to with the display and sharing of food (Wonderley 1991). The abstract nature of negative-painted decorations may convey a set of ideological principles that were not rooted in a particular place but were shared widely among people in a number of societies. Such beliefs could have facilitated intersocietal discourse, possibly accompanied by feasting (Wonderley 1991).

Although Usulutan ceramics are found in all investigated portions of Honduras that yield Late Preclassic remains, their prevalence in these collections varies somewhat. Allowing that frequency assessments are difficult to make from the available data, it is hard to miss the concentration of this pottery at Copan. Not only is Usulutan common in the Copan Valley but also vessels decorated in this manner found here assume the widest array of forms recorded for any location in Honduras (e.g., Longyear 1952; Viel 1983). Such diversity and numbers imply that Copan was an important node in the Usulutan distribution network, its Late Preclassic residents possibly maintaining close ties with Chalchuapa and/or Maya Highland sources of this pottery. The above interpretation is further suggested by the recovery of two pedestal stone sculptures in Highland Maya style from Copan (Fash 1991:74; see also B. Fash, this volume).

Negative-painted containers are some of the most elaborately decorated vessels found in Late Preclassic Honduran assemblages outside Chalchuapa. Painted bichromes are rare to absent in most areas, and trichromes as well as polychromes are virtually non-existent. Though the significance of this dearth is obscure, it at least implies that complex social messages were not being conveyed in pottery designs. Nor were they commonly transmitted in any other surviving media, such as the stone monuments that were becoming increasingly ubiquitous at nearby Chalchuapa and Highland Maya centers (Anderson 1978; Michels 1979; Sharer and Sedat 1987). One possible implication of this observation is that information relating to such features of the social landscape as political boundaries and hierarchical distinctions was not sufficiently salient to require statement and reinforcement in visible, overt forms.

The overall impression conveyed by Late Preclassic material culture from Honduras, therefore, is of a series of interlinked societies most of which were hierarchically organized. Status distinctions were not dramatically stated, and political frontiers were porous, with ideas and, presumably, people regularly passing among societies. This network was weakly (and very likely indirectly) tied into developments occurring in western El Salvador and the Maya Highlands, though its constituent polities did not adopt many of the more explicit material expressions of hierarchy found in those areas. The latter observation implies that political centralization was not as advanced as in neighboring zones to the south and west.

Developments at Los Achiotes and Cerro Chino in the Copan Valley generally conform to the above picture. Events transpiring on the Copan Valley floodplain, however, diverge from those recorded elsewhere, concentrating population where, throughout Honduras, settlements are dispersed, but lack the monumental signifiers of labor control. Similarly, floodplain denizens seem to have been more intensively involved with exchanges that linked them to Maya Highland and/or western Salvadoran societies than was the case for their neighbors. This asynchrony only becomes more pronounced in the succeeding Early Classic.

Early Classic Political Centralization and Intersocietal Contact

Many Late Preclassic Southeast Mesoamerican polities underwent processes of political decentralization during the Early Classic (see Figure 15.2 for the location of sites discussed). This sequence is most clearly expressed at Chalchuapa where Ilopongo's eruption in ca. A.D. 260 buried the center along with much of western El Salvador under deep ash deposits from which it took centuries to recover. Less dramatically, previously unified realms in the Comayagua, Naco, and, possibly, Sula Valleys fragmented as their capitals were either abandoned or survived as lower ranked settlements within the site hierarchy. These developments do not necessarily imply a resurgence of egalitarian principles. Small-scale monumental centers succeed primate settlements in both the Naco and Comayagua Valleys, for example (Dixon 1991; Urban 1986a, 1986b). Power differentials, therefore, may well have persisted on smaller spatial scales.

The situation on Lake Yojoa's northern shore is unclear, Los Naranjos likely remained a major political center but, without published settlement data for the rest of the area, we cannot say whether it continued to dominate its hinterland or shared it with usurpers.

Along the middle Ulua drainage, the Late Preclassic Baide site was apparently abandoned, its place taken by the newly emergent center of Gualjoquito ca. 12 km to the north (Ashmore et al. 1987; Schortman et al. 1986).

Early Classic Gualjoquito was considerably smaller and less impressive than its Late Preclassic predecessor; though it became the center of a major polity during the Late Classic (A.D. 600–950).

The case for the Sulaco drainage is unclear. First pioneered during the Late Preclassic, the recovery of over 500 pieces of jade and jadeite from the site of Salitron Viejo strongly argues for the presence of well-connected elites who could acquire this valued commodity from distant Guatemalan (middle Motagua) sources. Though Early Classic settlement patterns in the Sulaco drainage are still being reconstructed, it

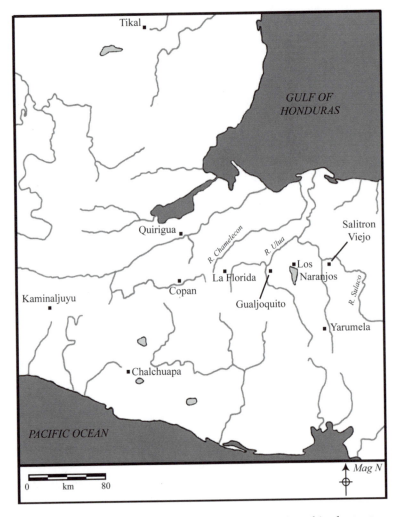

Figure 15.2 Location of Early Classic sites mentioned in the text.

seems that Salitron Viejo's residents were successfully advancing claims to political pre-eminence. Like Gualjoquito in the Ulua drainage, Salitron Viejo would become the capital of an extensive political unit during the succeeding Late Classic (Hirth et al. 1989).

In the La Florida Valley, about 35 km east/southeast of Copan, the site of the same name now occupied the apex of a two-tier settlement hierarchy (Nakamura et al. 1991). This development is all the more striking as it follows a period of apparent local population decline during the Late Preclassic.

The political picture is more complex than was the case for the Late Preclassic. While power is dispersed in some areas, in others the first steps toward centralization were being taken. In at least one case (the middle Ulua drainage) there was no obvious shift in the complexity of the settlement hierarchy but a definite change in the locus of power. Population decline is not clearly indicated in any of the investigated zones, nor can we say with certainty whether people were concentrating around newly founded capitals. For the moment we will argue that population nucleation is not strongly attested to anywhere in Early Classic Honduras beyond Copan and await the results of new and ongoing research to disprove this claim.

But what of contemporary developments in the Copan Valley? Initially, the Late Preclassic/Early Classic transition was marked by changes that occurred within the familiar southeast Mesoamerican framework. A relatively small center was established at the earlier floodplain settlement, its monumental buildings organized according to principles similar to those manifest earlier at Cerro Chino and Los Achiotes (Early Yune, Sedat and López, this volume). Whether this modest capital was the sole political focus within the valley remains uncertain. By the early 5th century A.D., however, the situation changed dramatically.

As our colleagues have amply demonstrated, after A.D. 426 Copan experienced an unprecedented period of construction and celebration of elite power focused on the site core, especially the Acropolis (Carrelli, this volume; Cheek 1983b; Fash 1991:72-76; Sedat and López, this volume; Sharer et al. 1992; Sharer, Traxler, et al. 1999). Large-scale constructions that dwarf anything known from elsewhere in Honduras at this time were now being raised, razed, and rebuilt at a dizzying pace. The scale and opulence of tombs housing the mortal remains of Copan's Early Classic rulers are equally impressive and lacking in Honduran analogues (Bell et al. and Reents-Budet et al., this volume). Not only did these scions succeed in capturing labor, but they also apparently attracted considerable portions of the total population to their capital (Fash 1991:75). Copan's rulers, in short, effectively moved to both concentrate supporters and control their labor. Though paramounts in the Sulaco drainage and in the nearby La Florida and middle Ulua Valleys were enjoying some success along these same lines, their achievements were profoundly overshadowed by developments at Copan.

The events noted above were occurring within a gradually changing matrix of intersocietal contacts. Usulutan ceramics continued to be found consistently throughout the area, their numbers augmented by the appearance of red-painted examples generally classed as "Chilanga" (Sharer 1978d:47). As was the case for the Late Preclassic, negative-painted vessels, including Chilanga containers, were particularly well represented at Copan. Orange and red-slipped monochromes remained important components of most collections as were unslipped, burnished vessels. Painted bichromes became more prevalent, however, and polychromes made their first unambiguous appearance throughout most of Honduras. Though we cannot decipher what was being "said" in these ceramics, it appears that pottery was being used to convey more, and more diverse, social information than had been the case during the Late Preclassic (Carr 1995).

Early Classic Honduran potters, therefore, continued to draw on a widespread array of decorative motifs maintained and spread through extensive intersocietal contacts. Usulutan vessels, still mostly open bowls though now often supported by large, hollow mammiform feet, apparently continued as elements in widely shared social behaviors. Painted bichromes and polychromes, however, at least had the potential to express, in highly visible ways, both political borders and intrasocietal hierarchical distinctions. Whether this latter potential was realized awaits analyses of larger collections to determine if regional stylistic patterns suggest the use of painted motifs to demarcate political frontiers (Blanton and Peregrine 1996). The only Honduran locale where elaborately decorated vessels were explicitly employed as status markers is Copan.

Ties between Honduras and the Maya Highlands persist throughout the Early Classic, though Copan's residents seem to have been more intensively involved in long-distance transactions than their Honduran contemporaries. *Talud-tablero* architecture, substantial adobe construction, hieroglyphic texts, distinctive goggle-eyed personages, architectonic stucco decorations, murals, vaulted tombs, and some pottery styles strongly argue for linkages between Copan's magnates and those of Kaminaljuyu, the Mexican Highlands, and the Maya Lowlands, especially Tikal (Agurcia F.; Reents-Budet et al.; B. Fash; Sedat and López; and Sharer, this volume).

Outside the Copan Valley, such ties are difficult to discern. Some of the jade and jadeite artifacts from Salitron Viejo on the Sulaco river are carved in styles reminiscent of examples found at Kaminaljuyu and Teotihuacan in the Valley of Mexico (Hirth 1988:308–309). Recovery at this center of green obsidian, probably from the Pachuca flows near Teotihuacan, *talud-tablero* architecture, and slipped orange monochromes that resemble Thin Orange Ware from Teotihuacan in their forms, color, and surface finish further suggests that Salitron Viejo's inhabitants enjoyed contacts with distant realms (Hirth 1988; Hirth et al. 1993:231). Most likely these ties were restricted to local elites and mediated through intermediaries, probably Copan's rulers and their agents.

Unlike the case in the Late Preclassic, Early Classic intersocietal transactions do not seem to have been equally accessible to wide segments of ancient populations. In fact, two interaction networks may have been emerging: one involving a wide range of people among whom ideas concerning ceramic decorative motifs and the use of

Usulutan pottery moved, the other restricted to magnates who dealt with, among other things, esoteric goods (such as jade) and concepts (such as those expressed in stucco decorations) that they alone possessed and understood. The former system operated throughout most of Early Classic Honduras, whereas in a few areas, especially Copan, aristocratic exchanges were also being pursued. Copan seems to have maintained its Late Preclassic position as a nexus through which Honduran societies were linked to networks extending into the Maya Highlands and Lowlands. As opposed to their Late Preclassic predecessors, however, these ties were now largely in the hands of powerful rulers.

What can account for the above-noted discrepancies between developments at Copan, on the one hand, and the rest of Honduras on the other? Although no definitive answer can be advanced at present, comparing these trajectories suggests some of the factors that might ultimately comprise an acceptable explanation.

Power Sources and Political Stability

Power can be achieved in a number of different ways. The wider the array of political assets a faction controls, the better able its members are to make demands on their followers and see them carried out. Power, however, is an abstract process embedded within social relations, and its sources in military, economic, and ideological processes can be difficult to read in the materials left behind by prehistoric societies. What follows, therefore, is an exercise in using ambiguous data to infer obscure processes, carried out in the hopes that others can build on this effort to create firmer interpretations.

The exciting research within the Copan Acropolis, coupled with extensive settlement pattern studies and excavations elsewhere in the Main Group, are building a picture of a powerful elite who manipulated economic, ideological, and, possibly, military processes to great advantage. The relatively small size of the Copan Valley, coupled with the concentration of the most fertile soils in the bottomlands, would have facilitated centralized control of the most productive tracts (Fash 1991:45-46; see also Carneiro 1970). Though it is impossible at this remove to describe Early Classic systems of land ownership, establishment of the Copan capital on the floodplain at least implies paramount efforts to assert claims to this highly valuable terrain. It may have also involved elite-directed efforts to control the area's volatile hydrology and reclaim its swamps (Hall and Viel, this volume).

The Naco, Comayagua, Sula, and La Florida Valleys are much larger and possess wider expanses of fertile land. Late Preclassic centers in the first three areas are situated on the margins of the most agriculturally productive zones, either at the base of the surrounding hills or, in the case of Yarumela, within a rain-shadow that made rainfall agriculture a risky proposition (Dixon 1992; Los Naranjos's position vis-a-vis subsistence resources is not known at present). Late Preclassic Los Achiotes and Cerro

Chino occupy similar positions within the Copan Valley (Canuto, this volume), as would any early center that might have existed beneath the modern town of Copán Ruinas (Fash 1991). There is no good reason to suppose that the available farming technology precluded settlement in more productive valley segments where Late Preclassic hamlets are indeed found (e.g., Pope 1987; Schortman and Urban 1994b). Whoever lived at these centers could not apparently assert claims to the best agricultural land by establishing residence on those tracts.

In all of the areas discussed, the Early Classic is marked by the appearance of monumental centers on the most fertile soils. Copan's rulers, however, enjoyed far more success than their counterparts elsewhere in capturing and channeling the labor of subordinates. Such triumphs may have been built, in part, on their ability to lay exclusive claims to the most productive fields within the narrowly circumscribed Copan Valley (Fash 1991:45–46). The more extensive tracts of arable terrain in other portions of Honduras possibly frustrated efforts at monopolization and so undermined paramount strategies of power concentration. Two of the three Honduran areas that supported modest signs of political centralization, the middle Ulua and Sulaco drainages, however, are also narrowly circumscribed environments in which developing centers are situated within the largest expanses of arable land in each zone. Here, what thwarted more rapid development of political centralization may have been the distribution of productive terrain in small, discontinuous segments. Such environments would have been inimical to population nucleation, an important process undergirding political centralization (de Montmollin 1989; Roscoe 1993).

Bridging the economic and ideological is the process of intersocietal exchange. Such transactions can be a means of acquiring foreign commodities whose value is based on their prosaic uses (such as obsidian nuclei imported for the fabrication of stone tools) and/or their association with high prestige, possibly supernaturally charged, distant realms (Helms 1979, 1988).

In either case, those who monopolize these contacts are in an excellent position to undercut their followers' autonomy as they are the sole source of items needed and valued by all (D'Altroy and Earle 1985; Earle 1997; Ekholm 1972; Friedman and Rowlands 1978; Peregrine and Feinman 1996). Clients surrender labor and its fruits in return for goods obtainable only from the monopolists. Such power is further enhanced if imports augment the charisma of potentates through the association of leaders with sacred locales. During the Late Preclassic, highly valued objects such as jadeite, marble vessels, and marine shell occur in small quantities at Yarumela but are not clearly attested to elsewhere in western and central Honduras (Dixon et al. 1994). Obsidian from various sources, including La Esperanza as well as El Chayal and San Martin Jilotepeque, is also found now in varying amounts at different Honduran sites (Hirth 1988). Contrasting with his picture of sporadic, low-volume exchanges is the aforementioned spread of ceramic designs and Usulutan pottery throughout Honduras.

Although future work may change this picture, it currently appears that inter-societal transactions were common, but did not generally involve the exchange of goods monopolized by elites. There was no basis here for power founded on exclusive control over imports.

The same can be said for the Early Classic—except at Copan and, to a lesser extent, Salitron Viejo. The findings from excavated tombs housing Copan's Early Classic rulers strongly argue for paramount control over a wide range of exotics (Bell et al. and Reents-Budet et al., this volume; Sharer, this volume; Sharer et al. 1992; Sharer, Traxler, et al. 1999). Most of these objects seem to have been badges of office that were the sole prerogatives of powerful aristocrats. Consequently, highly valued imports at Copan functioned more as expressions of the elite's external connections and the prestige derived from such contacts, than as the basis for dependency relations linking rulers and ruled through unequal exchanges (Sharer, Traxler, et al. 1999:20). Such a pattern implies that extra-societal transactions served more as ideological rather than as economic supports for elite pretensions. Restriction of exotic symbols to aristocratic architectural and mortuary contexts reinforces the notion that elites monopolized local participation in foreign ideologies and their material manifestations (B. Fash, this volume).

The concentration of jade and jadeite items at Salitron Viejo, along with other exotics such as marble, shell, and slate artifacts, suggests that similar processes were being instigated by emergent elites here as well (Hirth et al. 1993:231). That many of these items were found in caches, rather than burials (Hirth 1988:307), may imply that their acquisition was not strictly controlled by local magnates or that, once obtained, they were invested in rituals associated with the entire community and not in the aggrandizement of specific individuals.

Close juxtaposition of elite residences with temples at Copan, coupled with the explicit legitimation of power through the complex and dramatic iconographic statements inscribed on the latter, point to an explicit linkage between rulers and the sacred. Interment of potentates within hallowed spaces only reinforces the bond, transforming deceased rulers into supernaturally potent, possibly deified, ancestors (Agurcia Fasquelle, this volume).

The gradually expanding corpus of Early Classic hieroglyphic inscriptions from Copan, with their frequent references to rites conducted by paramounts, reinforces the impression that political power was based, in part, on prowess within the supernatural realm (B. Fash, this volume).

Most Late Preclassic monumental Honduran architecture probably served as venues for the performance of large-scale public rituals. There are a few signs of far less imposing residences in the environs of these buildings, and at least some of these likely housed the rulers who commissioned the nearby platforms and officiated at ceremonies performed on and around them (Dixon 1992; Dixon et al. 1994; Urban 1986b). Such a juxtaposition implies that elite power in Late Preclassic Honduras was

founded largely on associations with the supernatural through cult observances conducted on physically impressive platforms. The occasional burial found in these edifices is not sufficiently opulent to support an argument for the deification of ritual specialists, nor were these notables apparently capable of siphoning off commoner labor
for the creation of elaborate and imposing elite residences.

The situation in the Early Classic is less clear. General diminution of monumental architecture throughout Honduras (Hirth 1988) may hint at a dramatic reorgan-
ization of social and political relations, possibly implying the ascendancy of rulers
whose secular roles were at least as important as their religious obligations. Certainly,
by the Late Classic, elite residences of some size are found throughout Honduras, albeit
frequently associated with cult constructions. There is currently too little data available on Early Classic building functions for the area to do more than guess that a transition from religious to secular sources of power was in process. What is clear, however, is that no known Honduran potentates commanded the awe inspired by Copan's
Early Classic rulers.

Military prowess is difficult to ascertain in the archaeological record (Webster
1993:421–424). Though still limited, hieroglyphic inscriptions provide a glimpse of
Copan as an expanding realm whose magnates were capable of establishing control
over Quirigua, ca. 90 km to the north/northwest (Harris 1999:26; Looper 1995, 1999;
Sharer, Traxler, et al. 1999:20). Such a relationship need not have been the product of
military adventure, but establishment and maintenance of this outpost in Guatemala's
lower Motagua Valley arguably required at least a threat of force. Intriguing references
to possible hostilities in which the founder of Copan's Classic period dynasty, K'inich
Yax K'uk' Mo', might have engaged, imply that military force was wielded by, and
against, Copan's previous rulers (Harris 1999:24; Sharer 1999, this volume; Sharer,
Traxler, et al. 1999). As Sharer, writing for this volume, points out, hiatuses in Copan's
hieroglyphic record may well reflect the fortunes of war suffered by local notables as
allies of Tikal in its contests with Calakmul. The absence of hieroglyphic inscriptions in
Honduras outside Copan and Quirigua certainly hampers the identification of military
activities. Bearing this discrepancy in mind, however, we must still conclude that there
is no basis for asserting that other Honduran Early Classic leaders consistently wielded
military power or that it was an asset on which they relied in hierarchy building.

The data, though rarely as ample and unambiguous as we would like, suggest
that the unprecedented power exercised by Copan's Early Classic magnates was based
on their ability to harness economic, ideological, and military processes to achieve
political ends. This concentration of strategic assets in the hands of the royal dynasty
assured them a level of control over local populations unmatched elsewhere in contemporary Honduras. It also established the foundations for stable hierarchical relations that persisted until ca. A.D. 800. Conversely, the inability of Late Preclassic
Honduran magnates to employ more than ideological assets in their quest for power
weakened their claims to political preeminence. The polities they led, therefore, had

more fragile hierarchical structures than those noted at Early Classic Copan and were more vulnerable to pressures toward decentralization, whether arising from within or beyond polity boundaries. There is some evidence that the Early Classic successors of these Honduran realms were in the process of forming around rulers who were trying to stake claims to a wider range of political resources. Moving their capitals onto more agriculturally productive land might reflect elite efforts to capture an important economic resource, whereas the concentration of valuable exotics at Salitron Viejo bespeaks a move toward monopolizing control over extra-societal contacts. If this is, indeed, what was happening, the strategies did not bear immediate fruit. Some small polities of the Early Classic, however, would give rise to much larger Late Classic realms in which power was firmly concentrated in the hands of a ruling faction.[*] What distinguishes Copan from its Honduran neighbors, therefore, may have more to do with the pace of change than any basic incongruencies in the processes underlying those trajectories.

Summary

Developments in Late Preclassic to Early Classic Honduras can be described with varying degrees of confidence. That Copan's trajectory during this span runs counter to events attested to in most of the region seems fairly certain. That the noted discrepancies are due to the variable success experienced by rulers throughout the area in monopolizing economic, ideological, and military resources is a plausible, though not established, proposition. Even if this last interpretation is eventually established, we still have not seriously broached the question of why Copan's lords concentrated power so effectively and relatively rapidly.

Intense concentration of the most fertile soils within the Copan Valley might have facilitated their centralized control, as noted earlier. Even so, economic resources only become components of successful political strategies when their alienation and manipulation by a faction are written into the social charter and protected by the threat of force (Earle 1997). Presumably, armed combat played an integral role in sustaining elite preeminence in Copan. Threats alone do not inevitably, or often, lead to acquiescence, however. Creation of stable hierarchical relations depends at least as much on forging a consensus concerning the legitimacy of power differentials (Demarest and Conrad 1992). Establishing a close link between rulers and the sacred,

---

[*] La Sierra in the Naco Valley; Travesia, Curruste, La Guacamaya, Calabazas, and Mantecales in the Sula Plain; Salitron Viejo and Intendencia in the Sulaco and Humuya drainages, respectively; Gualjoquito along the middle Ulua; Las Tapias, Roncador, El Abra, El Puente, Nueva Suyapa, Los Higos, and Las Pilas in the adjoining La Florida and La Venta Valleys; and Los Naranjos on Lake Yojoa's northern shore (Ashmore et al. 1987; Baudez and Becquelin 1973; Henderson 1981; Hirth et al. 1989; Nakamura et al. 1991; Schortman and Urban 1994; Robinson 1987; Urban and Schortman 1986).

this tie made all the more intimate when the paramount's ancestors are deified, may be one step in this direction. Maintaining and physically proclaiming exclusive ties to distant, high-prestige realms is another strategy that might be used to sacralize inequality.

Whatever explanation is finally put forward to account for Copan's atonality within the symphony of Honduran developments must account for how the above-noted triad of power sources was successfully orchestrated within the valley. Equally important, this hypothesis must specify why military, economic, and ideological assets remained disarticulated in other portions of contemporary Honduras well into the Late Classic (e.g., the Comayagua Valley) or were relatively slow to cohere (as in the Sula, Naco, and Sulaco Valleys). It may well be that a crucial element in the Copanec transformation was the introduction of a blueprint for novel power relations by a forceful and charismatic agent, K'inich Yax K'uk' Mo'. An interloper's ideas might have catalyzed local political developments, demonstrating ways in which previously diffuse power sources could be successfully combined to advance and legitimize a wholly new form of political centralization. We still do not know what elements of Copanec Early Classic political structure facilitated K'inich Yax K'uk' Mo's success and why comparable incursions and metamorphoses were not experienced elsewhere in Honduras. Significant culture change requires both individual initiative and a context in which innovation is rewarded, or is at least allowed to disrupt preexisting relations leading to the creation of new configurations. Examining Copanec political processes in light of developments recorded elsewhere in contemporary Honduras helps to sharpen appreciation for the complex interplay between agency and structure (Bourdieu 1977). Ultimately, such comparisons will shed light on how strategies of political centralization were forged, advanced, and resisted across the cultural mosaic that was Early Classic Honduras.

Acknowledgments

We are very grateful to all who have made our work in Honduras over the past 25 years both possible and enjoyable. In particular, we extend our profound thanks to the National Science Foundation, National Endowment for the Humanities, National Geographic Society, Fulbright Foundation, Wenner Gren Foundation, The Margaret Cullinan Wray Foundation, and Kenyon College for generously providing the funds without which our work would have been impossible. The directors and staff of the Instituto Hondureño de Antropología e Historia have been, and remain, invaluable colleagues and collaborators in all of our investigations. We would like to single out for particular thanks, Drs. Cueva, Agurcia, Cruz, Casco, and Dra. Joya, former directors of the Institute, for their unfailing support as well as Licda. Fajardo, Dra. Lara, Dr. Hasemann, and Lics. Veliz and Durón for all of their help. People from all walks of life and backgrounds in the Naco Valley and middle Ulua drainage willingly contributed their hard and skillful labor to the research we directed in and around their communities and we are forever in their debt. We are also very grateful to all those who have taken time over the years to share their findings and help us craft better arguments, especially Joyce Marcus, Kent Flannery, Wendy Ashmore, Bob Sharer, George Hasemann, Gloria Lara, Boyd Dixon, Ken Hirth, Tony Wonderley, and John Henderson. And last, but definitely not least, thanks are due to Ellen Bell, Marcello Canuto, and Bob Sharer for inviting us to cast the diffuse, ambiguous light of Southeast Mesoamerican research on the stately development of Early Classic Copan. Any errors or confusions that have crept into this chapter despite the best efforts of all of the above people and institutions remain our sole responsibility.

16

The Early Classic and its Antecedents at Kaminaljuyu: A Complex Society with Complex Problems

Juan Antonio Valdés and Lori E. Wright

The Early Classic of Kaminaljuyu has been a key period of interest because of the Carnegie Institution of Washington excavations which discovered several *talud-tablero* style buildings that contained tombs rich in artifacts considered typical of Teotihuacan (Kidder et al. 1946). Years later, excavations by Cheek (1977) in the area known as the Palangana, and those by Brown (1977) at the peripheral site of Solano, ratified the presence of *talud-tablero* architecture. These discoveries led scholars to propose that Teotihuacanos had strongly influenced Kaminaljuyu over a period spanning 150 years, between A.D. 400 and 550 (Cheek 1977). By contrast, Shook and Hatch (1999) proposed that the Teotihuacan presence in highland Guatemala was brief, lasting 100 years or less.

The view that Teotihuacan contact had a lasting influence at Kaminaljuyu has predominated for 50 years, despite published excavations in diverse parts of the site carried out by Guatemalan archaeologists since the 1970s, which have broadened the panorama of information about the Preclassic and Classic period occupations at the city (Carpio Rezzio 1999; Fahsen 2000; Gutiérrez Mendoza 1989; Hatch 1993, 1996, 1997, 2000; Navarrete and Luján 1986; Ohi 2001; Ohi and Ito 1994; Shook and Hatch 1999; Valdés 1997, 1998; Valdés and Hatch 1996). Yet recent publications often repeat the traditional hypotheses about Teotihuacan influence or occupation at Kaminaljuyu and present an antiquated reconstruction of the site's history. Therefore, we review a number of the most important developments in the city's history, as well as the results of recent research, with the aim of better understanding this prehispanic city.

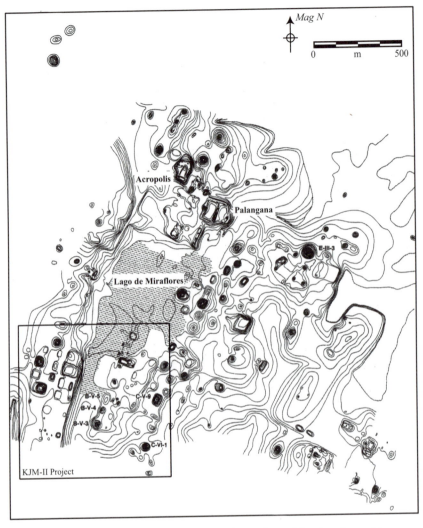

Figure 16.1 Kaminaljuyu, showing the main architectural groups mentioned in the text.

The Preclassic Period at Kaminaljuyu

Investigations by the Miraflores II and San Jorge projects have shown that the social complexity of the city began during the Middle Preclassic (Valdés 1997, 1998, 2001; Hatch 1993) and not during the Late Preclassic as is usually assumed from prior excavations (Michels 1979a). This early development was due in large part to the soil fertility and to the advantageous use of Lake Miraflores, which was the principal source of water for the center of the city (Figure 16.1), and also provided the city's occupants with dietary resources such as aquatic plants and animals (Emery n.d.).

Monumental architectural works began to be constructed in the Middle Preclassic period (Providencia phase; ca. 600–400 B.C.), when large plazas delimited by temples and residences first appeared. Ceremonial and artistic developments began to rapidly emerge in all sites across the valley, with the appearance of plain stelae and altars placed in front of principal buildings. As a sign of its emerging complexity, the first carved monument (Stela 9) was erected in Kaminaljuyu during this period. The achievements of the ruling class are also indicated by the complexity of emergent technology.

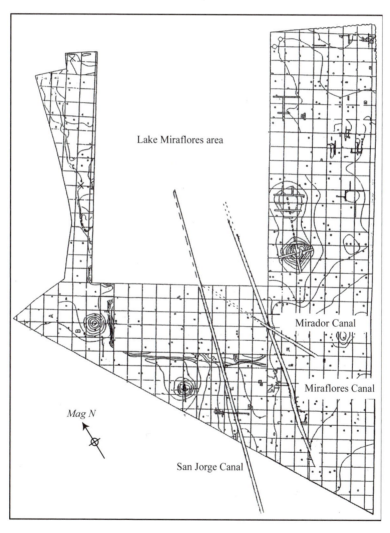

Figure 16.2 Three major canals at the site of Kaminaljuyu: San Jorge, Miraflores, and Mirador.

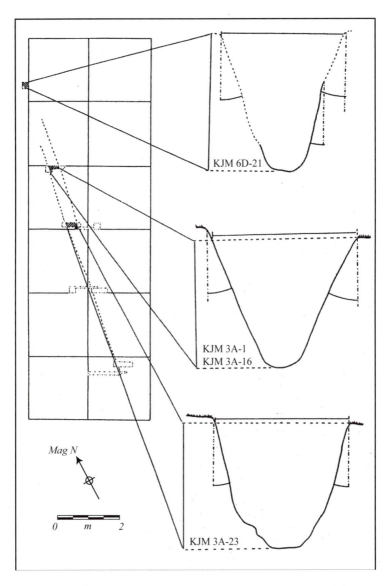

Figure 16.3 Plan and section of the beginning section of the
Miraflores canal, near the Miraflores lake.

Hydraulic engineering works were built to irrigate cultivated fields on the southern periphery of the city. Three enormous gravity-fed canals have been discovered in the southern part of the site: the Miraflores, San Jorge, and Mirador Canals (Figure 16.2). A fourth, the Mongoy Canal, is located near the northern limit of the city, next to mound B-I-1. The oldest of these is the Middle Preclassic Miraflores Canal; the other three canals are Late Preclassic in date (Hatch 1993, 1997; Ohi and Ito 1994; Valdés and Hatch 1996).

The Miraflores Canal was constructed around 600 B.C. and without doubt is the largest known from the Maya area for this time. It originated from the southern margin of Lake Miraflores and was excavated into the *talpetate* substratum along 1 km. The first section of the canal has a V shape, measuring 3.90 m in width by 5.8 m in depth (Figure 16.3). Farther along its length, as the rate of water flow became less critical, the canal increased in width and decreased in depth, taking on a U-shaped form, and reached a width of almost 8 m by only 1 m in depth (Barrientos 1997; Valdés and Hatch 1996; Valdés 1997, 1998, n.d.). We have suggested that there must have been a system of controlled flooding along the canal's trajectory to simulate a natural flood plain, given that the canal margins are of varying height.

This irrigation system was so effective that the network of canals was expanded during the following four centuries. The Miraflores Canal was gradually closed and filled with trash by ca. 200 B.C. (Verbena phase), even as a new larger canal system was constructed. The San Jorge Canal was the most impressive feature of the expanded system. It measured 18 m wide by 8 m deep, and ran nearly 2 km in length.

Various secondary canals have been detected, among them the smaller Mirador Canal. The importance of the Mirador Canal lies in its application of a new hydraulic technology. The angular form of the canal walls at several points indicates that wooden floodgates were used to restrict the channel and control the movement of water toward the agricultural fields (Valdés n.d.). Presumably the systems of intensive cultivation made possible by the canals increased yields of crops such as maize, beans squash, chile, avocado, anona, zapotes and possibly also cacao (Ivic 1988), improving the dietary diversity and security of the city's occupants.

During the Late Preclassic, there are indications that political power became concentrated in the hands of a supreme ruler, who surrounded himself by a court of close relatives and city leaders. This ruling elite could rely on sufficient authority to order the construction of large works of architecture and hydraulic engineering, to celebrate public ceremonies, as well as to control interregional commerce and the advantages that it conferred. The ruler's authority was represented in a triumphal manner on the carved monuments erected around the city.

The best evidence for centralized political authority comes from the elaborate contents of the two richest Late Preclassic tombs, discovered in Structure E-III-3 (Shook and Kidder 1952). The tombs were deposited at different times, but their proximity and similarity implies that the line of succession may well have been hereditary (Shook and Hatch 1999). Since Structure E-III-3 was the largest at the site, and more importantly, since it was the funerary monument for two great dignitaries, it is almost certain that its architectural group was the core of the Late Preclassic city.

Images of ruler-warriors in triumphal poses were sculpted in stone monuments, sometimes accompanied by representations of captives kneeling or in acts of humiliation. This indicates that competition between polities may have involved battles to obtain prestige-enhancing captives and territorial border skirmishes (Figure 16.4). Through epigraphic studies, Fahsen (1999, n.d.) has proposed that the Preclassic inhabitants of Kaminaljuyu were speakers of a Ch'olan language. The similarity of Ch'olan languages of central and eastern Guatemala would have facilitated communication among populations of the region and the expansion of commercial routes for the exchange of articles of jade, obsidian, basalt, ceramics, and cacao within the Miraflores interaction sphere (Demarest and Sharer 1986).

Around A.D. 100 or 200, the waters that fed Lake Miraflores began to diminish, and the water volume was no longer sufficient to keep the large canal systems functioning. It is not clear exactly what happened; perhaps the springs dried up or overexploitation caused sedimentation of the lake. As seismic shifting along a geologic fault is hypothesized to have been responsible for the formation of the lake, further activity may have again changed drainage patterns from the lake. What is certain is that the scarcity of water had fatal consequences for agricultural production and the basic diet, leading to population decline and perhaps popular discontent. This last stage of the Preclassic period is known as the Santa Clara phase (A.D. 100–200), and according to Shook and Hatch (1999), Kaminaljuyu fell into decline at this time, breaking off commercial connections with regions on the Pacific coast and in El Salvador. Agricultural production must have returned to more extensive methods, and as a consequence, crop yields declined. It is interesting to note that several carved monuments show evidence of damage and intentional desecration of the faces of the ancestral rulers.

The Early Classic and Its Effects on the People of Kaminaljuyu

As the curtain rose upon the Early Classic period (Aurora phase A.D. 200–400), Kaminaljuyu had lost its ancient prestige and power. Studying ceramics, Hatch (1993) proposed an intrusion of a group of Maya peoples from the western Guatemalan highlands, which she called the "Solano tradition" because the first evidence of this ceramic tradition was found at Solano, south of Kaminaljuyu. She argues that these migrants had originated in the area of Huehuetenango, and had advanced via what are now the Departments of Quiché, Chimaltenango, and Sacatepéquez to reach the central highlands. Fahsen (2000) considers that they were speakers of K'iche', for which reason we will refer to them as "Quicheans."

Regardless of their ethnic affiliation, it is certain that around approximately A.D. 200 this intrusive group had installed themselves at Solano and other strategic sites from which they could control routes between the highlands and the Pacific

Figure 16.4 Kaminaljuyu Monument 65, showing the ruler in the center and captives at his sides (drawing by J. Kaplan and L. F. Luin).

coast. The invaders displaced the ruling elite at Kaminaljuyu as well as a large number of its occupants. The presumed Ch'olan population of Kaminaljuyu was possibly displaced to the east or the southeast, toward Copan and Chalchuapa, where they might have been easily integrated because of their cultural similarity, allied traditions, and language.

The arrival of this "Quichean" migration coincides with the disappearance of writing and the cessation of monumental sculpture at Kaminaljuyu, for apparently the new arrivals did not participate in the emerging Classic period literary culture (Valdés 1997). It is almost certain that the change in leadership occurred abruptly, although customs changed more gradually among the non-elite population. Evidence of this gradual change comes from a transition in utilitarian ceramic wares from the Preclassic into the Early Classic period (Hatch 2000).

With the establishment of the new regime in Kaminaljuyu, relations shifted toward a completely different focus than they had during the Preclassic. The routes to the east were abandoned, and in their place interaction with the western highlands grew, especially with the regions that are now the departments of Chimaltenago and Sacatepéquez. However, this shift does not appear to have affected patterns of obsidian exchange, for obsidian from El Chayal (to the east) continued to predominate in Aurora phase deposits, while material from San Martín Jilotepeque (to the west) remained at low frequency (Braswell 1996).

At present, we still do not know the mechanism responsible for this expansionistic movement from the west into Kaminaljuyu and the central Highlands. There are no signs of military confrontation that might have resulted in mass burials or the destruction of architecture. Therefore, it may have been a gradual invasion, which led to the weakening of Kaminaljuyu's leaders by blocking their commercial relations with the Pacific Coast and El Salvador. The ceramic and architectural evidence indicate a notable decline in population in all sectors of the city, as indicated by the abandonment of many Preclassic buildings at the start of the Early Classic.

The most important constructions from this time period appear to have been structures D-III-1 and D-III-13, which show a previously unknown architectural style, with large masks and figures fashioned in clay on the façade, into which blocks of obsidian were set. Also for the first time, an altar or central block was set in the top of the stair, thereby dividing the access to the building. This seems to indicate that the seat of the new administration shifted to this part of the city, which supports our hypothesis of strong administrative changes within the polity.

One important point is that the drying of Lake Miraflores had significant consequences for the agricultural support of this Early Classic population. Although the poor preservation of human bone at Kaminaljuyu limits our ability to reconstruct dietary behavior from skeletal data, we have demonstrated the impact of the disappearance of the lake and its associated irrigated fields on the diet of Kaminaljuyu's inhabi-

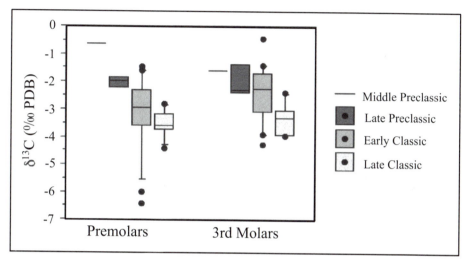

Figure 16.5 Carbon isotope composition of tooth enamel by time period
for Kaminaljuyu premolars and 3rd molars.

tants using carbon isotope analysis of tooth enamel. The carbon isotope ratios ($\delta^{13}C$)
of tooth enamel preserve an average of carbon sources in the diet during childhood
when the teeth developed. The $\delta^{13}C$ ratios of Kaminaljuyu teeth primarily reflect the
importance of maize versus other plants and animal foods in children's diets at the city.
Figure 16.5 illustrates the ratios observed in premolars, which form between roughly
2 and 6 years of age, and in 3rd molars, which form between 9 and 13 years of age.[*]
$\delta^{13}C$ is higher in teeth from Preclassic burials than in burials interred at later times. In
fact, the Preclassic and Late Classic mean $\delta^{13}C$ is statistically different ($p<0.01$) for
both premolars and 3rd molars, indicating that maize was more important in the
Preclassic diet than in the Late Classic one.

---

[*] We measured stable isotopes of carbon and oxygen in sections of tooth enamel that
span from the cusp to the cemento-enamel junction in each tooth. We ground the enamel, soaked
it in sodium hypochlorite, and then leached it in buffered acetic acid to remove diagenetic con-
taminants. Details of the sample preparation have been published elsewhere (Wright and
Schwarcz 1998). We reacted the enamel samples with orthophosphoric acid in an Isocarb carbonate device and measured isotope ratios of carbon dioxide gas evolved from the enamel in the
VG Optima mass spectrometer at McMaster University.

This decline in maize consumption appears to have begun by the Early Classic period, as Early Classic $\delta^{13}C$ is also lower than Preclassic $\delta^{13}C$. However, the Early Classic burial sample includes the skeletons of several foreigners, so cultural variation in childhood diets complicates this inference. Nonetheless, it seems likely that the decreased consumption of maize was a consequence of major changes to agricultural strategies precipitated by the desiccation of Lake Miraflores and the abandonment of the field systems it had irrigated.

The Enigmatic Esperanza Phase of the Early Classic Period

The later part of the Early Classic period (ca. A.D. 400 and 550) is known as the Esperanza phase. Although a new chapter would be written for Kaminaljuyu at this time, its leaders continued their close relationship with sites located to the west of the Valley of Guatemala. While the population gradually grew, it appears that the city remained smaller than during the Arenal phase, and was culturally impoverished. The tradition of erecting sculpted monuments did not resume until the Late Classic period (Shook and Hatch 1999:312).

The importance of the Esperanza phase is the apparently foreign cultural elements that were discovered at Kaminaljuyu in the mid-20th century (Kidder et al. 1946). These include five buildings that show *talud-tablero* architecture and several important tombs that contain stuccoed vessels and green obsidian; together they have spurred ongoing debate regarding the role of Teotihuacan at Kaminaljuyu. Although most emphasis has been placed on the materials from central Mexico in the tombs, the tomb offerings show that the Kaminaljuyu elite had widespread commercial connections. The Esperanza period tombs also contain polychrome vases from the Maya Lowlands, ceramics from Oaxaca, mirrors in the Tajin style of Veracruz, and jade from the Motagua Valley, as well as conch, turtle carapaces, and stingray spines from both the Pacific and Caribbean (Kidder et al. 1946; Shook and Hatch 1999).

Despite all the discussion about the role of Teotihuacan at Kaminaljuyu over the years, the exact nature of the relationship between the distant cities is still not satisfactorily resolved. Explanations range from full-blown military incursions to interaction that emphasized commercial motives to hypotheses that the foreigners at Kaminaljuyu were groups of acculturated Maya and that the interaction with central Mexico occurred strictly among the elite, and did not involve the non-elite population in any significant way (Braswell 2000; Brown 1977; Cheek 1977; Cowgill 2001; Demarest and Foias 1993; Hatch 1993, 1996; Kidder et al. 1946; Sanders and Michels 1979). What is certain is that this discussion has exaggerated the importance of Kaminaljuyu's association with Teotihuacan, while scholars have virtually ignored discoveries which demonstrate the dramatic local development of the city since Preclassic times, including its advances in hydraulic technology and its unprecedented number of carved and hieroglyphic monuments.

We also note that discussions about the role of war and militarism at Teotihuacan have reemerged with the discovery of more than 200 sacrificial victims in the temple of Quetzalcoatl (Sugiyama 1992), and in several deposits under the Temple of the Moon (Sugiyama 2001). However, Manzanilla (1998) has observed that this militarism at Teotihuacan may be overstated. A large number of these burials appear to be those of sacrificed women and were perhaps interred as part of a ritual carried out in the context of internal political change at Teotihuacan. Manzanilla also notes that depictions of warriors armed with dart-throwers do not appear until the end of Teotihuacan's history, as we might expect during a period of political instability when this central Mexican city was invaded and burned. This is interesting from the perspective of Kaminaljuyu, where the Teotihuacan elements are restricted to a very narrow elite segment of the site. This absence of foreign elements in the rest of the city is a strong indication that if any Teotihuacanos actually did reach Kaminaljuyu, their numbers were not large.

Despite some similarity to the architecture at Teotihuacan, detailed analysis of the Kaminaljuyu architecture reveals a significant difference in the proportions of the diagnostic *talud-tablero* façades. At Teotihuacan the ratio of talud to tablero ranges from 1:3 to 1:5; at Kaminaljuyu proportions of 1:1 were used. At Tikal proportions were intermediate at 1:2 and 1:3 (Laporte 1985), but show traditional features of Maya architecture, such as inset corners and aprons that differ markedly from the rectangular plan of basal platforms at Teotihuacan. In other words, the *talud-tablero* form is modified to conform to Maya stylistic norms. Moreover, the earliest *talud-tablero* buildings at Tikal date to shortly after A.D. 300, approximately a century before it appears at Kaminaljuyu and Copan, and much earlier than the appearance of Teotihuacan ceramic styles that use slab supports and stuccoed decoration.

The beginning of Teotihuacan's expansion is dated to about A.D. 300 (Millon 1981), but, significantly, this was also the time at which Tikal and the centers of the northeastern Petén expanded. Importantly, Maya Tzakol ceramics and Lowland cherts have been found at Teotihuacan, albeit in small quantities. It seems more likely that the Maya maintained mutual economic contacts with central Mexico by exporting a new product, ideology. In reference to this, Taube (2001) has identified the presence of Maya images, glyphs, and iconography in the murals of Tetitla, one of the largest palace groups at Teotihuacan.

More surprising is the presence in the Ciudadela of central Teotihuacan of an astronomical observation complex, or "E group," an architectural form that is widely known to have originated among the Maya (Fialko 1988). Although Group E at Uaxactun is the best-known example because it was the first identified, the antiquity of these groups is well documented. For instance, the complex in Mundo Perdido at Tikal dates to the Middle Preclassic (Fialko 1988; Laporte and Fialko 1995). The abundance of these complexes in the Petén soon led to their appearance in sites elsewhere, such Finca Acapulco in Chiapas and Kaminaljuyu in the Highlands (Murdy 1990; Valdés

1995). These complexes have also been referred to as "horizon observatories" (Galindo Trejo 2001), since their main function is to record solstices and equinoxes of the rising sun.

In Mexico, Classic Period E Groups have been reported at Xochicalco (Galindo Trejo 2001) and Monte Albán (Fahmel Beyer 1995). At Teotihuacan the complex is Early Classic, and located in the Ciudadela. It is focused on the Pyramid of the Feathered Serpent. To the east is a platform that supports three small temples. These temples have been dated to A.D. 300 (Jarquín Pacheco and Martínez Vargas 1982), a date that coincides very well with the first appearance of *talud-tablero* architecture at Tikal. The religious implications of these complexes transcend cultural differences since they focus on the annual sun cycle and relate to the passage of time, the calendar, mathematical calculations, and control of agriculture. These concepts had been firmly entrenched in Maya culture from Late Preclassic times, as seen in the iconography of building facades and masks (Valdés 1995).

It is likely that the relationship between the Maya and Teotihuacan was one of mutual adaptation to foreign ideological and economic interests. Similarly, Hatch (1993) proposes that a gradual acculturation of Kaminaljuyu's elite, through attempts to imitate or share stylistic elements from distant regions, is responsible for the appearance of foreign elements in the Esperanza period. Likewise, Demarest and Foias (1993) argue that the foreign elements at Kaminaljuyu are simply evidence of participation in a broad horizon style of elite interaction. In this respect, information obtained from chemical analysis of the skeletal remains in the Kaminaljuyu tombs that show the greatest concentration of Teotihuacan-style elements is of great importance. These analyses help us to infer the identity of the individuals interred within the tombs, and have implications for models that attempt to explain the role of Teotihuacan in Kaminaljuyu's history.

Who Was Interred in the Tombs of Mounds A and B?

The isotopic composition of the human remains from the Esperanza tombs sheds some light on the geographic origins of these individuals. We sampled teeth from a series of Kaminaljuyu skeletons, both those interred in the Esperanza tombs and from domestic burials that antedate and postdate this time of Teotihuacan contact. From tooth enamel carbonate, we obtain both carbon ($\delta^{13}C$) and oxygen ($\delta^{18}O$) isotopic ratios. As noted above, $\delta^{13}C$ serves as a measure of maize consumption at Kaminaljuyu. By contrast, the $\delta^{18}O$ of tooth enamel is determined by the composition of water imbibed. In general, enamel $\delta^{18}O$ reflects geographic differences in the $\delta^{18}O$ of rainwater, which varies with latitude and climate. Thus, skeletons that show outlying $\delta^{18}O$ values may be those of migrant individuals whose tissues formed in a different rainfall regime. Although the skeleton remodels throughout life and will equilibrate to local values with time, teeth retain the isotopic signals of childhood, so migrants may best

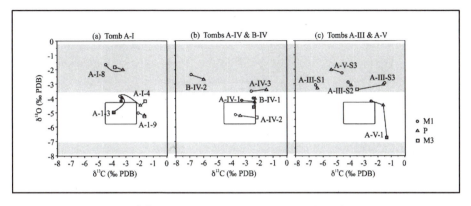

Figure 16.6 Stable isotopic composition of tooth enamel
from Mound A and B tombs.

be identified by anomalous isotopic compositions of the teeth. Although variation in diet within a culture can be substantial, outlying $\delta^{13}C$ ratios may also distinguish foreign skeletons that consumed disparate amounts of maize as compared to local children.

The Early Classic skeletons from Kaminaljuyu show the broadest spread of both $\delta^{13}C$ and $\delta^{18}O$ in tooth enamel of any time period at the site. Skeletons that show outlying values are found almost exclusively in the Esperanza tombs from Mounds A and B that were excavated by the Carnegie Institution; however, many of the tomb skeletons show local values. Figure 16.6 shows the isotope data for several of the tombs. Skeletons located centrally in the tombs are indicated by shaded symbols. In each case, symbols representing the composition of a 1st molar, a premolar, and a 3rd molar are joined by lines in the sequence of their development. Generally speaking, tooth enamel of 1st molars forms between birth and 2.5 years of age; premolar enamel forms between 2 and 6.5 years; and 3rd molar enamel forms between 9 and 13 years. Shifts in $\delta^{13}C$ between teeth of a skeleton indicate that most Kaminaljuyu residents consumed more maize in later childhood than at younger ages. Declines in $\delta^{18}O$ between 1st molars and later developing teeth are probably due to the decreasing intake of ^{18}O-enriched water from breastmilk in favor of other beverages (Wright and Schwarcz, 1998). Like most aspects of childhood, there is significant variation in dietary change among Kaminaljuyu skeletons. The square box in each graph in Figure 16.6 represents the ranges of Late Classic skeletons that were buried in domestic con-

texts. The shaded bar at the top of the graph represents the range observed in preliminary analyses of several burials from Classic period Tikal (Wright, unpublished data)
and Postclassic Topoxte (Wright, Schwarcz, and Acevedo 2000) but we note that the
lower border of the Lowland range is not yet well delimited. The lower bar represents
the range measured by White et al. (1998) for bone phosphate at Teotihuacan which
we have converted to the carbonate PDB scale. Local $\delta^{18}O$ of Kaminaljuyu tooth
enamel are intermediate to those at Teotihuacan and in the Maya Lowlands.

Oxygen isotope variation among the tomb skeletons hints at the presence of
several foreigners. The first graph (a) in Figure 16.6 illustrates skeletons sampled from
Tomb A-I, the earliest tomb in Structure A, in which skeletons were laid out in extended
fashion. The tomb may have been periodically opened to inter a new decedent, but since
many of the peripheral skeletons are of adolescents, they may have been sacrificial victims included as offerings to accompany the primary, central skeletons. The central skeleton (A-I-3) and two peripheral skeletons show local Kaminaljuyu isotope ratios, but one
peripheral adolescent skeleton has a lowland $\delta^{18}O$ value in all three teeth.

The central graph (b) shows isotope data for skeletons from Tombs A-IV and
B-IV; both contained a seated central skeleton, each accompanied by two peripheral
seated skeletons. The two central skeletons (both #1) have coincident local
Kaminaljuyu isotope values. Values for the peripheral skeleton A-IV-2 are also consistent with a childhood spent at Kaminaljuyu. Although A-IV-3 is higher on the $\delta^{18}O$
scale, we hesitate to identify it as a foreigner because its $\delta^{18}O$ are less than one permil
higher than other skeletons from this tomb. Skeleton B-IV-2 stands out both in its high
$\delta^{18}O$ and in the lower $\delta^{13}C$. Its oxygen isotope values are consistent with a childhood
spent in Petén, but the $\delta^{15}N$ of dentine collagen from this individual are extremely
high and imply that this child ate substantial amounts of marine fish. We suspect that
this individual lived a coastal childhood, perhaps in Belize or Yucatan, but, it is also pos-
sibile that this person may have originated on the Pacific coastal lowlands from where
we have no comparative oxygen isotope data.

The graph on the right shows skeletons from two tombs where the central
adult skeleton was seated tailor fashion and was accompanied by three decapitated
adolescent skulls. All of the teeth from the skulls have isotope compositions consistent with a childhood spent in the lowlands. Skeleton A-V-1 is unusual in having a local
Kaminaljuyu signal for the 1st molar and premolar, but a 3rd molar $\delta^{18}O$ that approaches the range measured at Teotihuacan (White et al. 1998). This might suggest that this
individual was born at Kaminaljuyu but was sent to central Mexico for adolescence
and ultimately returned to die at Kaminaljuyu (as inferred by White et al. 2000 from
phosphate $\delta^{18}O$). Although this might indicate some contact with Teotihuacan, we
expect $\delta^{18}O$ ratios to be very similar over a broad area, since they are determined by
rainfall patterning. Thus other areas may show similar signals to Teotihuacan.

In sum, the isotope data provides little support for the suggestion that the
tomb occupants might be migrants from Teotihuacan. Both the central occupants of

the earlier tombs, wherein skeletons were extended, and the later tailor-position central skeletons appear to have had a local childhood. The 3rd molar value of the skeleton A-V-1 might indicate contact with central Mexico, but cannot be taken as absolute evidence for that contact. Most of the foreign remains appear to have been from lowland areas, and it is likely that they represent at least two different locales, one coastal and one inland. Although the $\delta^{18}O$ values are similar to those found in the Maya Lowlands, we cannot exclude the possibility of an origin on the Pacific Coast at this time. We hope to glean further inferences on the identity of these skeletons through strontium isotope analyses of the teeth. Strontium isotope ratios in skeletal tissues are determined by the geological substrates on which foods are grown (see Buikstra et al. this volume). Preliminary strontium isotope ratios confirm the foreign origin of the crania in Tombs A-III and A-V and of skeleton B-IV-2. Like other aspects of the material culture from the tombs, the isotope data from these skeletons supports greater connection with nearby Maya cities than with distant Teotihuacan.

Connections Between Kaminaljuyu and Copan

Artifactual remains indicate that there was some contact between Kaminaljuyu and Copan, but we have no firm evidence as to the strength of these connections, whether their intensity varied over the centuries, or the exact nature of this contact. In Copan, excavations have recovered ceramics from highland Guatemala, obsidian from El Chayal, and jade from the Motagua Valley, as well as similar architectural systems, iconographic elements, funerary forms, and recently, the shared use of canals for the transport of water and for irrigation. Such elements may indicate some interaction between the cities. This evidence has been presented by Viel (1998), Viel and Hall (2000a) and Hall and Viel (this volume), thus we will make only a few additional observations here.

Excavations at Copan have recovered highland materials dating to very early times, whether it be in structure fill, middens, or as offerings in burials; these include both lithic and ceramic materials. In the Late Preclassic (400 B.C.–A.D. 200), Copan was but a small community in contrast to the metropolis of Kaminaljuyu, with its ideological and technological achievements. The southeast Maya zone saw substantial population movement (Viel and Hall 2000c), and it is curious that several later Copan inscriptions may refer to the origin of the Copan polity at A.D. 159/160 (Stuart, this volume). This raises the question of whether these dated events at Copan may have been related to the departure of the Ch'olan populations from Kaminaljuyu around A.D. 100 or 200. Could these same people have arrived to join the small Protoclassic population detected in excavations of the northwest platform of the Principal Group at Copan? Might these migrants have introduced the canal technology they knew so well to Copan?

These questions might be answered in the affirmative if we keep in mind the serious problems that must have afflicted the people of Kaminaljuyu with the declining levels of Lake Miraflores at this time. This might well explain the expansion of the Bijac phase population of Copan—the arrival of new peoples who occupied the southern and northwestern portions of the Main Group, and the modern village of Copán Ruinas (Viel 1998; Traxler this volume). These buildings were made of clay, the construction method of Kaminaljuyu. The population of Kaminaljuyu was well versed in the design and management of hydraulic canal systems, for which they may have undertaken the development of the bottomlands that surrounded the Main Group at Copan. Immigrants from Kaminaljuyu would have been easily assimilated into the local Copan population because of their shared Ch'olan-group language.

Things changed radically in A.D. 426 with the arrival of a group apparently from the central Maya Lowlands, led by one K'inich Yax K'uk' Mo', whose flashy debut was followed by his transformation into the sovereign of the growing city. The new leader began construction programs on a huge scale, without doubt to convey prestige on his new city in the eyes of his new neighbors. These earliest structures in the Acropolis show remarkable similarity to Early Classic Petén architecture, with stone walls finely decorated with multicolored painted stucco (Fash 1998, this volume; Sharer 1996; Sharer, Traxler, et al. 1999; Traxler, this volume). Moreover, the palaces of the northwest patio group (Traxler 1996, 2001) repeat a style common at Tikal during the later part of the Early Classic (A.D. 378–550), wherein palaces have three doors giving access at the front of the building and contain two or three interior rooms (Valdés 2000). At Copan, this is seen in Aguila Structure. Likewise, Sharer (1996) and Traxler (this volume) have noted that the construction techniques shown in the *talud-tablero* Hunal Structure are more akin to *talud-tablero* structures in Petén than to those at Kaminaljuyu, in that they employ stone and stucco. Moreover, the decorations do not completely surround the basal platform of Hunal Structure, and its *talud-tablero* proportions more closely resemble those at Tikal than at Kaminaljuyu. That K'inich Yax K'uk' Mo' ordered the construction of such distinctive architecture is not surprising if we recall that he may have spent his childhood at Tikal (Buikstra et al. this volume). Perhaps he had in mind the *talud-tablero* buildings of Mundo Perdido and Group 6C-16 at Tikal.

We can also see similarity between Kaminaljuyu and Copan in the content of the Early Classic tombs (Bell 2003; Bell et al., this volume; Sharer 2003a, 2003b). At both sites the tombs contain funerary offerings that show a mixture of local and foreign elements, including the conspicuous central Mexican stuccoed vessels (Kidder et al. 1946; Bell et al. this volume). Neutron activation analyses of the ceramics from the Hunal and Margarita Tombs show greater affiliation with sites in the Maya Highlands and Lowlands, despite the fact that many of them were stuccoed and carried Teotihuacan iconography (Reents-Budet et al., this volume).

Another oft-cited foreign feature of the Early Classic tombs both at Kaminaljuyu and Copan is the presence of skeletons seated in what has been called "tailor position" (Figure 16.7). The later tombs from Mounds A and B as well as the

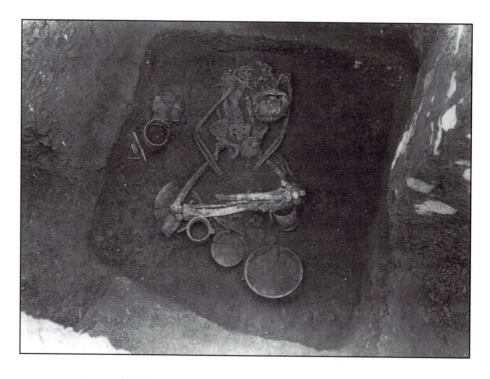

Figure 16.7 Burial in "tailor" position excavated at Kaminaljuyu
(photograph by E. Shook).

Palangana contain skeletons seated with their legs crossed (Cheek 1977; Braswell 2000). At Copan this position is seen in Tomb V-4 found in the east sector of the Great Plaza at Copan (Valdés and Cheek 1983), as well as the Motmot Tomb (Davis Salazar and Bell 1999; Fash and Fash 2000; W. Fash, this volume). At both sites, these burials date to the later part of the Early Classic. It is interesting to note that seated burials are rare at Tikal; the Early Classic burials that otherwise show striking similarity to the tombs at Kaminaljuyu and Copan contained extended skeletons, such as the Tikal Project Burial 10 (Coe 1990). Although the tailor position was thought to be a characteristic shared with Teotihuacan (Braswell 2000), in fact, seated burials at Teotihuacan seldom show the legs in this crossed position. Instead, the knees are raised vertically because they are placed in restricted vertical pits (see various chapters in Manzanilla and Serrano 1999). Similar vertically seated burials occur throughout the Maya area. However, the tomb recently excavated in the Pyramid of the Moon at Teotihuacan contains elaborately adorned skeletons seated in the tailor position and dates to A.D. 350—prior to the Kaminaljuyu tombs.

Although Sugiyama argues that this is evidence for a Teotihuacan presence at Kaminaljuyu, it is notable that the tailor position skeletons at Kaminaljuyu show local isotope ratios. A jade statuette found in the Teotihuacan tomb shows a seated man with realistic features, hair, and eyes, similar to the figurines of Kaminaljuyu. This new discovery further supports the inference of a Maya influence at Teotihuacan and implies a close interaction between the ruling elite of these distant cultures.

Rather than Teotihuacan, the stable isotope data for the skeletons in the Kaminaljuyu tombs confirm that many of the individuals may well have originated in a lowland area. At Copan, strontium and oxygen isotope analysis of tomb occupants hints at the presence of Lowland Maya individuals, most likely including K'inich Yax K'uk' Mo' himself (see Buikstra et al. this volume). With the exception of a single Kaminaljuyu child who may have spent his adolescence in central Mexico, it is significant that at Copan and Kaminaljuyu the results of both the ceramic neutron activation and the human stable isotopic analyses contradict the original proposed Teotihuacan intrusion, and demonstrate that Kaminaljuyu—much like Copan—maintained stronger connections with its Maya neighbors than with Teotihuacan. Although none of the seven Copan skeletons studied isotopically to date show an isotopic signal that would identify them as having spent their childhood at Kaminaljuyu, the preliminary strontium isotope data for a few of the foreigners at Kaminaljuyu is not inconsistent with Copan and might hint at greater interaction between these Maya cities than is indicated in the material culture. Ongoing work in mapping strontium isotope signatures across the Maya area should help further clarify these questions.

Conclusions

A new interpretation of the developmental history of Kaminaljuyu has emerged from excavations carried out since 1980. When combined with the emerging historical and archaeological data from Copan, it becomes clear that both Kaminaljuyu and Copan experienced fluctuating fortunes during the Late Preclassic and Early Classic periods. Furthermore, original populations at both cities had to accommodate the incursion of foreign peoples who brought with them foreign customs. For Kaminaljuyu, the Early Classic Esperanza Phase was a period of growth that followed severe decline, but it did not outshine the urban accomplishments of the city's Preclassic past. There is no doubt that Kaminaljuyu was in frequent contact with widespread areas of Mesoamerica, especially other Early Classic Maya cities, and this included some contact with Teotihuacan. But the oxygen isotope data from the Esperanza tombs refute the hypothesis that Kaminaljuyu served as a major port of entry for elite Teotihuacanos into the Maya realm. Instead these data support models that emphasize the importance of an elite ideology shared among neighboring Early Classic Maya polities that included both Teotihuacan and Maya elements. These data raise the question of whether migration between these not-so-distant Maya cities (especially Tikal and Copan) may have been more influential in the expression of the "Teotihuacanoid" characteristics seen at a number of Maya cities than was direct interaction with central Mexico. Ongoing isotopic research has been instrumental in clarifying many of these Early Classic intersite relationships, and may help to bring these connections into sharper focus in the near future.

Acknowledgments

The stable isotope research was funded by a grant awarded to Wright by the Wenner-Gren Foundation for Anthropological Research, and the analyses were carried out with the permission of the Peabody Museum of Archaeology and Ethnology and the Instituto de Antropología e Historia de Guatemala.

17

PRIMARY AND SECONDARY STATE FORMATION IN SOUTHERN MESOAMERICA

Joyce Marcus

"The assumption that there exists a realm of facts independent of theories which establish their meanings is fundamentally unscientific"—Blackburn (1972:10)

"Theory, on the other hand, cannot be treated without close reference to empirical data"—Claessen and Skalník (1978:4)

This volume's hard-won empirical data, when integrated with appropriate theory, has the potential to generate a more universally meaningful view of the ancient Maya than ever before. A new generation of researchers has obtained crucial data on the founding of the Copan dynasty at A.D. 426 and made Copan one of the most detailed case studies of state formation in the Maya region. By integrating multiple lines of investigation (survey, excavation, epigraphy, and some 3 km of tunnels that exposed otherwise inaccessible early buildings) and drawing on a wide range of analyses (instrumental neutron activation to determine clay sources, strontium isotope analyses to determine where buried individuals spent their early years, calculation of the man-hours needed to build different kinds of structures, pollen washes from the interior of tomb vessels to determine their former contents, dry residue analyses from floors and pottery vessels), the Copan team has written new and important chapters to that polity's history.

During the Early Classic (A.D. 200–600), many parts of the Maya region achieved statehood. Not all these occurrences, however, conform to what theorists call *primary* state formation. That term is usually reserved for cases where a state forms from simpler chiefly societies in the absence of a preexisting state that could serve as a

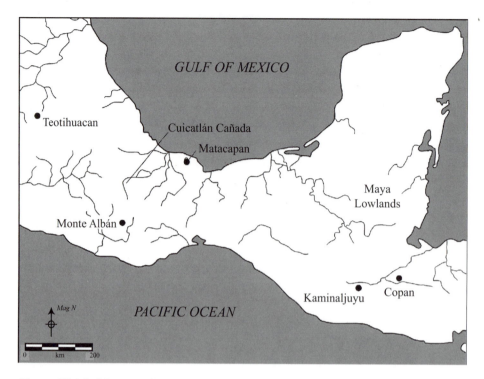

Figure 17.1 In Mesoamerica *primary* states arose in both the highlands and lowlands. Four examples of primary states include those administered by Teotihuacan and Monte Albán in the highlands and those controlled by Tikal and Calakmul in the lowlands. Copan, in the southeast corner of the Maya area, is an example of a *secondary* state. By comparing the primary state of Monte Albán with the *secondary* state of Copan, we can try to determine in what ways primary and secondary states are similar and in what ways they differ.

model. Once the first state has formed in a region, *secondary* states based on that pre-existing model can arise through a number of processes. In some cases neighboring chiefly centers might join forces and reorganize themselves to avoid being absorbed by an expanding primary state. In other cases a nearby chiefdom, desiring greater power, might ask an established state to send it a prince from the latter's royal house. For example, the Mexica of Tenochtitlan asked the more powerful ruler of Culhuacan to send them their first true "king," and thus it was that Acamapichtli came to be founder of the Mexica dynasty (Durán 1964:34). Although the Mexica began as a secondary state, they went on to be much more powerful than Culhuacan.

We can put the early Copan state into a broader framework by comparing it to the early Monte Albán state in Oaxaca (Figure 17.1). These are two of the most extensively investigated early states in all of southern Mesoamerica. Both areas have been the scene of full-coverage settlement pattern surveys (for the Copan Valley, see Baudez 1983; Braswell 1992; Fash 1983b, 1983c; Leventhal 1979; Webster 1985; Webster and Freter 1990a, 1990b; Webster et al. 1992; Willey et al. 1978; Willey and Leventhal 1979a; and for the Valley of Oaxaca, see Blanton et al. 1982, Feinman et al. 1985, and Kowalewski et al. 1989). Both valleys have seen more than 100 years of excavation, with work intensifying in recent decades within a framework of multidisciplinary anthropological archaeology.

One result of the recent intensive work is that we now see a number of similarities and differences between the Copan and Monte Albán states. An interesting difference results from the fact that Monte Albán seems to have been a primary state which arose from a group of chiefdoms, while Copan seems to have been a secondary state that formed with the arrival of a nobleman from a primary state (his exact place of origin is uncertain, although the consensus in this volume is that he came from the Tikal region). Some of the similarities between Copan and Oaxaca result from the fact that states, whether primary or secondary at their founding, eventually share a whole series of attributes or "archaeological signatures of the state" (Flannery 1998; Marcus 1993:115–116; Marcus and Flannery 1996:Ch.13–14; Spencer and Redmond 2001a; Wright and Johnson 1975). The archaeological signatures of the state are rules of thumb rather than immutable laws, and the more of them we find, the better the case for statehood. These can be generally applied to Copan and Monte Albán as follows:

1. Many states have an administrative hierarchy of at least four tiers of sites, one more tier than the typical "complex" or "paramount" chiefdom. Finding such a hierarchy begins with full-coverage survey, which allows one to produce a histogram of site sizes and search for a four-mode distribution. Since size alone is not proof of administrative function, the survey should be followed up by excavations aimed at the recovery of administrative buildings and artifacts. Simply put, sites at higher levels of the hierarchy should have a greater number and variety of administrative structures than sites at lower levels.

Because both valleys have received full-coverage survey, one would expect that comparisons would be easy. As we will see, however, past flooding and deposition of soils by the Copan River has made it impossible to recover as complete a record of Preclassic settlement patterns as can be done in the more arid Valley of Oaxaca. As for the ground plans of early monumental buildings, Copan may have the advantage; Monte Albán's earliest structures are often hidden under reconstructed Late Classic buildings, while Copan's are being exposed by tunnels.

2. The first appearance of a true palace is an important clue to the evolution of kingship. Here there are some real parallels between the two areas. In both valleys, it turns out that the earliest palaces were made of adobe, and it was not until the 1990s that they came to light. For this we can thank Loa Traxler at Copan (this volume) and Charles Spencer and Elsa Redmond (2001a) in Oaxaca.

3. The evolution of raiding into true warfare is yet another signature of the state, and in both regions, warfare was for too many decades ignored as an important process in the rise and expansion of early states. During the 1990s it became clear that conquests by Tikal, Calakmul, Copan, and Monte Albán were typical examples of early state expansion.

4. A widening social stratification, one manifestation of which is the spectacular royal tomb, is another clue to the prehispanic state. Both Copan and Monte Albán have produced some royal tombs, often including mural painting and hieroglyphic texts.

5. State-sponsored craft production is yet another archaeological signature, although the dividing line between chiefly support and kingly support of craftsmen is hard to draw. Craft activities occurred on so many levels, from household to palace, that the trick is to determine which crafts the state really cared about monopolizing. Copan may have taken over Quirigua to control the jade sources of the Motagua River valley. Monte Albán may have monopolized the production of certain "C" or *crema* pottery vessels, which they provided only to elite families who were their allies (Feinman 1982).

When all these signatures are present, there is a good chance that we are dealing with a state. However, that still does not tell us (1) the *exact order in which each signature appeared*, and (2) the *specific catalysts that brought the state into existence*. Given the long ceramic periods often defined in Mesoamerica (e.g., 200–300 years), some or all of the elements listed above may seem to occur simultaneously, when in fact they appeared in succession. Future work in the Maya area, with the aid of texts and AMS radiocarbon dates, has the potential to document each step in the rise of the state more precisely. The specific sequence may, however, vary from region to region within the Maya area (Marcus 1992a, 1993, 1998; Sanders 1974).

The Valley of Oaxaca: "Sawtoothed" Ascent to the Primary State

One difference between primary and secondary states is that there are more ways in which the latter can form. Once a template for the operation of a state exists in a region and its advantages have become clear, there are a variety of ways in which secondary states can arise. (The founders of secondary states usually knew *a priori* that they were trying to found states; founders of primary states almost certainly thought they were just creating a larger, more powerful chiefdom.)

Recently, Flannery (1999) compared five historically documented cases in which a known actor or agent created a state out of several formerly autonomous chiefdoms. Those five examples were part of a larger sample of cases in which powerful leaders created a state in the absence of preexisting models. In every case, state formation was preceded by a long period of chiefly cycling (Anderson 1994; Wright

1984), a process by which a group of rival chiefdoms takes turns rising, peaking, collapsing, and sometimes rising again. At each peak there might be an attempt to incorporate neighboring chiefdoms into a larger polity, but such larger entities eventually broke down. For this reason, the ascent from chiefdom to state can be called "sawtoothed," rather than smooth, including some attempts at consolidation that failed (Carneiro 1969, 1991; Marcus 1992a, 1998; Nicolis and Prigogine 1977; Sharer 1991).

Eventually, in the historical cases mentioned, a powerful individual succeeded in unifying several previously autonomous chiefdoms into a polity so large that it could no longer be administered as a chiefdom. All of the cases matched the model scenario by Cohen (1978:49), who suggested that significant increases in interpolity conflict were one catalyst leading to state formation, and that a defining characteristic of the newly formed state was its ability to overcome the "fissiparous tendencies" that had caused previous attempts at consolidation to break down (Cohen 1978:35).

It is worth noting that in *none* of the cases examined by Flannery could unification be described as "voluntary"; it was always accomplished by some military or demographic advantage. Autonomy is rarely surrendered without a fight (Carneiro 1970, 1981, 1992; Cohen 1974; Webster 1977, 1993). Nor did any of the cases suggest "corporate government" or "multiple pathways" to primary state formation; Flannery (personal communication 2001) suggests that to the extent that such alternate pathways exist, they are more likely to be found in the formation of second-generation or third-generation states.

The Preclassic Valley of Oaxaca provides many examples of pre-state chiefly cycling. Between 1150 and 850 B.C., the site of San José Mogote appears to have been the valley's largest chiefdom. Between 850 and 700 B.C. it declined somewhat as new chiefly centers like Huitzo rose to power. Between 700 and 500 B.C. San José Mogote grew to prominence once again, but it seems at that time to have had rivals powerful enough to succeed in burning its major temple (Marcus and Flannery 1996:128).

From 700 to 500 B.C. there were approximately 80 communities in the valley and a site-size hierarchy of three tiers. San José Mogote in the northern valley, San Martín Tilcajete in the southern valley, and Yegüih in the eastern valley were the key villages in three rival chiefdoms (see Figure 17.2). San José Mogote, which appears to have been defended by a wooden palisade as far back as the Early Preclassic, had moved its most important elite residences and public buildings to the top of a more easily defended hill. Its most prominent feature was a Middle Preclassic acropolis of whitewashed adobe buildings set on platforms built of huge limestone blocks. At about the time its main temple was burned to cinders, San José Mogote evidently scored a victory of its own: a naked sacrificial victim, whose name was carved between his feet, is depicted on a stone in the corridor between two Middle Preclassic platforms (Marcus and Flannery 1996:129).

One elite residence on the acropolis consisted of adobe rooms surrounding a patio, beneath which was a stone tomb. The adobe walls, the private patio, and the

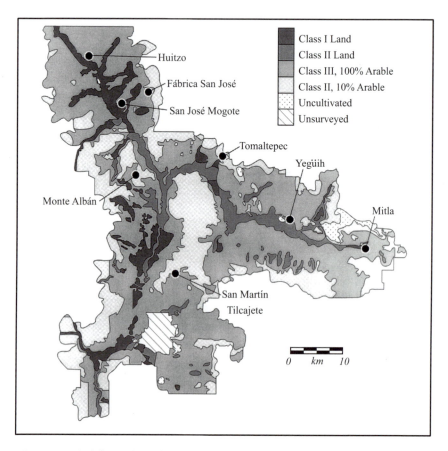

Figure 17.2 The Valley of Oaxaca, cradle of Zapotec civilization, consists of 2100 km^2 in the southern highlands of Mexico. Before 500 B.C.—when Monte Albán was founded—the Valley of Oaxaca was politically divided into three rival chiefdoms of unequal size (San José Mogote, Yegüih, and San Martín Tilcajete), each located in a different arm of the valley (redrawn and modified from Marcus and Flannery 1996:123).

two-chambered tomb all anticipate later Zapotec royal residences, but they do not constitute a true palace. The chiefly family who lived here had deformed skulls, jade necklaces, bloodletting "stingray spines" chipped from obsidian, and anthropomorphic censers in which the smoke from burning incense emanated from eyes and mouth (Marcus and Flannery 1996:127, 132).

Second-tier villages like Tomaltepec had smaller public buildings and were probably headed by a subchief (Whalen 1981); some of their public buildings had dedicatory sacrificial victims incorporated into them.

Third-tier sites tended to be small villages or hamlets and seem to lack the public buildings of Tier 1 and 2 sites (although none have been fully excavated). Some subordinate sites may have been linked to chiefly centers by hypogamy. One woman at Fábrica San José had cranial deformation and was buried with a large hollow figurine, marine shells, and six fine gray vessels (Drennan 1976). This high-status female may have been sent from nearby San José Mogote to marry one of the village leaders, a longstanding pattern at this Tier 3 site (Marcus and Flannery 1996:134).

A number of the higher-status residences at Fábrica San José appear to have been deliberately burned; in fact, the period 700–500 B.C. was characterized by unusually high quantities of burnt house daub, which (along with the evidence for raiding at San José Mogote) suggests the kind of "significant increases in interpolity conflict" predicted by Cohen. Despite its 70 ha size, San José Mogote was in a relatively vulnerable position near the Atoyac River.

At roughly 500 B.C., San José Mogote and a number of its satellite villages—in all, a group of settlements including an estimated 2,000 people—abandoned the northern valley and moved 15 km south to a 400-m-high mountain called Monte Albán. It appears that virtually the entire San José Mogote chiefdom had moved to a defensible location from whence it could begin to expand against rivals such as Tilcajete and Yegüih. Some of those rivals resisted, while others saw the advantage of capitulating (Spencer and Redmond 1997, 2001a, 2001b).

Once on Monte Albán, the new arrivals began to build 3 km of defensive walls on the more easily climbed slopes. By concentrating thousands of potential warriors within its walls, Monte Albán had achieved a demographic advantage over its rivals. As Carneiro (1992:131) has emphasized, "so great is the competitive advantage conferred by large size that the larger a society becomes through successful warfare, the likelier it is to become even larger."

It is significant that the earliest stone monuments at Monte Albán include a gallery of prisoners—more than 300 carved stones arranged in four rows, each depicting a naked sacrificed captive. There can be little doubt that this gallery of 300 victims sent a powerful message to all who might resist Monte Albán's expansion. But despite the military propaganda evident in Monte Albán's early monuments and hieroglyphic texts, its strategy for consolidation and expansion was more complex than that. Monte Albán's hinterland consisted of (1) a few powerful and uncooperative nearby rivals like Tilcajete, (2) a larger number of polities organized only as simple chiefdoms, and (3) more distant regions like Sola de Vega which were almost unpopulated (see Figure 17.3). Like the later Mexica, the early Zapotec began their strategy of consolidation by taking a detour around each of their strongest opponents in their efforts to bring weaker neighbors under control.

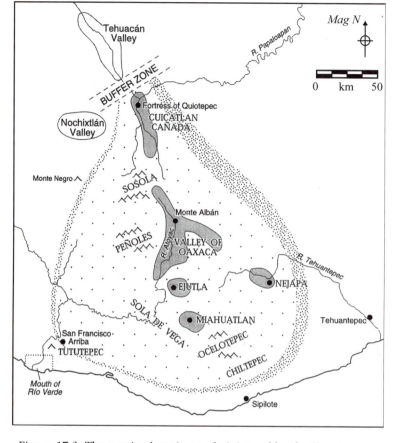

Figure 17.3 The maximal territory administered by the Zapotec capital of Monte Albán was about 20,000 km². This expansion into valleys outside the Valley of Oaxaca was achieved sometime between A.D. 100 and 200 (redrawn from Marcus 1998:fig. 3.3).

The Cuicatlan Cañada, a region that could provide Monte Albán with tropical products, appears to have been subdued by force. Spencer and Redmond (1997) have documented the way the Zapotec burned villages, created skull racks from the heads of resisters, built a fortress, and reorganized the irrigation systems of Cuicatlan. Its place glyph appears on a list of subject places carved on Monte Albán's Building J (Marcus 1980, 1992a). On the other hand, the valleys of Ejutla and Miahuatlan seem to have been brought under Monte Albán's hegemony without evidence of conflict, perhaps through political marriage alliances (Feinman and Nicholas 1990, 1993; Marcus and Flannery 1996:200). In the case of Sola de Vega, Monte Albán seems simply to have colonized it by sending settlers into the sparsely occupied valley (Balkansky 1998a, 2002).

To be sure, Monte Albán could not rest until it had subdued its most powerful rivals inside the valley. In preparation for this it encouraged the growth of a ring of 155 satellite villages, encircling Monte Albán at distances of only 10-15 km. Because many of these villages were in irrigable piedmont locations, Kowalewski et al. (1989) have referred to this as "the piedmont strategy." In this way Monte Albán had sufficient farmers, warriors, and craftsmen concentrated near at hand to support its expansion.

Thanks to recent excavations by Spencer and Redmond (2001a), we now know how Monte Albán's strongest rival, San Martín Tilcajete, was eventually overcome. It is worth noting that the process took several centuries and could not have been detected through surface survey; instead, years of meticulous excavation were required.

Tilcajete, only 25 km south of Monte Albán, had been an important piedmont community since at least 1000 B.C. The archaeological site consists of three discrete areas on successively higher hills. Between 700 and 500 B.C. a 25-ha community occupied the hill called El Mogote, a low-lying (and hence less easily defended) piedmont spur with streams that could be used to irrigate the alluvium below. By 500-300 B.C.—the period of Monte Albán's founding—Tilcajete had grown to 52.8 ha and was not about to surrender its autonomy. It had built for itself a 160 x 140 m plaza, with buildings delimiting its four sides, and two additional mounds in the plaza. On the plaza's east side was an apparent temple; on the north side was an elite residence consisting of three structures around a patio. Radiocarbon dates indicate that this plaza was completely burned at ca. 300 B.C., the first archaeological manifestation of Monte Albán's campaign against Tilcajete. Not surprisingly, Tilcajete's ceramic assemblage at this time is virtually lacking in the elite cream wares which Feinman (1982) has shown were produced near Monte Albán. Tilcajete also has a paucity of obsidian from distant sources which were traded to Monte Albán. Communities that had capitulated to Monte Albán received their share of such imports, but enemies did not.

Even after their plaza had been burned, the inhabitants of Tilcajete did not give up. Instead, they moved the center of their community 800 m uphill to a rise called El Palenque, where they built a new plaza with precisely the same orientation and layout as the earlier El Mogote version. El Palenque covered 71.5 ha and was defended by stone and earth walls. Tilcajete's continued growth, its refusal to give up its ceremonial layout and orientation, and its willingness to rebuild and defend itself against Monte Albán contrast sharply with the takeover of the Cuicatlan Cañada, where Monte Albán seems to have encountered much less resistance. One reason for this may be demographic; Spencer (personal communication 2000) suspects that there may then have been more people living at Tilcajete than in the largely rural Cañada.

Despite Tilcajete's resistance, Spencer and Redmond (2001a) report that hostilities increased and the El Palenque community was attacked and burned at ca. 100 B.C. The main target of the attack was the residence of the community leader, and because El Palenque was abandoned following the conflagration, Spencer and Redmond were able to expose fully our oldest accessible Zapotec "palace." (Undoubtedly there were comparable palatial residences at Monte Albán, but without tunnel excavations like those at Copan, we will never recover such early and deeply buried elite residences.)

The "palace" at El Palenque consists of 8 rooms arrayed around an interior patio, set on a 16 x 16 m masonry platform. Left behind in the fire were fallen carbonized roof beams, dense quantities of burned adobe, and whole vessels and ground stone tools lying on the burned floors of the rooms and patio. This raid seems to have ended Tilcajete's attempts to preserve its autonomy.

Following the abandonment of El Palenque, settlement at Tilcajete shifted to SMT-23, a nearby mountaintop. Excavations there by Christina Elson (personal communication 2000) are likely to reveal that a victorious Monte Albán had made it a second-tier administrative center. An ancient road leads from SMT-23 in the direction of Monte Albán, which is visible in the distance. From 100 B.C. to A.D. 200 the flow of elite Monte Albán ceramics (including cream wares) to SMT-23 is impressive, as if Tilcajete were at last part of the Monte Albán hegemony.

By this time, Monte Albán had succeeded in pacifying its entire 2100 km^2 valley. It now dominated a four-tier settlement hierarchy with secondary centers, tertiary centers, and villages and was extending its hegemony to areas up to 150 km outside the Valley of Oaxaca (see Figure 17.3). The Main Plaza we see today had been leveled and dozens of public buildings constructed on it, including the multifunctional North Platform, many two-room temples, a ballcourt, *adoratorios*, and an arrowhead-shaped building with stone inscriptions commemorating 40 places claimed by Monte Albán as the borders of its territory. The sheer variety of institutions represented by these building types, together with evidence of a four-tier administrative hierarchy, suggest that Monte Albán had become the capital of a mature state (Flannery and Marcus 1976; Marcus and Flannery 1994, 1996).

Clearly, the process of state formation in Oaxaca took several centuries and involved many steps. All the evidence from surveys and excavations, however, shows that this state formed in the absence of a preexisting model. As was true of the earliest states of the Zulu, Ashante, Hunza, Malagasy, and Hawaiians, the state formed in Oaxaca when one member of a group of competing chiefdoms succeeded in creating a larger polity by bringing its rivals (and other neighbors) together under its control (Flannery 1999). This was done by a long-term strategy of military force, diplomacy, colonization, and (probably) political marriages. The first "king" of the Zapotec, whatever his name, could not have been sent from a preexisting state, since we know of none. Nevertheless, once the Zapotec state had formed it shared many structural features with the Copan state.

Was There a Period of Chiefly Cycling in the Copan Valley?

It is very likely that state formation at Copan was preceded by an era during which complex Preclassic chiefdoms rose, peaked, and collapsed against a background of simpler chiefdoms (Fash 2001; Urban and Schortman 1986). Unless the Copan Valley is very different from other areas of Mesoamerica, some of those complex chiefdoms may have come close to achieving unification of the region, only to break down. Unfortunately our view of this crucial period is incomplete because, as Hall and Viel show in this volume, we still know so little about Preclassic political organization and settlement hierarchy of the Copan Valley.

While excavating a series of caves in the Copan Valley in the 1890s, George Byron Gordon found Preclassic ceramics. At that time, one might have predicted that it would be easy to find additional material, but it has proved more difficult than Gordon could have guessed. Not until 1978, when Fash was excavating in the center of Patio A, Group 9N-8, 600 m east of Copan's Principal Group, did anyone come upon material as old as that found by Gordon. Then, in 1981, Fash found even earlier material just 10 m away (Fash 1991:65). These materials included the earliest house known so far from the Copan Valley, dating to the Rayo phase (1300–900 B.C.). The next phase, Uir (900–400 B.C.), has distinctive burial vessels that constitute the "Gordon" sub-complex, named after George Byron Gordon because its ceramics look like those he recovered in the 1890s. Significantly, the Gordon ceramics feature shapes and pan-Mesoamerican motifs that are particularly well known from the highlands of Mexico (Flannery and Marcus 2000).

Such tiny windows into the Early and Middle Preclassic are tantalizing, but limited. Why is it so difficult to find Early and Middle Preclassic villages? Hall and Viel suggest that the course of the Copan River has changed a number of times, with seasonal flooding possibly burying hamlets. In addition, some past excavations might not have been deep enough to reach Preclassic levels (indeed, some of Hall and Viel's excavations revealed thick sterile levels covering artifact-bearing strata). Thus, while both the Copan and Oaxaca Valleys had long sequences of Early and Middle Preclassic chiefdoms, there is no question that sites of that era are easier to find in Oaxaca.

As we move to the Late Preclassic in the Copan Valley (Chabij phase, 400 B.C.–A.D. 100), the situation becomes more promising, thanks to Marcello Canuto's excavations at Los Achiotes (this volume) and those of David Carballo (1997) at Cerro Chino. Canuto suggests that the similar hilltop location and layout at both sites indicate that Late Preclassic site planning was different from that imposed later by the founder of the Copan state. Los Achiotes represents a stage when important ritual seems to have been removed from individual households and centered in public buildings or spaces; the only dedicatory caches found so far were in the ballcourt. Villages of this era may have been located on hilltops both for defensive reasons, and to avoid seasonal flooding on the alluvium below.

During the Late Preclassic Copan was not yet part of a state, but later hieroglyphic texts refer retrospectively to events at 321 B.C., A.D. 159, A.D. 160, and A.D. 376 (Morley 1920; Riese 1992:132–133; Schele and Freidel 1990:fig. 8:2; Stuart 1992, this volume). Although we do not know what these early events were, they suggest the presence of individuals whose actions were important enough to be referred to by later rulers. Some may have been events in a series of cycles during which Late Preclassic and Protoclassic leaders attempted—evidently unsuccessfully—to unify the Copan Valley.

Primary State Formation in the Petén

While increasingly complex societies developed in the Copan Valley during the Protoclassic (A.D. 1–250), a few primary states may have been forming to the north. The first hints come from the impressive chiefly centers of El Mirador, Tikal, and Calakmul (Coe 1990; Folan et al. 1995; Harrison 1970, 1999; Matheny 1980, 1986; Sharer 1991). Huge pyramids at El Mirador and Calakmul show us that their early leaders could attract large numbers of followers and command them to build immense public works. Since so few signatures of the state have been documented at El Mirador, scholars disagree as to whether it was part of an early state or a paramount chiefdom (Matheny 1986; Sharer 1991). In addition, the fact that El Mirador collapsed at the very time that Tikal rose to prominence suggests that any attempts El Mirador made to consolidate the region ultimately failed.

Most Mayanists agree that if El Mirador was not the capital of a state, the agent who could be credited with founding the first primary Maya state was Yax Eb Xok of Tikal, who ruled sometime between A.D. 50 and 100. Unfortunately, his reign is also missing some signatures of statehood—for example, no palace can as yet be associated with Yax Eb Xok, or for that matter with Foliated Jaguar, who ruled Tikal around A.D. 150. In the absence of conclusive evidence at any of the three large centers at this time, we can at least point to the fact that Tikal (and perhaps Calakmul) overcame the "fissiparous tendencies" mentioned by Cohen (1978), while El Mirador did not.

Secondary States, Including the Copan Case

Many of Mesoamerica's secondary states were created by princes from preexisting states who, for one reason or another, could not expect to ascend to the throne of their native polity. This process could (and did) continue in third- and fourth-generation states. A well-known example is the Mixtec ruler 8 Deer Jaguar Claw, born in Tilantongo in A.D. 1063. Because 8 Deer was the son of his father's second wife, he was outranked as heir apparent by a half-brother. He left Tilantongo for Tututepec, a town to which his mother had connections, where he began a three-stage strategy—military conquest, the sacrifice of rivals, and royal marriages with women from subjugated towns. Eventually he established an expansionist state larger than his father's; codices suggest that he conquered as many as 100 places. 8 Deer's military expansion ended only when he was captured in battle and sacrificed by his rivals in A.D. 1115 (Smith 1973). The history of Mesoamerica provides many cases of such men, almost always using military skills to overcome their lack of genealogical credentials. Such military strategy may well have been employed by the founder of the Copan state, although we do not know whether he was invited (like Acamapichtli) or simply arrived as a usurper.

As many as 300 years may have elapsed between the formation of a primary state at Tikal and the establishment of a secondary state in the Copan Valley. So little is known about the relations among sites in the Copan Valley during the two centuries preceding state formation that it is difficult to describe the political situation from A.D. 225 to 425. In 1920 Morley speculated that immigrants from Tikal had reached Copan before A.D. 435, and less than 30 years later Copan was the capital of its valley (Morley 1920:416). Building on Morley's observations, I suggested in 1976 that Copan was reorganized politically when one dynasty rose to exert control and that the probable source of that dynasty was the Petén. I presented this "Petén hypothesis" by saying that "contact with non-Copan Valley populations (e.g., Tikal) may have taken the form of a marriage or arrival of a Petén woman or the arrival of a younger brother from the northeast Petén" (Marcus 1976:124). Contributors to the present volume now suggest, with much more solid evidence, that the scenario of a nobleman coming from Tikal may be correct.

According to the hieroglyphic inscriptions of Copan, the founder of its first royal dynasty was a lord named K'uk' Mo' who arrived in A.D. 426. We are told this on Altar Q, a monument commissioned in A.D. 776, which depicts Yax Pasaj Chan Yoaat and the 15 rulers who preceded him. The text on the top of Altar Q says, "on September 6, A.D. 426, Lord K'uk' Mo' took the K'awiil scepter in the Crossed Bundles House." The hieroglyph of "seizing the scepter" is often interpreted as accession to the throne (Marcus 1976:134–135; Schele and Freidel 1990:317); thus this date in A.D. 426 is considered to mark the founding of the Copan dynasty.

Three days later K'uk' Mo' came away from Crossed Bundles House, having received his full royal name of K'inich Yax K'uk' Mo'; this acquisition of a new name is also consistent with having taken office. Next comes an important passage which states that K'inich Yax K'uk' Mo' had reached Copan after a trip of five months. Speaking of this passage, Stuart (this volume) speculates that K'inich Yax K'uk' Mo's "supposed journey from the 'Crossed Bundles House' was the return leg of a longer jaunt, and that his ultimate starting point may have been Copan, or just possibly some other Maya site." The bone chemistry of the Hunal interment, thought to be the skeleton of K'inich Yax K'uk' Mo', suggests that the second alternative is correct.

If the identification of the Hunal Tomb occupant as K'inich Yax K'uk' Mo' is correct (Bell et al., this volume; Reents-Budet et al. this volume; Sharer, Fash et al. 1999; Sharer, Traxler, et al. 1999), based on analyses of his bones we can say that he had sur-

began their tunneling. Prior to that, we knew of this dynastic founder only from the retrospective references of his successors. So important was K'inich Yax K'uk' Mo' in the history of Copan that he was still featured by the 16th ruler of his dynasty who lived three-and-a-half centuries later (Marcus 1994:257–258).

The Copan Valley is roughly a third the size of the Valley of Oaxaca. However, K'inich Yax K'uk' Mo' and his immediate successors expanded well beyond it, putting together a state covering ca. 10,000 km^2. Their realm remained large until A.D. 738, at which point Quirigua's ruler claims in a text to have defeated the king of Copan in battle, thereby achieving his city's independence (Marcus 1976, 1992a, 1998). From that time on, Quirigua embarked on its own ambitious flurry of construction and monument carving (Sharer 1990, 1991). Despite their shrinking realm, later rulers at Copan continued to link themselves to the founder of their dynasty.

The Future of Work at Copan

We have come a long way since George Byron Gordon worked on the Hieroglyphic Stairway at Copan, John Longyear studied the ceramics, and George Guillemin opened up the first 100 m of tunnels. One of the things we have learned is that a region like the Copan Valley, intensively researched for many decades, eventually becomes a case study that transcends its region. One need no longer be a Mayanist to find the Copan story compelling. It is now one of the most detailed archaeological examples of secondary state formation from anywhere in the prehistoric world.

In 1991 Fash and Sharer, borrowing a term from Walter W. Taylor (1948), called for a "conjunctive approach" in which multiple lines of evidence—settlement pattern studies, large-scale excavation, epigraphic studies, biological anthropology, bone chemistry, materials analysis, and other approaches—would be brought to bear on the Copan Valley to achieve a common goal.

By comparing Oaxaca and Copan, we see two pathways to the state. Each was preceded by a long period during which egalitarian societies were transformed into rank societies, and eventually into stratified (or nearly stratified) societies with a belief in the divine descent of the elite (see both Agurcia F. and Taube, this volume). Because of the humidity of the Copan Valley and the volatility of its major river, we have fewer details of this period than we do in arid Oaxaca. This is a problem for future investigators in the Copan Valley to solve.

In Oaxaca, after a long period of escalating conflict among rival chiefdoms, one of the participants seized a defensible mountaintop and set about converting its formerly autonomous rivals into subject provinces of a much larger polity. This is how primary states form, and once they have produced the template, we can see neighboring regions deliberately creating rival states. Huamelulpan may belong in the latter category, since it even borrowed Zapotec-style writing (Gaxiola 1976; Marcus 1983b). It probably formed by consolidating the local population and moving to a mountaintop to avoid being incorporated by the expanding Monte Albán state (Balkansky 1998b).

In the Maya region, primary states seem to have formed at places like Calakmul and Tikal (Folan et al. 1995; Harrison 1999; Marcus 1995, 1998). While we are still a long way from knowing the details, it would seem that those early states formed much as the Monte Albán state did, by military and political consolidation of previously autonomous rival chiefdoms. (Judging by the immense public buildings in the lowlands, the last of those chiefdoms were very complex and powerful.) A future task for Maya archaeologists, therefore, will be to determine why those areas of the Petén achieved statehood so early, at least relative to the rest of the Maya region. Such a task will take long-term multidisciplinary projects, like the one at Copan (e.g. Andrews and Fash 1992; Baudez 1983, 1994; Fash 2001; Fash and Sharer 1991; Riese 1992; Sharer, Fash et al. 1999).

Founded perhaps 300 years after the primary states of the Petén, Copan became a secondary state with the arrival of a prince from the royal house of one of those preexisting states. While we do not know whether Lord K'uk' Mo' was an invited prince or a usurper, it appears that he may have used political marriage, ambitious construction, and military expansion to legitimize himself. Although he reigned for only a decade, his impact on Copan was so lasting that 350 years later he was still featured on monuments commissioned by the current ruler of the dynasty he founded. K'inich Yax K'uk' Mo' brought the template of a powerful preexisting state with him and established a grand architectural plan, one that was maintained throughout the history of the Copan Acropolis. We should remember, however, that we know this only because the team of archaeologists working at Copan refused to content themselves with the retrospective hieroglyphic comments of K'inich Yax K'uk' Mo's successors. They kept digging—literally and figuratively—until they had K'inich Yax K'uk' Mo' himself, and could read in his healed wounds the price of creating a state through military expansion.

REFERENCES

Abrams, Elliot M.
1984   Systems of Labor Organization in Late Classic Copan, Honduras: The Energetics of Construction. Ph.D. dissertation, Department of Anthropology, Pennsylvania State University.
1994   *How the Maya Built Their World: Energetics and Ancient Architecture.* Austin: University of Texas Press.

Agrinier, P.
1963   Nuevos casos de mutilaciones dentarias procedentes de Chiapas, Mexico. *Anales del INAH* 15(4):229-243.

Agurcia F., Ricardo
1996   Rosalila, el corazón de la Acrópolis, El templo del Rey-Sol. *Yaxkin* 14:5-18.
1997a   Il tempio del Re Sole e la sua evoluzione nell'acropoli di Copan. In *I Maya di Copan: l'Atene del Centroamerica*, edited by G. Orefici, pp. 99-108. Milan: Skira Editore.
1997b   Le temple du roi Soleil et son évolution au coeur de l'acropole de Copan. In *Les Mayas au Pays de Copan*, pp. 91-100. Milan: Skira Editore.
1997c   Rosalila, An Early Classic Maya Cosmogram from Copan. *Symbols* (Spring):32-37.
1998   Copan: Art, Science and Dynasty. In *Maya*, edited by P. Schmidt, M. de la Garza, and E. Nalda, pp. 336-355. New York: Rizzoli.

Agurcia F., Ricardo, Donna K. Stone, Alfonso Morales, D. W. Kluth, and C. Leroux
1989   Estructura 10L-16 (OP. 41), Informe del Campo, Temporada 1989. Manuscript on file at the Instituto Hondureño de Antropología e Historia, Tegucigalpa and Copan.

Agurcia F., Ricardo, Donna K. Stone, and Jorge Ramos
1996   Tierra, tiestos, piedras, estratigrafía, y escultura: Investigaciones en la
        Estructura 10L-16 de Copan. In *Visión del Pasado Maya*, edited by W. L. Fash
        and R. Agurcia Fasquelle. Tegucigalpa: Asociación Copan.

Agurcia F., Ricardo, and Juan Antonio Valdés
1994   *Secretos de Dos Ciudades Mayas/Secrets of Two Maya Cities: Copan y/and
        Tikal.* San Pedro Sula, Honduras: Centro Editorial.

Agurcia F., Ricardo, and William L. Fash
1991   Maya Artistry Unearthed. *National Geographic Magazine* 180(3):94-105.
1992   *Historia Escrita en Piedra: Guía al Parque Arqueológico de las Ruinas de
        Copan.* Tegucigalpa: Asociación Copan, Instituto Hondureño de Antropología
        e Historia.

Anderson, Dana
1978   Monuments. In *The Prehistory of Chalchuapa, El Salvador*, vol. 1, edited by
        R. J. Sharer, pp. 155-180. Philadelphia: University of Pennsylvania Press.

Anderson, David G.
1994   *The Savannah River Chiefdoms.* Tuscaloosa: University of Alabama Press.

Andrews, E. Wyllys V, and Barbara W. Fash
1992   Continuity and Change in a Royal Maya Residential Complex at Copan.
        Ancient Mesoamerica 3(1):63-88.

Anton, Ferdinand F., Frederick J. Dockstader, Margaret Trowell, and Hans Nevermann
1979   *Primitive Art: Pre-Columbian, North American Indian, African, and
        Oceanic.* New York: Abrams.

Aoyama, Kazuo
1996   Exchange, Craft Specialization, and Ancient Maya State Formation: A Study of
        Chipped Stone Artifacts from the Southeast Maya Lowlands. Ph.D. disserta-
        tion, Department of Anthropology, University of Pittsburgh.
1999   *Ancient Maya State, Urbanism, Exchange, and Craft Specialization:
        Chipped Stone Evidence from the Copan Valley and the La Entrada Region,
        Honduras.* University of Pittsburgh Memoirs in Latin American Archaeology
        No. 12. Pittsburgh, PA: University of Pittsburgh Department of Anthropology.

Apostolides, Alex
1987   Chalcatzingo Painted Art. In *Ancient Chalcatzingo*, edited by D. C. Grove, pp.
        171-199. Austin: University of Texas Press.

Ashmore, Wendy
1991   Site-Planning Principles and Concepts of Directionality among the Ancient
        Maya. *Latin American Antiquity* 2(3):199-226.

Ashmore, Wendy, Edward M. Schortman, Patricia A. Urban, Julie Benyo, John M. Weeks, and Sylvia Smith
1987   Ancient Society in Santa Bárbara, Honduras. *National Geographic Exploration & Research* 3:232-254.

Balandier, Georges
1970   *Political Anthropology*. New York: Pantheon.

Balkansky, Andrew K.
1998a   The Origin and Collapse of Complex Societies in Oaxaca (Mexico): Evaluating the Era from 1965 to the Present. *Journal of World Prehistory* 12:451-493.
1998b   Urbanism and Early State Formation in the Huamelulpan Valley of Southeastern Mexico. *Latin American Antiquity* 9:37-67.
2002   *The Sola Valley and the Monte Albán State: A Study of Zapotec Imperial Expansion*. Ann Arbor: University of Michigan Museum of Anthropology.

Ball, Joseph W.
1983   Teotihuacan, the Maya, and Ceramic Interchange: A Contextual Perspective. In *Highland-Lowland Interaction in Mesoamerica: Interdisciplinary Approaches*, edited by A. G. Miller, pp. 125-145. Washington, DC: Dumbarton Oaks.

Barrientos, Tomás
1997   Desarrollo evolutivo del sistema de canales hidráulicos en Kaminaljuyu. Tesis de Licenciatura en Arqueología. Guatemala City: Universidad del Valle de Guatemala.

Baudez, Claude F.
1966   Niveaux ceramiques au Honduras: une reconsideration de l'evolution culturelle. *Journal de la Société des Américanistes* 55:299-341.
1994   *Maya Sculpture of Copan: The Iconography*. Norman: University of Oklahoma Press.

Baudez, Claude F., ed.
1983   *Introducción a la Arqueología de Copan, Honduras*, tomos I, II, III. Tegucigalpa: Proyecto Arqueológico Copan, Secretaría de Estado en el Despacho de Cultura y Turismo.

Baudez, Claude F., and Pierre Becquelin
1973   *Archéologie de los Naranjos, Honduras*. Mexico City: Mission Archéologique et Ethnologique Française au Mexique.

Becker, Marshall J.
1971   The Identification of a Second Plaza Plan at Tikal, Guatemala, and its Implications for Ancient Maya Social Complexity, Ph.D. dissertation, Department of Anthropology, University of Pennsylvania.

Bell, Ellen E.
2001   The Engendering of a Dynasty. In *Ancient Maya Women*, edited by T. A.
        Ardren, pp. 89-104. Walunt Creek, CA: Altamira.
2003   Early Classic Ritual Deposits in the Copan Acropolis: The Material
        Foundations of Political Power at a Classic Period Maya Center. Ph.D. disserta-
        tion, Department of Anthropology, University of Pennsylvania.

Bell, Ellen E., Loa P. Traxler, David W. Sedat, and Robert J. Sharer
1999   Uncovering Copan's Earliest Royal Tombs. *Expedition* 41(2):29-35.

Bell, Ellen E., Robert J. Sharer, David W. Sedat, Marcello A. Canuto, and Lynn A. Grant
2000   The Margarita Tomb at Copan, Honduras: A Research Update. *Expedition*
        42(3):21-25.

Benyo, Julie C., and Thomas Melchionne
1987   Settlement Patterns in the Tencoa Valley, Honduras: An Application of the
        Coevolutionary Systems Model. In *Interaction on the Southeast
        Mesoamerican Frontier: Prehistoric and Historic Honduras and El
        Salvador*, vol. 1, edited by E. J. Robinson, pp. 49-64. BAR International Series
        327. Oxford: British Archaeological Reports.

Berlo, Janet
1983   The Warrior and the Butterfly: Central Mexican Ideologies of Sacred Warfare
        and Teotihuacan Iconography. In *Text and Image in Pre-Columbian Art:
        Essays on the Interrelationship of the Visual and Verbal Arts*, edited by J.
        Berlo, pp. 79-117. BAR International Series 180. Oxford: British Archaeological
        Reports.
1984   *Teotihuacan Art Abroad: A Study of Metropolitan Style and Provincial
        Transformation in Incensario Workshops*. BAR International Series 199. 2
        vols. Oxford: British Archaeological Reports.

Bill, Cassandra R.
1997   Patterns of Variation and Change in Dynastic Period Ceramics and Ceramic
        Production at Copan, Honduras. Ph.D. dissertation, Department of
        Anthropology, Tulane University.

Bishop, Ronald L., and Marilyn Beaudry
1994   Appendix B, Chemical Compositional Analysis of Southeastern Maya
        Ceramics. In *Ceramics and Artifacts from Excavations in The Copan
        Residential Zone*, edited by G. R. Willey, R. M. Leventhal, A. A. Demarest, and
        W. L. Fash, pp. 407-444. Papers of the Peabody Museum of Archaeology and
        Ethnology No. 80. Cambridge, MA: Peabody Museum of Anthropology and
        Ethnology.

Bishop, Ronald, and Hector Neff
1989   Multivariate Analysis of Compositional Data in Archaeology. *Archaeological
        Chemistry IV*, edited by R. O. Allen, pp. 576-586. Advances in Chemistry Series
        220. Washington, DC: American Chemical Society.

Bishop, Ronald L., Robert L. Rands, and George R. Holley
1982   Ceramic Compositional Analysis in Archaeological Perspective. In *Advances in Archaeological Method and Theory*, vol. 5, edited by M. Schiffer, pp. 275–330. New York: Academic.

Black, Stephen L.
1990   Field Methods and Methodologies in Lowland Maya Archaeology. Ph.D. dissertation, Department of Anthropology, Harvard University.

Blackburn, Robin, ed.
1972   *Ideology in Social Science: Readings in Critical Social Theory*. New York: Pantheon.

Blackman, M. James
1986   Precision in Routine INAA over a Two-Year Period at the NBSR. In *NBS Reactor: Summary of Activities July 1985 Through 1986*, edited by F. J. Shorten, pp. 122–126. NBS Technical Note 1231. Washington, DC: U.S. Department of Commerce, National Bureau of Standards, U.S. Government Printing Office.

Blanton, Richard E.
1994   *Houses and Households: A Comparative Study*. New York: Plenum.

Blanton, Richard E., and Peter Peregrine
1997   Main Assumptions and Variables or Economic Analysis Beyond the Local System. In *Economic Analysis Beyond the Local System*, edited by R. Blanton, P. Peregrine, D. Winslow, and T. Hall, pp. 3–12. Lanham, MD: University Press of America.

Blanton, Richard E., Stephen A. Kowalewski, Gary M. Feinman, and Jill Appel
1982   *Monte Albán and its Hinterland, Part I: Prehispanic Settlement Patterns of the Central and Southern Parts of the Valley of Oaxaca, Mexico*. Memoirs of the University of Michigan Museum of Anthropology No. 15. Ann Arbor: University of Michigan Museum of Anthropology.

Boldsen, Jesper L.
1997   Transition Analysis: A Method for Unbiased Age Estimation from Skeletal Traits. *American Journal of Physical Anthropology Supplement* 24:79.

Boldsen, Jesper L., G. R. Milner, L. W. Konigsberg, and J. W. Wood
2002   Transition Analysis: A New Method for Estimating Age From Skeletons. In *Paleodemography: Age Distributions from Skeletal Samples*, edited by R. D. Hoppa and J. W. Vaupel, pp. 73–106. Cambridge: Cambridge University Press.

Boone, Elizabeth H.
2000   *Stories in Red and Black: Pictorial Histories of the Aztecs and Mixtecs*. Austin: University of Texas Press.

Bourdieu, Pierre
1973   The Berber House. In *Rules and Meanings*, edited by M. Douglas, pp. 98-110. Harmondsworth, UK: Penguin.
1977   *Outline of a Theory of Practice*, translated by R. Nice. Cambridge: Cambridge University Press.
1990   *The Logic of Practice*. Palo Alto, CA: Stanford University Press.

Braswell, Geoffrey E.
1992   Obsidian Hydration Dating, the Coner Phase, and Revisionist Chronology at Copan, Honduras. *Latin American Antiquity* 3:130-147.
1996   A Maya Obsidian Source: The Geoarchaeology, Settlement History, and Ancient Economy of San Martín Jilotepeque, Guatemala. Ph.D. dissertation, Department of Anthropology, Tulane University.
2000   Un acercamiento a la interacción entre Kaminaljuyu y el centro de México durante el Clásico Temprano. In *XIII Simposio de Investigaciones Arqueológicas en Guatemala, 1999*, edited by J. P. Laporte, H. L. Escobedo, A. C. de Suasnávar, and B. Arroyo, pp. 115-126. Guatemala City: Museo Nacional de Arqueología y Etnología.
2003   Teotihuacan and the Maya: Reinterpreting Early Classic Interaction. In *Teotihuacan and the Maya: Reinterpreting Early Classic Interaction*, edited by G. Braswell. Austin: University of Texas Press.

Brown, Kenneth L.
1977   The Valley of Guatemala: A Highland Port of Trade. In *Teotihuacan and Kaminaljuyu*, edited by W. T. Sanders and J. Michels, pp. 205-396. University Park: Pennsylvania State University Press.

Brumfiel, Elizabeth M., and John W. Fox, eds.
1994   *Factional Competition and Political Development in the New World*. Cambridge: Cambridge University Press.

Bryant, J. Daniel, and Philip N. Froelich
1995   A Model of Oxygen Isotope Fractionation in Body Water of Large Mammals. *Geochimica et Cosmochimica Acta* 59(21):4523-4537.
1996   Oxygen Isotope Composition of Human Tooth Enamel from Medieval Greenland: Linking Climate and Society. *Geology* 24(5):477-478.

Buikstra, Jane E.
1996   Estudio Piloto de Enterramientos de la Acrópolis. Apéndice II. In Programa de Investigación de la Acrópolis Temprana (PIAT), Proyecto Arqueológico Acrópolis Copan, Informe Preliminar de la Temporada del 1996, edited by R. J. Sharer. Manuscript on file at the Instituto Hondureño de Antropología e Historia, Tegucigalpa and Copan.
1997   The Bones Speak: High-Tech Approach to the Study of our Ancestors. Lecture presented for the Loren Eiseley Associates of the University of Pennsylvania Museum of Archaeology and Anthropology, Philadelphia.

Buikstra, J. E., and J. H. Mielke
1985   Demography, Diet and Health. In *The Analysis of Prehistoric Diets*, edited by R. I. Gilbert and J. H. Mielke, pp. 359-422. New York: Academic.

Buikstra, Jane E., and Mark Swegle
1989   Bone Modification Due to Burning: Experimental Evidence. In *Bone Modification*, edited by R. Bonnichsen and M. Sorg, pp. 247-258. Orono, ME: Center for the Study of the First Americans.

Buikstra, Jane E., and Douglas H. Ubelaker, eds.
1994   *Standards for Data Collection From Human Skeletal Remains.* Arkansas Archaeological Survey Research Series No. 44. Fayetteville: Arkansas Archaeological Survey.

Buikstra, Jane E., T. Douglas Price, Lori E. Wright, and James H. Burton
2000   The Early Classic Royal Burials at Copan: A Bioarchaeological Perspective. Paper presented at the 65th Annual Meeting of the Society for American Archaeology, Philadelphia, PA.

Burke, W. H., R. E. Denison, E. A. Hetherington, R. B. Koepnick, H. F. Nelson, and J. B. Otto
1982   Variation of Seawater 87Sr/86Sr throughout Phanerozoic Time. *Geology* 10:516-519.

Cabrera Castro, Rubén
1992   A Survey of Recently Excavated Murals at Teotihuacan. In *Art, Ideology, and the City of Teotihuacan*, edited by J. C. Berlo, pp. 113-128. Washington, DC: Dumbarton Oaks.
1993   Human Sacrifice at the Temple of the Feathered Serpent: Recent Discoveries at Teotihuacan. In *Teotihuacan: Art from the City of the Gods*, edited by K. Berrin and E. Pasztory, pp. 100-107. San Francisco: Fine Arts Museums of San Francisco.

Cabrera Castro, R., M. E. Ruiz Gallut, and M. A. Trinidad Meléndez
1996   Murales del acervo de la zona arqueológica de Teotihuacan: Devolución reciente. In *La Pintura Mural Prehispánica en México, Teotihuacan*, vol. 1, tomo 2, edited by B. de la Fuente, pp. 465-474. Mexico City: Universidad Nacional Autónoma de México.

Canby, Joel S.
1949   Excavations at Yarumela, Spanish Honduras. Ph.D. dissertation, Department of Anthropology, Harvard University.
1952   Possible Chronological Implications of the Long Ceramic Sequence Recovered at Yarumela, Spanish Honduras. In *The Civilizations of Ancient America: Selected Papers of the XXIXth International Congress of Americanists*, edited by S. Tax, pp. 79-85. Chicago: University of Chicago Press.

Canuto, Marcello A.
1997   Investigaciones Arqueológicas en Los Achiotes, Honduras. Manuscript on file
        at the Instituto Hondureño de Antropología e Historia, Tegucigalpa and
        Copan, Honduras.
1998   Survey and Excavation at El Raizal, Honduras: Final Report, 1998 Season.
        Report submitted to the Foundation for the Advancement of Mesoamerican
        Studies, Crystal River, FL.
1999a   El asentamiento rural en los alrededores de Copan: Un desarrollo precoz.
        Paper presented at the VII Seminario de Antropología de Honduras,
        Tegucigalpa.
1999b   Survey and Excavation in the Rural region of Copan, Honduras, Final Report, 1999
        Season. Report submitted to the National Science Foundation, Washington, DC.
2002   A Tale of Two Communities: Social and Political Transformation in the
        Hinterlands of the Maya Polity of Copan. Ph.D. dissertation, Department of
        Anthropology, University of Pennsylvania.

Canuto, Marcello A., and Ellen E. Bell
2003   Informe Preliminar 2003: Proyecto Arqueológico Regional El Paraíso,
        Department de Cópan, Honduras. Ms. on file at the Instituto Hondureno de
        Antropología e Historia, Tegucigalpa, Copan, and El Paraíso.

Canuto, Marcello A., and William J. McFarlane
1999   Una comunidad rural en los alrededores de Copan: Un desarrollo precoz. In
        XIII Simposio de Investigaciones Arqueológicas en Guatemala. Guatemala
        City: Ministerio de Cultura y Deportes, Instituto de Antropología e Historia, y
        Asociación Tikal.

Canuto, Marcello A., and Jason Yaeger, eds.
2000   The Archaeology of Communities: A New World Perspective. London:
        Routledge.

Carballo, David M.
1997   Investigaciones Arqueológicas en Cerro Chino, Honduras. Manuscript on file at
        the Instituto Hondureño de Antropología e Historia, Tegucigalpa and Copan.

Carneiro, Robert L.
1969   The Measurement of Cultural Development in the Ancient Near East and in
        Anglo-Saxon England. Transactions of the New York Academy of Sciences,
        Series II 31:1013–1023.
1970   A Theory of the Origin of the State. Science 169:733–738.
1981   The Chiefdom: Precursor of the State. In The Transition to Statehood in the
        New World, edited by G. D. Jones and R. R. Kautz, pp. 37–79. Cambridge:
        Cambridge University Press.
1991   The Nature of the Chiefdom as Revealed by Evidence from the Cauca Valley
        of Colombia. In Profiles in Cultural Evolution, edited by A. T. Rambo and K.
        Gillogly, pp. 167–190. Anthropological Paper 85. Ann Arbor: University of
        Michigan Museum of Anthropology.

1992   The Role of Natural Selection in the Evolution of Culture. *Cultural Dynamics*
        5:113-140.

Carpio Rezzio, E.
1999   *La Relación Kaminaljuyu-Teotihuacan.* Guatemala City: Instituto de
        Investigaciones de la Escuela de Historia, Universidad de San Carlos de
        Guatemala, Guatemala.

Carr, Christopher
1995   A Unified Middle-Range Theory of Artifact Design. In *Style, Society, and
        Person*, edited by C. Carr and J. Neitzel, pp. 171-258. New York: Plenum.

Carrasco Vargas, Ramón
2000   Tumbas reales de Calakmul: Ritos funerarios e estructura de poder.
        Arqueología Mexicana 7(42):28-33.

Carrelli, Christine W.
1997   Análisis Preliminar de la Construcción de la Acrópolis de Copan en el Clásico
        Temprano. *Yaxkin* 16:16-23.
1998   Architectural Construction as an Index of Culture Change: A Case Study of
        Royal Maya Architecture at Copan, Honduras. Paper presented at the
        Conference on Culture Change in the Ancient World, Center for Ancient
        Studies and Department of Anthropology, University of Pennsylvania,
        Philadelphia.
1999   La Arquitectura Real de Copan: Energética, Maniobra, y Construcción. Paper
        presented at the VII Seminario de Antropología de Honduras, Tegucigalpa.

Cheek, Charles D.
1977   Excavations at the Palangana and the Acropolis, Kaminaljuyu. In *Teotihuacan
        and Kaminaljuyu*, edited by W. T. Sanders and J. W. Michels, pp. 1-204.
        University Park: Pennsylvania State University Press.
1983a   Excavaciones en la Plaza Principal. In *Introducción a la Arqueología de
        Copan, Honduras*, tomo II, edited by C. F. Baudez, pp. 191-289. Tegucigalpa:
        Proyecto Arqueológico Copan, Secretaría de Estado en el Despacho de
        Cultura y Turismo.
1983b   Excavaciones en la Plaza Principal: Resumen y Conclusiones. In *Introducción
        a la Arqueología de Copan, Honduras*, tomo II, edited by C. F. Baudez, pp.
        319-348. Tegucigalpa: Proyecto Arqueológico Copan, Secretaría de Estado en
        el Despacho de Cultura y Turismo.
1986   Construction Activity as a Measurement of Change at Copan, Honduras. In
        The Southeast Maya Periphery, edited by P. A. Urban and E. M. Schortman,
        pp. 50-72. Austin: University of Texas Press.

Cheek, Charles D., and Veronica Kennedy Embree
1983   Estructura 10L-2. In *Introducción a la Arqueología de Copan, Honduras*,
        tomo II, edited by C. F. Baudez, pp. 93-141. Tegucigalpa: Proyecto
        Arqueológico Copan, Secretaría de Estado en el Despacho de Cultura y
        Turismo.

Cheek, Charles D., and Daniel E. Milla Villeda
1983   Estructura 10L-4. In *Introducción a la Arqueología de Copan, Honduras*, tomo II, edited by C. F. Baudez, pp. 37-91. Tegucigalpa: Proyecto Arqueológico Copan, Secretaría de Estado en el Despacho de Cultura y Turismo.

Cheek, Charles D., and Mary L. Spink
1986   Excavaciones en el Grupo 3, Estructura 223 (Operación VII). In *Excavaciones en el Area Urbana de Copan*, tomo II, edited by W. T. Sanders, pp. 27-154. Tegucigalpa: Proyecto Arqueológico Copan, Segunda Fase, Secretaría de Cultura y Turismo, Instituto Hondureño de Antropología e Historia.

Cifuentes Aguirre, O.
1963   *Odontología y mutilaciones dentarias mayas*. Guatemala City: Editorial Universitaria.

Claessen, Henri J. M., and Peter Skalník
1978   The Early State: Theories and Hypotheses. In *The Early State: Theories and Hypotheses*, edited by H. J. M. Claessen and P. Skalník, pp. 3-29. The Hague: Mouton.

Coe, Michael D.
1965   The Olmec Style and Its Distribution. In *Archaeology of Southern Mesoamerica, Part 2*, edited by G. R. Willey, pp. 739-775. Handbook of Middle American Indians, vol. 3, R. Wauchope, general editor. Austin: University of Texas Press.

Coe, William R.
1990   *Excavations in the Great Plaza, North Terrace, and North Acropolis of Tikal*. Tikal Report 14. University Museum Monograph 61. Philadelphia: University of Pennsylvania Museum of Archaeology and Anthropology.

Coggins, Clemency C.
1975   Painting and Drawing Styles at Tikal: An Historical and Iconographic Reconstruction. Ph.D. dissertation, Department of Anthropology, Harvard University.
1979   A New Order and the Role of the Calendar: Some Characteristics of the Middle Classic Period at Tikal. In *Maya Archaeology and Ethnohistory*, edited by N. Hammond, pp. 38-50. Austin: University of Texas Press.
1988   On the Historical Significance of Decorated Ceramics at Copan and Quirigua and Related Classic Maya Sites. In *The Southeast Classic Maya Zone*, edited by E. H. Boone and G. R. Willey, pp. 95-124. Washington, DC: Dumbarton Oaks.

Coggins, Clemency C., and Orrin C. Shane
1984   *Cenote of Sacrifice: Maya Treasures from the Sacred Well at Chichen Itza*. Austin: University of Texas Press.

Cohen, Anthony P.
1985   *The Symbolic Construction of Community*. London: Routledge.

Cohen, Ronald
1974   The Evolution of Hierarchical Institutions: A Case Study from Biu, Nigeria. *Savanna* 3(2):153-174.
1978   State Origins: A Reappraisal. In *The Early State: Theories and Hypotheses*, edited by H. J. M. Claessen and P. Skalník, pp. 31-75. The Hague: Mouton.

Cowgill, George L.
2001   Clásico Temprano 150/200-600 d.C. *Arqueología Mexicana* 8(47):20-27.

Culbert, T. Patrick
1993   *The Ceramics of Tikal: Vessels from the Burials, Caches, and Problematical Deposits*. Tikal Report No. 25, Part A, University Museum Monograph No. 81. Philadelphia: University of Pennsylvania Museum of Archaeology and Anthropology.

Culbert, T. Patrick, ed.
1991   *Classic Maya Political History*. Cambridge: Cambridge University Press.

D'Altroy, Terence N., and Timothy K. Earle
1985   Staple Finance, Wealth Finance, and Storage in the Inka Political Economy. *Current Anthropology* 26(2):187-206.

Danforth, Marie Elaine
1999   Coming up Short: Stature and Nutrition among the Ancient Maya of the Southern Lowlands. In *Reconstructing Ancient Maya Diet*, edited by C. D. White, pp. 103-117. Salt Lake City: University of Utah Press.

Davis-Salazar, Karla L., and Ellen E. Bell
2000   Una comparación de los depósitos funerarios de dos mujeres en la acrópolis de Copan, Honduras. In *XIII Simposio de Investigaciones Arqueológicas en Guatemala*, edited by J. P. Laporte, H. L. Escobedo, A. C. de Suasnávar, and B. Arroyo, pp. 1113-1128. Guatemala City: Ministerio de Cultura y Deportes, Instituto de Antropología e Historia, y Asociación Tikal.

de Marrais, Elizabeth, Luis Jaime Castillo, and Timothy Earle
1996   Ideology, Materialization, and Power Strategies. *Current Anthropology* 37:15-31.

de Montmollin, Olivier
1989   *The Archaeology of Political Structure*. Cambridge: Cambridge University Press.

Demarest, Arthur A., and Antonia Foias
1993   Mesoamerican Horizons and the Cultural Transformations of Maya Civilization. In *Latin American Horizons*, edited by D. Rice, pp. 147-192. Washington, DC: Dumbarton Oaks.

Demarest, Arthur A., and Geoffrey W. Conrad
1992   *Ideology and Pre-Columbian Civilizations.* Santa Fe, NM: SAR.

Demarest, Arthur A., and Robert J. Sharer
1982   The Origin and Evolution of Usulután Ceramics. *American Antiquity* 47:810–822.
1986   Late Preclassic Ceramic Spheres, Culture Areas, and Cultural Evolution in the Southeastern Highlands of Mesoamerica. In *The Southeast Maya Periphery*, edited by P. A. Urban and E. M. Schortman, pp. 194–223. Austin: University of Texas Press.

Dembo, A., and José Imbelloni
1938   *Deformaciones intencionales del cuerpo humano de carácter ethnico.* Buenos Aires: José Anesi.

DePalma, Anthony F.
1983   Surgery of the Shoulder, 3rd ed., pp. 362–371. New York: Lippincott.

Dixon, Boyd
1992   Prehistoric Political Change on the Southeast Mesoamerican Periphery. *Ancient Mesoamerica* 3(1):11–25.

Dixon, Boyd, L. R. V. Joesink-Mandeville, Nobukatsu Hasebe, Michael Mucio, William Vincent, David James, and Kenneth Petersen
1994   Formative-Period Architecture at the site of Yarumela, Central Honduras. *Latin American Antiquity* 5(1):70–87.

Drennan, Robert D.
1976   *Fábrica San José and Middle Formative Society in the Valley of Oaxaca.* Memoirs of the University of Michigan Museum of Anthropology No. 8. Ann Arbor: University of Michigan Museum of Anthropology.

Durán, Diego
1964   *The Aztecs: The History of the Indies of New Spain*, translated by D. Heyden and F. Horcasitas. London: Cassell.
1994   *The History of the Indies of New Spain*, translated by D. Heyden. Norman: University of Oklahoma Press.

Earle, Timothy K.
1997   *How Chiefs Come to Power: The Political Economy of Prehistory.* Palo Alto, CA: Stanford University Press.

Edmunson, Munro S.
1982   *The Ancient Future of the Itza: The Book of Chilam Balam of Tizimin.* Austin: University of Texas Press.

Ekholm, Gordon
1961   Some Collar-Shaped Shell Pendants from Mesoamerica. In *Homenaje al Pablo Martinez del Río*, pp. 287-293. Mexico City: Instituto Nacional de Antropología e Historia.

Erasmus, Charles J.
1965   Monument Building: Some Field Experiments. *Southwestern Journal of Anthropology* 21:277-301.

Ericson, Jonathan E.
1985   Strontium Isotope Characterization in the Study of Prehistoric Human Ecology. *Journal of Human Evolution* 14:503-514.

Fahmel Beyer, Bernd
1995   *En el cruce de caminos: Bases de la relación entre Monte Albán y Teotihuacan*. Mexico City: Instituto de Investigaciones Antropológicas, Universidad Nacional Autónoma de México.

Fahsen, Federico
1988   *A New Early Classic Text from Tikal*. Research Reports on Ancient Maya Writing No. 17. Washington, DC: Center for Maya Research.
1999   Sistemas de escritura Maya. In *Los Mayas, Ciudades Milenarias de Guatemala*, edited by G. M. Cosme, C. V. Lorenzo, and J. A. Valdés, pp. 57-64. Zaragoza, Spain: Ayuntamiento de Zaragoza.
2000   Kaminaljuyu y sus vecinos. In *XIII Simposio de Investigaciones Arqueológicas en Guatemala, 1999*, edited by J. P. Laporte, H. L. Escobedo, A. C. de Suasnávar, and B. Arroyo, pp. 57-84. Guatemala City: Museo Nacional de Arqueología y Etnología.
n.d.   Análisis Epigráfico de los Monumentos de Kaminaljuyu. In *Excavaciones en Kaminaljuyu: Proyecto Miraflores II, 1994-1996*, edited by J. A. Valdés. Guatemala City: Universidad de San Carlos de Guatemala.

Fahsen, Federico, Linda Schele, and Nikolai Grube
1995   *The Tikal-Copan Connection: Shared Features, Version 2*. Copan Note 123. Austin, TX: Copan Acropolis Archaeological Project, Instituto Hondureño de Antropología e Historia.

Farriss, Nancy M.
1987   Remembering the Future, Anticipating the Past: History, Time, and Cosmology among the Maya of Yucatan. *Comparative Studies in Society and History* 29(3):566-593.

Fash, Barbara W.
1997a   La scultura del mondo classico Maya. In *I Maya di Copan: l'Atene del Centroamerica*, edited by G. Orefici, pp. 79-98. Milan: Skira Editore.
1997b   Sculpting the Maya Universe: A New View on Copan. *Symbols* (Spring):18-21.

Fash, Barbara W., William L. Fash, Sheree Lane, Rudy Larios, Linda Schele,
        Jeffery Stomper, and David Stuart
1992   Investigations of a Classic Maya Council House at Copan, Honduras. *Journal
        of Field Archaeology* 19(4):419-442.

Fash, William L.
1983a   Deducing Social Organization from Classic Maya Settlement Patterns: A Case
        Study from the Copan Valley. In *Civilization in the Ancient Americas*, edited
        by R. M. Leventhal and A. L. Kolata, pp. 261-288. Albuquerque, NM, and
        Cambridge, MA: University of New Mexico Press and Peabody Museum of
        Archaeology and Ethnology.
1983b   Maya State Formation: A Case Study and Its Implications. Ph.D. dissertation,
        Department of Anthropology, Harvard University.
1983c   Reconocimiento y Excavaciones en el Valle. In *Introducción a la Aqueología
        de Copan, Honduras*, tomo I, edited by C. F. Baudez, pp. 229-470.
        Tegucigalpa: Proyecto Arqueológico Copan, Secretaría de Estado en el
        Despacho de Cultura y Turismo.
1988   A New Look at Maya Statecraft from Copan, Honduras. *American Antiquity*
        62:157-169.
1991   *Scribes, Warriors, and Kings: The City of Copan and the Ancient Maya.*
        London: Thames and Hudson.
1997c   Il progetto archeologico dell'acropoli di Copan e il retaggio della civiltá
        maya. In *I Maya di Copan: l'Atene del Centroamerica*, edited by G. Orefici,
        pp. 61-78. Milan: Skira Editore.
1998   Dynastic Architectural Programs: Intention and Design in Classic Maya
        Buildings at Copan and Other Sites. In *Function and Meaning in Classic
        Maya Architecture*, edited by S. D. Houston, pp. 223-270. Washington, DC:
        Dumbarton Oaks.
2001   *Scribes, Warriors and Kings: The City of Copan and the Ancient Maya*, rev.
        ed. London: Thames and Hudson.
2002   Religion and Human Agency in Ancient Maya History: Tales from the
        Hieroglyphic Stairway. *Cambridge Archaeological Journal* 12(1):5-19.

Fash, William L., Harriet F. Beaubien, Catherine Magee, Barbara W. Fash,
        and Richard V. Williamson
2001   Trappings of Kingship among the Classic Maya: Ritual and Identity in a Royal
        Tomb from Copan. In *Fleeting Identities: Perishable Material Culture in
        Archaeological Research*, edited by P. B. Drooker. Carbondale: Center for
        Archaeological Investigations, Southern Illinois University.

Fash, William L., and Barbara W. Fash
1996   Building a World-View: Visual Communication in Classic Maya Architecture.
        RES: Anthropology and Aesthetics 29/30:127-147.
2000   Teotihuacan and the Maya: A Classic Heritage. In *Mesoamerica's Classic
        Heritage: From Teotihuacan to the Aztecs*, edited by D. Carrasco, L. Jones, and
        S. Sessions, pp. 433-464. Boulder: University Press of Colorado.

Fash, William L., and Robert J. Sharer
1991   Sociopolitical Developments and Methodological Issues at Copan, Honduras:
       A Conjunctive Perspective. *Latin American Antiquity* 2:166-187.

Fash, William L., and David Stuart
1991   Dynastic History and Cultural Evolution at Copan, Honduras. In *Classic Maya
       Political History: Hieroglyphic and Archaeological Evidence*, edited by T. P.
       Culbert, pp. 147-179. Cambridge: Cambridge University Press.

Fash, William L., Richard V. Williamson, Carlos Rudy Larios, and Joel Palka
1992   The Hieroglyphic Stairway and Its Ancestors: Investigations of Copan
       Structure 10L-26. *Ancient Mesoamerica* 3:105-116.

Feinman, Garry M.
1982   Ceramic Production Sites in Monte Albán and its Hinterland, Part I:
       Prehispanic Settlement Patterns of the Central and Southern Parts of the
       Valley of Oaxaca, Mexico. In *Memoirs of the University of Michigan
       Museum of Anthropology No. 15*, edited by R. E. Blanton, S. Kowalewski, G.
       Feinman, and J. Appel, pp. 389-386. Ann Arbor: University of Michigan
       Museum of Anthropology.

Feinman, Garry M., Stephen A. Kowalewski, Richard E. Blanton, Laura Finsten,
       and Linda M. Nicholas
1985   Long-Term Demographic Change: A Perspective from the Valley of Oaxaca.
       Journal of Field Archaeology 12:333-362.

Feinman, Gary M., and Linda M. Nicholas
1990   At the Margins of the Monte Albán State: Settlement Patterns in the Ejutla
       Valley, Oaxaca, Mexico. *Latin American Antiquity* 1(3):216-246.
1993   Shell-Ornament Production in Ejutla: Implications for Highland–Coastal
       Interaction in Ancient Oaxaca. *Ancient Mesoamerica* 4:103-119.

Fialko, Vilma
1988   Mundo Perdido, Tikal: un ejemplo de complejos de conmemoración
       astronómica. *Mayab* 4:14-21.

Fitzsimmons, James L.
1998   Classic Maya Mortuary Anniversaries at Piedras Negras, Guatemala. *Ancient
       Mesoamerica* 9(2): 271-278.

Flannery, Kent V.
1972   The Cultural Evolution of Civilizations. *Annual Review of Ecology and
       Systematics* 3:399-426.
1998   The Ground Plans of Archaic States. In *Archaic States*, edited by G. M.
       Feinman and J. Marcus, pp. 15-57. Santa Fe, NM: SAR.
1999   Process and Agency in Early State Formation. *Cambridge Archaeological
       Journal* 9(1):3-21.

Flannery, Kent V., and Joyce Marcus
1976   Evolution of the Public Building in Formative Oaxaca. In *Cultural Change and Continuity*, edited by C. Cleland, pp. 205-221. New York: Academic.
2000   Formative Mexican Chiefdoms and the Myth of the "Mother Culture." *Journal of Anthropological Archaeology* 19:1-37.

Folan, William J., Joyce Marcus, and W. Frank Miller
1995   Verification of a Maya Settlement Model through Remote Sensing. *Cambridge Archaeological Journal* 5(2):277-283.

Foncerrada de Molina, Marta
1980   Mural Painting in Cacaxtla and Teotihuacan Cosmopolitism. In *Third Palenque Round Table, 1978: Part 2*, edited by M. G. Robertson. Austin: University of Texas Press.

Fox, John G.
1996   Playing with Power: Ballcourts and Political Ritual in Southern Mesoamerica. *Current Anthropology* 37:483-509.

Freidel, David A., and Linda Schele
1988   Symbol and Power: A History of the Lowland Maya Cosmogram. In *Maya Iconography*, edited by E. Benson and G. Griffin, pp. 45-95. Princeton, NJ: Princeton University Press.

Freidel, David A., Linda Schele, and Joy Parker
1993   *Maya Cosmos: Three Thousand Years on the Shaman's Path*. New York: William Morrow.

Freidel, David A., Charles K. Suhler, and Rafael Cobos Palma
1998   Termination Ritual Deposits at Yaxuna: Detecting the Historical in Archaeological Contexts. In *The Sowing and the Dawning: Termination, Dedication, and Transformation in the Archaeological and Ethnographic Record of Mesoamerica*, edited by S. B. Mock, pp. 135-144. Albuquerque: University of New Mexico Press.

Freter, AnnCorinne
1988   The Classic Maya Collapse at Copan, Honduras: A Regional Settlement Perspective. Ph.D. dissertation, Department of Anthropology, Pennsylvania State University.
1994   The Classic Maya Collapse at Copan, Honduras: An Analysis of Maya Rural Settlement Trends. In *Archaeological Views from the Countryside*, edited by G. M. Schwartz and S. E. Falconer, pp. 160-176. Washington, DC: Smithsonian Institution Press.
1996   Rural Utilitarian Ceramic Production in the Late Classic Period Copan Maya State. In *Arqueología Mesoamericana: Homenaje a William T. Sanders*, edited by A. G. Mastache, J. R. Parsons, R. S. Santley, and M. C. Serra Puche, vol. 2, pp. 209-229. Mexico City: Instituto Nacional de Antropología e Historia.

Friedman, Jonathan, and Michael J. Rowlands
1978   Notes Towards an Epigenetic Model of the Evolution of Civilization. In *Theory and Explanation in Archaeology: The Southampton Conference*, edited by J. Friedman and M. J. Rowlands, pp. 201-276. New York: Academic.

Gaffney, V. L., and M. Tingle
1988   Maddle Farm (Berks.) Project and Micro-Regional Analysis. In *Archaeological Field Survey in Britain and Abroad*, edited by S. M. and F. H. Thompson, pp. 67-73. Occasional Paper (New Series) 6. London: Society of Antiquaries of London, Thames and Hudson.

Gaffney, C. F., and V. L. Gaffney
1988   Some Quantitative Approaches to Site Territory and Land Use From the Surface Record. In *Conceptual Issues in Environmental Archaeology*, edited by J. L. Bintliff, D. A. Davidson, and E. G. Grant, pp. 82-90. BAR International Series. Edinburgh: Edinburgh University Press.

Galindo, Juan
1835   The Ruins of Copan in Central America. *Archaeología Americana. Transactions and Collections of the American Antiquarian Society* 2:543-550.
1945   Informe de la comisión científica formada para el reconocimiento de las antigüedades de Copan, por decreto de 15 de enero de 1834, del C. gefe supremo del estado de Guatemala Dr. Mariano Gálvez. *Anales de la Sociedad de Geografía e Historia de Guatemala*:217-228.

Galindo Trejo, Juan
2001   La observación celeste en el pensamiento prehispánico. *Arqueología Mexicana* 8(47):29-35.

Galindo Trejo, J., and M. E. Ruiz Gallut
1998   Bonampak: Una confluencia sagrada de caminos celestes. In *Area Maya, Bonampak*, edited by L. S. Cicero, pp. 137-157. La pintura mural prehispánica en México, tomo II, B. de la Fuente, general editor. Mexico City: Universidad Nacional Autónoma de México.

Galloway, Alison, ed.
1999   *Broken Bones: Anthropological Analysis of Blunt Force Trauma*. Springfield, IL: Charles C Thomas.

García de Palacio, Diego
1983   [1576]   *Carta-relación de Diego García de Palacio a Felipe II sobre la provincia de Guatemala, 8 de marzo de 1576*. Mexico City: Universidad Nacional Autónoma de México.

Gaxiola González, Margarita
1976   Excavaciones en San Martín Huamelulpan, Oaxaca, 1974. Tesis profesional. Mexico City: Escuela Nacional de Antropología.

Genovés Tarazaga, Santiago
1967   Proportionality of the Long Bones and their Relation to Status among
        Mesoamericans. *American Journal of Physical Anthropology* 26:67-77.

Giles, Eugene, and Linda L. Klepinger
1988   Confidence Intervals for Estimates Based on Linear Regression in Forensic
        Anthropology. *Journal of Forensic Sciences* 33(5):1218-1222.

Gillespie, Susan D.
2001a   Personhood, Agency, and Mortuary Ritual: A Case Study from the Maya Area.
        Journal of Anthropological Archaeology 20:73-112.
2001b   Rethinking Ancient Maya Social Organization: Replacing "Lineage" with
        "House." *American Anthropologist* 102(3):467-484.

Girard, Rafael
1949   *Los Chortis ante el problema Maya*. Mexico City: Editorial Cultura.

Glascock, Michael D.
1992   Characterization of Archaeological Ceramics at MURR by Neutron Activiation
        Analysis and Multivariate Studies. In *Chemical Characterization of Ceramic
        Pastes in Archaeology*, edited by H. Neff. Monographs in World Archaeology
        No. 7. Madison, WI: Prehistory Press.

Golden, Charles W.
2002   Bridging the Gap Between Archaeological and Indigenous Chronologies: An
        Investigation of the Early Classic/Late Classic Divide at Piedras Negras,
        Guatemala. Ph.D. dissertation, Department of Anthropology, University of
        Pennsylvania.

Gonlin, Nancy
1993   Rural Household Archaeology at Copan, Honduras. Ph.D. dissertation,
        Department of Anthropology, Pennsylvania State University.
1994   Rural Household Diversity in Late Classic Copan, Honduras. In
        Archaeological Views from the Countryside, edited by G. M. Schwartz and S.
        E. Falconer, pp. 177-197. Washington, DC: Smithsonian Institution Press.

Goss, Thomas P.
1992   Fractures of the Glenoid Cavity: Current Concepts Review. *Journal of Bones,
        Joints and Surgery* 74A:299-305.
1995   Fractures of the Shoulder Complex. In *Upper Extremity Injuries in the
        Athlete*, edited by A. M. Pappas and J. Walzer, pp. 259-276. New York: Churchill
        Livingstone.
1996   The Scapula: Coracoid, Acromial, and Avulsion Fractures. *American Journal of
        Orthopedics* 25:106-115.

Gordon, George Byron

1896   *Prehistoric Ruins of Copan, Honduras: A Preliminary Report on Explorations, 1891-1895.* Memoirs of The Peabody Museum of Archaeology and Ethnology, no. 1. Cambridge, MA: Peabody Museum of Archaeology and Ethnology, Harvard University.

1902   *The Hieroglyphic Stairway, Ruins of Copan.* Memoirs of The Peabody Museum of Archaeology and Ethnology, vol. 1, no. 6. Cambridge, MA: Peabody Museum of Archaeology and Ethnology, Harvard University.

Graham, Ian

1963   Juan Galindo, Enthusiast. *Estudios de Cultura Maya* 3:11-36.

1982   *Yaxchilan.* Corpus of Maya Hieroglyphic Inscriptions, no. 3. Cambridge, MA: Peabody Museum of Archeology and Ethnology, Harvard University.

Graham, Ian, and Eric von Euw

1977   *Yaxchilan.* Corpus of Maya Hieroglyphic Inscriptions, no. 1. Cambridge, MA: Peabody Museum of Archeaology and Ethnology, Harvard University.

Grove, David C.

1981   Olmec Monuments: Mutilation as a Clue to Meaning. In *The Olmec and Their Neighbors,* edited by E. P. Benson, pp. 49-68. Washington, DC: Dumbarton Oaks.

Grube, Nikolai

1990   *A Reference to Waterlily Jaguar on Caracol Stela 16.* Copan Note 68. Austin, TX: Copan Acropolis Archaeological Project, Instituto Hondureño de Antropología e Historia.

1992   Classic Maya Dance. *Ancient Mesoamerica* 3:201-218.

Grube, Nikolai, and Werner Nahm

1994   A Census of Xibalba: A Complete Inventory of "Way" Characters on Maya Ceramics. In *The Maya Vase Book,* edited by B. Kerr, pp. 686-715. New York: Kerr Associates.

Grube, Nikolai, Linda Schele, and Federico Fahsen

1995   *The Tikal-Copan Connection: Evidence from External Relations, Version 2.* Copan Note 121. Austin, TX: Copan Acropolis Archaeological Project, Instituto Hondureño de Antropología e Historia.

Gutiérrez Mendoza, E.

1988   Cocinas comunales asociadas con agricultura intensiva (sistema de irrigación), en el sitio arqueológico de Kaminaljuyu / San Jorge. Tesis de Licenciatura en Arqueología. Guatemala City: Escuela de Historia, Universidad de San Carlos.

Hall, Jay, and René Viel
1994   Searching for the Preclassic Maya at Coopan, Honduras: Results of the 1993
        University of Queensland Field Season. In *Archaeology of the North*, edited by
        M. Sullivan, S. Brockwell, A. Webb, and F. D. McCarthy, pp. 381–393. Darwin,
        Northern Territory: Australian National University, North Australian Research
        Unit.
1998   The Formative of Copan. Paper presented at the 63rd Annual Meeting of the
        Society for American Archaeology, Seattle, WA.

Hammond, Norman
1991   *Cuello: An Early Maya Community in Belize.* Cambridge: Cambridge
        University Press.

Harbottle, Garman
1976   Activation Analysis in Archaeology, in *Radiochemistry*, G. W. A. Newton, editor.
        London: The Chemical Society.

Harris, John F.
1999   Dynasty Founder Yax K'uk' Mo' According to the Inscriptions. *Expedition*
        41(2):22–28.

Harrison, Peter D.
1970   The Central Acropolis, Tikal, Guatemala: A Preliminary Study of the Functions
        of Its Structural Components during the Late Classic Period. Ph.D. disserta-
        tion, Department of Anthropology, University of Pennsylvania.
1999   *The Lords of Tikal: Rulers of an Ancient Maya City.* London: Thames and
        Hudson.

Hatch, Marion Popenoe de
1993   *Inferencias de la economía y la organización sociopolítica en
        Kaminaljuyu durante los períodos Preclásico y Clásico Temprano.* Segundo
        y Tercer Foro de Arqueología de Chiapas, Serie Memorias, pp. 33–42. Mexico
        City: Gobierno del Estado de Chiapas, Instituto Chiapaneco de Cultura.
1996   The Highlands During the Classic Period. In *Piezas Maestras Mayas, Galería
        Guatemala III*, pp. 108–118. Guatemala City: Fundación G & T.
1997   *Kaminaljuyu / San Jorge: Evidencia arqueológica de la actividad
        económica en el Valle de Guatemala 300 a.C. a 300 d.C.* Guatemala City:
        Universidad del Valle de Guatemala.
2000   Kaminaljuyu Miraflores II: La naturaleza del cambio político al final del
        Preclásico. In *XIII Simposio de Investigaciones Arqueológicas en
        Guatemala, 1999*, edited by J. P. Laporte, H. L. Escobedo, A. C. de Suasnávar,
        and B. Arroyo, pp. 11–28. Guatemala City: Museo Nacional de Arqueología y
        Etnología.

Haviland, William A.
1988   Musical Hammocks at Tikal. In *Households and Community in the Mesoamerican Past*, edited by R. R. Wilk and W. Ashmore, pp. 121-134. Albuquerque: University of New Mexico Press.

Headrick, Annabeth E.
1999   The Street of the Dead . . . It Really Was: Mortuary Bundles at Teotihuacan. *Ancient Mesoamerica* 10:69-85.

Hellmuth, Nicholas M.
1975   *The Escuintla Hoards: Teotihuacan Art in Guatemala*. Foundation for Latin American Research Progress Reports 1, no. 2. Guatemala City: Foundation for Latin American Research.
1987   *Monsters und Menschen ib der Maya-Kunst*. Graz, Austria: Akademische Druck-u, Verlagsanstalt.

Helms, Mary W.
1979   *Ancient Panama: Chiefs in Search of Power*. Austin: University of Texas Press.
1988   *Ulysses' Sail: An Ethnolgraphic Odyssey of Power, Knowledge, and Geographical Distance*. Princeton, NJ: Princeton University Press.
1993   *Craft and the Kingly Ideal: Art, Trade, and Power*. Austin: University of Texas Press.

Henderson, John S.
1984   *Archaeology in Northwestern Honduras: Interim Reports of the Proyecto Arqueológico Sula 1*. Ithaca, NY: Intercollege Program in Archaeology, Cornell University.

Henderson, John S., and Marilyn Beaudry-Corbett, eds.
1993   *Pottery of Prehistoric Honduras*. Los Angeles: University of California, Los Angeles.

Hendon, Julia A.
1987   The Uses of Maya Structures: A Study of Architecture and Artifact Distribution at Sepulturas, Copan, Honduras. Ph.D. dissertation, Department of Anthropology, Pennsylvania State University.
1989   Elite Household Organization at Copan, Honduras: Analysis of Activity Distribution in the Sepulturas Zone. In *Household and Communities: Proceedings of the 21st Annual Chacmool Conference*, edited by S. MacEachern, D. J. W. Archer, and R. D. Garvin, pp. 371–380. Calgary, Alberta: Archaeological Association of the University of Calgary.

Herscovici, Dolfi Jr., Alberic G. Fiennes, M. Allgower, and Thomas P. Ruedi
1992   The Floating Shoulder: Ipsilateral, Clavicle, and Scapular Neck Fractures. *Journal of Bones, Joints and Surgery* 74B:362-364.

Hillson, Simon
1996   *Dental Anthropology*. Cambridge: Cambridge University Press.

Hirth, Kenneth G.
1988   Beyond the Maya Frontier: Cultural Interaction and Syncretism along the Central Honduran Corridor. In *The Southeast Classic Maya Zone*, edited by E. H. Boone and G. R. Willey, pp. 297-334. Washington, DC: Dumbarton Oaks.

Hirth, Kenneth G., Nedenia Kennedy, and Maynard Cliff
1993   El Cajón Region. In *Pottery of Prehistoric Honduras*, edited by J. S. Henderson and M. Beaudry-Corbett, pp. 214-232. Institute of Archaeology Monograph 35. Los Angeles: University of California, Los Angeles.

Hirth, Kenneth G., Gloria Lara Pinto, and George Hasemann, eds.
1989   *Archaeological Research in the El Cajon Region, Volume 1: Prehistoric Cultural Ecology*. Pittsburgh, PA: Department of Anthropology, University of Pittsburgh.

Houston, Stephen D.
1998   Classic Maya Depictions of the Built Environment. In *Function and Meaning in Classic Maya Architecture*, edited by S. D. Houston, pp. 333-372. Washington, DC: Dumbarton Oaks.
2000   Into the Minds of the Ancients: Advances in Maya Glyph Studies. *Journal of World Prehistory* 14(2):121-201.

Houston, Stephen D., and David Stuart
1989   *The Way Glyph: Evidence for 'Co-essences' among the Classic Maya*. Research Reports on Ancient Maya Writing No. 30. Washington, DC: Center for Maya Research.
1998   The Ancient Maya Self: Personhood and Portraiture in the Classic period. *RES: Anthropology and Aesthetics* 33:73-101.
2000   Peopling the Classic Maya Court. In *Royal Courts of the Ancient Maya*, edited by T. Inomata and S. D. Houston, pp. 54-83. Boulder, CO: Westview.

Houston, Stephen D., and Karl Taube
2000   An Archaeology of the Senses: Perception and Cultural Expression in Ancient Mesoamerica. *Cambridge Archaeological Journal* 10:253-288.

Ideberg, Rolf S., Sven Grevsten, and Sune Larsson
1995   Epidemiology of Scapular Fractures: Incidence and Classification of 338 Fractures. *Acta Orthopaedica Scandinavica* 66:395-397.

Imbelloni, José
1925   Sobre el Número de Tipos Fundamentales a los que Deben Referirse las
        Deformaciones Cráneas de los Pueblos Indígenas de Sud América: Algunos
        Resultados de una Nueva Aplicación de Morfología Exacta o
        Craneotrigonometría. *Anales de la Sociedad Argentina de Estudios
        Geográficos* 1(3):183–199.

Inomata, Takeshi, and Stephen D. Houston
2000   Opening the Royal Maya Court. In *Royal Courts of the Ancient Maya*, edited
        by T. Inomata and S. D. Houston, pp. 3–26. Boulder, CO: Westview.

Ivic, M.
1988   Proyecto Kaminaljuyu / San Jorge: algunos resultados e interpretaciones. In
        Primer Simposio de Investigaciones Arqueológicas en Guatemala, 1987,
        edited by J. P. Laporte and H. Escobedo, pp. 67–73. Guatemala City: Ministerio
        de Cultura y Deportes, Instituto de Antropología e Historia, y Asociación Tikal.

Jarquín Pacheco, Ana María, and Enrique Martínez Vargas
1982   Exploraciones en el lado Este de la Ciudadela (Estructuras 1G, 1R, 1Q y 1P).
        In *Memoria del Proyecto Arqueológico Teotihuacan 80-82*, edited by R.
        Cabrera, I. Rodríguez, and N. Morelos, pp. 19–47. Mexico City: Universidad
        Nacional Autónoma de México.
1991   Sacrificio de niños: Una ofrenda a la deidad de la lluvia en Teotihuacan.
        Arqueología 6:69–84.

Joesink-Mandeville, Leroy R. V.
1987   Yarumela, Honduras: Formative Period Cultural Conservatism and Diffusion.
        In *Interaction on the Southeast Mesoamerican Frontier*, edited by E. J.
        Robinson, pp. 196–214. BAR International Series 327. Oxford: British
        Archaeological Reports.

Johnston, Kevin J., and Nancy L. Gonlin
1998   What Do Houses Mean? Approaches to the Analysis of Classic Maya
        Commoner Residences. In *Function and Meaning in Classic Maya
        Architecture*, edited by S. D. Houston, pp. 141–185. Washington, DC:
        Dumbarton Oaks.

Jones, Christopher
1979   Tikal as a Trading Center. Paper presented at the 43rd International Congress
        of Americanists, Vancouver.
1991   Cycles of Growth at Tikal. In *Classic Maya Political History: Hieroglyphic
        and Archaeological Evidence*, edited by T. P. Culbert, pp. 102–127.
        Cambridge: Cambridge University Press.

Jones, Christopher, and Linton Satterthwaite
1982   *The Monuments and Inscriptions of Tikal: The Carved Monuments. Tikal Report No. 33, Part A*, University of Pennsylvania Museum Monograph 44. Philadelphia: University of Pennsylvania Museum of Archaeolgy and Anthropology.

Jones, Christopher, and Robert J. Sharer
1980   Archaeological Investigations in the Site Core of Quirigua. *Expedition* 23(1):11-19.

Kennedy, Nedenia
1981   The Formative Period Ceramic Sequence from Playa de los Muertos, Honduras. Ph. D. dissertation, Department of Anthropology, University of Illinois.

Kerr, Justin
1990   *The Maya Vase Book 2*. New York: Kerr Associates.
1992   *The Maya Vase Book 3*. New York: Kerr Associates.
2000   *The Maya Vase Book 6*. New York: Kerr Associates.

Kidder, Alfred V.
1940   Archaeological Problems of the Highland Maya. In *The Maya and Their Neighbors: Essays on Middle American Anthropology and Archaeology*, edited by C. L. Hay, R. L. Linton, S. K. Lothrop, H. L. Shapiro, and G. C. Vaillant, pp. 117-125. New York: Dover.

Kidder, Alfred V., Jesse D. Jennings, and Edwin M. Shook
1946   *Excavations at Kaminaljuyu, Guatemala*. Publication 561. Washington, DC: Carnegie Institution of Washington.

Killion, Thomas W.
1990   Cultivation Intensity and Residential Site Structure: An Ethnographic Examination of Peasant Agriculture in the Sierra de los Tuxlas, Veracruz, Mexico. *Latin American Antiquity* 1:191-215.
1992   Residential Ethnoarchaeology and Ancient Site Structure: Contemporary Farming and Prehistoric Settlement Agriculture at Matacapan, Veracruz, Mexico. In *Gardens of Prehistory: The Archaeology of Settlement Agriculture in Greater Mesoamerica*, edited by T. W. Killion, pp. 119-149. Tuscaloosa: University of Alabama Press.

Kolb, Michael J., and James E. Snead
1997   It's a Small World After All: Comparative Analysis of Community Organization in Archaeology. *American Antiquity* 62:609-628.

Kowalewski, Stephen A., Gary M. Feinman, Laura Finsten, Richard E. Blanton, and Linda M. Nicholas
1989   *Monte Albán's Hinterland, Part II: Prehispanic Settlement Patterns in Tlacolula, Etla, and Ocotlan, the Valley of Oaxaca, Mexico*. Memoirs of the University of Michigan Museum of Anthropology No. 23. Ann Arbor: University of Michigan Museum of Anthropology.

Krueger, Harold W.
1985   Sr Isotopes and Sr/Ca in Bone. Paper presented at the Bone Mineralization Conference, Warrenton, VA.

Kubler, George
1967   *The Iconography of the Art of Teotihuacan*. Washington, DC: Dumbarton Oaks.
1984   *The Art and Architecture of Ancient America*. Middlesex, Harmondsworth: Penguin.

Landa, Diego de
1938   *Relación de las Cosas de Yucatán*. Mérida: Edición Yucateca.

Langley, James C.
1992   Teotihuacan Sign Clusters: Emblem or Articulation? In *Art, Ideology, and the City of Teotihuacan*, edited by J. C. Berlo, pp. 247–280. Washinton, DC: Dumbarton Oaks.

Laporte, Juan Pedro
1985   Arquitectura Clásica Temprana de Tikal y el modo Talud-Tablero. *Antropología e Historia de Guatemala* 8:3–48.
1989   *Alternativas del Clásico Temprano en la Relación Tikal-Teotihuacan: Grupo 6C-XVI, Tikal, Guatemala*. Mexico City: Universidad Nacional Autónoma de México.

Laporte, Juan Pedro, and Vilma Fialko
1990   New Perspectives on Old Problems: Dynastic References for the Early Classic at Tikal. In *Vision and Revision in Maya Studies*, edited by F. Clancy and P. Harrison, pp. 33–66. Albuquerque: University of New Mexico Press.
1995   Un Reencuentro con Mundo Perdido, Tikal, Guatemala. *Ancient Mesoamerica* 6:41–95.

Larios, Rudy, David W. Sedat, and Fernando López
1993   Consolidación e investigación en el corte arqueológico de la acrópolis de Copan, Honduras. In *VI Simposio de Investigaciones Arqueológicas en Guatemala, 1992*, edited by J. P. Laporte, H. L. Escobedo, and S. Villagran de Brady, pp. 517–526. Guatemala City: Ministerio de Cultura y Deportes, Instituto de Antropología e Historia, y Asociación Tikal.

LeCount, Lisa
1999   Polychrome Pottery, Primitive Wealth and Social Power in the Late and
        Terminal Classic Lowland Maya Society. *Latin American Antiquity*
        10(3):239-258.

Leventhal, Richard M.
1979   Settlement Patterns at Copan, Honduras. Ph.D. dissertation. Department of
        Anthropology, Harvard University.

Leyenaar, Ted J. J.
1978   *Ulama: The Perpetuation in Mexico of the Pre-Spanish Ball Game
        Ullamaliztli*. Leiden, The Netherlands: Rijksmuseum voor Volkenkunde.

Linné, Sigvald
1942   *Mexican Highland Cultures: Archaeological Researches at Teotihuacan,
        Calpulalpan, and Chalchicomula in 1934-1935*. Publication No. 7.
        Stockholm: Ethnographic Museum of Sweden.

Longinelli, Antonio
1984   Oxygen Isotopes in Mammal Bone Phosphate: A New Tool for
        Paleohydrological and Paleoclimatological Research? *Geochimica et
        Cosmochimica Acta* 48:385-390.

Longyear, John M.
1952   *Copan Ceramics: A Study of Southeastern Maya Pottery*. Publication 597.
        Washington, DC: Carnegie Institution of Washington.

Looper, Mathew G.
1995   The Sculpture Programs of Butz'-Tiliw, An Eighth-Century Maya King of
        Quirigua, Guatemala. Ph.D. dissertation, Department of Anthropology,
        University of Texas at Austin.
1999   New Perspectives on the Late Classic Political History of Quirigua,
        Guatemala. *Ancient Mesoamerica* 10:263-280.

López Austin, Alfredo
1987   The Masked God of Fire. In *The Aztec Templo Mayor*, edited by E. H. Boone,
        pp. 257-291. Washington, DC: Dumbarton Oaks.

López Olivares, Nora M.
1997   Cultural Odontology: Dental Alterations from Petén, Guatemala. In *Bones of
        the Maya: Studies of Ancient Skeletons*, edited by S. Whittington and D. M.
        Reed, pp. 105-115. Washington DC: Smithsonian Institution Press.

Loten, H. Stanley, and David M. Pendergast
1984   *A Lexicon for Maya Architecture*. Archaeology Monograph 8. Toronto: Royal
        Ontario Museum.

Lounsbury, Floyd G.
1989   The Names of a King: Hieroglyphic Variants as a Key to Decipherment. In
        Word and Image in Maya Culture, edited by W. Hanks and D. S. Rice, pp.
        73–91. Salt Lake City: University of Utah Press.

Lovejoy, C. Owen, Richard S. Meindl, Thomas R. Pryzbeck, and Robert P. Mensforth
1985   Chronological Metamorphosis of the Auricular Surface of the Ilium: A New
        Method for the Determination of Adult Skeletal Age at Death. *Journal of
        Physical Anthropology* 68: 15–28.

Manahan, Kam
2003   Reevaluating the Decline of Classic Maya Kingdoms: A Case Study from
        Copan, Honduras. Ph.D. dissertation. Department of Anthropology, Vanderbilt
        University.

Mann, Michael
1986   *The Sources of Social Power: Volume 1, A History of Power from the
        Beginning to A.D. 1760.* Cambridge: Cambridge University Press.

Manzanilla, Linda
1998   El Estado Teotihuacano. *Arqueología Mexicana* 6(32):22–31.

Manzanilla, Linda, and Carlos Serrano, eds.
1999   *Prácticas Funerarias en la Ciudad de los Dioses: Los Enterramientos
        humanos de la Antigua Teotihuacan.* Mexico City: Instituto de
        Investigaciones Antropológicas, Universidad Nacional Autónoma de México.

Marcus, Joyce
1976   *Emblem and State in the Classic Maya Lowlands.* Washington, DC:
        Dumbarton Oaks.
1980   Zapotec Writing. *Scientific American* 242:50–64.
1983a   Lowland Maya Archaeology at the Crossroads. *American Antiquity*
        48:454–488.
1983b   The Style of the Huamelulpan Stone Monuments. In *The Cloud People:
        Divergent Evolution of the Zapotec and Mixtec Civilizations*, edited by K.V.
        Flannery and J. Marcus, pp. 125–126. New York: Academic.
1992a   Dynamic Cycles of Mesoamerican States. *National Geographic Research &
        Exploration* 8:392–411.
1992b   *Mesoamerican Writing Systems: Propaganda, Myth, and History in Four
        Ancient Civilizations.* Princeton, NJ: Princeton University Press.
1993   Ancient Maya Political Organization. In *Lowland Maya Civilization in the
        Eighth Century A. D.*, edited by J. A. Sabloff and J. S. Henderson, pp. 111–183.
        Washington, DC: Dumbarton Oaks.
1994   A Zapotec Inauguration in Comparative Perspective. In *Caciques and their
        People*, edited by J. Marcus and J. F. Zeitlin, pp. 245–274. University of
        Michigan Museum of Anthropology Anthropological Paper 89. Ann Arbor:
        University of Michigan Museum of Anthropology.

1995 Where Is Lowland Maya Archaeology Headed? *Journal of Archaeological Research* 3(1):3–53.
1998 The Peaks and Valleys of Ancient States: An Extension of the Dynamic Model. In *Archaic States*, edited by G. M. Feinman and J. Marcus, pp. 59–94. Santa Fe, NM: SAR.
2003 Teotihuacan and the Maya. In *Teotihuacan and the Maya: Reinterpreting Early Classic Interaction*, edited by G. Braswell. Austin: University of Texas Press.

Marcus, Joyce, and Kent V. Flannery
1994 Ancient Zapotec Ritual and Religion: The Application of the Direct Historical Approach. In *The Ancient Mind: Elements of Cognitive Archaeology*, edited by C. Renfrew and E. B. W. Zubrow, pp. 55–74. Cambridge: Cambridge University Press.
1996 *Zapotec Civilization: How Urban Society Evolved in Mexico's Oaxaca Valley*. London: Thames and Hudson.

Martin, Simon
1997 The Painted King List: A Commentary on the Codex-style Dynastic Vases. In *The Maya Vase Book: A Corpus of Rollout Photographs of Maya Vases*, vol. 5, edited by J. Kerr, pp. 847–863. New York: Kerr Associates.
2000 Court and Realm: Architectural Signatures in the Classic Maya Southern Lowlands. In *Royal Courts of the Ancient Maya, Volume 1: Theory, Comparison, and Synthesis*, edited by T. Inomata and S. D. Houston, pp. 168–194. Boulder, CO: Westview.

Martin, Simon, and Nickolai Grube
1995 Maya Superstates. *Archaeology* 48(6):41–46.
2000 *Chronicle of Maya Kings and Queens*. London: Thames and Hudson.

Martínez López, M. W., and P. A. Juárez
1995 Entierros humanos del Proyecto Especial Monte Albán 1992–1994. In *Entierros humanos de Monte Albán: Dos Estudios*, edited by M. Winter, pp. 79–244. Oaxaca City, Mexico: Instituto Nacional de Antropología e Historia.

Mata Amado, G., and R. E. Hansen
1992 El diente incrustado temprano de Nakbe. In *V Simposio de Investigaciones Arqueológicas en Guatemala, 1993*, edited by J. P. Laporte and H. Escobedo, pp. 237–242. Guatemala City: Ministerio de Cultura y Deportes, Instituto de Antropología e Historia, y Asociación Tikal.

Matheny, Ray T.
1980 *El Mirador, Petén, Guatemala: An Interim Report*. Papers of the New World Archaeological Foundation No. 45. Provo, UT: Brigham Young University.
1986 Investigations at El Mirador, Petén, Guatemala. *National Geographic Research & Exploration* 2:332–353.

Mathews, Peter

1985   Maya Early Classic Monuments and Inscriptions. In *A Consideration of the Early Classic Period in the Maya Lowlands*, edited by G. R. Willey and P. Mathews, pp. 5–54. Albany, NY: Institute for Mesoamerican Studies, SUNY.

Matos Moctezuma, Eduardo

1988   *The Great Temple of the Aztecs: Treasures of Tenochtitlan*. London: Thames and Hudson.

Maudslay, Alfred P.

1886   Explorations of the Ruins and Site of Copan, Central America. *Proceedings of the Royal Geographical Society* 8:568–594.

1889   *Biologia Centrali-Americana: Contributions to the Knowledge of the Fauna*
–1902   *and Flora of Mexico and Central America*. London: R. H. Porter and Dulau.

McFarlane, William J., and Marcello A. Canuto

2000   Analysis of the Lithics from Los Achiotes, Honduras: Considering a Preclassic Community. Paper presented at the 65th Annual Meeting of the Society for American Archaeology, Philadelphia, PA.

Merbs, Charles F.

1989   Trauma. In *Reconstrution of Life from the Skeleton*, edited by M. Y. Iscan and K. A. R. Kennedy, pp. 161–189. New York: Alan R. Liss.

Merwin, Raymond E., and George C. Valliant

1932   *The Ruins of Holmul, Guatemala*. Memoirs of the Peabody Museum of Archaeology and Ethnology, 3, no. 2. Cambridge, MA: Peabody Museum of Archaeology and Ethnology, Harvard University.

Michels, Joseph W., ed.

1979a   *Settlement Pattern Excavation at Guatemala*. University Park: Pennsylvania State University Press.

Michels, Joseph W.

1979b   *The Kaminaljuyu Chiefdom*. University Park: Pennsylvania State University Press.

Miller, Arthur G.

1973   *The Mural Painting of Teotihuacan*. Washington, DC: Dumbarton Oaks.

1986   *Maya Rulers of Time: A Study of Architectural Sculpture at Tikal, Guatemala*. Philadelphia: University of Pennsylvania Musuem of Archeology and Anthropology.

Miller, Arthur G., ed.

1983   *Highland-Lowland Interaction in Mesoamerica: Interdisciplinary Approaches*. Washington, DC: Dumbarton Oaks.

Miller, Mary Ellen
1986a Copan, Honduras: Conference with a Perished City. In *City States of the Maya: Art and Architecture*, edited by E. P. Benson, pp. 72–108. Denver, CO: Rocky Mountain Institute for Pre-Columbian Studies.
1986b *The Murals of Bonampak*. Princeton, NJ: Princeton University Press.

Miller, Virginia E.
1991 *The Frieze of the Palace of the Stuccoes, Acanceh, Yucatan, Mexico*. Studies in Pre-Columbian Art and Archaeology 31. Washington, DC: Dumbarton Oaks.

Miller, W. E., and J. Ada
1992 Injuries to the Shoulder Girdle. In *Skeletal Trauma: Fractures, Dislocations, Ligamentous Injuries*, edited by D. G. Browner, J. B. Jupiter, A. M. Levine, and P. G. Trafton, pp. 1291–1310. Philadelphia: Saunders.

Millon, René
1981 Teotihuacan: City, State, and Civilization. In *Supplement to the Handbook of Middle American Indians: Archaeology*, edited by J. Sabloff, pp. 198–243. Handbook of Middle American Indians 1, V. R. Bricker, general editor. Austin: University of Texas Press.

Milner, George R., and Jesper L. Boldsen
n.d. Estimated Ages of Two Copan Skeletons. Manuscript in preparation.

Milner, George R., Jesper L. Boldsen, and Bethany M. Usher
1997 Age-at-Death Determination Using Revised Scoring Procedures for Age-Progressive Skeletal Traits. *American Journal of Physical Anthropology, Supplement* 24:170.

Milner, G. R., J. L. Boldsen, and J. W. Wood
2000 Paleodemography. In *Biological Anthropology of the Human Skeleton*, edited by M. A. Katzenberg and S. R. Saunders, pp. 467–497. New York: Wiley-Liss.

Molloy, John P., and William L. Rathje
1974 Sexploitation among the Late Classic Maya. In *Mesoamerican Archaeology, New Approaches*, edited by N. Hammond, pp. 431–444. Austin: University of Texas Press.

Morales, Alfonso
1989 Reporte de Excavación Lado Norte de la Estructura 10L-16. Manuscript on file at the Instituto Hondureño de Antropología e Historia, Tegucigalpa and Copan.

Morales, Alfonso, Julia C. Miller, and Linda Schele
1990 *The Dedication Stair of "Ante" Temple*. Copan Note 76. Austin, TX: Copan Acropolis Archaeological Project, Instituto Hondureño de Antropología e Historia.

Morley, Frances R., and Sylvanus G. Morley
1938   *The Age and Provenance of the Leyden Plaque*. Publication 509. Washington, DC: Carnegie Institution of Washington.

Morley, Sylvanus G.
1920   *The Inscriptions at Copan*. Publication 219. Washington, DC: Carnegie Institution of Washington.
1939   Recent Epigraphic Discoveries at the Ruins of Copan, Honduras. In *So Live the Works of Men*, edited by D. D. Brand and F. E. Harvey, pp. 277-293. Albuquerque: University of New Mexico Press.

Murdy, Carson N.
1990   Tradiciones de arquitectura prehispánica en el Valle de Guatemala. *Anales de la Academia de Geografía e Historia de Guatemala* 54:349-397.

Murillo, Saul
1989   Investigaciones de corte arqueológico, Ruínas de Copan. Manuscript on file at the Instituto Hondureño de Antropología e Historia, Tegucigalpa and Copan.

Museé Rath
1998   *Mexique: Terre des Dieux*. Geneva: Musées d'Art et d'Histoire.

Nakamura, Seiichi
1991   Conclusiones. In *Investigaciones Arqueológicas en La Región de La Entrada*, vol. 2, edited by S. Nakamura, K. Aoyama, and E. Uratsuji, pp. 251-291. San Pedro Sula, Honduras: Instituto Hondureno de Antropología e Historia and Servicio de Voluntarios Japoneses para la Cooperación con el Extranjero.
2000   Informe Preliminar: Las Excavaciones de Rescate en el Cuadrante 10J, al sur de las Estelas 5 y 6, Copan, Honduras. Manuscript on file at the Instituto Hondureño de Antropología e Historia, Tegucigalpa and Copan.

Nakamura, Seiichi, Kazuo Aoyama, and Eiji Uratsuji
1991   *Investigaciones Arqueológicas en La Región de La Entrada*, tomos I, II, III. San Pedro Sula, Honduras: Instituto Hondureño de Antropología e Historia and Servicio de Voluntarios Japoneses para la Cooperación con el Extranjero.

Navarrete, Carlos C., and L. Luján Muñoz
1986   *El gran montículo de La Culebra*. Mexico City: Academia de Geografía e Historia, Universidad Nacional Autónoma de México.

Neer, Charles S., and Charles A. Rockwood
1984   Fractures and Dislocations of the Shoulder. Part I: Fractures about the Shoulder. In *Fractures in Adults*, edited by C. A. Rockwook and D. P. Green, pp. 675-721. Philadelphia, PA: Lippincott.

Neff, Hector
2000   Neutron Activation Analysis for Provenance Determination in Archaeology. In *Modern Analytical Methods in Art and Archaeology*, edited by E. Ciliberto and G. Spoto. Chemical Analysis, vol. 155, Winefordner, general editor. New York: Wiley.

Netting, Robert M., Richard R. Wilk, and Eric J. Arnould, eds.
1984   *Households: Comparative and Historical Studies of the Domestic Group.* Berkeley: University of California Press.

Nicolis, G., and I. Prigogine
1977   *Self-Organization in Nonequilibrium Systems.* New York: Wiley.

Ohi, Kuniaki
2001   *La Culebra, Kaminaljuyu.* Tokyo: Museo del Tabaco y Sal.

Ohi, Kuniaki, and Nobuyuki Ito
1994   Relación entre las estructuras y los objetos encontrados en Mongoy, Kaminaljuyu. In *Kaminaljuyu*, edited by K. Ohi, pp. 177-182. Tokyo: Museo del Tabaco y Sal.

Olson, Gerald W.
1979   Effects of Activities of the Ancient Maya upon Some of the Soils in Central America. *Mexicón* 1:20-22.

Pahl, Gary W.
1976   A Successor-Relationship Complex and Associated Signs. In *The Art, Iconography, and Dynastic History of Palenque, Part 3*, edited by M. G. Robertson, pp. 35-44. Pebble Beach, CA: Robert Louis Stevenson School.

Palmer, M. R., and H. Elderfield
1985   Sr isotope Composition of Sea Water over the Past 75 Myr. *Nature* 314:527-529.

Parsons, Lee A.
1986   *The Origins of Maya Art: Monumental Stone Sculpture of Kaminaljuyu, Guatemala, and the Southern Pacific Coast.* Studies in Precolumbian Art and Archaeology No. 28. Washington, DC: Dumbarton Oaks.
1988   The Iconography of Blood and Sacrifice in the Murals of the White Patio, Atetelco, Teotihuacan. Ph.D. dissertation, Department of Anthropology, University of Texas at Austin.

Pasztory, Esther
1976   *The Murals of Tepantitla, Teotihuacan.* New York: Garland.
1998   *Pre-Columbian Art.* Cambridge: Cambridge University Press.

Pauketat, Timothy R.

1994   *The Ascent of Chiefs: Cahokia and Mississippian Politics in Native North America.* Tuscaloosa: University of Alabama Press.

2000   Politicization and Community in the Pre-Columbian Mississippi Valley. In *The Archaeology of Communities: A New World Perspective*, edited by M. A. Canuto and J. Yaeger, pp. 16–43. London: Routledge.

Paynter, Robert

1989   The Archaeology of Equality and Inequality. *Annual Review of Anthropology* 18:369–399.

Perlman, Isadore, and Frank Asaro

1969   Pottery Analysis by Neutron Activation*I. *Archaeometry* 11:21–52.

Pendergast, David M.

1972   Altun Ha, Honduras (Belize): Temporada 1966–1968. *Estudios de Cultura Maya* 8:35–56.

1988   *Lamanai Stela 9: The Archaeological Context.* Research Reports on Ancient Maya Writing No. 20. Washington, DC: Center for Maya Research.

Peraza Lope, Carlos A.

1999   Mayapan: Ciudad-capital del Posclásico. *Arqueología Mexicana* 7(37):48–53.

Peregrine, Peter

1991   Prehistoric Chiefdoms on the American Midcontinent: A World System Based on Prestige Goods. In *Core/Periphery Relations in Precapitalist Worlds*, edited by C. Chase-Dunn and T. Hall, pp. 193–211. Boulder, CO: Westview.

Peregrine, Peter, and Gary M. Feinman

1996   *Pre-Columbian World Systems.* Madison, WI: Prehistory Press.

Perry, Clayton R., John A. Elstrom, and A. M. Pankovich, eds.

1995   *Handbook of Fractures.* New York: McGraw Hill.

Phenice, Terrall

1969   A Newly Developed Visual Method of Sexing the Os Pubis. *American Journal of Physical Anthropology* 30:297–301.

Pope, Kevin O.

1987   The Ecology and Economy of The Formative–Classic Transition Along the Ulua River, Honduras. In *Interaction on the Southeast Mesoamerican Frontier*, edited by E. J. Robinson, pp. 95–128. BAR International Series 327. Oxford: British Archaeological Reports.

Price, Barbara J.
1978   Secondary State Formation: An Explanatory Model. In *Origins of the State: The Anthropology of Political Evolution*, edited by R. Cohen and E. R. Service, pp. 161–186. Philadelphia, PA: Institute for the Study of Human Issues.

Price, T. Douglas, Gisela Grupe, and Peter Schrörter
1994a   Reconstruction of Migration Patterns in the Bell Beaker Period by Stable Strontium Isotope Analysis. *Applied Geochemistry* 9:413–417.
1998   Migration and Mobility in the Bell Beaker Period in Central Europe. *Antiquity* 72:405–411.

Price, T. Douglas, Clark M. Johnson, Joseph A. Ezzo, Jonathan A. Ericson, and James H. Burton
1994b   Residential Mobility in the Prehistoric Southwest United States: A Preliminary Study Using Strontium Isotope Analysis. *Journal of Archaeological Sciences* 24:315–330.

Price, T. Douglas, Linda Manzanilla, and William D. Middleton
2000   Immigration and the Ancient City of Teotihuacan in Mexico: A Study Using Strontium Isotopes Ratios in Human Bone and Teeth. *Journal of Archaeological Sciences* 27:903–913.

Proskouriakoff, Tatiana
1950   *A Study of Classic Maya Sculpture*. Publication 593. Washington, DC: Carnegie Institution of Washington.
1993   *Maya History*, edited by R. Joyce. Austin: University of Texas Press.

Puleston, Dennis E.
1979   An Epistemological Pathology and the Collapse, or Why the Maya Kept the Short Count. In *Maya Archaeology and Ethnohistory*, edited by N. Hammond and G. R. Willey, pp. 63–71. Austin: University of Texas Press.

Rands, Robert L., and Ronald L. Bishop
1980   Resource Procurement Zones and Patterns of Ceramic Exchange in the Palenque Region, Mexico. In *Models and Methods in Regional Exchange*, edited by R. E. Fry, pp. 19–46. SAA Paper No. 1. Washington, DC: Society for American Archaeology.

Rathje, William L.
1983   To the Salt of the Earth: Some Comments on Household Archaeology among the Maya. In *Prehistoric Settlement Patterns: Essays in Honor of Gordon R. Willey*, edited by E. Z. Vogt and R. M. Leventhal, pp. 23–34. Albuquerque, NM, and Cambridge, MA: University of New Mexico Press and Peabody Museum of Archaeology and Ethnology.

Rattray, Eveyn C., and Garman Harbottle
1992   Neutron Activation Analysis and Numerical Taxonomy of Thin Orange
        Ceramics from the Manufacturing Sites of Río Carnero, Puebla, Mexico. In
        Chemcal Characterization of Ceramic Pastes in Archaeology, edited by H.
        Neff, pp. 221-232. Monographs in World Archaeology No. 7. Madison, WI:
        Prehistory Press.

Reents-Budet, Dorie, Joseph W. Ball, Ronald L. Bishop, Virginia Fields, and Barbara
        MacLeod
1994a   *Painting the Maya Universe: Royal Ceramics of the Classic Period.* Durham,
        NC: Duke University Press.

Reents-Budet, Dorie, Joseph W. Ball, Jennifer Taschek, and Ronald L. Bishop
2000   Out of the Palace Dumps: Ceramic Production and Use at Buenavista del
        Cayo, Belize. *Ancient Mesoamerica* 11:99-121.

Reents-Budet, Dorie, Ronald L. Bishop, and Barbara MacLeod
1994b   Painting Styles, Workshop Locations and Pottery Production. In *Painting the
        Maya Universe: Royal Ceramics of the Classic Period*, edited by D. Reents-
        Budet, pp. 164-233. Durham, NC: Duke University Press.

Reents-Budet, Dorie, and T. Patrick Culbert
1999   Las ofrendas del período Clásico Temprano de Tikal y Kaminaljuyu:
        Relaciones regionales e 'internacionales.' In *XIII Simposio de
        Investigaciones Arqueológicas en Guatemala*. Guatemala City: Ministerio de
        Cultura y Deportes, Instituto de Antropología e Historia, y Asociación Tikal.

Reents-Budet, Dorie, Simon Martin, Richard D. Hansen, and Ronald L. Bishop
in press Codex-Style Pottery: Recovering Context, Narrative, and Meaning. *Ancient
        Mesoamerica*.

Renfrew, Colin
1972   *The Emergence of Civilization: The Cyclades and the Aegean in the Third
        Millennium B.C.* London: Methuen.
1973   Monuments, Mobilization, and Social Organization in Neolithic Wessex. In *The
        Explanation of Culture Change: Models in Prehistory*, edited by C. Renfew,
        pp. 539-558. Pittsburgh, PA: University of Pittsburgh Press.
1986   Introduction: Peer Polity Interaction and Socio-Political Change. In *Peer Polity
        Interaction and Socio-Political Change*, edited by C. Renfrew and J. Cherry,
        pp. 1-18. Cambridge: Cambridge University Press.

Reyna Robles, Rosa María, and Felipe Rodríguez Betancourt
1990   La época clásica en el estado de Guerrero. In *La Epoca Clásica: Nuevos
        Hallazgos, Nuevas Ideas*, edited by A. C. de Méndez, pp. 221-236. Mexico
        City: Instituto Nacional de Antropología e Historia.

Reynolds, J.
1979   Residential Architecture at Kaminaljuyu. In *Settlement Pattern Excavation at Kaminaljuyu*, edited by J. Michels, pp. 223-276. University Park: Pennsylvania State University Press.

Rice, Prudence
1999   Rethinking Classic Lowland Maya Pottery Censers. *Ancient Mesoamerica* 10:25-50.

Riese, Berthold
1986   Late Classic Relationship Between Copan and Quirigua: Some Epigraphic Evidence. In *The Southeast Maya Periphery*, edited by P. A. Urban and E. M. Schortman, pp. 94-101. Austin: University of Texas Press.
1988   Epigraphy of the Southeast Classic Maya Zone in Relation to Other Parts of Mesoamerica. In *The Southeast Classic Maya Zone*, edited by E. H. Boone and G. R. Willey, pp. 67-94. Washington, DC: Dumbarton Oaks.
1992   The Copan Dynasty. In *Epigraphy*, edited by V. R. Bricker, pp. 128-153. Supplement to the Handbook of Middle American Indian 5, V. R. Bricker, general editor. Austin: University of Texas Press.

Robertson, Merle Greene
1985   *The Late Buildings of the Palace.* The Sculpture of Palenque 3. Princeton, NJ: Princeton University Press.

Robicsek, Francis, and Donald M. Hales
1981   *The Maya Book of the Dead: The Ceramic Codex*. Charlottesville: University of Virginia Art Museum.

Robinson, Eugenia J., ed.
1987   *Interaction on the Southeast Mesoamerican Frontier*. Oxford: British Archaeological Reports.

Rogers, J. Daniel, and Bruce D. Smith, eds.
1995   *Mississippian Communities and Households*. Tuscaloosa: University of Alabama Press.

Rodgers, Lee F.
1982   *Radiology of Skeletal Trauma*. New York: Churchill Livingstone.

Romano, A.
1987   Inconografía cefálica maya. In *Memorias del Primer Coloquio Internacional de Mayistas*, pp. 1413-1474. Mexico City: Universidad Nacional Autónoma de México.

Romero Molina, Javier
1958   *Multilaciones Dentarias Prehispánicas de México y América en general*. Mexico City: Instituto Nacional de Antropología e Historia.

1986a   *Catálogo de la colección de dientes mutilados prehispánicos, IV parte.* Mexico City: Instituto Nacional de Antropología e Historia.
1986b   Nuevos datos sobre la mutilación dentaria en Mesoamérica. *Anales de Antropología* 23:349-365.

Roscoe, Paul
1993   Practice and Political Centralization: A New Approach to Political Evolution. *Current Anthropology* 94:640-656.

Rose, Jerome C., Keith Condon, and Alan H. Goodman
1985   Diet and Dentitions: Developmental Disturbances. In *The Analysis of Prehistoric Diets*, edited by R. I. Gilbert and J. H. Mielke, pp. 281-306. New York: Academic.

Roys, Ralph L.
1967   *The Book of Chilam Balam of Chumayel.* Norman: University of Oklahoma Press.

Rue, David J.
1987   Early Agriculture and Early Postclassic Occupation in Western Honduras. *Nature* 326:285-286.

Runciman, Walter G.
1982   Origins of States: The Case of Archaic Greece. *Comparative Studies in Society and History* 24:351-377.

Sabloff, Jeremy A.
1990   *The New Archaeology and the Ancient Maya.* New York: Freeman.

Sabloff, Jeremy A., ed.
2003   *Tikal: Dynasties, Foreigners, & Affairs of State: Advancing Maya Archaeology.* Santa Fe, NM: SAR.

Sahagún, Fray Bernadino de
1950   *Florentine Codex: General History of the Things of New Spain.* Translated by A. J. O. Anderson and C. E. Dibble. Santa Fe, NM: SAR.

Sanders, William T.
1974   From Chiefdom to State: Political Evolution at Kaminaljuyu, Guatemala. In *Reconstructing Complex Societies*, edited by Charlotte B. Moore. Supplement to Bulletin of the American Schools of Oriental Research 20:97-116.
1981   Classic Maya Settlement Patterns and Ethnographic Analogy. In *Lowland Maya Settlement Patterns*, edited by W. Ashmore, pp. 351-369. Albuquerque: University of New Mexico Press.
1989   Household, Lineage, and the State in 8th-century Copan. In *House of the Bacabs, Copan, Honduras: A Study of the Iconography, Epigraphy, and Social Context of a Maya Elite Structure*, edited by D. L. Webster, pp. 89-105. Washington, DC: Dumbarton Oaks.

Sanders, William T., ed.
1986   *Excavaciones en el Área Urbana de Copan: Proyecto Arqueológico Copan,
        Fase II*, tomos I, II, III. Tegucigalpa: Proyecto Arqueológico Copan, Segunda
        Fase, Secretaría de Cultura y Turismo, Instituto Hondureño de Antropología e
        Historia.

Sanders, William T., and Joseph W. Michels, eds.
1977   *Teotihuacan and Kaminaljuyu: A Study in Prehistoric Culture Contact.*
        University Park: Pennsylvania State University Press.

Sanders, William T., and Barbara J. Price
1968   *Mesoamerica: The Evolution of a Civilization.* New York: Random House.

Sanders, William T., and David L. Webster
1998   The Mesoamerican Urban Tradition. *American Anthropologist* 90:521-546.

Santley, Robert S., Michael J. Berman, and Rani T. Alexander
1991   The Politicization of the Mesoamerican Ballgame and Its Implications for the
        Interpretation of the Distribution of Ballcourts in Central Mexico. In *The
        Mesoamerican Ballgame*, edited by D. R. Wilcox and V. L. Scarborough, pp.
        3-24. Tucson: University of Arizona Press.

Saturno, William A.
1996   Archaeological Investigations at Río Amarillo, Honduras, 1996 Season.
        Manuscript on file at the Instituto Hondureño de Antropología e Historia,
        Tegucigalpa and Copan.
2000   In the Shadow of the Acropolis: Río Amarillo and its Role in the Copan Polity.
        Ph.D. dissertation, Department of Anthropology, Harvard University.

Saul, Frank P.
1972   *The Human Skeletal Remains of Altar de Sacrificios: An Osteobiographic
        Analysis.* Memoirs of the Peabody Museum of Archaeology and Ethnology,
        vol. 63, no. 2. Cambridge, MA: Peabody Museum of Archaeology and
        Ethnology, Harvard University.

Saul, Frank P., and Julie M. Saul
1989   Osteobiography: A Maya Example. In *Reconstruction of Life from the
        Skeleton*, edited by M.Y. Iscan and K.A. R. Kennedy, pp. 287-302. New York:
        Liss.

Schele, Linda
1987a   *The Protagonist and Dating of Stela E.* Copan Note 25. Austin, TX: Copan
        Acropolis Archaeological Project, Instituto Hondureño de Antropología e
        Historia.
1987b   *Stela I and the Founding of the City of Copan.* Copan Note 30. Austin, TX:
        Copan Acropolis Archaeological Project, Instituto Hondureño de Antropología
        e Historia.

1989 *A Brief Commentary on the Top of Altar Q*. Copan Note 66. Austin, TX: Copan Acropolis Archaeological Project, Instituto Hondureño de Antropología e Historia.

1990a *The Early Classic Dynastic History of Copan: Interim Report, 1989*. Copan Note 70. Austin, TX: Copan Acropolis Archaeological Project, Instituto Hondureño de Antropología e Historia.

1990b *Early Quirigua and the Kings of Copan*. Copan Note 75. Austin, TX: Copan Acropolis Archaeological Project, Instituto Hondureño de Antropología e Historia.

1990c *The Founders of Lineages at Copan and Other Sites*. Copan Note 8. Austin: Copan Acropolis Archaeological Project, Instituto Hondureño de Antropología e Historia.

1990d *Two Early Monuments from Copan*. Copan Note 82. Austin, TX: Copan Acropolis Archaeological Project, Instituto Hondureño de Antropología e Historia.

1992 The Founders of Lineages at Copan and Other Maya Sites. *Ancient Mesoamerica* 3:135-144.

Schele, Linda, and David A. Freidel
1990 *A Forest of Kings: The Untold Story of the Ancient Maya*. New York: William Morrow.

Schele, Linda, and Nikolai Grube
1992 *The Founding Events at Copan*. Copan Note 107. Austin, TX: Copan Acropolis Archaeological Project, Instituto Hondureño de Antropología e Historia.

Schele, Linda, Nikolai Grube, and Federico Fahsen
1993 *The Tikal-Copan Connection: The Copan Evidence, Version 2*. Copan Note 122. Austin, TX: Copan Acropolis Archaeological Project, Instituto Hondureño de Antropología e Historia.

1994 *The Xukpi Stone: A Newly Discovered Early Classic Inscription from the Copan Acropolis: Part II: The Epigraphy*. Copan Note 114. Austin, TX: Copan Acropolis Archaeological Project, Instituto Hondureño de Antropología e Historia.

Schele, Linda, and Peter Mathews
1998 *The Code of Kings*. New York: Simon and Schuster.

Schele, Linda, and Mary Ellen Miller
1986 *The Blood of Kings: Dynasty and Ritual in Maya Art*. Fort Worth, TX, and New York: Kimball Art Museum and George Braziller.

Schortman, Edward M., and Seiichi Nakamura
1991 A Crisis of Identity: Late Classic Competition and Interaction on the Southeast Maya Periphery. *Latin American Antiquity* 2:311-336.

Schortman, Edward M., and Patricia A. Urban
1991   Patterns of Late Preclassic Interaction and the Formation of Complex Society in the Southeast Maya Periphery. In *The Formation of Complex Societies in Southeastern Mesoamerica*, edited by W. R. Fowler, Jr., pp. 121–142. Boca Raton, FL: CRC Press.
1994a Living on the Edge: Core/Periphery Relations in Ancient Southeastern Mesoamerica. *Current Anthropology* 35(4):410–413.

Schortman, Edward M., and Patricia A. Urban, eds.
1994b Sociopolitical Hierarchy and Craft Production: The Economic Bases of Elite Power in a Southeast Mesoamerican Polity, Part III (The 1992 Naco Valley Season). Manuscript on file at the Instituto Hondureño de Antropología e Historia and Kenyon College, Tegucigalpa and Gambier, OH.

Schortman, Edward M., Patricia A. Urban, Wendy Ashmore, and Julie Benyo
1986   Interregional Interaction in the SE Maya Periphery: The Santa Barbara Archaeological Project, 1983–1984 Seasons. *Journal of Field Archaeology* 13:259–272.

Schwartz, Glenn M., and Steven E. Falconer, eds.
1994   *Archaeological Views from the Countryside*. Washington, DC: Smithsonian Institution Press.

Sealy, J. C., N. J. van der Merwe, A. Sillen, F. J. Kruger, and H. W. Krueger
1991   87Sr/86Sr as a Dietary Indicator in Modern and Archaeological Bone. *Journal of Archaeological Science* 18:399–416.

Sedat, David W.
1996   Etapas tempranas en la evolución de la Acrópolis de Copan. *Yaxkin* 14:19–27.
1997a *The Earliest Ancestor to Copan Str. 10L-16*. ECAP Paper No. 3. Philadelphia, PA: Instituto Hondureño de Antropología e Historia and the University of Pennsylvania Museum Early Copan Acropolis Program.
1997b *The Founding Stage of the Copan Acropolis*. ECAP Paper No. 2. Philadelphia, PA: Instituto Hondureño de Antropología e Historia and the University of Pennsylvania Museum Early Copan Acropolis Program.
1997c *Margarita Structure: New Data and Implications*. ECAP Paper No. 6. Philadelphia, PA: Instituto Hondureño de Antropología e Historia and the University of Pennsylvania Museum Early Copan Acropolis Program.
1997d *Vessel 1 from the Margarita Tomb*. ECAP Paper No. 7. Philadelphia, PA: Instituto Hondureño de Antropología e Historia and the University of Pennsylvania Museum Early Copan Acropolis Program.
1997e *Yehnal Structure: An Early Dynastic Structure at Copan*. ECAP Paper No. 4. Philadelphia, PA: Instituto Hondureño de Antropología e Historia and the University of Pennsylvania Museum Early Copan Acropolis Program.

Sedat, David W., and Fernando López
1999   Tunneling into the Heart of the Copan Acropolis. *Expedition* 41(2):16-21.

Sedat, David W., and Robert J. Sharer
1994   *The Xukpi Stone: A Newly Discovered Early Classic Inscription from the Copan Acropolis: Part I: The Archaeology*. Copan Note 113. Austin, TX: Copan Acropolis Archaeological Project, Instituto Hondureño de Antropología e Historia.
1997   Evolución de la Acrópolis de Copan durante el Clásico Temprano. Los Investigadores de la Cultura Maya 5:383-389. Campeche, Mexico: Universidad Autónoma de Campeche.

Segovía Pinto, V.
1981   Kohunlich: Una Ciudad Maya del Clásico Temprano. In *Kohunlich: una Ciudad Maya del Clásico Temprano*, edited by E. F. Torrijos, pp. 213-297. Mexico City: San Angel Ediciones.

Séjourné, Laurette
1964   La simbólica del fuego. *Cuadernos Americanos* 135:149-178.
1966   *Arquitectura y Pintura en Teotihuacan*. Mexico City: Siglo XXI Editores.
1976   *Burning Water: Thought and Religion in Ancient Mexico*. Berkeley, CA: Shambhala.

Seler, Eduard
1902-
  1923 *Gesammelte Abhandlungen zur Amerikanischen Sprach- und Altertumskunde*. Berlin: Ascher.

Sempowski, Margaret
1992   Economic and Social Implications of Variations in Mortuary Practices at Teotihuacan. In *Art, Ideology, and the City of Teotihuacan*, edited by J. C. Berlo, pp. 27-58. Washington, DC: Dumbarton Oaks.

Service, Elman R.
1978   Classical and Modern Theories of the Origins of Government. In *Origins of the State: The Anthropology of Political Evolution*, edited by R. Cohen and E. R. Service, pp. 21-33. Philadelphia, PA: Institute for the Study of Human Issues.

Sharer, Robert J.
1974   The Prehistory of the Southeastern Maya Periphery. *Current Anthropology* 15(2):165-187.
1978a Archaeology and History at Quirigua, Guatemala. *Journal of Field Archaeology* 5:51-70.
1978b Culture History of Chalchuapa and the Southeastern Maya Highlands. In *The Prehistory of Chalchuapa, El Salvador 3*, edited by R. J. Sharer, pp. 208-215. Philadelphia: University of Pennsylvania Press.

1978c   Excavations in the El Trapiche Group. In *The Prehistory of Chalchuapa, El Salvador 1*, edited by R. J. Sharer, pp. 61–87. Philadelphia: University of Pennsylvania Press.

1978d   Pottery. In *The Prehistory of Chalchuapa, El Salvador 3*, edited by R. J. Sharer, pp. 2–128. Philadelphia: University of Pennsylvania Press.

1978e   Summary of Architecture and Constructional Activity. In *The Prehistory of Chalchuapa, El Salvador 1*, edited by R. J. Sharer, pp. 121–132. Philadelphia: University of Pennsylvania Press.

1988   Quirigua as a Classic Maya Center. In *The Southeast Classic Maya Zone*, edited by E. H. Boone and G. R. Willey, pp. 31–65. Washington, DC: Dumbarton Oaks.

1990   *Quirigua: A Classic Maya Center and Its Sculptures*. Durham, NC: Carolina Academic.

1991   Diversity and Continuity in Maya Civilization: Quirigua as a Case Study. In *Classic Maya Political History*, edited by T. P. Culbert, pp. 180–198. Cambridge: Cambridge University Press.

1992   The Preclassic Origin of Lowland Maya States. In *New Theories on the Ancient Maya*, edited by E. Danien and R. Sharer, pp. 131–136. Philadelphia: University of Pennsylvania Museum of Archaeology and Anthropology.

1993   The Social Organization of the Late Classic Maya: Problems of Definition and Approaches. In *Lowland Maya Civilization in the Eighth Century A.D.*, edited by J. A. Sabloff and J. S. Henderson, pp. 91–110. Washington, DC: Dumbarton Oaks.

1995   *The Ancient Maya*. 5th ed. Palo Alto, CA: Stanford University Press.

1996   Los patrones del desarrollo arquitectónico en la Acrópolis de Copan del Clásico Temprano. *Yaxkin* 14:28–34.

1997a   *Formation of Sacred Space by the First Kings of Copan*. ECAP Paper No. 10. Philadelphia, PA: Instituto Hondureño de Antropología e Historia and the University of Pennsylvania Museum Early Copan Acropolis Program.

1997b   The Foundation of the Ruling Dynasty at Copan, Honduras: The Early Acropolis and Mesoamerican Interaction. Paper presented at A Tale of Two Cities: Copan and Teotihuacan, Department of Anthropology, Harvard University, Cambridge, MA.

1997c   K'inich Yax K'uk' Mo' and the Genesis of the Copan Acropolis. Paper presented at A Tale of Two Cities: Copan and Teotihuacan, Department of Anthropology, Harvard University, Cambridge, MA.

1997d   *Political and Ideological Power and the Origins of the Acropolis*. ECAP Paper No. 1. Philadelphia, PA: Instituto Hondureño de Antropología e Historia and the University of Pennsylvania Museum Early Copan Acropolis Program.

1997e   *The Tombs of the Copan and Quirigua Founders*. ECAP Paper No. 9. Philadelphia, PA: Instituto Hondureño de Antropología e Historia and the University of Pennsylvania Museum Early Copan Acropolis Program.

1999   Archaeology and History in the Royal Acropolis, Copan, Honduras. *Expedition* 41(2):8–15.

2003a   Founding Events and External Interaction at Copan, Honduras. In *Teotihuacan and the Maya: Reinterpreting Early Classic Interaction*, edited by G. Braswell, pp. 143–165. Austin: University of Texas Press.

2003b Tikal and the Copan Dynastic Founding. In *Tikal: Dynasties, Foreigners, & Affairs of State: Advancing Maya Archaeology*, edited by J. A. Sabloff, pp. 319-353. Santa Fe, NM: SAR.

Sharer, Robert J., William L. Fash, David W. Sedat, Loa P. Traxler, and Richard V. Williamson
1999 Continuities and Contrasts in Early Classic Architecture of Central Copan. In *Mesoamerican Architecture as Cultural Symbol*, edited by J. K. Kowalski, pp. 220-249. Oxford: Oxford University Press.

Sharer, Robert J., and James C. Gifford
1970 Preclassic Ceramics from Chalchuapa, El Salvador, and their Relationships with the Maya Lowlands. *American Antiquity* 35:441-462.

Sharer, Robert J., Julia C. Miller, and Loa P. Traxler
1992 Evolution of Classic Period Architecture in the Early Acropolis, Copan: A Progress Report. *Ancient Mesoamerica* 3:145-159.

Sharer, Robert J., and David W. Sedat
1987 *Archaeological Investigations in the Northern Maya Highlands, Guatemala: Interaction and Development of the Maya Civilization.* University Museum Monograph 59. Philadelphia: University of Pennsylvania Museum of Archaeology and Anthropology.

Sharer, Robert J., David W. Sedat, Loa P. Traxler, Christine W. Carrelli, Ellen E. Bell, and E. Christian Wells
1998 Report of the 1998 Field Season of the Early Copan Acropolis Program. Manuscript on file at the University of Pennsylvania Museum of Archaeology and Anthropology, Philadelphia.

Sharer, Robert J., Loa P. Traxler, David W. Sedat, Ellen E. Bell, Marcello A. Canuto, and Christopher Powell
1999 Early Classic Architecture Beneath the Copan Acropolis: A Research Update. *Ancient Mesoamerica* 10:3-23.

Shipman, Pat, Giraud Foster, and Margaret Schoeninger
1984 Burnt Bones and Teeth: An Experimental Study of Color, Morphology, Crystal Structure and Shrinkage. *Journal of Archaeological Science* 11:307-325.

Shook, Edwin M., and Marion Popenoe de Hatch
1999 Las Tierras Altas Centrales: Períodos Preclásico y Clásico. In *Historia General de Guatemala*, tomo I, pp. 295-318. Guatemala City: Asociación de Amigos del País, Fundación para la Cultura y el Desarrollo.

Shook, Edwin M., and Alfred V. Kidder
1952 Mound E-III-3, Kaminaljuyu, Guatemala. In *Contributions to American Anthropology and History 11*, no. 53, pp. 33-128. Washington, DC: Carnegie Institution of Washington.

Shook, Edwin M., and Tatiana Proskouriakoff
1956   Settlement Patterns in Meso-America and the Sequence in the Guatemalan
        Highlands. In *Prehistoric Settlement Patterns in the New World*, edited by G.
        R. Willey, pp. 93–100. Viking Fund Publications in Anthropology 23. New York:
        Wenner-Gren Foundation for Anthropological Research.

Smailus, Ortwin
1975   *El Maya-Chontal de Acalan: Análisis Lingüístico de un Documento de los
        Años 1610-1612.* Centro de Estudios Mayas, Cuaderno 9. Mexico City:
        Universidad Nacional Autónoma de México.

Smith, A. Ledyard
1950   *Uaxactun, Guatemala: Excavations of 1931-1937.* Publication 588.
        Washington, DC: Carnegie Institution of Washington.

Smith, Mary Elizabeth
1973   *Picture Writing from Ancient Southern Mexico: Mixtec Place Signs and
        Maps.* Norman: University of Oklahoma Press.

Smith, Robert E.
1955   *Ceramic Sequence at Uaxactun, Guatemala.* 2 vols. Publication 20. New
        Orleans, LA: Middle American Research Institute, Tulane University.

Spencer, Charles S., and Elsa M. Redmond
1997   *Archaeology of the Cañada de Cuicatlán, Oaxaca.* Anthropological Paper
        80. New York: American Museum of Natural History.
2001a   The Chronology of Conquest: Implications of New Radiocarbon Analyses
        from the Cañada de Cuicatlán, Oaxaca. *Latin American Antiquity*
        12:182-201.
2001b   Multilevel Selection and Political Evolution in the Valley of Oaxaca, 500–100
        B.C. *Journal of Anthropological Archaeology* 20:195-229.

Spinden, Herbert J.
1913   *A Study of Maya Art: Its Subject Matter and Historical Development.*
        Memoirs of the Peabody Museum of Archaeology and Ethnology, vol. 6.
        Cambridge, MA: Peabody Museum of Archaeology and Ethnology, Harvard
        University.

Stephens, John L., and Frederick Catherwood
1963   *Incidents of Travel in Central America, Chiapas, and Yucatan.* New York:
[1841] Dover.

Stephens, N. G., A. S. Morgan, P. Corvo, and B. A. Bernstein
1995   Significance of Scapular Fracture in the Blunt-Trauma Patient. *Annals of
        Emergency Medicine* 26:439-442.

Stone, Andrea
1989   Disconnection, Foreign Insignia, and Political Expansion: Teotihuacan and the
        Warrior Stelae of Piedras Negras. In *Mesoamerica after the Decline of
        Teotihuacan*, edited by R. A. Diehl and J. C. Berlo. Washington, DC: Dumbarton
        Oaks.

Stone, Donna K., and David W. Kluth
1989   1989 Season Field Report: Operation 41, Sub-operation 5 & 8. Manuscript on
        file at the Instituto Hondureño de Antropología e Historia, Tegucigalpa and
        Copan.

Storey, Rebecca
1985   Pre-Columbian Child and Infant Mortality in Teotihuacan and Copan.
        American Journal of Physical Anthropology 66:234-235.
1992   The Children of Copan: Issues in Paleopathology and Paleodemography.
        Ancient Mesoamerica 3(1):161-168.
1997   Individual Frailty, Children of Privilege and Stress in Late Classic Copan. In
        Bones of the Maya: Studies of Ancient Skeletons, edited by S. L. Whittington
        and D. M. Reed, pp. 116-126. Washington, DC: Smithsonian Press.
1999   Late Classic Nutrition and Skeletal Indicators at Copan, Honduras. In
        Reconstructing Ancient Maya Diet, edited by C. D. White, pp. 169-179. Salt
        Lake City: University of Utah Press.

Strömsvik, Gustav
1935   Copan. *Carnegie Institution of Washington Yearbook* 34:118-120.
1941   *Substela Caches and Stela Foundations at Copan and Quirigua.*
        Contributions to American Anthropology and History No. 37. Washington, DC:
        Carnegie Institution of Washington.
1952   *The Ball Courts at Copan, with Notes on Courts at La Unión, Quirigua,
        San Pedro Pinula, and Asunción Mita.* Contributions to American
        Anthropology and History No. 55. Washington, DC: Carnegie Institution of
        Washington.

Stuart, David
1986   *The Chronology of Stela 4 at Copan.* Copan Note 12. Austin, TX: Copan
        Acropolis Archaeological Project, Instituto Hondureño de Antropología e
        Historia.
1989   *The "First Ruler" on Stela 24.* Copan Note 7. Austin, TX: Copan Acropolis
        Archaeological Project, Instituto Hondureño de Antropología e Historia.
1992   Hieroglyphs and Archaeology at Copan. *Ancient Mesoamerica* 3(1):169-184.
1996   Kings of Stone: A Consideration of Stelae in Classic Maya Ritual and
        Representation. *RES: Anthropology and Aesthetics* 29/30:148-171.
1997   Smoking Frog, K'inich Yax K'uk Mo', and the Epigraphic Evidence for ties
        between Teotihuacan and the Classic Maya. Paper presented at A Tale of Two
        Cities: Copan and Teotihuacan, Department of Anthropology, Harvard
        University, Cambridge, MA.

1998   "The Fire Enters His House": Architecture and Ritual in Classic Maya Text. In
        Function and Meaning in Classic Maya Architecture, edited by S. D.
        Houston, pp. 373-425. Washington, DC: Dumbarton Oaks.
2000   "The Arrival of Strangers": Teotihuacan and Tollan in Classic Maya History. In
        Mesoamerica's Classic Heritage: From Teotihuacan to the Aztecs, edited by
        D. Carrasco, L. Jones, and S. Sessions, pp. 465-514. Boulder: University Press of
        Colorado.

Stuart, David, and Linda Schele
1986a   *Interim Report on the Hieroglyphic Stair of Structure 26*. Copan Note 17.
        Austin, TX: Copan Acropolis Archaeological Project, Instituto Hondureño de
        Antropología e Historia.
1986b   *Yax-K'uk'-Mo', The Founder of the Lineage of Copan*. Copan Note 6. Austin,
        TX: Copan Acropolis Archaeological Project, Instituto Hondureño de
        Antropología e Historia.

Stuart, David, Nikolai Grube, Linda Schele, and Floyd Lounsbury
1989   *Stela 63, A New Monument from Copan*. Copan Note 56. Austin, TX: Copan
        Acropolis Archaeological Project, Instituto Hondureño de Antropología e
        Historia.

Stuart, George
1997   The Royal Crypts of Copan. *National Geographic* 192(6):68-93.

Suchey, Judy M., and D. Katz
1986   Skeletal Age Standards Derived from an Extensive Multiracial Sample of
        Modern Americans. Paper presented at the 55th Annual Meeting of the
        American Association of Physical Anthropologists, Albuquerque, NM.

Suchey, Judy M., P. A. Owings, D. V. Wiseley, and T. T. Noguchi
1984   Skeletal Aging of Unidentified Persons. In *Human Identification: Case
        Studies in Forensic Anthropology*, edited by T. A. Rathburn and J. E. Buikstra,
        pp. 278-297. Springfield, IL: Charles C Thomas.

Sugiyama, Saburo
1992   Rulership, Warfare, and Human Sacrifice at the Ciudadela, Teotihuacan: An
        Iconographic Study of Feathered Serpent Representations. In *Art, Ideology,
        and the City of Teotihuacan*, edited by J. Berlo, pp. 205-230. Washington, DC:
        Dumbarton Oaks.
2001   Dedication Burials and State Symbolism Materialized at the Moon Pyramid,
        Teotihuacan. Paper presented at the 66th Annual Meeting of the Society for
        American Archaeology, New Orleans, LA.

Sugiyama, Saburo, and Rubén Cabrera Castro
1999   Se descubren dos ofrendas de notable importancia en la Pirámide de la Luna
        en Teotihuacan. *Arqueología Mexicana* 7(40):71-73.

Tate, Carolyn
1992   *Yaxchilan:The Design of a Maya Ceremonial City*. Austin: University of
        Texas Press.

Taube, Karl
1992a   Iconography of Mirrors at Teotihuacan. In *Art, Ideology, and the City of
        Teotihuacan*, edited by J. C. Berlo, pp. 169-204.Washington, DC: Dumbarton
        Oaks.
1992b   *The Major Gods of Ancient Yucatan*. Studies in Pre-Columbian Art and
        Archaeology No. 32.Washington, DC: Dumbarton Oaks.
1992c   The Temple of Quetzalcoatl and the Cult of Sacred War at Teotihuacan. *RES:
        Anthropology and Aesthetics* 21:53-87.
1994   The Birth Vase: Natal Imagery in Ancient Maya Myth and Ritual. In *The Maya
        Vase Book*, vol. 4, edited by J. Kerr, and B. Kerr, pp. 652-685. New York: Kerr
        Associates.
1997   Transformations and Use of Teotihuacan Symbolism at Copan and Other Maya
        Cities. Paper presented at A Tale of Two Cities: Copan and Teotihuacan,
        Department of Anthropology, Harvard University, Cambridge, MA.
1998a   Iconographic Investigations of Structure 10L-16, Copan, Honduras: Report of
        the 1995-1997 Field Seasons. Manuscript on file at the Instituto Hondureño
        de Antropología e Historia,Tegucigalpa and Copan.
1998b   The Jade Hearth: Centrality, Rulership, and the Classic Maya Temple. In
        Function and Meaning in Classic Maya Architecture, edited by S. D.
        Houston, pp. 427-478.Washington, DC: Dumbarton Oaks.
2000a   Lightning Celts and Corn Fetishes:The Formative Olmec and the
        Development of Maize Symbolism in Mesoamerica and the American
        Southwest. In *Olmec Art and Archaeology: Social Complexity in the
        Formative Period*, edited by J. E. Clark and M. Pye, pp. 297-337.Washington,
        DC: National Gallery of Art.
2000b   The Turquoise Hearth: Fire, Self-Sacrifice, and the Central Mexican Cult of War.
        In *Mesoamerica's Classic Heritage: From Teotihuacan to the Aztecs*, edited
        by D. Carrasco, L. Jones, and S. Sessions, pp. 269-340. Boulder: University
        Press of Colorado.
2000c   *The Writing System of Ancient Teotihuacan*.Ancient America No. 1.
        Barnardsville: Center for Ancient American Studies.
2001   La Escritura Teotihuacana. *Arqueología Mexicana* 8(48):58-63.

Taylor, Walter W.
1948   *A Study of Archaeology*.American Anthropologist Memoir 69, no. 3, part 2.
        Washington, DC:American Anthropological Association.

Tiesler Blos,V.
1998   *La costumbre de la deformación cefálica entre los antiguos Mayas:
        Aspectos morfológicos y culturales*. Mexico City: Instituto Nacional de
        Antropología e Historia.
1999   *Rasgos bioculturales entre los antiguos Mayas*. Mexico City: Universidad
        Nacional Autónoma de México.

Todd, T. Wingate
1921a Age Changes in the Pubic Bone I: The Male White Pubis. *American Journal of Physical Anthropology* 3:285-334.
1921b Age Changes in the Pubic Bone III: The Pubis of the White Female. *American Journal of Physical Anthropology* 4:26-39.
1921c Age Changes in the Pubic Bone IV: The Pubis of the Female Negro-White Hybrid. *American Journal of Physical Anthropology* 4:40-70.

Tozzer, Alfred M.
1941 *Landa's Relación de las Cosas de Yucatán*. Papers of the Peabody Museum of Archaeology and Ethnology No. 18. Cambridge: Peabody Museum of Archaeology and Ethnology, Harvard University.

Traxler, Loa P.
1994 A New Discovery at Copan. *Expedition* 35(3):57-62.
1996 Grupos de patios tempranos de la Acrópolis de Copan. *Yaxkin* 14:35-54.
1997 Connections Buried Beneath the Dancing Jaguars at Copan Honduras. Paper presented at A Tale of Two Cities: Copan and Teotihuacan, Department of Anthropology, Harvard University, Cambridge, MA.
2001 The Royal Court of Early Classic Copan. In *Royal Courts of the Ancient Maya 2*, edited by T. Inomata and S. D. Houston, pp. 47-73. Boulder, CO: Westview.
2003 At Court in Copan: Palace Groups of the Early Classic. In *Maya Palaces and Elite Residences*, edited by J. Christie. Austin: University of Texas Press.

Trigger, Bruce G.
1990 Monumental Architecture: A Thermodynamic Explanation of Symbolic Behaviour. *World Archaeology* 22(2):119-132.

Trik, Aubrey S.
1939 *Temple XXII at Copan*. Publication 509. Washington, DC: Carnegie Institution of Washington.

Trotter, Mildred
1970 Estimation of Stature from Intact Long Bones. In *Personal Identification in Mass Disasters*, edited by T. D. Stewart, pp. 71-83. Washington, DC: National Museum of Natural History.

Trotter, Mildred, and Goldine C. Gleser
1958 A Re-evaluation of Stature Based on Measurements of Stature Taken During Life and of Long Bones after Death. *American Journal of Physical Anthropology* 16:79-123.

Turner II, B. L., W. Johnson, O. Mahood, F. Wiseman, and J. Poole
1983 Habitat y Agricultura en la Región de Copan. In *Introducción a la Arqueología de Copan, Honduras*, tomo I, edited by C. F. Baudez, pp. 35-142. Tegucigalpa: Proyecto Arqueológico Copan, Secretaría de Estado en el Despacho de Cultura y Turismo.

1986a   Precolumbian Settlement in the Naco Valley, Northwestern Honduras. In *The Southeast Maya Periphery*, edited by P. A. Urban and E. M. Schortman, pp. 275-295. Austin: University of Texas Press.

1986b   Systems of Settlement in the Precolumbian Naco Valley, Northwestern Honduras. Ph.D. dissertation, Department of Anthropology, University of Pennsylvania.

1993   Naco Valley. In *Pottery of Prehistoric Honduras*, edited by J. S. Henderson and M. Beaudry-Corbett, pp. 30-63. Institute of Archaeology Monograph 35. Los Angeles: University of California, Los Angeles.

Urban, Patricia A., and Edward M. Schortman, eds.
1986   *The Southeast Maya Periphery*. Austin: University of Texas Press.

Valdés, Juan Antonio
1991   Los Mascarones del Grupo 6C-XVI de Tikal: Análisis Iconográfico para el Clásico Temprano. *Estudios de Cultura Maya* 18:233-262.

1995   Desarrollo cultural y señales de alarma entre los Mayas: el Preclásico Tardío y la transición hacia el Clásico Temprano. In *The Emergence of Lowland Maya Civilization*, edited by N. Grube, pp. 71-86. Acta Mesoamericana 8. Möckmühl, Germany: Verlag Anton Saurwein.

1997   El Proyecto Miraflores II dentro del Marco Preclásico de Kaminaljuyu. In *X Simposio de Investigaciones Arqueológicas en Guatemala, 1997*, edited by J. P. Laporte and H. L. Escobedo, pp. 81-91. Guatemala City: Ministerio de Cultura y Deportes, Instituto de Antropología e Historia, y Asociación Tikal.

1998   Kaminaljuyu, Guatemala: Descubrimientos recientes sobre poder y manejo hidráulico. In *Memorias del Tercer Congreso Internacional de Mayistas, 1995*, pp. 752-770. Mexico City: Centro de Estudios Mayas, Universidad Nacional Autónoma de México.

2000   El surgimiento de palacios y tronos en las cortes reales de las Tierras Bajas Mayas. *U tz'ib* 10:11-32.

2001   Water Management at Kaminaljuyu: The Beginnings of Power and Ideology in the Guatemalan Highlands. Paper presented at the 66th Annual Meeting of the Society for American Archaeology, New Orleans, LA.

Valdés, Juan Antonio, and Charles D. Cheek
1983   Excavaciones en el Sector Este de la Plaza Principal. In *Introducción a la Arqueología de Copan, Honduras*, tomo II, edited by C. F. Baudez, pp. 291-318. Tegucigalpa: Proyecto Arqueológico Copan, Secretaría de Estado en el Despacho de Cultura y Turismo.

Valdés, Juan Antonio, and Marion Popenoe de Hatch
1996   Evidencias de poder y control social en Kaminaljuyu: Proyecto Arqueológico Miraflores II. In *IX Simposio de Investigaciones Arqueológicas en Guatemala, 1995*, edited by J. P. Laporte and H. L. Escobedo, pp. 377-396. Guatemala City: Ministerio de Cultura y Deportes, Instituto de Antropología e Historia, y Asociación Tikal.

van Vark, G. N.
1974   The Investigation of Human Cremated Skeletal Material by Multivariate
        Statistical Methods, I. Methodology. *Ossa* 1:63–95.

Viel, René
1983   Evolución de la Cerámica en Copan: Resultados Preliminares. In *Introducción
        a la Arqueología de Copan, Honduras,* tomo I, edited by C. F. Baudez, pp.
        471–549: Proyecto Arqueológico Copan, Secretaría de Estado en el Despacho
        de Cultura y Turismo.
1993a   Copan Valley. In *Pottery of Prehistoric Honduras,* edited by J. S. Henderson
        and M. Beaudry-Corbett, pp. 12–18. Institute of Archaeology Monograph 35.
        Los Angeles: University of California, Los Angeles.
1993b   *Evolución de la Cerámica de Copan, Honduras.* Tegucigalpa: Instituto
        Hondureño de Antropología e Historia.
1998   Interacción entre Copan y Kaminaljuyu. In *XI Simposio de Investigaciones
        Arqueológicas en Guatemala, 1997,* edited by J. P. Laporte and H. L.
        Escobedo, pp. 427–430. Guatemala City: Ministerio de Cultura y Deportes,
        Instituto de Antropología e Historia, y Asociación Tikal.
1999a   El Período Formativo de Copan. In *XII Simposio de Investigaciones
        Arqueológicas en Guatemala, 1998,* edited by J. P. Laporte, H. L. Escobedo,
        and A. C. Monzón, pp. 99–104. Guatemala City: Ministerio de Cultura y
        Deportes, Instituto de Antropología e Historia, y Asociación Tikal.
1999b   The Pectorals of Altar Q and Structure 11: An Interpretation of the Political
        Organization at Copan, Honduras. *Latin American Antiquity* 10(4):377–399.

Viel, René, and Charles D. Cheek
1983   Sepulturas. In *Introducción a la Arqueología de Copan, Honduras,* tomo I,
        edited by C. F. Baudez, pp. 551–609. Tegucigalpa: Proyecto Arqueológico
        Copan, Secretaría de Estado en el Despacho de Cultura y Turismo.

Viel, René, and Jay Hall
1994   Le Projet Préclassique de Copan. *Trace* (25):13–20.
1998   The Chronology of Copan, Honduras: An Update and Discussion. Paper pre-
        sented at the 63rd Annual meeting of the Society for American Archaeology,
        Seattle, WA.
2000a   Factional Competition at Copan, Honduras. Paper presented at the 65th
        Annual Meeting of the Society for American Archaeology, Philadelphia, PA.
2000b   Informe Preliminar: Temporada 2000. Manuscript on file at the Instituto
        Hondureño de Antropología e Historia, Tegucigalpa and Copan.
2000c   Las relaciones entre Copan y Kaminaljuyu. In *XIII Simposio de
        Investigaciones Arqueologicas en Guatemala, 1999,* edited by J. P. Laporte,
        H. L. Escobedo, A. C. de Suasnávar, and B. Arroyo, pp. 127–134. Guatemala
        City: Ministerio de Cultura y Deportes, Instituto de Antropología e Historia, y
        Asociación Tikal.

Vlcek, David T., and William L. Fash
1986   Survey in the Outlying Areas of the Copan Region, and the Copan-Quirigua
         "Connection." In *The Southeast Maya Periphery*, edited by P. A. Urban and E.
         M. Schortman, pp. 102-113. Austin: University of Texas Press.

Von Winning, Hasso
1987   *La Iconografía de Teotihuacan: Los Dioses y los Signos*. Mexico City:
         Universidad Nacional Autónoma de México.

Webster, David
1977   Warfare and the Evolution of Maya Civilization. In *The Origins of Maya
         Civilization*, edited by R. E. W. Adams, pp. 335-372. Albuquerque: University
         of New Mexico Press.
1985   Recent Settlement Survey in the Copan Valley, Honduras. *Journal of New
         World Archaeology* 5(4):39-51.
1993   The Study of Maya Warfare: What It Tells us about the Maya and What It Tells
         us about Maya Archaeology. In *Lowland Maya Civilization in the Eighth
         Century A.D.*, edited by J. A. Sabloff and J. S. Henderson, pp. 415-444.
         Washington, DC: Dumbarton Oaks.
1998   Classic Maya Architecture: Implications and Comparisons. In *Function and
         Meaning in Classic Maya Architecture*, edited by S. D. Houston, pp. 5-47.
         Washington, DC: Dumbarton Oaks.
1999   The Archaeology of Copan, Honduras. *Journal of Archaeological Research*
         7(1):1-53.

Webster, David, ed.
1989   *House of the Bacabs, Copan, Honduras: A Study of the Iconography,
         Epigraphy, and Social Context of a Maya Elite Structure*. Washington, DC:
         Dumbarton Oaks.

Webster, David, and AnnCorinne Freter
1990a   The Demography of Late Classic Copan. In *Precolumbian Population
         History in the Maya Lowlands*, edited by T. P. Culbert and D. Rice, pp. 37-61.
         Albuquerque: University of New Mexico Press.
1990b   Settlement History and the Classic Collapse at Copan: A Redefined
         Chronological Perspective. *Latin American Antiquity* 1:66-85.

Webster, David, AnnCorinne Freter, and Nancy Gonlin
2000   *Copan: The Rise and Fall of an Ancient Maya Kingdom*. Orlando, FL:
         Harcourt.

Webster, David, and Nancy Gonlin
1988   Household Remains of the Humblest Maya. *Journal of Field Archaeology*
         15:169-190.

Webster, David, Barbara Fash, Randolph Widmer, and Scott Zeleznik
1998   The Skyband Group: Investigation of a Classic Maya Elite Residential Complex at Copan, Honduras. *Journal of Field Archaeology* 25(3):319-343.

Webster, David, William T. Sanders, and Peter van Rossum
1992   A Simulation of Copan Population History and its Implications. *Ancient Mesoamerica* 3:185-197.

Whalen, Michael
1981   *Excavations at Santo Domingo Tomaltepec: Evolution of a Formative Community in the Valley of Oaxaca, Mexico.* Memoirs of the Univerisity of Michigan Museum of Anthropology No. 12. Ann Arbor: University of Michigan Museum of Anthropology.

White, Christine D., Michael W. Spence, Fred J. Longstaffe, and Kimberly R. Law
2000   Testing the Nature of Teotihuacan Imperialism at Kaminaljuyu using Phosphate Oxygen-Isotope Ratios. *Journal of Anthropological Research* 56:535-558.

White, Christine D., Michael W. Spence, Hillary Le Q. Stuart-Williams, and Henry P. Schwarcz
1998   Oxygen Isotopes and the Identification of Geographical Origins: The Valley of Oaxaca versus the Valley of Mexico. *Journal of Archaeological Science* 25(7):643-655.

Whittington, Stephen L.
1989   Characteristics of Demography and Disease in Low Status Maya from Classic Period Copan, Honduras. Ph.D. dissertation. Department of Anthropology, Pennsylvania State University.
1991   Enamel Hypoplasia in the Low Status Maya Population of Copan, Honduras, around the Time of the Collapse. *American Journal of Physical Anthropology* 85:167-184.
1992   Enamel Hypoplasia in the Low-Status Maya Population of Prehispanic Copan, Honduras. *Journal of Paleopathology Monograph Publications* 2:185-205.
1999   Caries and Antemortem Tooth Loss at Copan: Implications for Commoner Diet. In *Reconstructing Ancient Maya Diet*, edited by C. D. White, pp. 151-167. Salt Lake City: University of Utah Press.

Whittington, Stephen L., and David M. Reed
1997   Commoner Diet at Copan: Insights from Stable Isotopes and Porotic Hyperostosis. In *Bones of the Maya: Studies of Ancient Skeletons*, edited by S. L. Wittington and D. M. Reed, pp. 157-170. Washington, DC: Smithsonian Institution Press.

Wilk, Richard R., and William L. Rathje
1982   Household Archaeology. In *Archaeology of the Household: Building a Prehistory of Domestic Life*, edited by R. R. Wilk and W. L. Rathje, pp. 617-639. American Behavioral Scientist 25, No. 6. Beverly Hills, CA: Sage.

Willey, Gordon R.

1974 The Classic Maya Hiatus: A 'Rehearsal' for the Collapse? In *Mesoamerican Archaeology: New Approaches*, edited by N. Hammond, pp. 417-430. Austin: University of Texas Press.

1980 Towards a Holistic View of Ancient Maya Civilization. *Man* 15:249-256.

Willey, Gordon R., William R. Coe, and Robert J. Sharer

1976 Un Proyecto para el Desarrollo de Investigación y Preservación Arqueológica en Copan (Honduras) y Vecindad. *Yaxkin* 1:10-29.

Willey, Gordon R., and Richard M. Leventhal

1979a Prehistoric Settlement at Copan. In *Maya Archaeology and Ethnohistory*, edited by N. Hammond, pp. 75-102. Austin: University of Texas Press.

Willey, Gordon R., Richard M. Leventhal, Arthur A. Demarest, and William L. Fash

1994 *Ceramics and Artifacts from Excavations in The Copan Residential Zone*. Papers of the Peabody Museum of Archaeology and Ethnology No. 80. Cambridge, MA: Peabody Museum of Archaeology and Ethnology, Harvard University.

Willey, Gordon R., Richard M. Leventhal, and William L. Fash

1978b Maya Settlement in the Copan Valley. *Archaeology* 31:32-43.

Willey, Gordon R., and Peter Mathews, eds.

1984 *A Consideration of the Early Classic Period in the Maya Lowlands*. Institute for Mesoamerican Studies Publication No. 10. Albany: State University of New York at Albany.

Williamson, Richard V.

1996 Excavations, Interpretations, and Implications of the Earliest Structures Beneath Structure 10L-26 at Copan, Honduras. In *Eighth Palenque Round Table, 1993*, edited by M. G. Robertson, M. J. Macri, and J. McHargue, pp. 169-175. San Francisco, CA: Pre-Columbian Art Research Institute.

1997 Los Orígenes de la Complejidad Social en Copan: Excavaciones debajo de la Estructura 10L-26 en Copan, Honduras. *Yaxkin* 16:31-39.

Wills, W. H., and R. D. Leonard, eds.

1994 *The Ancient Southwestern Community*. Albuquerque: University of New Mexico Press.

Wingard, John D.

1996 Interaction Between Demographic Processes and Soil Resources in the Copan Valley, Honduras. In *The Managed Mosaic: Ancient Maya Agriculture and Resource Use*, edited by S. L. Fedick, pp. 207-235. Salt Lake City: University of Utah Press.

Wisdom, Charles

1961 *Los Chortis de Guatemala*. Guatemala City: Ministerio de Educación Pública.

Wonderley, Anthony
1991   Late Preclassic Sula Plain, Honduras: Regional Antecedents to Social Complexity and Interregional Convergence in Ceramic Style. In *Formation of Complex Society in Southeastern Mesoamerica*, edited by W. Fowler, pp. 143–169. Boca Raton, FL: CRC Press.

Wright, Henry T.
1984   Prestate Political Formations. In *On the Evolution of Complex Societies: Essays in Honor of Harry Hoijer*, edited by T. Earle, pp. 41–77. Malibu, CA: Undena Press.

Wright, Henry T., and Gregory A. Johnson
1975   Population, Exchange, and Early State Formation in Southwestern Iran. *American Anthropologist* 77:267–289.

Wright, Lori E.
1999   Los niños de Kaminaljuyu: Isótopos, dieta y etnicidad en el altiplano de Guatemala. In *XII Simposio de Investigaciones Arqueologicas en Guatemala, 1998*, edited by J. P. Laporte, H. L. Escobedo, and A. C. Monzón, pp. 485–497. Guatemala City: Ministerio de Cultura y Deportes, Instituto de Antropología e Historia, y Asociación Tikal.

Wright, Lori E., José V. Genovez, Mario Vásquez, Bento Burgos, Inés Guerrero, and Henry P. Schwarcz
1998   La osteología de rescate en Kaminaljuyu y algunas observaciones acerca de la dieta prehispánica en el Valle de Guatemala. In *XI Simposio de Investigaciones Arqueológicas en Guatemala, 1997*, edited by J. P. Laporte and H. L. Escobedo, pp. 419–426. Guatemala City: Ministerio de Cultura y Deportes, Instituto de Antropología e Historia, y Asociación Tikal.

Wright, Lori E., and Henry P. Schwarcz
1998   Stable Carbon and Oxygen Isotopes in Human Tooth Enamel: Identifying Breastfeeding and Weaning in Prehistory. *American Journal of Physical Anthropology* 106:1–18.
1999   Correspondence Between Stable Carbon Oxygen and Nitrogen Isotopes in Human Tooth Enamel and Dentine: Infant Diets and Weaning at Kaminaljuyu. *Journal of Archeological Science* 26:1159–1170.

Wright, Lori E., Henry P. Schwarcz, and R. Acevedo
2000   La Dieta de los Habitantes de Topoxté: Una Reconstrucción Isotópica. In *El Sitio Maya de Topoxté: Investigaciones en una Isla del Lago Yaxhá, Petén, Guatemal*, edited by W. Wurster, pp. 158–164. Mainz, Germany: Verlag Philipp von Zabern.

Yaeger, Jason
2000   The Social Construction of Communities in the Classic Maya Countryside. In *The Archaeology of Communities: A New World Perspective*, edited by M. A. Canuto and J. Yaeger, pp. 123–142. London: Routledge.

Yaeger, Jason, and Marcello A. Canuto
2000   An Introduction to the Archaeology of Communities. In *The Archaeology of Communities: A New World Perspective*, edited by M.A. Canuto and J.Yaeger, pp. 1–12. London: Routledge.

Yoffee, Norman
1991   Maya Elite Interaction: Through a Glass, Sideways. In *Classic Maya Political History: Hieroglyphic and Archaeological Evidence*, edited by T. P. Culbert, pp. 285–310. Cambridge: Cambridge University Press.

Zuckerman, J. D., A. S. Morgan, and F. Cuomo
1993   Fractures of the Scapula. *Instruction Course Lectures* 42:271–281.

Contributors

RICARDO AGURCIA FASQUELLE is Director of the Associación Copan, Copán Ruinas, Honduras.

RONALD L. BISHOP is Senior Research Archaeologist at the Smithsonian Center for Materials Research and Education, Washington, DC.

ELLEN E. BELL is a Visiting Adjunct Instructor of Anthropology at Kenyon College, Gambier, OH.

JANE E. BUIKSTRA is Professor of Anthropology at the University of New Mexico, Albuquerque.

JAMES A. BURTON is Senior Scientist at the Laboratory of Archaeological Chemistry, University of Wisconsin-Madison.

MARCELLO A. CANUTO is Assistant Professor of Anthropology at Yale University, New Haven, CT.

CHRISTINE W. CARRELLI is Assistant Professor of Anthropology at Ocean County College, Toms River, NJ.

KARLA L. DAVIS-SALAZAR is a Post-Doctoral Research Associate in the Department of Anthropology and the Archaeological Research Institute at Arizona State University, Tempe, AZ.

BARBARA W. FASH is Senior Researcher at the Peabody Museum of Archaeology and Ethnology, Harvard University, Cambridge, MA.

WILLIAM L. FASH is Bowditch Professor of Anthropology at Harvard University, Cambridge, MA.

LYNN A. GRANT is Conservator at the University of Pennsylvania Museum of Archaeology and Anthropology, Philadelphia, PA.

JAY HALL is Senior Lecturer in the Department of Anthropology and Sociology and at the University of Queensland, Brisbane, Australia.

FERNANDO LÓPEZ is Supervisor of Architectural Consolidation for the Instituto Hondureño de Antropología e Historia and the Programa Integrado de Conservación del Proyecto Arqueológico Copán.

JOYCE MARCUS is Professor of Anthropology at the University of Michigan, Ann Arbor.

T. DOUGLAS PRICE is Weinstein Professor of European Archaeology and Director of the Laboratory of Archaeological Chemistry at the University of Wisconsin-Madison.

DORIE REENTS-BUDET is Co-Director of the Maya Ceramics Database Project at the Smithsonian Institution, Washington, DC.

EDWARD M. SCHORTMAN is Professor of Anthropology at Kenyon College, Gambier, OH.

DAVID W. SEDAT is Research Specialist at the University of Pennsylvania Museum of Archaeology and Anthropology, Philadelphia, PA.

ROBERT J. SHARER is Shoemaker Professor of Anthropology and Curator of the American Section of the University of Pennsylvania Museum of Archaeology and Anthropology, Philadelphia, PA.

DAVID STUART is Senior Researcher at the Peabody Museum of Archaeology and Ethnology, Cambridge, Harvard University, MA.

KARL TAUBE is Professor of Anthropology at the University of California, Riverside.

LOA P. TRAXLER is Assistant Curator of PreColumbian Studies at Dumbarton Oaks, Washington, DC.

PATRICIA A. URBAN is Professor of Anthropology at Kenyon College, Gambier, OH.

JUAN ANTONIO VALDÉS is former Director of the Instituto de Antropología e Historia de Guatemala.

RENÉ VIEL is Researcher at the University of Queensland, Brisbane, Australia.

LORI E. WRIGHT is Assistant Professor of Anthropology at Texas A&M University, College Station, TX.

INDEX